INSANITY
INSIDE
OUT

INSANITY INSIDE OUT

by Kenneth Donaldson

CROWN PUBLISHERS, INC.
NEW YORK

Printed in the United States of America

Published simultaneously in Canada by General Publishing Company Limited

Designed by Ruth Smerechniak

Library of Congress Cataloging in Publication Data

Donaldson, Kenneth.
Insanity inside out.

1. Psychiatric hospital care—Personal narra-
tives. 2. Mental illness—Public opinion.
3. Donaldson, Kenneth. 4. Insanity—Jurisprudence—United States. I. Title. [DNLM:
1. Mental disorders. WM100 D676i]
RC439.D66   362.2'1'0926   76-5862
ISBN 0-517-52531-3

TO CARTER, NARREL, TRANCIE, *and* VITTORIO

ACKNOWLEDGMENTS

There are three friends, listed chronologically, who made this ultimate triumph a reality. There is Morton Birnbaum, dedicated fighter, who over the years made the final outcome in the courts possible; Ruth Aley, wonderful agent, who engineered the long road to successful publication; Sig Moglen, inspiring editor, whose determination matched my own. For them, the only words available at the moment are, thank you, friends. Special thanks are also due Bruce Ennis for his masterful handling of the battle in the courtroom. And to each of the following people, who gave encouragement and concrete help during the long struggle, my sincere thanks:

Jackson G. Beatty
Shirley Burghard
Charles M. Butterworth III
Emil Colozzi
George Dean
Eugene Z. DuBose, Jr.
Raymond D. Fowler
Walter Fox
Paul R. Friedman
James M. Hanley

Jack
Hegel Kirk
John H. Lembcke
Richard T. McSorley
Nell Foster Rogers
Lawrence Al Siebert
Margery Sonnleitner
George B. Stallings, Jr.
Zena

CONTENTS

KENNETH DONALDSON HAS WRITTEN A REMARKABLE BOOK. ON A PERSONAL level it is a moving account of a man who survived fifteen years of unwanted and unwarranted confinement. From a social perspective the book is important: it raises in dramatic fashion the critical question of how society treats (or mistreats) people who need (or are mistakenly thought to need) mental health care and treatment.

Driven by an understandably fanatical desire not only to regain his liberty, but also to preserve his integrity, Donaldson overcame adversities where others surely would have given way. For years his eloquent pleas went unanswered: to his doctors these plaints were nothing more than further proof of his "paranoia"; to the courts they were largely the musings of a madman, typically not even worthy of a response from the state that was depriving him of his liberty.

In the end Donaldson was vindicated. Assisted by Dr. Morton Birnbaum, a physician who is also a practicing attorney, and Bruce Ennis, an activist civil liberties lawyer, his case ultimately reached the Supreme Court of the United States, which ruled that Donaldson had been denied his constitutional right to liberty.

What is significant about the decision in Donaldson's case is not that the Court ruled for Donaldson. In view of the extreme facts of the case, how could it have done otherwise? Donaldson was incarcerated for fifteen years even though he was an articulate, white, essentially middle-class, educated man with no history of violating the law. Moreover, even though he was plainly able to care for his own needs, he was being warehoused in a debilitating institution under the supervision of doctors whose care bordered on malpractice. That Donaldson had to be so indefatigable to vindicate his rights is truly a sad reflection on our society.

We must not fail to distinguish, moreover, between the condition of a Donaldson—intelligent and in command of the complexities of his incarceration and assisted by two such able champions as Birnbaum and Ennis—and the condition of most people who, because of illness or for economic or intellectual reasons, can't help themselves. Those without voices they can raise, those submerged by what has engulfed them—it is those people we must attend.

The simple, if distressingly troubling, fact is that the American judiciary has, with rare exception, steadfastly turned its back on the plight of our confined mentally ill. In our country's two-hundred-year history, Donaldson's is the first case where the Supreme Court was willing to take even a brief look at the quality of life behind the institutional door. As Justice Blackmun recently pointed out:

> The States have traditionally exercised broad power to commit persons found to be mentally ill. . . . Considering the number of persons affected, it is perhaps remarkable that the substantive constitutional limitations on this power have not been more frequently litigated.

Yet, even in the face of this paucity of judicial guidance, the Court, when given the opportunity in Donaldson's case, took only the most tentative of steps, carefully assuring that its decision was limited to the very narrow facts immediately before it. As for the plight of the many other patients not covered by the *Donaldson* decision, that will have to await another day.

This judicial abdication results, I believe, from an unwillingness to confront the difficult ethical and moral questions presented by the imposition of institutional care on an unwilling patient. Rather than agonize over these trying issues, courts have all too readily turned the decisions over to medical experts whose authoritative-sounding diagnoses and prognoses often camouflage a lack of factual investigations or behavioral knowledge.

Doctors, in turn, have wittingly or unwittingly invited this transfer of responsibility. For them, mental illness and treatability are medical questions; the law's involvement is seen (or rationalized) only as an impediment to effective care. What these doctors fail to realize, however, is that coercive psychiatry presents moral and social issues that go well beyond the ken of their medical expertise. It raises questions such as the following: What does it mean to say that a particular person is mentally ill? What impact does his perceived illness have on his behavior? If the person is incarcerated, how will he be benefitted? Are there treatments available that can help him? Are there resources available to ensure that such treatments will be forthcoming? Is the patient confined because society refuses to pay for the setting up of adequate alternative care? What will be the wider costs to the person if he is confined? Is the person being confined because others—his family, perhaps—want to be rid of him? Is he being confined because he is thought to be dangerous? If so, what do we mean by dangerous? On what basis do we rest our prediction that he is likely to engage in harmful behavior? Why do we distinguish between a person's right to ignore a physical diagnosis but not a mental one, even if there is no alleged danger?

To be sure, medical input is essential to these inquiries. But, by itself, it is not sufficient. Also at stake are fundamental moral questions involving a balance between individual and social rights. To the extent that these latter issues are submerged in seemingly clinical judgments, the potential for abuse is manifest.

Recently, as a member of an ad hoc committee of the American Psychiatric Association reviewing the use of psychiatric facilities in the Soviet Union, I was exposed to the most serious conflicts in loyalty among institutional professionals. The medical model of "sickness" could be and was perverted to conform to judgments of what the bureaucracy found to be politically acceptable behavior. This same abuse can, and I would suggest sometimes does, occur in our own society, although it may be more visible as it bears on social, rather than political, conformity.

In raising this series of questions posed by coercive psychiatry, I do not mean to suggest that the answers are readily ascertainable. On the contrary, contemporary understanding of human behavior is too tentative and incomplete to allow for any measure of certainty. This, however, makes the challenge more important, not less. For, despite our uncertainty, we are continually making decisions that have serious effects on the lives of many people. We cannot, therefore, wistfully hope for the day when greater certainty exists. We must instead at least try to make the "best" decision humanly possible, given present knowledge and resources.

Failure to meet this challenge, I fear, may result in a strong social backlash against institutional psychiatry. Cases such as Donaldson's are sure to fuel the movement of those who, like Dr. Thomas Szasz, would abolish all forms of coercive psychiatry. This, in my view, would be a mixed blessing at best. For, while I have no doubt that there are others like Donaldson, who are even now being improperly confined, I am equally confident that there are still others for whom release from mental institutions will mean little more than further abandonment. Indeed, in those states that have recently discharged large numbers of mental patients with the intention of benefitting them through a return to their communities, studies show that a sizable proportion have ended up adrift in our blighted urban ghettos. In short, they have been shunted from the "back wards" to the "back alleys" as the "promise of freedom" has often proved to be as chimerical as the "promise of treatment."

My quarter century's experience as a jurist at the center of legal issues concerning the interplay of law and mental health convinces me that there is no single solution to the problems of coercive psychiatry. Individual needs are too varied, and behavioral knowledge too uncertain to allow for a panacea—be it institutionalization or deinstitutionalization. Rather, I am inclined to agree with Dr. Leon Eisenberg of Harvard, who has recently written:

> The fact that psychiatry can be abused does not make psychiatry an abuse. Scientists can be suborned, but science remains essential to human welfare. I join the call for ethical vigilance in medicine and science, not the Luddite appeal for wrecking the machinery in the vain hope of returning to a sinless Eden.

The problem remains, of course, of how to preserve the contributions of psychiatry, while also curbing its abuses, be they deliberate or unintended.

The "answer" to this question lies not in a particular substantive solution. Rather, I would suggest that it rests in a reassessment of the social process by which we determine when and how mental health treatment shall be imposed on an unwilling subject. Such an assessment must, I would submit, begin with the recognition that the ultimate decision whether to impose treatment is a legal, not a medical, question.

As I indicated earlier, this is not to suggest that medical input is not critical to the decision. It is. But such input must rest on fully candid expert testimony, subject to the rigors of the adversary system, so that doctors are forced to explain what they do *not* know, as well as what they do know, and why.

Many doctors, perhaps due to their lack of understanding, react unfavorably to the adversary system. This is unfortunate. The adversary system, as I have often noted, does not create adversity (*i.e.*, conflict and opposition). It is rather a decisional mechanism for attempting to resolve adversity which necessarily exists when parties present competing claims. Likewise, cross-examination, the most effective tool of the adversary system, is more than a license for lawyers to engage in legitimized hostility. It is a means by which the biases and conflicts of interests of any witness can be surfaced so that the decision maker can see as much as possible of the total picture before arriving at a conclusion.

That there are competing claims in the imposition of involuntary treatment is obvious. Any doubt on this score is put to rest by this book. Equally apparent, although perhaps not as well recognized, is that institutional psychiatrists have biases and conflicts of interest. They are biased in that their training predisposes them toward seeing pathology and wanting to treat it. And, they are subject to conflicting interests because they have allegiances to the institutions, which pay their salaries, as well as to the individuals whom they seek to serve. If these considerations, as they bear on a specific case, are not revealed to the decision maker, the decision inevitably suffers.

Given the constitutional dictate that courts must resolve the questions raised by coercive psychiatry, mental health professionals face an important choice: either they can open up their processes to the scrutiny of judicial analysis and public concern, or they can simply refuse to participate. Admittedly, the former choice will not be wholly pleasant for these professionals. It will mean that their insecurities, their doubts, and their mistakes will be aired for public viewing. No one welcomes such a prospect.

As troubling as participation in the judicial process might seem, however, it is far better than the alternative of withdrawal. Such withdrawal might bolster professional self-image by preserving the mystique of psychiatry; but it will also assuredly undermine the cause of people who genuinely need help. I say this because I am convinced that psychiatry has a significant body of knowledge that can and should be brought to bear on the difficult questions involved in involuntary treatment. If this knowledge does not enter the courtroom, judicial decisions, which also seek to help people in need, will be correspondingly impoverished.

I would hope then that, among its other contributions, *Insanity Inside Out* becomes the occasion for a reevaluation by judges and mental health professionals alike of their respective roles in the commitment process. For, if we are to have fewer Donaldsons in the future—be they people who are improperly confined or people who are needlessly abandoned—we will need a judiciary that is willing to accept its constitutional responsibility, and a mental health profession that is willing to attempt to ensure that this responsibility is responsibly exercised. These are large demands, but the problems cannot be met with less.

DAVID L. BAZELON
Chief Judge
U.S. Court of Appeals
Washington, D.C.

TO SPEND AN HOUR WITH KEN DONALDSON IS TO KNOW THAT YOU HAVE met an extraordinary man. To spend a year with him—as I just have—is to appreciate the depth of his qualities.

And when you measure Ken's virtues—his gentleness, his perspicacity about people, his honesty, his easy mirth—when you measure these against the starkness of his experience, you are forced to thoughts about character and adversity.

The adversity Ken has borne is detailed in these pages. The strengths of the man radiate between the words. Indeed, there is present a fortitude which some would call recalcitrance, obsession, illness. Surely it is intense self-possession—call it obsession if you will—that would make a man resist the assembled judgment of Chattahoochee for so achingly long when freedom might be had through following it. So too has he resisted many of my attempts to distinguish possibility from probability.

Donaldson marshalls his antagonists' charges—with all their harshness—as carefully as his own. He offers without prettification his account of events as they were experienced by him. He knows full well what judgments may be drawn, but his conviction is that his history must be delivered without evasion.

That is the point I wish to emphasize, and that is my reason for laying aside conventional editorial reticence. By consciously exposing his own vulnerability, Ken Donaldson adds to the value of this volume. *Insanity Inside Out* not only reveals treatment conditions which we must ameliorate, but it raises directly the need to rethink our too pat definitions of mental illness. That so partial a categorization should deprive a man of Ken's creativity and nobility of his freedom to function demeans and deprives us as well.

As that unsung advocate of the ill and abused, Morton Birnbaum, is fond of saying, "The light of a thousand candles casts no shadows." The array of mental health problems has many shadows, and the more brightly lit these recesses, the better. Ken Donaldson's classic book will be more than a candle—it will be a spotlight. We must look where it points.

SIG MOGLEN

CHAPTER 1

A Rupture

THE DAY THE FIFTEEN YEARS WENT DOWN THE DRAIN WAS DECEMBER 10, 1956.

As the State of Florida looked out over the Gulf of Mexico, there was hardly a ripple in the wake of the setting sun. It was an evening meant for contentment and reflection over iced tea.

A dozen streets in from the Gulf, I let my eyes rest a moment on the coleus up against the white clapboards of the cabaña on my parents' trailer.

It had been a busy day: packing, sorting papers, making a first draft on my income tax report; in two weeks I was to start on a kitchen job for the season at a hotel at Boca Grande. The iced tea I would drink later, alone, over in my cottage on the south street of the court while I read law books.

It saddened me to face my parents at the table. In their late seventies, they seemed to have outgrown the age of understanding. They even seemed hostile to my autobiography, which I had sent three days previously to an editor. They wished neither to read it nor discuss it. This mystified me because we were a family which took interest in one another's projects and not inclined to argue. Always before, except once, my parents had been a comfort over the bumps of a rather rough life. So, after several years of my knocking about the country, divorced, I had hoped for a few quiet evenings of the kind of understanding talk that is more valuable than all the oil deposits of the world.

As it was, I stepped into the cabaña, not with a feeling of dread, but with the wish the hotel job had already started. Dad was on the sofa in the trailer. I spoke to him and turned toward the kitchen. There was a knock on the screen door. As Dad did not get up, I answered.

There were two men in sport shirts. The tall one spoke: "You Kenneth Donaldson?"

"Yes." I stepped outside.

"You're under arrest." He showed his badge.

"For what?"

"Somebody told the sheriff some things and he got an order from the judge."

"I'm not trying to be funny, please understand, but I would like to see the order."

"No. We're deputies. We want to talk to you at the jail."

"We can talk here." I took a hold of the doorknob.

The second deputy said, "Go ahead, show it to him."

So the first pulled a paper from inside his shirt and read off my name and said it was signed by Jack White, Pinellas County Judge.

It didn't seem exactly proper. But, not knowing Florida law, I would go down as a law-abiding citizen and talk to somebody. "Let me say good-by to my mother."

Nodding, they waited outside.

I stopped on the trailer step, maybe to remain in sight of the deputies.

"I've been arrested," I said. It sounded hollow.

Mother did not look up from the stove.

"They're taking me to jail."

She raised her hands with the spoon but did not turn her white head—mysterious as the arrest itself.

"I'm going now," I said, stunned. "If I'm not right back, will you get a lawyer down first thing in the morning?"

She turned around, but the expression through her silver-rimmed glasses was unreadable, angled slightly to my left, the first time she had ever done this when talking to me. And she said, "The one you talked to?"

"No—not the state's attorney—any other one. Good-by."

"Do you have to go now, just before supper?"

From the striking blueness of a vacation sky to the stygian blackness of a basement ceiling, I had come to be the guest of Pinellas County in the "hole" of their new jail, because "somebody had told the sheriff something."

It was a 7 × 10-foot dark green box with a 3 × 10-inch slit glassed at eye level and one open at waist height. A grille, top and bottom, let light shadow in from a drop bulb by the door to the stairs, also locked. The other cell was empty. I held my breath to try to catch the sound of traffic, church bell, or train whistle. The lone sound all night was somebody walking behind the cell once and flushing the seatless toilet from the outside.

"So this is how they talk to you!" I thought over and over.

Anger subsided after hours of walking the rough floor. My guesses during the sleepless night as to why I was there seemed absurd. They don't put you in jail for sending a book to a publisher, do they? Or did Dad, who thought everybody was on the level, think that his son was not?

But, no, it was all a practical joke these crackers had cooked up to initiate a visiting Yankee—like the snipe hunts in South Carolina; and in the morning the lawyer would be there, and I would go back to the cottage, pick up the papers filed all over the bed, pack the lawbooks in a suitcase, and give my toolboxes a final inspection. My carpenter tools I would leave with the folks. I was clearing out of this state on the first bus back to Philadelphia.

Sitting on the edge of the bunk, I felt the cell's walls pressing in toward dark green claustrophobia. I had to get up and walk. Many have felt that weight. It cuts across nerves like a steamroller, crushing normal attitudes, leaving the humiliation of total defeat. The weaklings meet it with a life of crime.

The shock of blank unbelief at finding myself in jail, which a friend later described as enough in itself to cure you of anything, had changed to anger by the next morning. But paroxysms of anger cannot last for two days, this side of insanity.

I knew the waiting in the interminable darkness would sometime end. I also knew that no lawyer was coming; so I gave the jailer fifteen cents, all I had in my pocket, to call the Methodist minister across the square. It was several hours before the jailer happened to come downstairs again. He told me no one had answered the phone at the parsonage. Before I could say anything, he said, "You're incommunicado," and like a child getting away from the spook in the closet he locked the door and went back up.

I knew it was late afternoon when the pan of supper was shoved onto the ledge of the open slit. This time I drank the warm tea, my first caffeine in months. A half hour after disembodied hands had removed the dishes, the evening jailer opened the cell. A slight elderly man, he was smiling.

"You're not crazy," he said. "You don't belong locked up like an animal. I'm moving you upstairs to the hospital block. Had to go over the desk. They had a hold on you—to keep you down here—but I went over their heads."

My father would not have done that, put me in the hole.

At the top, the third floor, there was glorious blindness as I stepped from the elevator into full sunshine from over the Gulf. I was the only one up there, in maximum security, six double cells.

By the time fifteen-watt shadows from the bars, front and back, crossed in wide angles on my dusty shoes, I had cleared away the grease and dried egg on the steel table with soap and rags that a trusty poked in.

In the morning I felt like a caged crow. Yet I would stand on my dignity, and I regarded with suspicious bitterness the uniformed deputy who entered to serve a paper. It ordered Kenneth Donaldson to a sanity hearing.

The deputy waited. "Understand it?"

"Yes."

He tried again before clanking shut the gate. "Sure you don't want me to read it for you?"

"No."

I waited five agonizing days for the date set, the 18th. When nobody came for me then, I assumed they were of a mind with the old jailer and had dropped the crazy charges. A release could be coming any minute.

Once a person gets over the shock of being condensed into $10 \times 10 \times 8$ feet, his need to exist takes over, makes quick adjustments. Thoughts go out to loved ones, their problems returning to perspective. I even figured it would cure the ills of mankind to lock everyone up, let everyone have a taste of it, say, in two equal batches, changing places every six months.

I took an interest in the other souls being added. We were lost souls, isolated even from the rest of purgatory, the two floors below us. But one Sunday evening the heavy doors at each end were left open and we heard a church choir singing carols downstairs.

Our contacts with the rest of the jail were the circumspect Negro trusties, who brought the two scanty and greasy meals. They relayed our notes to the desk, brought our newspapers, and got other things for us at the stores. The evening monotony was broken by the arrival of the snack cart.

A trusty brought me five dollars, leaving thirty-five in my billfold at the desk, more than enough for a bus ticket to Philadelphia. I ordered a daily paper. From the snack cart I bought writing paper, toothbrush and paste, and two coconut bars for a laxative.

We were so forgotten that we could have burned the place down, had there been much to burn. A drunk fired his mattress one night, bathing us in smoke until the smoldering was doused in the morning.

By this time I had several neighbors, though I scarcely caught a glimpse of them, because they were added or subtracted usually in early morning or late evening when I was on my bunk. About all I saw was the arms on each side, as we swapped newspapers or as I passed my coffee around the solid-steel side of the cell.

My first neighbor, on the right, worked in a finance company office. His mother brought him an article on brain blocks. He knew positively that a brain block was my trouble. I don't remember what he himself had bugged out to avoid, but he said he would be there only two days and two days it was.

My next neighbor replaced him on my right. The day after I drew the five from the desk, he was leaving penniless for the state penitentiary and put the bite on me for two bucks. There was no reticence between two helpless souls. I even bought him a pint of ice cream in a kind of noncelebration.

On my left arrived the squeaky voice that was George. Usually he was locked up for drunkenness. This time the charge was incompetency, because he had driven through the ditch, stone sober, around a police roadblock on his street.

"My mother'll be down tomorrow," he said. "I'm writing a writ for Circuit Court—habeas corpus. She'll file Monday and I'll walk out free. Costs eighteen dollars. Whyn't you do the same? I'd dictate it."

"In the first place they know by now that I'm not nuts," I said.

"You don't know these people. They'll put you in Chattahoochee. You can't get out."

"What's Chattahoochee?"

"The insane asylum."

"They couldn't do that."

"Better get the writ."

"Wouldn't be enough for the bus then."

"Ask your mother."

"Never." But I did not tell George that my parents had now piled on the last straw by failing to send a lawyer to my jail cell. We had once been a devoted family. Then they had almost alienated me completely, a few years previously, by abetting the spread of malicious gossip about me (though they had done so innocently). At that time they wanted me given electroshock treatments. I consequently blew my stack and drew away from them.

"Ask her, man—or you'll be out of circulation for years."

I was indignant, not worried. They couldn't keep me forever. Someone in authority would have to talk to me. I wrote Governor Collins. I wrote many others, including the Salvation Army, a friend, vicinity newspapers. Nobody answered except Travelers Aid, Philadelphia. They said: "You would do better to stay in Florida. . . ." It was so much easier to help a soul stranded without funds between trains than to help one lost in a "Mexican jail."

Well, I damn sure would ask somebody else. In the meanwhile, I had worn a hole in the sole of my shoe on the concrete floor, walking and thinking. I was determined to go down to the *Evening Bulletin* upon reaching Philadelphia and have them take a picture of the way I had been so summarily treated in Florida. It made no difference that a safety razor was passed along the cells each week, I would have a beard for the picture. One thin knee of my khaki pants had caught on the corner of the bunk, ripping a four-inch flap. What a picture—beard, rip, hardened eyes!

By now, all six cells were full. My new neighbor on the right, Jody, had a big black arm that received my coffee. He had been returned from Raiford Penitentiary to stand trial on another charge. In a way, we were all waiting like animals in a barn on a remote farm, whose caretaker lay dead from a stroke of lightning. Yet, we just couldn't lie down and die. To keep up our spirits and take up some of the slack in our afternoons, I taught them to play the Big Depression game "Battleships."

Another help was the woman put at the far end, Mabel. She told us her story. She had sunbathed in the altogether, this in her own yard in St. Petersburg and shielded from her neighbors' eyes, but their just knowing she was doing it was enough for her arrest. They put her first in the St. Pete jail in a strip cell, without clothes or food or water. She caught urine in her hands to drink. Now, with never a hearing, she was destined for Chattahoochee.

Her story brought sorrow to the cellblock, but she also brought sympathy for our hearts, leading, in a sweet throaty voice each evening, the songs from her huge store, religious to bawdy.

Next to her was Albert, about thirty. He had killed his wife and two children with a butcher knife as they slept. He was heartsick. His story was on the front pages, but we did not talk about it in the cellblock. He sent out for ice cream twice a day and ate nothing else. At night he started the singing in his good baritone and hated to knock it off for bed. His especial favorite, which haunts me today, was the beautiful hymn, "An Evening Prayer." Over and over, with her heart in it, silky, silvery Mabel led: "If I have wounded any soul today. . . ."

Albert asked for a trial, he wanted the chair. Two psychiatrists sat before his cell and interviewed him. In the other cells, we overheard only once, his voice coming from the depths: "I had a compulsion." The newspapers said the doctors urged him to claim insanity. He insisted on the chair. The judge gave him life.

Over in the women's quarters, there was a shower and no women; so a jailer took us over in pairs one night, though Mabel was not paired and got no wash-down. Albert was my partner. The reaction on first coming face to face with a maniacal killer, in a shower of all places, was to glue eyes on him until his manner reassured. He was skin and bones, polite and friendly.

"Want to see the steel plate in my head?" he asked and bent his close-cropped head to give me a look. "From Okinawa with the Marines."

Another sad case was nineteen-year-old Billy, on my left, being put away by his mother, after his threatening her at the beach. While he was far from sane, as retardation looked to me then at the beginning of my long education in insanity, he amazed me by discussing TV programs rationally by the hour with Mabel and Albert. But to his mother, he was just a heartache. "The doctors down here don't know what to do for him," she told me, "but they say the doctors up there do."

Billy did not rail at his mother. When she was gone, he would say, over and over, "This is the end of the line." Both visiting days each week, she brought him goodies and, at Christmas, homemade cookies for us others too, as well as a stack of paperbacks for me.

"You probably need treatment of some kind," she said as she handed over the books. That surprised me. As I look back, that was my second diagnosis, one that could easily pass as the official version. Would one be locked up if he didn't need treatment?

Billy did not stay with us long. In his loneliness he would cry out, "Boozhwaaaah!" At night he would spend hours noisily dipping out the toilet bowl with his metal cup while crying, "I'm dead. You hurt me but good. Boozhwaaah!" One night he woke me from sleep. I yelled at him and he cried out, "I'm not bothering anybody down here, God."

"Well, this is God," I intoned in my deepest voice. "Stop that damned racket down there."

Billy went to bed.

The next night there was no stopping him. He yelled and dipped, and he banged his cup on the bars, the universal call for the jailer; however, through the steel doors no jailer heard. But the neighbors across the street did. In the morning Billy went to the hole.

I thought then that Billy was funny. I bristled because his mother and others had put me in the same category. So, when a plump matron called hello, one day, and said the doctor would be by on his rounds, I said: "I don't care about a doctor. But would you call a priest for me?"

"I'd be glad to," she said.

That was it. At long last someone intelligent, someone dissociated from this crazy business, would be up to see me. I'd be out in a day or two. In the meantime, bring on your doctor.

I had not been reduced to the point of losing my civility toward everyone, but people thinking I was sick made the sight of a doctor sour.

"I'm a doctor," the short man in a dark suit greeted me pleasantly.

"I don't need a doctor," I said firmly, and, alas, dangerously more firmly than necessary. "I need a lawyer."

"So, you don't need a doctor?" he mimicked, catching my underlying hostility. Then scorning the observation, he asked, "Do you happen to know where you are?"

"In the Pinellas County jail," I said, but too late, ingratiatingly.

"Know why?" The professional smile could have been sardonic.

"On a writ of *Inquisition of Incompetency.*"

"Who got the writ?"

"I don't know."

"No idea at all?"

I hated to go further, fearing a misconstruing; but I needed to be helpful fast, so I explained, "I would think it is because of the autobiography I sent to an editor three days before I was locked up. You see, a group of people have slandered me. I wrote a book to expose them. I can conceive of no one else who would want me locked up."

The doctor edged over in front of the next cell. That gave me some concern. But surely he couldn't possibly think I was sick, I thought in 1956. Probably he was just busy and saw that everything was okay. Eventually, I knew, this thing would have to wind down.

When the white-uniformed matron happened by to see Mabel next day, I called down, "Did you call the priest?"

"Oh, I can't do that."

"Would you take this note to the captain then?"

"Oh, I'd be glad to."

A few days later, when an old man had a heart attack in the end cell, his doctor looked in on me before going back downstairs.

"How are you doing?" he said warmly, seeming unruffled by being called out at breakfast.

"All right—for here," I said.

"Know what day it is?"

"Tuesday, 5 January."

"Is it raining out?"

"No."

"How did you happen to get in here?"

I repeated the story told the other doctor. I proceeded with some confidence, taking his intentness for deep understanding.

"Don't you think your mother might have done it?" he asked.

"We had no quarrel. There is no reason under the sun for my being behind bars."

Total time: two minutes.

I congratulated myself on making headway. Two doctors now knew that I knew what day it was. What more was needed?

With the new year, new hopes: a tall gray-haired man appeared with a clipboard.

Without waiting for me to get up to the bars, he read off: "Kenneth Donaldson?" His thin mouth barely moved.

"Yes sir."

"Age fifty?"

"No—forty-eight."

"Residing on A Street, Belleaire Village Court?"

"B Street. And who are you?"

"I am Judge White. You were in a New York State asylum in 1945?"

"No—1943."

The judge pulled an envelope from his left coat pocket, read the back and crumpled it into his pocket. He raised an eyebrow and looked up for the first time, over his glasses. "The doctors find you evasive and I find you combative. I am sending you to the state asylum."

They can't do that! My head pounded. The judge was turning away.

"I want a real hearing," I blurted out.

"You've just had your hearing," the office of authority said scornfully.

"I mean a public one." There were still the guarantees of the United States Constitution.

"What do you want? One on the courthouse steps?" his words came trailing back.

"That would be better than this!" In twenty more feet the judge would be out of the cellblock. I yelled, "I want a lawyer!"

Majesty was gone.

But miracle, he came back. "I'll let you have a lawyer. What one?"

"I don't know any here. Would you send me one, please?"

"Do what I can," he said gruffly.

I didn't hear my neighbors' indignation. I was a hunk of jello clinging by two celery stalks to the bars.

The following week, a young man, 140 pounds, handed through the bars his business card: "Milton D. Jones, Attorney-at-Law."

"Oh—you're from the judge," I said. "Sure glad to see you."

He backed off to avoid shaking hands. "I'll arrange a hearing for thirty-five dollars."

"Fair enough." But at that stage in my indoctrination into the ways of Florida, the coincidence of its being exactly what I had downstairs worried me. More than half would be needed for the bus. "Would you take a check for part—on my Philadelphia bank? I don't know about Greyhound's taking one. I'll give you fifteen dollars cash and a check."

"That's all right. Do you have a check?"

"No."

He started down for one.

"Just a minute," I said. I wanted to face the doctors before the judge. That was okay with him. He'd get the check and we'd have the hearing.

"Not without the doctors," I said.

"I'll call them," he said. Returning in twenty minutes, he said the doctors could not come for two weeks.

That was okay with me. The first two days I had paid the price. Two more weeks wouldn't make much difference—now.

"No," he said, "the judge is ready. If it's necessary, we'll have another hearing with them."

"But I'll not pay without the doctors."

I thought that was the end of it, but five minutes later a jailer took me down and locked me in the wire-caged platform at one side of the visitor's room. Two yellow oak desks faced me outside. Judge and lawyer came quietly to the desks. The lawyer sat with his eyes down. There was no introduction.

"Tell me about your case," said the judge, looking gravely over his glasses for a moment, then looking at the wall. He represented the only way out through the solid wall of public apathy. Was it fear that made them put me in a cage? Was it distaste that made them look away? What was it that made them throw one in the hole and then forget? Was mine a special case? The judge's face was immobile. Behind it I would have to find the answers, but I could not ascertain how much intelligence he had.

I would get one thing straight at the beginning. Looking the judge in the eye, I said, "I told Mr. Jones I did not want a hearing without the doctors who say I'm nuts. Furthermore, I told him I would not pay until they were here." Despite the magnitude of my predicament, I was quite calm.

The lawyer said nothing and continued staring at the floor.

"Tell me your story," said the judge, possibly bored, his voice showing no awareness of anything out of the way.

"I don't know who is responsible," I said, "for putting me in here." All sorts of possibilities flashed before my imagination.

"Your father is the only signer of the paper," the judge said.

"We had no quarrel. . . ." I thought of my father's aversion to even reading the letters I had received in answer to my own from the White House, from Senator Russell, from George Meany. But there was no point in bringing that up.

At this point in my recital, the lawyer did a remarkable thing: without having said aye, yes, or no, he walked out.

I continued explaining to the judge. To show there was no psychiatric problem, I told about my recent examination at the psychiatric clinic in Philadelphia. Then I talked about my last-minute decision to visit my parents for a few months, planning on getting some respite as well as doing a few things for the folks.

"So you see, Your Honor," I said, "doctors up there examined me and found me okay. Here no doctors examined me, yet they say I am crazy. This is ridiculous. I am no crazier today than when I left Philadelphia. That's where I belong—where people know I'm all right."

The judge walked around and unlocked the cage and stood with me in the center of the large room. "You were in a mental institution once before and your father doesn't think you are ready to go on your next job. It was a hotel job? Therefore," the judge said, for a moment letting me think an arm would be put around my shoulders, "for these two reasons I am sending you to Chattahoochee."

"But I'm not sick, Your Honor."

"A few weeks up there. Take some of that new medication—what's the name of it?—and you'll be back."

He rang for the jailer.

It gave me the feeling of expecting the Grand Canyon to shed a tear if someone happened to get shoved over the south rim.

Yet my belief was strong that there was enough common sense in the world to prevent one's being stonewalled, literally. And as several days passed without further threat to my welfare, I was encouraged to try something more. On a Sunday, I talked to Jody's father and mother, who stopped after church. The father, with dark gray suit and white kinky hair, listened gravely with his hat in his hand. The mother, in a dark print dress, said that their kind had to be careful in Pinellas County, but on the next visiting day she trudged through exceptional heat to the Catholic priest four blocks away. Then, as nobody came to see me, a week later she went to the Christian Science church for me.

On Sunday after services, a Scientist couple came. I apologized for the torn pants and explained about the beard. They heard my story out.

"You seem all right to us," Mr. and Mrs. Jenn said. "This is a misunderstanding. Yes, we'll see the judge—and your mother. One thing we do know, you don't belong in jail."

Lying on the bed that night, I remembered the stranger coming up to the gas pump in Philadelphia, the day before I left for Florida, and saying, "They've got a funny law down there."

"Poof!" I thought, before falling off to sleep. "This is America, not Russia."

This is a copy of the paper that was served on me upon my arrest, December 10, 1956:

IN THE COURT OF THE COUNTY JUDGE,
IN AND FOR _____Pinellas_____ COUNTY,

STATE OF FLORIDA.

INQUISITION OF INCOMPETENCY
(Petition by member of family
or next of kin)

_____Kenneth Donaldson_____

TO _____Hon. Jack F. White_____, COUNTY JUDGE IN AND FOR THE COUNTY AFORESAID:

Your petitioner respectfully represents unto your Honor that ___he is the_____ **father** _____of_____ **Kenneth Donaldson** , *who is* _____**50**_____ *years of age, and whose address is* _____**Belleaire Village Trailer Court, Largo (A St.)**_____ , *Florida. The said* _____**Kenneth Donaldson**_____ *is believed to be incompetent within* the intent and meaning of Section 394.20, Florida Statutes, 1941, as amended by Chapter 23157, Laws of 1945, and the nature of h **is** disability is_____ **Persecution complex, increasing signs of paranoid delusions, petitioner believes him to be potentially dangerous.**

The members of the family of the said **Kenneth Donaldson** *with their addresses, are as follows:*

Members of Family	Relationship	Addresses
William T. Donaldson	Father	**Belleaire Village**
Marjorie K. Donaldson	Mother	**Trailer Court, A Street, Largo, Florida**

WHEREFORE, your petitioners pray that an examination be made as to the mental and physical condition, or both, of the said **Kenneth Donaldson**, *as provided by law, and that an order be entered adjudging the said* **Kenneth Donaldson** *to be incompetent, if_____ he is so found.*

/s/ **William T. Donaldson**

STATE OF FLORIDA
COUNTY OF_____ **Pinellas**
William T. Donaldson *being sworn by me, the undersigned officer, says on oath that the statements contained in the foregoing petition are true, to the best of h* **is** *knowledge and belief.*

/s/ **William T. Donaldson**
Sworn to and subscribed before me **at Clearwater, Fla.,**
this 10th day of December A. D. **1956.**
(Notarial Seal) /s/ **Ruby W. Breaker**

Notary Public, State of Florida
at large. My commission expires
Jan. 18, 1960. Bonded by
American Surety Co. of N.Y.

Filed Dec. 10, 1956
Jack F. White, County Judge
By R. W. Breaker, Clerk.

CHAPTER 2

A Previous
Rupture

ON A DREARY WINTER MORNING IN 1943, I STOOD BEFORE AN Onondaga County judge in the stately courthouse of Syracuse, New York, before the regular session came to order. I was not a criminal. I was there to ask the judge's advice on a matter that had come up on my job at a defense plant. I had had some trouble and felt that I could not go back to work again. But the law said that I could not quit a defense job. The judge said it was a matter for the doctors. He advised me to sign myself in at a psychiatric observation center for ten days. On my decision voluntarily to place my fate in the hands of doctors lies the wreckage of my life, traumatizing everyone else in my family as well.

In 1943 I was thirty-four years old. I was physically run down. In a span of twelve months, my wife had been operated on; one of our three children had been in an oxygen tent for weeks; and I had had two herniotomies. We were saddled with doctor bills, some being relics of the Big Depression, in the form of judgments held by collection agencies. I was working on the second shift at General Electric's new defense plant in Syracuse, operating a milling machine. Then from midnight to 4:00 A.M., I went to adult-education machine shop classes to prepare for a better job. That would mean something better on the table for the wife and me (the children got their orange juice and milk) than the omnipresent macaroni and potatoes. In my "spare time," I thought I could make a few dollars for Christmas by assembling and selling fluorescent lamps, which I bought from a mail-order house; however, fluorescents were not catching on fast and my sales were nil.

Then one night I blacked out going home from work. Today I know that sheer physical exhaustion alone could have accounted for it. At the time, I believed that I had had a nervous breakdown.

With my memory complete today, except for eight hours from one night and a few hours from the next week, I can tell what happened in 1943. With my natural manual dexterity and the increased proficiency from night school, I was able to turn out more work than my neighbors. I thought this a patriotic thing to do, with our boys fighting on foreign shores; however, there are some things a war does not change, one being the work habits of the masses. Some blue-collar benefits are, as I had myself seen, won at great price. It seemed, though, that in a war emergency there could be some relaxation in piecework schedules. But the foreman put me straight.

Coming by after supper, he said: "Donaldson, you've turned in extra pieces for two nights. The other men aren't going to like this. I can't have any trouble here."

"All right," I said. "But, say, I've been going to night school on West Genesee for three months. I'm working on a lathe now. Is there any chance I could get a better job here?"

"We're opening a new bank of vertical lathes soon. I'll put you on days with one of the old-timers to break in. I'll let you know."

It was a time of public tension, if not among all the factory workers, at least in the press and on the radio. Usually, the young man, at the machine to my right, and I talked about the ebb and flow of the war. We always returned to President Roosevelt's policies, disagreeing heatedly about some. "What we ought to do," I said, "would be to let Stalin and Hitler knock each other off, first. One is as bad as the other." "No," my neighbor argued vehemently.

On the last night before I was to start on the new lathes, I noticed that men and women on the other mills were watching me. I cut short my talking with my neighbor. I was wondering what it was I had said that might have disturbed them. Some of the men grouped near me in the washroom, but no one said anything to me.

Then, as we waited in our street clothes, sitting in front of our machines in the vast stillness of the building, anticipating the whistle, there were curses in back of me disconnected from any conversation. They could have been directed at anybody. I merely noted the oddity of their occurrence. On the way to the time clock, there was no longer any question about the remarks being directed at me: "Put the son of a bitch in the army for a couple of years." "We'll get the bastard in the parking lot."

In the darkness of late winter, I remember avoiding our car pool and walking away between the rows of cars.

Friends say that I might have got a blow on the head. Whatever, my next memory is of downtown. Before the first grayness of dawn, with the ground frozen but with no snow on the shoulders of the statue of Chief Eckel in the park, my father and my wife pulled up to the curb in Vanderbilt Square where I was walking past storefronts. They were relieved at finding me, but upset that I could not explain what had happened. I said only that I could not go back to work. Over coffee at a beanery, I could not tell them why, for I did not really know myself. I did not want to tell them that I would get beat up if I went back. But beat up for what? A man is not going to walk into a beating without knowing what it is for.

Nor have the intervening years given me the answer. I have learned only one other fact: the union at GE, which was the United Electrical Workers, was Communist controlled. It is no more than speculation, a searching for a needle in the haystack of time, to wonder if my neighbor ran to the union steward to get even with me or if someone else did, believing either that I was a Communist or a non-Communist, as the case may have been.

As I look back, I see that the logical solution would have been to call in sick for a couple of days, after which with renewed strength I could have faced any unpleasantness. But there is an equally logical reason why neither I nor my family even thought for a moment of that simple solution. I come from a long line of proud industrious workers to whom it was inconceivable to call in sick as long as one could stand on his two feet. That is why, as I was still on my feet but refused to go to work, my family took me before the judge.

I knew that I was not nuts. But I knew nothing about

"official" insanity; my family knew only that I had acted "crazy"; the judge knew it should be left up to the doctors.

The judge had given me a third choice: enlisting in the army. But that was foreign to my way of life, which had been centered on books and academic things, before I had turned to manual work to support my family. Obviously, I needed time to think.

I found that time in a tiny locked room, with no doorknob on my side. In the second day, my plain common sense saw that there would be no problem: I would just go back to work after these ten days.

After the fifth day, I was allowed to sit around with other men in a small parlor. I remember, also, getting an angry reprimand from the nurse, who walked us for a few minutes every day in the frosty air on a tiny porch, bricked up above our heads. I was not walking fast enough, my shoulders were not back, my head was not up. My couldn't-care-less reply amounted to a personal insult to her.

One day I was called down to the second floor for an interview by a doctor, who happened to be a woman. Her tone was overbearing, as if people bored her. It suddenly all seemed so childish in the cold light from her forbidding eyes.

I said, "I've thought it over for a week. I don't want to talk about it."

"See here, I'm a doctor," she snapped. "Do you understand that? Why didn't you go back to work?"

"I don't want to talk about it."

"Then we'll have to help you."

On the tenth day I was driven with others, men, women, and children, sitting on wooden benches in a windowless van, and I was let out in the custody of a white-uniformed employee at the front building of Marcy State Hospital, near Utica. It was a three-story brick building, as I recall, with a front porch, at the top of a long sloping lawn.

Tragedy at the whim of a bureaucrat? Pulling petals from a flower? One goes free and one goes—

In 1943, I was busy thinking about how to save my own skin, as I sat for two days in a huge dayroom, with its strong smells and loud noises, amid unhappy men milling about in ill-fitting pants and hospital gowns, a few naked, nearly all barefoot. At almost any hour, some healthy soul would be urinating on the floor, striking the same attitude I had to the nurse at the Observation Center.

Someone else would scream and jump, and someone would writhe and run into another patient, knocking him down.

Forty-eight hours later, as soon as there was room, I was moved to the open ward on the first floor. The quiet bedroom was eight tight rows each way. On my first walk, I looked into the store in a corner of the basement. I longed for a candy bar, but my money had not been returned on my leaving the Observation Center.

Up to this point in my life, it had never occurred to me that I was not a human being. But it must be that I had ceased to be one; otherwise, the doctor, who trotted through this ward every morning, would have thrown out a word or two to me, as he did to others on his dash..

Several of the men, following me to the porch or rocking with me in the parlor, exchanged hometowns and sizes of families. Why was I there? I really couldn't tell them, but I was sure somebody would soon acknowledge the mistake of putting a sane person in a crazy house.

In looking back through my hospital record, I find these words: "He still resides on Ward A-2, but may cause some difficulties in his management occasionally, because he is some-what surly and domineering now." That probably followed the day that the "patient boss" on the ward took down my hand-kerchiefs, which I had hung to dry, and threw them away. When he turned around and asked me to run an errand for the ward, I told him to go shaft himself. Surly? Surely, I had a right to be— anywhere except on a funny farm.

I bored the men and women at my table in the dining room with my gripes on the food. Open-ward women, from the other half of the first floor, ate with us. We picked our own places at round tables with white cloths. This was at a time when the only good dish was a tureenful of boiled potatoes in a milky solution, while at the same time the newspapers were commending the state farms on raising the best of food for the state institutions. They did not report that only the entrails came down to the patients' tables.

Outraged, I gave a soliloquy against the politicians, causing the friendliest girl at the table to tell me, as we carried up our dirty dishes: "The only thing wrong with you, Kenneth, is that you talk too damn much."

That was my first aboveboard diagnosis. But recognizing the disease was not also a cure, as I demonstrated a few days later.

One noon, a nurse met me at the dining room entrance and took me to the adjoining room where I was to run the dishwasher. The cardinal rule was to have clean dishes and silver at all times for the doctors' and nurses' dining room, off on another side. She left me to tackle mountains of dishes caked with egg and oatmeal. I was working along in steam up to my eyeballs, with a new batch of dirty plates now pouring in from the patients, when the friendly girl called me over to the opening. She had fixed me a plate before everything had gone. I was taking a few fast mouthfuls with my fingers when the nurse popped back.

"What's this?" she said angrily. "You've let the machine stop—and the doctors without plates."

"I was just getting something before it was too late," I said.

"You're not to eat that stuff anymore. Here—see this chop?" She handed me her dirty plate. "There's plenty of meat on it yet. That's what you're going to eat. We want to fatten you up. Now get busy or I'll have to call one of the doctors."

I was supposed to eat out of their dirty dishes like a dog? I'd be damned! "You can tell the doctor I don't eat like that."

"You mean you're too good to eat after us? You're the first one we ever had trouble with. This is the best job in the hospital."

"You'd better get somebody else then."

I walked out and she stacked dishes.

Winter-gray monotony followed: reading the morning paper on the ward, buying *Time* at the basement store with the dollar from home, walking when it was not storming.

All I wanted to talk about on Sundays, when my wife visited, was getting signed out. At her second request, the doctor put me before staff.

Eight doctors sat behind a table on the stage of the auditorium, above the dining room. I sat in the second row of the orchestra, with an attendant behind me.

I did not know it at the time, but the doctors were working with a half-dozen facts, garnered by social workers in interviews with my wife and mother at their homes, plus these two women's opinions of why I had "cracked up." My wife thought my mother had been too strict with me and that my parents valued my brother more than me. My mother thought I did not get along well with my father and that I was jealous of my brother's success in his career. Nonetheless, I do not fault my family. They were trying to help the doctors understand my "breakdown." On their part, the doctors "interpreted" my dropping out of college and staying around the house for a couple of years as a depression, I see only now from the record.

"You were cared for at home?" they asked me.

For several years I lived with my parents without paying board. Yes, I was cared for at home! And except for not paying my way, I was a loving and dutiful son. I wrote my first novel during those years. I studied drawing with a mail-order course and at a local high school. I edited our church newspaper. When I got married, it was still the Depression. I went from job to job trying to make more money.

I answered the doctors' questions, fully, about my discouragements and aspirations. I was naïve. We were talking about two different things. To the doctors I was "dull . . . manic . . . schizoid." I have my complete Marcy file in front of me as I write this.

(Incidentally, Marcy would never let me see my own record, though they always remained ready to show it to "any interested party." In 1972 they released a copy to the State of Florida, whose lawyers were fishing to get something on me. But Marcy had to give a copy to my lawyers too!)

I find my Marcy record to be untrue to the extent that it is an "interpretation" made by the doctors, not a verbatim transcript. I learned in Chattahoochee how this is done. In the matter of staff, after the patient leaves the room, the doctors call in a stenographer and dictate the interview.

At Marcy, the doctors at staff had found out about the factory workers' threats on my last night at GE. When the staff questioned me, I felt instinctively that they would not understand what actually had happened, and so I lied. I told them it had all been in my imagination, expecting them to see that I was now recovered. A friend has pointed out that the lie might have been a critical mistake for me. On the other hand, I see the situation as a dilemma. The doctors gave no credence to anything else I told them anyway.

Everything else I told them honestly. I was trying to reason it out with them. Those days locked up had been the first in years in which I had been able to sit down quietly and think. Naïvely, in answering the doctors' questions, I was thinking aloud. I covered the events leading up to my status of not-well-to-do machine operator and my disappointment in not having arrived at a more prestigious position. These were my thoughts, not all of which were covered at staff. But there was no doubt in my mind that doctors, any doctors, would see that my confusion was not from fantasy but from events.

Here, in part, are the doctors' conclusions, taken from my Marcy file:

> This man has made a very poor adjustment in life. He shows illogic and ulterior thinking. He is not satisfied with any of his work and always has some other dreams and delusions about the future of what he could become. He wants to be a lawyer and writer. . . .

> . . . He was overactive but this is more than a manic patient. For no apparent reason he was restless. He is still a seclusive, dull individual. In reference to his delusional ideas, I think we have to deal with schizoid. . . . Dementia praecox, mixed type. I think he should have electric shock treatment. . . .

> . . . Manic depressive type, would probably hold two or three jobs, but he couldn't hold one. I don't think we are dealing with a manic, I think he is a praecox. . . .

> . . . I notice in the family history, the patient's father, although he liked him very much, they couldn't seem to get along together. His mother was very devoted but would pick on him. That makes for a bad start and with most cases of dementia praecox they get into various difficulties. . . . I think he is a case of dementia praecox. It is not out of the way for them to be depressed or grandiose. He does a lot of altruistic thinking, is paranoid. He says that he has insight into his condition. I don't think he appreciates the seriousness. . . .

On the basis of that hearing, which was the first time I had ever talked to any doctor at Marcy, I was put down for electroconvulsive therapy. And, also, it was, except for a couple of minutes at the Observation Center, the first time I had talked to a doctor since the judge suggested putting the matter in their hands.

There is nothing in the hospital record of what I said that would warrant my receiving any kind of treatment whatsoever. I say that there is nothing in my last thirty-two years—nothing in what I have said, written, or done—that would warrant my being locked up, least of all given electroshock.

My disease was wholly in the minds of others—in the minds of the informants and the doctors. I needed electroshock as much as a gnat needs a rock rammed up its anus. I was only the second one in Marcy to take them: the doctors wanted to study their effect.

It is my judgment that the shocks were punishment for my run-in with the nurse at the dishwasher. In truth, all my trouble can be laid to half a pork chop, as a reporter for the Los Angeles *Times* pointed out while interviewing me in 1975.

If I had known how much trouble that pork chop would be, I would not have refused to talk about it with the doctors. "It was too hot in there," was the only reason I gave for quitting my job on the dishwasher. "That's not the way we heard it," the doctors told me. "We'll put you someplace where it won't be too hot!" I was sent the next day to the refrigerated butchershop and in another few days I got my first shock. There is not a word of all that in the file.

What happened to me is not unusual. A recent experiment was described in an article in *Science,* January 19, 1973, by David L. Rosenhan, a professor of psychology and law at Stanford University. He and seven other sane people signed themselves into twelve mental hospitals across the country, state and private. They found that psychiatrists and other staff members cannot tell the difference between the sane and insane.

Rosenhan wrote: "The hospital itself imposes a special environment in which the meanings of behavior can easily be misunderstood." The eight researchers found that their most commonplace actions on the wards were "interpreted" into disease symbols, as their taking notes for their later article being classified as compulsive writing. All seven were released (after from seven to fifty-two days) as "schizophrenics in remission," despite their best efforts to convince the hospital staff of their sanity.

"We continue," the article said, "to label patients 'schizophrenic,' 'manic-depressive,' and 'insane' as if those words had captured the essence of understanding.... We have known for a long time that our diagnoses are not useful or reliable, but we have nevertheless continued to use them."

In making the charge that my ECT was more for punishment and experiment, I do so not as much in self-justification or in apology for the unsatisfactory life that resulted for me, as in condemnation of the continued use of electroshock on helpless people by doctors who do not know what they are doing and who often couldn't care less. The doctors no more understood a need for electroshock for me than earlier doctors did a need for exorcising the humors in the Middle Ages.

Even the "barbaric" Russians stopped using them as therapy (before I was admitted to Chattahoochee in 1957) because they damage the brain. Recently, they have been used again in Russia, but this time as punishment for political dissidents.

In 1943 I felt that my wife could put a stop to my treatments. She took it up with our family doctor. He told her I needed a rest and that that was the only way I would get one.

Again, we have a long-distance "scientific" diagnosis.

"But I don't need a rest. I am working a full day here in the butchershop. I could work outside," I said.

"But your doctor here—" she said.

"He doesn't know me. He never talked to me until he stopped to tell me he was writing you about shock. Why, I don't even know his name."

"But you went to staff. Those doctors must know what they're doing."

"I told you about that."

She left, close to tears, then gave authorization for ECT.

After she had gone, a fellow patient brought me the front page of the Sunday supplement to a London newspaper, a full-size sheet. It featured a picture story of a London stockbroker who, every time he became excited about the market, would take a course of ECT. "So," the other patient said, continuing the softening-up process, "you'll really be glad you took them."

I was taken, first, to see patients strewn on the floor in coma from insulin shock. I was offered a choice. I certainly would not allow what I had just seen, when ECT sounded so attractive in London. I was congratulated on my perspicacity and assured that nothing could result except great benefit to me.

The first tender victim of ECT in Marcy, at his last treatment, like the Judas goat, led me over to a building at the back of the oval. From then on, I walked alone, figuratively and literally. After passing hundreds of retarded and crippled men, like those on my first day in Marcy, I arrived in a small section of an upper floor. I would disrobe and don a hospital gown. A nurse would grease my temples and adjust the electrodes to either side while I lay on a gurney. Her rubbing the electrodes in to assure contact hurt more than the treatment itself. Then she would wheel the black box up to the gurney and plug in, and together with three male attendants hold me down while the doctor, arriving at the last second, twirled the rheostat. There would be a painless flash like a bad dream that goes pop. It was more frightening in contemplation before and after. After a shock I would come to, groggily struggling over a footrail of one of twenty beds touching sides. An attendant steadied me the first time, until he was sure I could stand alone, a matter of five seconds.

Midway in the course of treatments, I would see, before climbing on the gurney, about a dozen men from the back wards, who had preceded me to the black box. They would be thrashing about and foaming at the mouth.

After twice-a-week shocks (up to twenty-three the record says) the doctors held another staff hearing for me and decided they had helped me enough.

I was given two days off from work. While I was waiting around for my wife to come on the weekend, the guys on the ward began arguing about catching a goldfish on a safety pin without bait. Someone bet me I couldn't do it. I thought the insane asylum was an ideal place to make such an experiment, for I was already labeled "crazy." So with the doctor's permission (he would stop now and listen to me) one morning for a couple of hours, I dangled a pin in a small circular concrete pool down toward the road. I caught only the biting remarks of another doctor and the lighthearted sneers of other passersby.

On Saturday morning, I was allowed to shave myself. In walking to the parking lot with my wife, I pointed out the pool, laughing at my exploit. (Today, sitting in front of the hospital record, I revel in the fact that, dulled as I was from the electricity, the psychiatrists could not burn out of me my temptation to "illogical thinking," which was their term for my lifelong propensity for trying something new. And as against their experiment on me, my experiment did not hurt the fish.) But the look in my wife's eyes warned me to be careful; nevertheless, she handed me the keys to the car and I drove the thing home to Auburn.

[I do not know how these pieces of misinformation arose. Perhaps my wife, in her desire to help me, had provided innocent speculation which the doctors had twisted into something else.]

MARCY STATE HOSPITAL
ABSTRACT OF COMMITMENT PAPER

NAME: W. Kenneth Donaldson

Brought from Syracuse Psychopathic Hospital by J. Mezza in hospital car driven by R. Sears.

ADMITTED: March 12, 1943.

PETITION STATES: Olive J. Donaldson—Petitioner—Wife.

Patient has had a previous episode for which he was not hospitalized. In January 1943 he stated that he was being followed and that people were after him. Patient believes that he has committed a serious crime and that the F.B.I. is after him. He later said that the Government had provided Army and Navy men to look after him. Patient has run away from home on two occasions and has frequently talked about this.

FINANCIAL STATUS: None.

ABSTRACT OF MEDICAL CERTIFICATE: Olive J. Donaldson—Wife—Informant.

HISTORY OBTAINED BY PHYSICIANS:

Patient is at Syracuse Psychopathic Hospital, county of Onondaga. Nativity: Pennsylvania. Date of birth: May 22, 1908. He is a citizen of U.S. He is a legal resident of New York State. Has resided in New York State 28 years. Male. White. Milling Machine Operator. Methodist. Birthplace of parents: Kingston, N.Y. No mentally sick relatives. Patient has been considered of normal mental standard. No treatment for syphilis. Present attack began: January 1943. Characterized by: Delusions, fearfulness; ran away from home. First noticed: Delusions.

EXAMINATION BY PHYSICIANS:

Physical condition: Tall, thin, no somatic complaints. Heart regular. Slightly accelerated. B. P. 100/55. Blood Wasserman and urine negative. Mental condition: Restless, overactive shallow emotionally affect at times inappropriate. Prior to admission thought men were following him to kill him and that he was being protected by many men; now he tends to minimize these ideas but apparently still is suspicious of others. He makes rather grandiose plans; is very changeable in mood; often absorbed.

<u>Patient said</u>: I'm feeling very well—I was upset when I came at cross purposes, didn't know just what to do. It was probably in my head—I thought people were laughing at me.

Signed: Mary F. Brew, M.D.
Jerome E. Alderman, M.D.

Dated: March 11, 1943
Dated [sic] :   Frank P. Malpass
Judge of County Court of Onondaga Co.

CHAPTER 3

1943-1950

A Case
History

IN THE LAZINESS OF THE FIRST SUNDAY MORNING AT HOME FROM THE asylum, my wife pulled me back onto the mattress when I raised my shoulders to get up.

"Not yet, dear," Olive said. "Just let me sleep a little longer."

Six mornings a week saw her hurrying through breakfast to ride with her father to American Locomotive, the diesel-engine plant, in Auburn where they both worked. She had moved back to her parents' farm with the children and gone to work, because my disability check from GE was too small to run a household.

I had been lying awake an hour, since 5:30, the getting-up time at the asylum. Out the front bedroom window in the new light, I could see fresh spring snow, like sponge on the phone wires running from the house. The smell of bacon frying no longer came through the floor register, which opened above the living-room stove. My father- and mother-in-law had long since gone to the barn. They had welcomed me back almost as though nothing had happened since my last visit to the farm in February.

I sank back in the featherbed, leaving a corner of the quilt turned down and watching the slate sky mix in some blue. I thought of the interview I was to have Wednesday at American Locomotive, where Olive was a welder, the only job open for women when she applied. She had put on overalls and helmet, and stood quietly in a booth behind a curtain, afraid to light the torch in her hands. When the group leader found her out, he laughed hilariously at this 5-foot-2, 100-pound bombshell. Instead of crying, she had to laugh too.

Thinking of the coming interview and wondering if I would do as well made me restless. I could lie still no longer. Olive came fully awake, pulling on my arm before my feet hit the slippers.

"Do you know something, Kenny?" Her eyes were now half closed. "I've been looking forward to this morning."

I jerked my arm out of her grasp, not angrily but with a spontaneous determination to finish what I had started out to do— walk to my clothes at the register.

"Oh!" She dropped to the pillow. I got dressed. As I passed the foot of the bed on the way to the stairs, she said, "What's the matter, dear?"

"Why, nothing." I was surprised; it had not occurred to me that I had done anything special.

"You never did this before."

"What?"

"Don't you know what I got married for? What every woman wants?"

"Oh, that! It's dead—something the hospital did."

She sat up.

"I think," I said, "maybe they operated."

"They couldn't! You'd have known!"

"Not when unconscious—in shock."

That was the first thing I noticed that had been altered in me. Such temporary impotence, caused by one thing or another which the hospital does, becomes a prime worry of most male patients, as I learned during fifteen years in Chattahoochee. Fortunately, after Marcy, all my glands began working in a short time.

Pulling away from my wife was only one of the changes after the shock treatments. I was unable to accept even the slightest restriction on my movements, except from those in a position of authority. Of authority figures I was actually fearful, afraid lest I draw their attention to my inadequacies. I was acutely sensitive to ridicule. Inside of me, something wanted to stand proudly, but my head could only hang. It might not show on the outside, but coloring everything was the fear of being revealed as a cripple. Instinctively, I knew that such discovery would be another mule kick to the temples, a continuation of ECT.

I was experiencing what everyone who goes through electroshock does. I experienced exactly what those with jangled nerves or emotional crises do, but without their interfering preoccupations. For that reason I am able to measure, in years, the depth of the abuse, not least of which is the accompanying stigma.

Of course, neighbors and relatives of shock victims don't understand shock. But neither do the doctors who twirl the dials on the black boxes, anymore than do the judges who send people away to such punishment or the public who "welcomes" the victims home.

During the thirty-two years of my quarantine by society, there has been little letup in the abhorrence my status occasions in most people. With those few who recognized my potentialities and tried to help me, there was a universal ignorance of what had to be overcome. Even I, then, did not know. Friends made good jobs available to me, and advantageous business associations. I declined them all in the knowledge that I was not ready. Next, these well-meaning people, in these liberated times, then turned to sex as my cure. Their hounding me on this score from 1950 to 1975 has been brutal. It was not that I was against sex, it was only that I was angered at their interference in my private life. I fought back. My only weapon was to dissociate myself from them—avoid them, move away, refuse to work for them. Their reactions were like a scorned woman's. In frustration, they could think of nothing better than to try to force psychiatric treatment on me, especially more ECT. Their belligerence drove me into a world of my own, a desert where I could lick my wounds and feel the itch of returning health.

When I first came home from Marcy, I met my formerly familiar world with a new response. There was a translucent barrier, through which I could not always pass. My children, parents, and in-laws were familiar; but some things were completely forgotten until I saw them, or sometimes heard them spoken of, whereupon they were instant old friends, assuming their normal places as if never absent. For months faces were without names. A cousin, who came out to Auburn, I knew I should know, yet I didn't until Mother filled me in.

I was the trained seal who had forgotten his routines. Other relatives discussed my experience at length. In the otherwise uneventful lives around me, I was the hors d'oeuvre served up by the medical profession as a conversation piece. Yet with some people, distaste made their tongues fumble. Within the family, love tempered curiosity.

Olive and her mother noticed my slowness in making decisions. So they made helpful suggestions like a couple of mother birds: "Wouldn't you like to look at the paper?" (when I stood looking out the kitchen window); or, "Wouldn't you like to take a nap?" (when I stood looking out the front-room window). But soon they fluttered off about their own business, leaving me to take a walk through the fields with one of the children.

On the first Wednesday morning, Olive insisted on going in late, so as to be with me outside the personnel office until it opened at 8:00. The ivy-clad offices abutted on the sidewalk. I felt eyes in every window, watching Olive kiss me good-by in the middle of the street. I needed most of all to show I could stand on my own two feet.

American Locomotive could not have been more understanding. The personnel man did not ask about the institutionalization— Olive must have seen to that. I was taken like any other human being to my foreman in the Navy Shop, a new cavernous concrete-and-steel structure, whose noise was a welcome part of getting back to productive activity.

I was assigned to the burring bench. There was work for four men smoothing 3-foot-high piston rods for the diesel engines going into PT boats. The bench boss put one on the bench with the electric hoist and showed me how to hold the bastard file. He did one rod, then stood back to watch me.

The force of the shock treatments hit home. I had to send my left arm a special message to raise the file into position. Then I had separately to instruct the right arm to move the file. The boss had to finish the first one for me and touch up the next couple. Olive came over for the coffee break. At the afternoon break, the foreman ran her off. At quitting time, the bench boss told me to come back the next day. Within two months I was promoted to the gear hobs on the night shift. I earned several raises, but I could not compute a setup, even with the evening inspector twice volunteering to check my figures. I could read the formulas; but the simplest mathematical operations wound up in meaningless errors. My attempts at correction produced fives in place of sevens where sixes were called for. When the plant was shut, during the two steelworkers' strikes following the war, I went to work as a union carpenter and was elected a trustee of the local.

During those years, while I was slow to catch on, I held my own in output with fellow workers. Reading was something else again. *Time* piled up by the foot, unread. I took two extension courses from the state agricultural college at Cornell. I knew the answers to the questions on the examination papers so well that I could taste them, but I had to look in the books for a picture of the words to put on paper. Doing that lowered my self-respect; it was like lying down and not putting my shoulder to the world, pleading illness.

When I came home from Marcy, Dad had given us a three-room cottage on five acres. For three years, working on it gave me the most meaningful period in my life. Dad and I put up rafters in the sun and flooring when it rained. Olive climbed the ladder with tools and served lemonade or coffee and cookies on the aromatic sloping roofing boards.

I stole time out for a big garden. I couldn't get enough of corn picked five minutes before it was served steaming. It was this city man's first flirtation with Mother Nature; I fell for her completely. As each crop came in—kohlrabi, brussels sprouts—I was lost in the wonder of it all, forgetting, for the first time, my fear that the next person I met might say, "Oh, yes, you're the one from Marcy."

Despite the healthful laughter of summer, an aura of the institutionalization hung in the air over family, neighbors, the State of New York. My wife was the only one to see the indirect antagonism festering inside me. It was fed by the realization that I was not normal. The children were dear to me, but there was time to do no more than give a few words of praise for one of their drawings from school, never time to help the older boy assemble a model plane. I was always behind schedule with the garden and the house. I woke up tired every morning. Over and over I asked myself, "Why did they do it? Why did they do it?"

Hoping to combat my inner festering, my wife persuaded me to sell the place and travel west in a house trailer. You might say it was a direct result of the Marcy shock table's reaching out and tearing at the entrails of a happy family.

A good piece past the Mississippi, the spaciousness was like a cool stream watering a seed of hope and faith, someplace in the body, separate from the brain. The clamps the doctors had fastened on me were loosening. Trailer-court proprietors, even transients from the East as well, exuded the friendliness of the Old West and unknowingly helped me shuck my old skin. Tucson was made up of such people. They and the sun were taking the corkscrews out of my head.

After a couple of months of steady work as carpenter, I was caught in a general layoff by the big contractors in December. Because people kept asking me about repairs on their trailers and others asking for bids on new houses, I talked with Olive about going into business for myself. I remember the two weeks of indecision before I dared to place an ad in the newspaper and the trepidation I felt until my contractor's license actually hung on the trailer wall. This is something I have seen in other victims of electroshock. The more treatments, the greater the loss of self-confidence. It derives, I believe, from a subconscious pathological fear of being caught in a mistake. It is a fear that the mistake will alert some onlooker to the queerness the doctors have fashioned for you, something which can be smelled as the Orientals smell meat-eating Occidentals.

That paper on the wall meant more than any school diploma. It marked a more important milestone: I was coming out from under. I knew that I would right the keel one day. Then I would go back to New York and tell the doctors something. My wife did not know what I was going through. And if a wife cannot, then no one can tell what a shock victim is experiencing.

There were forces at work which in our everyday lives we do not usually take time to identify, like the seasonal cycles that give the blade of grass strength to force its way up through a blacktopped parking lot. I had been drawn to a group of men (carpenters) with an appealing spirit of independence. Job seniority and wage increments bothered few of them. A man who knows his trade takes no more guff than he cares to, as work beckons no farther away than the next street. Soaking up this spirit had been the first tonic for my mental jelly.

But while Mother Nature was working, I kept trying too. When I attended a brush-up school, which the carpenter's union conducted evenings, I was determined to make changes more far-reaching than just the miles from Auburn. Back there, it had been much like when I started out at age eighteen and had argued with fraternity brothers at college over the direction one should spoon soup to keep the chin dry. I had argued with some of the old carpenters on the job, even argued compulsively with my dad for my right to do things my own way. But now I was so eager to learn that I modified my reactions, respectfully trying out the suggestions of my fellow workers. But the shock table had still more disappointments to hand out. One night it was as if I were blind to the 3 × 12-foot brown paper on which were sketched out the rafters and cuts for a five-gable roof with dormers. It was work I would have zipped through in high school. I looked down at my paper disconsolately, last week's multiplication still unfinished, as a fellow in the back called out that he had completed his last angle.

Still, I did not tell Olive. But she could not fail to feel the intensity of my determination. What went wrong was her applying the heat, from the still nebulous star I was following, to herself as guilt. It showed at the most unusual times. Once it was after sex.

"You haven't forgiven me, have you?" she said.

I did not comprehend. "What?"

"About the hospital."

"You never should have let them give me shock."

"But every doctor said they would help you."

"You should have used your own good sense."

"Kenny! How was I to know?" She spoke through tears. "Do you feel you are over them?"

"No."

Simple, honest "no" was more than her spirit could take. She finally broke, the week before Christmas. We were getting ready to move into our half-finished concrete-block house in time for the holiday. This was quite feasible in a climate where you can practically live outdoors all year. The windows were not glazed when a hop-skip-jump desert devil lifted the roof a hundred feet out in the desert, dumping it upside down in one piece, cracked down the middle. Anchor bolts went too, tearing out the walls. The corners were left standing.

Olive's hysterics subsided into aversion toward me. After a week of her nagging, I agreed to a divorce. There was no rancor then; there is no bitterness now. There is only pity for the victims of the "black box," in this case, not me, as I had the strength to see it through, but pity for her, our children, my parents, her parents, our children's children. Only now with the production of this book will they have available the balm of understanding.

Losing the children was a harder blow than the shock treatments. When I came home from work in the early darkness of winter, I wanted, in my heart, to drive over and bring *my* family back to where they belonged. Instead, after feeding an old tramp tiger cat, Mama Mia, sardines and top milk, the two of us paced the scar across the desert that was the street, Mama Mia at my heels, purring out her love to the clamorous accompaniment of the polished stars, while the silent saguaro held its breath to listen.

Within a few months, I went back to Syracuse. I worked as a carpenter while putting my parents' house in top shape for sale. By December, Dad had retired and the three of us were living in a small cottage in a trailer court in Tucson. I was working on plans for a retirement home for the folks, which we got started soon, along with my contract work.

One afternoon at the library while gathering an armload on contemporary houses, I browsed along the stacks, sniffing a little of the enthusiasm from college days. My eyes fell on William James's *Principles of Psychology,* a book I had always meant to read. I read late into that night. We use only 10 percent of our minds, I learned. When the brain is injured, it can repair itself. Those words, in bold gold letters on a green-black sky, ruled my mind.

I had this new beacon when I became enmeshed in the plans of Elletta, the thrice-divorced daughter of the court's proprietors. She already had four small children. One evening, after taking a dozen of the small fry from the court for a potato roast up in the foothills, Elletta and I walked out on the flat floor of Nature's planetarium.

"What is it you want out of life?" Elletta asked.

"I don't know now," I said.

"We all want happiness, Kenny. Is there another way to find it? Without a wife, I mean."

But a wife was out of the question. I was behind in payments for my children. My mother and father deserved some repayment for their help after Marcy. And sex alone was not enough to invite carrying a millstone around my neck.

"Kenny," Elletta said, taking my hand, "you'll get over it. You'll make it again."

"It's not Olive," I said.

"I know. Your mother told me about the hospital."

I was stunned and sick at heart. What I so desperately believed needed to be kept secret in my new environment had instead been broadcast.

That week I had a call about a kitchen remodeling, from Mrs.

Odessa Stronth, an arthritic widow. It was suppertime. After looking at the kitchen, we were standing on opposite sides of the wooden gate in the adobe fence. I pointed to the emerald lawn, a thick mat, and to the red and purple and every shade of yellow flowers along house and fence. "You've created a thing of beauty here."

"An army colonel gave the house its start," she said. "I'm lucky he was transferred. But it isn't home. I'd go back to Kentucky tomorrow if my doctor would let me. Here, I feel my arthritis has put me in a prison inside this fence. It would almost be worth the pain to see the dome of the courthouse again."

"I've noticed how those forced to stay here hate it—almost invariably—while those like myself, who chose it by free will, see beauty at every hand. Take the sky—did you ever see a bluer sky? Of course, there's dust everywhere, but still the sky's clear. There's not a profusion of plants, but each has a beautiful blossom in the spring. You've seen across the valley after a spring rain—it turns from brown to green and a riot of blooms. But even dry, it's a perfect color scheme—tans, browns, purple grays under a cobalt sky."

"You make it sound different through your eyes." She sighed.

"Yet, best of all to me is the feeling of freedom—of wide-open spaces. It's done something for me. I wouldn't want to leave ever."

I stayed for sandwiches and iced tea. A week later I stopped around in the evening to talk. We told each other what had led up to Tucson.

"Long before I came out here," she said, "our house burned down. The big old trees were scarred their whole length. They reminded me so much of my own fingers. When my husband passed, I couldn't seem to find the will to keep going. Then one day my doctor told me to look into Christian Science, and in three years I had the courage to come out here."

Some weeks later, candles were lit on the table by the end kitchen windows and the best silver laid. We watched the mountains across the valley turn from diffused pink to deepest purple.

"What table manners," she remarked. "Where did a carpenter learn to use a fork like that?"

"I have played other parts," I said.

"What happened? Do you mind telling me?"

I thought some moments. "I've been through the mill." I

flushed and apologized for spoiling a wonderful meal.

"You haven't. Why not tell me? Have you ever talked it all out?"

We sat with elbows on the table, watching the stars course from peak to peak.

"I had always wanted to be a lawyer and a writer," I reminisced. "Things fell apart. I lost my faith and never got started again. I've sort of drifted up to this point. And now I've been crippled by doctors. I'm free at last to do what I want—but I have lost something."

She had been silent for a half hour. "Isn't that a good reason for looking for help outside of yourself?"

"But where does one find such a person?"

"Let me tell you what happened when our home burned down. My husband let me rent a room on the next street. I stayed there alone, day after day, just looking out the window. One day the buds came out. The buds always come out again, Kenneth. You'll find help when you turn back to God."

I did not go to church with her that week, though soon I was going regularly. Bit by bit, my understanding grew and an inner peace and an inner strength grew, which have never left me through a quarter century.

I called on Odessa often. We talked of "cabbages and kings." In trying to build memories wiped out by ECT, we discussed what might have led to my being put away in 1943. It was far from clear then. She wanted to know what had made me leave American Locomotive.

"Are you sure there was nothing?" she prodded.

"It had nothing to do with my leaving," I said, "but there was one unusual happening. It was the night that word came over the radio that President Roosevelt had died. There was a hush in the vast Navy Building as most of the machines shut down. In the stillness, I let out three cheers."

"Kenneth!" Odessa was shocked. "You mustn't. Somebody might hear you."

"I've got a right to." Then I said it again.

"But respect for the office!"

"He besmirched the office himself—by becoming infallible."

From then on, there was intensive questioning on President Truman. Did I really think he was a little man? More often now, she was saying: "I hadn't thought of it that way. You really do have a solution for things." She wanted to introduce me to important people, knowing many from her days in Alben W. Barkley's office before he became vice-president and later in the Navy Department in Washington; however, I put it off because, though my brain was accurate, it was slow.

Trivial as mention of Roosevelt was at the time, I feel it was taken as a challenge by some of Odessa's friends, with whom she had gossiped about me, causing them to retaliate slanderously. Stories began to reach my ears, painting me incongruously as a homosexual. She herself took up this line for questioning and hounded me until I gave her the name of the person who once tried to have homosexual relations with me, when I was seventeen.

Tucson was a small town then. With retirees sitting around with nothing to do, it was the perfect setting for scandal, real or imaginary. The retirees at the court were midwesterners. To them, Christian Science equated with lunacy. They were going to save me from both. And Elletta was going to save me from *that* woman. "Two and two make four. You know that," she told me.

This casual slander, which I could not account for, this trivial thing grew into something bigger than any desert devil. The sky fell in. What was bugging them? I had done nothing to anybody.

Then Brothers of the Forge, the name I am using for a social fraternity, and Sisters of the Skillet, an auxiliary, got into the act, seemingly to save my parents as well as Odessa, who were all members, from some unnamed evil on my part. Then, as the stories going the rounds of the lumberyard and the court got dirtier, I offered to marry Odessa to protect her name. But she would marry none but a Forger. I said I would not join before marrying. Her grocer had been a Vulcan of the Forge back East. He asked her, so she told me, for a candid evaluation of me, so he could report back to Elletta's father, who also had been a Vulcan, back in Indiana.

Odessa took her coffee black, my mother with cream. At the weekly court suppers I was forced to make a choice. To show my respect to a truly great lady, who had put some meaning in my life, and with not the least slight intended for my mother, I took mine black. The next time, my coffee was accompanied by an avalanche of insults and the spilling by a serving lady of a cup of the hottest in my lap. That was my last supper.

My ex-wife came up to me on the job one day and confessed that she had done something awful to me, without telling what. It is my guess, today, that she had given my life history to her new husband, as she had once given it to the doctors at the hospital. Then he must have slandered me to the working people in town. The barbers started calling me a sex deviant. Men on the job played tricks, like removing the support under a scaffold plank so that I fell six feet to the ground. Why would strangers suddenly do this to me?

When someone is in an atmosphere such as this, how could one prevent imagining something?

While my only crime was to be the victim of an insane asylum, it was enough to make me wish I were dead. More than one morning when I took a break for a Coke at the drugstore, crossing vacant lots to the next street, I prayed for the ground to open and swallow me up.

Hindsight is so much easier. Remember, in Tucson I was only a few years out of Marcy where I had been only the second one to have electroshock. Tucson residents must have thought I was only a temporarily subdued maniac. Even today, a quarter century later, the country was afraid of having Eagleton as vice-president. "What if he assumed the presidency and suddenly became unstable?" was the thought in people's minds.

One day my mother said she had checked my books and found no record of the hundred dollars she had given me for the house. "Elletta says you spent it on the woman," she said.

That evening, a war was waging inside me, between weariness with the world and the urge for survival. I was slumped in a rocker, no doubt with a woebegone look on my face, when Odessa came with a tray of coffee and cookies. She put down the tray and slapped my face hard. I sat up bristling.

"That's the way I like to see you look," she said. "That's what General Patton did to the boy in the hospital. Did he do wrong?"

My good sense had to admit that it was good medicine sometimes.

Ladies at the court, in their small-town bigotry, were going to save me from further defiling myself and dishonoring my parents. I overheard them talking about putting something in my food to curb my sex life. I went to a doctor to find out what they might use and how to counteract it. He was alarmed and steered me hurriedly to the police, who dismissed the matter as being out of their jurisdiction.

Things were getting out of hand. I had had no sex relations with the widow. It was all incomprehensible to me. I went to my lawyer to see what he could make of it. I told him Odessa seemed to offer sex, then refused. But as soon as I mentioned the shock treatments, he sent me straight to his psychologist friend, under the threat of having the police take me if I did not go.

The psychologist asked if I thought it were a physical possibility for someone to climb up on the roof outside his window and peer in at us. Yes, it was a physical possibility, I said. In fact, at that moment, a workman came out of a skylight to work on the roof.

The doctor was convinced I needed more shock treatments. He even urged my parents to force them on me; however, at that time, my parents still had the same common sense they had always shown before leaving Syracuse.

Let us go back to Syracuse for a moment. In the year before my parents and I drove to Arizona, I worked forty hours a week as a carpenter. I supported my children and paid for their summer vacation in Syracuse. Every night and weekend, I worked on the folks' house, reshingling, remodeling the kitchen, painting inside and out, refinishing floors. We had no arguments, no disagreements of any kind. Our trip west was nothing but pleasure in anticipation of settling near my children. I spent weeks drawing plans for an ideal two-bedroom retirement house for them and built much of it with my own hands, besides carrying on my general contracting.

But another whole field was opening for me, in politics, through Odessa's top-brass friends in both parties. I could have had a career in either party; however, I put off meeting these close friends of hers until I would be completely recovered from shock. But first she had quizzed me in minute detail on most of my life. I had no recall, as yet, of many of the years preceding Marcy. My answers were speculation and deduction. Nevertheless, my thinking was clear and logical, and my predictions of political events to come unusually accurate.

I did not realize at the time that I had exercised a profound influence on Odessa, causing her to change from Democrat to Republican. That act and her championing my beliefs among her friends is the only thing that could have triggered the coincident outburst of nastiness around town directed at me. Someone asked me if I were the father of my brother's daughter. Another man asked if my father had not stolen all his tools from the firm where he had worked for thirty years.

In this book, I do not want to catalog the scurvy innuendoes on the job. There, harassment also fed on itself. Some of the cracks, cancerlike, grew out of control, losing any connection to their original perpetrators. Guys on the job, seeing that they could bother me, carried it on just for the sake of tormenting someone.

I could see no way to close the gap of misunderstanding, but I drove Odessa over to talk to my father in my attempt to close it. Mother refused flatly to see "the witch."

Odessa told me that my mother would be glad to lick my boots someday. I saw no reason for such a remark.

The whole summer was saturated with such surprises. Truth is stranger than fiction; however, given my Marcy background, the truth was seen only as fiction by my lawyer. Life is also more involved than any inkblots; thus, the psychologist, coming in contact with something more involved than his own product, had no place else to put down my harassment than as asylum lore.

What does all this have to do with insanity? Precisely this: if I had not been carrying the label from Marcy, people would have talked to me on my own level and I would have gotten help to stop the slanderers. Because they refused to talk to me, staying behind their antiseptic cloak of sanism, I was reduced to wondering all sorts of things in the absence of straight answers. (*Sanism* is the word coined by Dr. Morton Birnbaum to describe the assumption of the "sane" world that because the patient is in a state mental institution he is therefore sick and belongs there.)

Nevertheless, above all, I knew that I was not "seeing and hearing things." I also knew a change of scene would give me a better chance to win my battle.

CHAPTER 4

1950-1956

A Case
(continued)

Autumn in St. Louis, 1950, was beautiful. There were many delightful days in the sunshine canvassing for a sewing machine company. Six evenings a week I made sales pitches and collections, so that I hardly had time to look beyond the next pay envelope.

Sundays were something else. There were the Sunday papers, church, and the zoo. But in the crowds I was lonely. Yet I wanted to be alone, having no desire for companions of either sex. Letters from Odessa cheered me. They contained no scriptural passages and no admonitions on churchgoing, but they led to my walking out Delmar Boulevard to the Christian Science church in University City.

Sun came through tall open windows, tinting pastel green walls and the white proscenium arch with the same gold as the young soprano's head. One day her solo was, "Open my eyes that I may see." I was glad I had gone up to the balcony where only three others sat, because all of a sudden tears coursed down my cheeks. It was the first time anything had touched me since the shock table. The words of the lesson-sermon, following, fell on deaf ears. I thought of Odessa in Tucson, who had made me believe it was not too late for whatever I set my mind to.

Walking back down Delmar I knew now what Christian Science meant. Each one as he is able advances in Science. The vegetable spaded out of the asylum dunghill was forever after immune to the wilt of despair, the mold of defeat. I had a vision, seeing my last night at work at General Electric, hearing the whir of cutters, the threats of men. I saw that I was blameless of illness or error.

But I could still be the prey of our sanist society, using its leverage of my former hospitalization to put me away again.

Being put away is something that could happen to you tomorrow, not because of anything you did but because of something somebody said you did. And once you have been victimized, you are trapped. If you try to fight it by exposing it, you only spread it, making it much worse. Evil travels much too fast for truth ever to catch up.

I started out in St. Louis with VIP treatment at Morgus Sewing Machine Company. They sent a brand-new Dodge truck for me and a special trainer from the regional office, out to the branch store on Delmar, around the corner from where I lived on Clara. When I made a trip to the regional office, to pick up some things for the store, an outsider might have thought from the way I was treated that I was the Prince of Wales.

Everything seemed to promise well for my future in St. Louis. My sales were going well, I even had a wealthy businessman propose to me that he fund a "Donaldson Sewing Machine Company." But I began to suspect Odessa's string-pulling in other ways when I did not go along with the tenets of either major party completely. I was treated with less deference at Morgus (whose president was one of the largest Republican contributors), a supervisor was familiar with my personal mail, strangers came up to me in the street with no purpose other than to be insulting. When I went to the toilet, noise would be made to taunt me.

These things were distinct from the few incidents growing out of my Marcy hospitalization. It amused me to have a plainclothesman interrogate me at the newsstand on the morning after some oil tanks were blown up on the south side, and to have deputy sheriffs "visit" with me on a suburban street on the week of a vicious sex attack on a small girl. But it dismayed and irritated me to have the restaurateur talking about someone with bees in his bonnet and a new fellow salesman discussing the possibility of committing "someone." Thus, hovering over every working hour was an uneasiness about being railroaded again. No one could say I was nuts, but the extreme hateful hazing visited on me forewarned that people's natural fear of ex-asylum inmates could mesh with the slander into something dreadful.

I left St. Louis the following winter. Plagued by a recurring bladder condition in the cold dampness, for which two doctors could suggest no remedy, I decided to move to a warm clime. My parents having sold their place in Tucson and moved to Largo, Florida, I visited them and took a hotel job downstate for the winter. In the spring, I had a pleasant interlude with Odessa, then I settled in Savannah, Georgia, to sell and collect for Nestors Mercantile Company days and to study law nights.

Summer was full upon the city and mayflies heralded each dusk on the streets near the river, before I had put together the money to buy a correspondence course from Blackstone School of Law, Chicago. At 8:00 o'clock, after making my last collection on the route, I would sit down in hundred-degree heat with a pitcher of ice water and read one paragraph slowly, then the next. Then reread the two. Without benefit of dictionary, which I could not afford, I fought for general meaning. I spent five nights on the first set of two pages. Each sentence by itself was understandable. It was the nuances of the "ifs," "buts," and "ands" in conjunction with the next sentence, which threw me. The sweat was not all from the weather. At midnight I would lie exhausted in sleep. In four weeks I sent in the first lesson. It came back marked "B-." This was the second milestone since Marcy State Hospital.

I would win. I was remembering the principles of what I read. One day the terminology would stick in my mind too. That would be the day I would go back to New York—just for a visit—and show them.

I had been so beaten down that it was a big step when I got the courage to send a suggestion on foreign policy to the White House. I received a response from the State Department which elated me.

But unhappily, there followed another outpouring of unpleasantries, leading me to seek the advice of a young Catholic priest. He advised me to change my name and go away to a large city.

I had enough money to get as far as Columbia, South

Carolina. In Richland County Court, I dropped my first initial and took the last name of McCullough, an old family name. At first I made good money, then I fell into the same abuse as in Savannah, this time following my attempted intercession with the editors of two newspapers about the brutal slaying of a teen-age Negro by deputy sheriffs in Walterboro. The whites thought I was black. What the Negroes thought, they were afraid to tell me. It was also evident that I was no longer free, being under constant surveillance as a potential maniac.

When Columbia, within a few months, turned into a repeat performance of Savannah, I decided to go back to New York to see if there was something in my hospital record which was feeding the troublemakers.

I settled down to a summer of canvassing for a siding company in Syracuse, to earn money for my next trip west. The boss, who was well connected in the Republican party, and other businessmen started ridiculing me because I shunned sex. At the Seymour Hotel, a workingman's hotel on East Onondaga Street, a horn blew each time, all through the summer, that I used the hall toilet.

But those were things I was prepared to live with, during my single-minded drive to the source. I phoned our family doctor to learn what he knew about my commitment. He said he did not know me. The Observation Center set up an appointment for me at the downtown office of Doctor Foreband, now in private practice, who had been head of the Center in 1943. This was to be my first encounter with a psychiatrist in the free world.

The next afternoon, Doctor Foreband said, "Mr. Mc-Cullough—that is the name, isn't it?—my secretary got a transcription of your case from the Observation Center, but there is nothing I can tell you, as we are not at liberty to disclose confidential files."

"But I am the patient whose file you have. Certainly I am the one entitled to know."

"It's confidential."

"That's ridiculous. Why are you allowed to see it then? I'm studying law and I'm sure there's no such provision in the law." I had raised my voice.

"You had better leave, Mr. McCullough, or I'll have to call assistance."

I got up.

"But first," said Foreband, asking me to be seated again, "I expect you to pay my fee. That will be forty dollars."

"I didn't come here for treatment."

"It makes no difference. You made an appointment and took my time."

"But I told your secretary exactly what I wanted."

"You pay the forty dollars and get out!"

"I'll tell you what," I said coolly, "you mail me the bill tonight and I promise I'll send my check just as soon as I get the bill tomorrow."

But the post office never had a letter from Foreband for me.

Back in Tucson, Odessa was on a bed of pain, with a nurse in constant attendance. I tried to find work, even canvassing house to house trying to sell screen-door grilles for a friend. The only work available was carpentry. I said no to that. Because I had once been turned down at the bank and laughed out of town as a builder, I vowed not to move back to Tucson until I had the money to build without asking any bank. I was not going to start all over again from the very bottom, swinging a hammer and saw amid their laughter.

I told Odessa I was leaving.

She did the unexpected, got up in her wheelchair and sent the nurse to a matinee. We faced each other in the living room.

"You've got money now," she said.

"I can't build a house for four hundred dollars." That was the proceeds from selling a lot I owned.

"Work by the hour. Are you too proud?"

"Not here, I won't. When I can come back and show these comedians—"

"You don't know what you've done to me. All my friends—"

"You won't marry me."

"If you leave me, Kenneth—" Her voice bit it off with all her remaining strength.

"What do you expect?" I too was hot.

"If you leave me—you're a young man yet—you've got most of your life before you. But I warn you—if you leave me, I'll make you sorry. You'll never live to forget it!"

There is no answer to threats from one you love.

She squeezed her eyes shut and turned the wheelchair to the wall.

I did not let the door slam.

I was fired from my first job in Los Angeles, as shipping clerk at Grant Piston Ring Company when I failed to show up at their Christmas party. This was because I was tired of the same old sex malarkey. It was not particularly disgusting at Grant's, but enough was enough. What spilled over into the marketplace was pretty strong and soon there were a lot of stores and banks I refused to enter again because of the hazing by employees. At my next job, running a table saw at a Northrop Aircraft warehouse in Lynwood, there was little hazing by fellow workers.

I was still writing letters to important people. These letters were suggestions, freely given with no expectation of reward other than the feeling of having done one's part. There seemed increasing interest by strangers and by all employers in my ideas. In Los Angeles, my papers were ransacked in my desk drawer and there was cigarette smoke in the room, though neither the maid nor I smoked. I was writing to some senators and labor leaders, as well as the White House. A more baffling interference was someone's putting medicine in my food in a Lynwood restaurant. Working with a doctor and a laboratory, we found codeine in my urine. I talked to the Lynwood police chief. I asked a half dozen state and county authorities to help me, besides a newspaper and the FBI.

I told no one what Odessa had said: "You're a young man yet, but—" But the Lynwood police evidently had heard. First, they ran me in for two hours, for eating my lunch on the edge of the railway right-of-way, which actually was outside the Lynwood city boundaries. I moved the next day to Huntington Park, but the arrest had nullified my pending promotion at Northrop.

Back in Lynwood something more had been prepared for me.

At ten minutes past midnight on a Thursday, in going home from work, I was still five blocks from the bus stop to catch the 12:15 to Huntington Park. There were no stars over the sleeping county and sidewalks were shaded from corner lights by leafy trees. Somewhere behind me a car started up and burned rubber rounding a corner. It turned abruptly into a driveway toward me and shook to a stop with the lights all but brushing my pants. Men jumped out on either side. A piece of blunt steel was rammed into my backbone.

"Stick 'em up!"

The second man was in the headlights now. It was a
policeman with leveled gun! My fright turned to incredulity as
they frisked me.

"What's all this about?" I asked.

They took turns speaking. "What were you doing on the side
street?"

"I wasn't on any side street."

"We saw you."

"I just crossed over kitty corner so as—"

"We've been waiting for you."

The one in the back took my billfold and handed it to the
other, who inspected its contents in the headlight.

I said, "There's my paycheck. I just left Northrop and was
going over to catch the bus." I moved to step away from the
prodding revolver, which hurt.

"Stand still or I'll shoot!"

I remembered Clarence Darrow's lecture, "Don't argue with
the criminal with the gun."

"And keep 'em up." The gun jabbed harder.

"Take me back to the warehouse, then, and I'll prove it."

"There's nobody there—it's been closed for hours."

"I just punched out. My foreman would still be there."

"Get in back. We're going for a ride."

They drove down a winding street with a center parkway,
circled the end, and came back about two blocks. Both officers got
out, the driver going up to a house, the other standing by the open
door with gun drawn on me. A woman peeked out and opened the
door wide when she saw it was police, but kept the screen hooked. I
remember every incongruous detail vividly. The gabled white
entrance was bordered with the same red bricks as the semicircular
steps. It was seventy feet from house to car, where I sat under the
feeble dome light.

The policeman at the house said, "Can you identify him?"

"I can't see him," she said, and opened the screen enough to
peer around it while still hanging fast to it.

"Is this the one?" the policeman near me said.

With the overhead light in her eyes, she said, "I can't see too
good."

The officer made me stick my head out. "That's the one all
right, isn't it?"

"I'm not too sure."

"But it could be, couldn't it?" the one beside her said.

"It might," she said.

"Thank you, ma'am."

They drove off with me.

At the station the only thing the deskman asked was, "Weren't you in a state hospital, McCullough? Well, I understand these things. I worked with cases like yours in the army for a year."

Before he would take my case, which was a Peeping Tom charge, Attorney Edwin C. Boehler made me have a psychiatric examination. A Pasadena doctor gave me a clean bill of health.

The complaining witness, the dumpy timid housewife, could make no identification and one of the arresting officers committed perjury on the stand. It took the jury less than ten minutes to acquit me.

But now I was saddled with an arrest record to be noted on every application for the rest of my life. And the Internal Revenue Service had zeroed in, while I was saddled with the expenses of the trial, and threatened court action to get the small tax due from my self-employment in South Carolina. Possibly this was actualizing Odessa's threat of "If you leave me. . . ."

Then the district attorney's assistant said he'd lock me up again "and then let's see you get free," if I persisted in taking action about the policeman's perjury.

Two things were evident: first, changing my name had done nothing except lay my children open to the shame that their father had to run and hide, and so I changed my name back to Donaldson in Superior Court; and second, here was one more city that didn't need me.

I went to Charleston, South Carolina. It was a repetition of Columbia, with the added attraction of preparations for the second War Between the States. Then I spent two weeks in Florida, unable to find a really good job, before heading for Philadelphia.

I met wonderful people in Philadelphia. They gave me the first help I got in any city against the troublemakers. Postal inspectors put an immediate end to the four-years-long delaying and stealing of my mail. And fatherly white-haired lawyer Richard T. McSorley counseled me to patience and offered the use of his library in my studies. And Travelers Aid, whom I had approached on the advice of a priest in Jacksonville, said they would help me get a job where I would not be harassed. First, they made me show them my correspondence with the White House and others and then submit to two days of outpatient psychological and psychiatric tests by at least eight doctors at the Psychiatric Clinic of Philadelphia General Hospital.

When I went back the following day, Miss Gray, a gracious Quaker interviewing at Travelers Aid, told me I had been given a clean bill of health. But, also, I had a letter from my parents, saying they needed some work done on their place, and I opted to go to Florida for the winter. Miss Gray said Travelers Aid stood ready to help me anytime I returned to Philadelphia.

I had started to write a book in Los Angeles, to expose what was being done to me. I spoke to an editor, Day Edgar at *The Saturday Evening Post,* and he said the *Post* might want to print excerpts from the book prior to publication. In Florida, while I worked days at bread-and-butter jobs, I studied law and completed the book at night.

I was most surprised that my parents were not interested in my correspondence with famous people, nor would they look at the reports from the psychiatrists in Los Angeles and Philadelphia. I even brought out the laboratory report showing codeine, in an effort to explain my gathering-no-moss rolling around the country. Instead, as in Tucson, they were thinking about shock treatments again for me. Accidentally, I overheard my mother talking to a doctor about me. I had had it. That was why, when I broke out in a nervous sweat at night, I wondered whether a neighbor, the doctor's cousin, was putting medicine in the casseroles she was sending over regularly. Then it was that I talked to the state's attorney. Finally, I told my parents I was taking a hotel job and packing back to Philadelphia immediately after the season.

I wasn't my "dear old sweet self" by this time, I can assure you, and I gave curt answers to many a stranger. When a St. Petersburg bank refused to cash my paycheck, drawn on them, I must have really sounded off.

I felt like driving one morning, just to look over the land. Here it was almost Christmas again. I was completely over the shock treatments, but another year was gone with little accomplished. I stopped to watch flamingos wading in blue water. There was so much beauty. The sunshine was wonderful. But one can't live on beauty alone. Ripples in the lagoon caught my thoughts. The people of Florida seemed nice enough. Only in Pinellas County were there all those suspicious eyes. Yet I couldn't eat flamingos. I had to hurry with the book and then make some money. I was told

I could save a thousand dollars in tips at the hotel. That would be enough to print my book in the spring, back in Camden.

That, and that alone, constitutes my entire case of paranoia.

LABORATORY REPORT

Dr. _____ O. H. Mueller _____ Lab. No. _____ 2088 _____

Patient _____ Kenneth McCullough _____ Date _____ 2-4-54 _____

Specimen:

Examination for: Poison Screening:

Report:

Trychnene	Negative
Arsenic	"
Lead	"
Cyanide	"
Mercury	"
Chloral hydrate	"
Cantharides	"
Codeine	Positive

BY _____ K. L. Dieterle, M.D.

MEDICAL DIAGNOSTIC LABORATORY
736 South Flower Street, Los Angeles 17
Telephone TRinity 8471

CHAPTER 5

A Fly on a
Basketball Hoop

IN THE DEPTH OF THE NIGHT, I HAD A DREAM THAT SOMEONE WAS shining a flashlight in my eyes, almost resting it on my nose, while at the same time somebody out in the fifteen-watt dimness of the corridor was telling me to get up. Crazy, yes, and confusing, even for a dream. I was glad it was my first one in jail.

Then the flashlight poked me in the shoulder. "Get up, he-ah? And be damned quick." Its voice was loveless. It took a shape as large as a man and there was another such at the open door of the cell. The flashlight snapped off. Sitting up, I saw they were deputies.

"We're going for a ride," said the one standing close.

"Where to?"

"The asylum. Cut the stalling. Be ready when we come back."

As I was escorted out, Albert stood in undershorts, reaching through the bars to shake hands. "Take care of yourself, old buddy. And be sure to say good-by to Mabel."

She was in bare feet and in a shapeless bundle of red-and-green zigzags, held closed with both hands. "I'm sorry, Kenny," she said and hoisted the lapels up to her eyes.

Downstairs I was told to stay put on a straight chair, which stood alone against a wall of the lobby. I was suddenly overcome with a violent shaking inside, righteous indignation about to boil over. It was such heartless terror. I had fought so hard for thirteen years and had overcome the crippling effects of Marcy. I was halfway through the law course and starting to be realized. No! NO! They can't do this! This is not Russia!

But I mustn't let the deputies see my shaking. I was six feet from a drinking fountain and the deputies were out of sight. I took a couple of slugs of ice water. They were ineffective. So I started walking back and forth from fountain to chair.

That brought a deputy on the run. "See here, if you can't sit quiet, we'll put you in a straitjacket. Think you can?"

I gritted my teeth into immobility.

I was joined by three other prisoners, put against the other walls. Each went to the desk, as his name was called, to sign out his personal effects. I got permission to inquire about mine. After a search, the counterman said, "Nope, there's nothing of yours here."

At 4:00 A.M., we were herded into a private two-door sedan. I sat between the deputies, astraddle the gear hump. At the city line a fog picked us up and stayed on, way after the January dawn. Occasionally the white line in the two-lane road looked up through the enfolding dough. The car was smoothly earning its payments at so much a head until we hit the shoulder on a turn with a set of lights momentarily flying by in the opposite direction. I was horrified to see the speedometer on 80, where it hung for four hours. I thought that if I did get to the asylum it would be God's will.

What the others thought, I did not find out until later. No one was talking. The youngest one, in his twenties, was going back for his second or third time, out of an eventual half dozen. He was the only prisoner who was indifferent to the morning's ordeal. Suffering an undisclosed trauma from his days in the service, he would, as I saw some months later, shadowbox in front of a mirror while muttering incomprehensibly and laughing. He was normal in all other ways and certainly not dangerous to himself or others. There was no need to lock him up, but as long as he did not care I can see no need to make an argument against his commitment.

Of the other prisoners in the car, yes, I can argue their cases. There was no need to put them away. Their plight is the plight of the other 850,000 involuntarily committed every year in this country. It is the spur for writing this book.

The oldest one that morning, in his late seventies, was sure he was going to his death. He had money in the bank and lived in his own house in St. Petersburg. Four times a year he might have an epileptic spell. Distant relatives, or his neighbors, or maybe some all-knowing caseworkers, thought it would be a terrible thing if he should lie alone, in his own house, unattended for fifteen minutes during a seizure. But he himself knew the difference between lying on his own rug and lying unattended on the worn wooden floors of the snake pit. He did not want the latter.

The other prisoner, Carter, a red-faced white-haired Irishman, was ten years older than I. Healthy, normally ebullient, he was to become my invaluable friend. He owned several building lots in Philadelphia and a nice house on the south side of St. Pete. Retired from the steel mills and construction work in Philly, he kept happily occupied, doing small bricklaying jobs. His son and daughter were married and had families in St. Pete. His son-in-law was an attendant on the psychiatric wards of the VA hospital at Bay Pines and regaled Carter's wife with stories from the wards. You never could be sure, he often said; some people gave the appearance of being harmless. Carter's wife, who had developed into a nervous nellie long before this, was also meeting with sympathetic neighbors to decry the pandemic of mental illness. She began to see neurotic tendencies in Carter, who was Protestant, when he argued hotly against supporting some special activity of the Catholic parish. She asked her priest's advice, who reasoned that it would not hurt to have Carter sent up for an examination.

When Carter was tossed in the jail, Judge White set him free on condition he go back to Philadelphia. After two months with his sister and brothers up there, with no word from home, he could not overcome his homesickness. Despite his sister's and brothers' warning, he went back down to Florida and knocked on his own locked front door. It was never opened before the police got him. Now, he had been committed without seeing judge or doctor.

In fact, I was the only one who had seen either judge or doctor prior to our reckless race through the fog. Furthermore, my reading of the law had revealed no grounds for either my own commitment or that of my companions.

About two hours up the road, the deputies told the men in

back to open the bag of sandwiches. Carter obliged. He twice tapped me on the shoulder with one in a waxed-paper envelope, saying, "They're mighty good."

But I had no stomach for food, though I did have a cup of coffee shortly afterward at a truck stop. The sensual warmth of coffee was incongruous in this nightmare. I had just watched one deputy outside the men's room with hand on revolver, until we all were reunited at the counter.

There were a few minutes to stretch in the cool dampness, while the deputies shot the breeze with a bunch from Tampa, bound for the penitentiary. I strolled to the end of the building. It wasn't fifty feet to the highway, where an occasional tractor-trailer roared by, incognito in the fog. The deputies were engrossed in chitchat. If I darted out in front of those big tires . . . it would be over in seconds. What did I want most? It was a tug to put an end to Rupture No. 2. Two trucks were barreling down the road. Fifteen seconds. Ten. I guess my mind was determined first to expose the perpetrators of this crime.

The fog raised quickly under the nine o'clock sun. Acres of lawn, buildings freshly painted white, trees, and winter flowers on tall stems in circular plots beckoned us in from the traffic light of a small town. Azaleas and camellias were showing color around the two-story building where we pulled up on the wrong side of the street.

Anger had shaken me in the lobby of the jail. That anger was now fear, and there was no shaking. I made a cool appraisal. Thirty feet in from the curb stood a living death. The deputies were waiting on either side of the walk. It was 150 feet to the corner of the building. I was in good health. I could make a dash to the woods and might escape the bullets; besides, only a fool stays in a crooked card game expecting to get even. Yet it was not fear that stayed my legs nor foolhardiness that led me in. Like the helpless victims of Auschwitz, hoping to the bitter end for justice and retribution, it was natural to obey.

"Auschwitz" inside was alive with red cushions and rubber plants and ferns in the sun by open windows. A smiling female at a high counter took the papers and one deputy took us down a corridor past closed doors, at the end pounding on a big gray green metal door.

The oldest and youngest of our group seemed insensible to our going behind the green door. But Carter and I smelled scorched brimstone. It was too late to worry, we would be fending off pitchforks. We were instant buddies.

It was 9:20. Inmates were in the dayrooms. A male attendant in white shirt and pants took us gleefully—at this rate they'd need more help and he'd get his promotion. Down the wet red-and-black tile floor we went. You could have heard an electric carving knife. Twenty men in a small dayroom looked at us with none of life's feverish interest.

Sitting in the hall, the four of us watched another attendant busy over a filing cabinet in the plexiglassed chart room. From time to time a nurse came from the front chart room. Four pairs of eyes watched for some hint.

In a little hall room, we were stripped, weighed, measured, blood tested, and typhoid shot. Carter and I skipped the state BVDs. Then the three of them went to the doctor up front.

I helped the attendant and patients string together small tables and chairs for twelve in the hall. When the rest of the ward traipsed past to the dining room next door, I got up, only to be shoved back by an attendant.

The screen of indefiniteness, of wondering how bad it could be, which had hung over the morning, was now ripped off. A one-legged man in a wheelchair headed the table, I next, opposite a little old man putting half the food from his tray into his hat and then trying to stuff the rest into his glass of milk. These conditions were something concrete to cope with.

Roast beef and mashed potatoes, I had two helpings all around, including ice cream, glad to be filling in the twenty pounds lost in jail.

I helped clean up the hall before getting new orders: "Stay in the alcove." There was no pain connected to it, of course, but I felt the weight of the world on my head. This was at the bottom of the standardized sinkhole of civilization. It was incredible that I was caught in this eddy.

The morning attendant took me to the little room and filled out a medical history questionnaire. He was wearing the Forge ring, a gold anvil inset in a large purple stone. I was prepared for anything but what happened next. He turned from the pencil sharpener to say, "We're getting tired of having so many railroaded here." That did not sound like persecution. My relief was immediate.

We were nearly through the questionnaire when Miss Neglaw, RN, threw the door open. "Who did you assign him to, Mr. Shast?" Her voice was imperative.

"Why, Doctor Eaton, of course."

"I want him changed to Doctor Adair."

Shast stood up, disbelief on his face. "But, Mis' Neglaw, we've always given this type to Eaton."

"No difference. Adair should be getting some of the younger men. You've been giving them all to Eaton."

Shast's face was red. "Is it all right if I start with the next one—all the forms are made out and the schedule posted?"

She grabbed the forms and stuffed them in the wastebasket. "You start now, he-ah?"

I had an hour alone in the alcove to savor the mixed blessings of a portentous start. A little old man, dragging one foot, brought two *Christian Science Sentinel*s. Then the housekeeper chased him out.

It was after 2:00 before Doctor Adair summoned me to the little room for a physical. A short neat man in his late thirties, with horn-rimmed glasses, he proceeded without fuss. Then we went back to the chart room, and I looked out at the twenty old men, some drooling, some shaking. These were Adair's type?

I recited my piece word-perfectly. I had gone over it so many times in the jail, my condensation was much improved but still not singsongy. The doctor accepted it. I tacked on what the Christian Science couple had said: "It's a misunderstanding. A misunderstanding by someone in Clearwater. Can't you discharge me now?"

"It will take some weeks at the earliest."

Then I said, "I'm a student of Christian Science, Doctor, and would appreciate your not forcing me to take medication."

There was no quibbling. He said, "You won't have to, as long as you don't cause trouble on the ward."

"Thank you. Another thing—I had thirty-five dollars at the desk in the jail. It wasn't there when I left this morning. None of my personal effects were. Is it all right to write the jailer for them?"

"Certainly, you have my permission."

Carter and I were exhausted when the bedrooms were unlocked at 6:00, but I fought off sleep for another hour, while Carter dropped off fully clothed. There were four beds. Across the outside wall ran wide-louvered windows, opened to catch the silence of winter swamp and forest and at lights out at 9:00 to let soft starlight fall on our faces.

At 9:30 the ceiling fluorescent lights snapped back on, and an attendant stood in the doorway yelling till Carter took off his clothes.

At 2:00 A.M. the one man at the other end started screaming. Carter and I jumped out of bed. The man thrashed from side to side and moaned. Then, of a sudden, he bounced three feet, so it seemed, up off the mattress, turned in midair with a bloodcurdling scream, and landed facing the other way.

"My God!" Carter whispered. "Did you see that?" He put his pants back on and his shoes too, before crawling under the spread. "I'm going to be ready!"

We got through two days somehow. The blind spot of each morning, 10:00 to 11:00, seemed long enough to drive from New York to Washington. Long days, longer nights. Days of fantasy—a seeming impossibility, dumping someone overnight into such a far-out place, neither hospital nor dungeon, but rather a third entity, horrible in its own right.

Sometimes I was told to sit in the back dayroom. The old men stared at my beard, a wavy reddish golden brown. One patient, after studying it, announced that he himself was Jesus Christ. Maybe they thought I was John the Baptist.

I went looking for attendant Shast to get it cut off. Shast laughed. "The doctor gave permission for you to keep it, but in here it would be better—off." With dull sheers and clippers it got whacked down, ready for the barber.

I visited with everyone. Carter said little about his case, but the rest were only too willing to talk. Old men had been shoved out of the way by their children, husbands by wives, children by parents. But surprisingly, in all the wailing, there were many calm, apparently normal men.

After breakfast I helped with the mopping and other chores like making out the laundry list for an unlettered attendant. But by 10:00 I had read through the morning paper with nothing else to do. Carter was often gone for some test or interview, other times snoozing under heavy medication, his face a pleasant red up past the roots of his snow-white hair. So it was with relief that I came to know Mr. Damascus.

Damascus had been sleepy, bothering no one, but one morning, as I put down the paper, he beckoned. His black hair had less gray than mine, though he was over sixty.

"I'm Narrel Damascus. Could you find time to talk?"

"That's all I've got." I laughed.

"Good," he said, not disposed to be jolly. "Mind if I call you Kenneth?"

"Call me Ken."

"Where you from, Kenneth?"

"Philadelphia."

"I mean Florida."

"Pinellas County—Clearwater."

"Charges?"

"No. You?"

"They won't let me face them. Ever hear of the Stockade? It's a hole. I was born in Tampa, but I can tell you I'm ashamed of it for the Stockade."

His manner was impressive. He sank back in the air cushions and blew a speck off his rimless glasses.

"I've sized you up, Kenneth. Want to help me get things done?"

"I'm going back to Philadelphia." I thought this a clever way to duck an involvement in an insane asylum.

"We'll have a mutual-help club," he said.

Ah, I felt on safer grounds. "I'd be glad to help. I was railroaded and half the others were, but I don't see how I could help from up there."

"You could do more. You'd be safe from these dishonest judges and untrustworthy doctors. They couldn't hurt you and you could cut them to pieces."

That was appealing.

Narrel added: "Remember the fellow who came in last night? I was in the hospital with him in Tampa. No charges—only mad about being locked up."

"Yeah, he made a racket."

"Three attendants took him into the utility room and worked him over. You didn't see him again because they gave him a shot and tied him down in bed. He's upstairs now. That's one thing we could stop. What do you say?"

But it still seemed farfetched to help from up north.

"Think it over," Narrel said. He pulled out his billfold and from it a small clipping from the Tampa *Tribune* about his case, how he was being held on a morals charge. His voice rose. "I'm an officer in the sheetmetal local. We've been fighting the *Tribune*. They said they'd get me."

Narrel held his hands to his head. "I've got a dilly of a hangover. Adair put me on Thorazine—250, four times a day. But it's mild compared to that stuff in City Hospital. Do you see now, Kenneth, what needs to be done? Some organization to step in for us little people?"

"I'll help. First I'm going to write a book about this and call it *Jackass Heaven.*"

"That won't go. Too many people would be offended."

"But it accurately—"

We were interrupted. Nurse Neglaw was calling the mail. She handed me a business letter. One end had been snipped off neatly. I showed it to her. "Why, Mr. Donaldson! No one in Chattahoochee would do such a thing!" It had been forwarded from the jail. What a disappointment to the snipper, for it was just an answer from *Time* saying they would be pleased to hold my subscription until I got back to Philadelphia.

Letters from my mother I tore up unread.

On dental run, twenty-four of us sat from 8:00 till noon, closely packed on high-backed mahogany-stained benches in a room no bigger than a cobbler's shop, in a small white building. I visited with a tall toothless tobacco chewer from the long-term wards, who had tobacco juice in his yellow-gray hair. His pants, changed that morning, were a mess of creases from the laundry and eight inches too short, and he had no socks.

"I'm from Denver," he said with a twang. "Ever been to Denver? Wonderful city. I hope you get to Denver. You're at the receiving ward? I live at the place down the street. Wonderful food there. You'd like it there. Well, been nice meeting you."

In the course of the first two weeks, I wrote three letters to Pinellas County, to the jailer, the sheriff, and the state's attorney about my money. None answered. Then Carter learned from a third-shift attendant how mail went into File 13. Carter and I watched. For two nights, the letters which were in the mailbox in the evening (a cigar box on the ledge inside the plexiglass) would be gone in the morning, and nobody got an answer. Carter, happening to be on doctor's call about his medication, saw one of his letters in the wastebasket near the door. To the doctor's mild amusement, Carter retrieved it. The doctor said some fool must have done it and called an attendant to mail it.

After a first conversation with each new arrival, there was nothing to talk about that wasn't a constant repetition of the injustices of a hard cruel world. What to do then? Whom to talk to? The idiots, like the one who ate newspapers as he walked the floor? The attendants, like the one who sat down with the newspaper for an hour every afternoon, only one day going through page after page of the same paper he had gone through page after page the day before, the second time upside down? Or the criminals, whose interests ran to remote places? Like the one who showed me how to put two cakes of soap in a sock—"You can kill with it." Like another who, in trembling voice, alone in a room with me after supper, told about guards at the state prison cracking his skull, and whose dark eyes flashed with plans to kill those guards when he was shipped back? Or like a third who tried to interest me in standing back of a cardplayer and signalling what opponents held, explaining, "We'll split," and promising five dollars a day apiece? He got out in two weeks.

To counteract the oppression of self-pity, a few of us gathered in a bedroom for an hour after supper. We played the fool and lampooned everything about Chattahoochee. I told them how Billy had yelled in the jail and how one day while reading in the front·dayroom I had heard "boozhwaaaah!" echo up the hall. Hurrying back, I had to wait for the second whoop. It came from the six-foot-three rack of bones draped over a four-foot settee, violently rolling. His long face hit the brown-leather back, then almost hit the floor. This rolling, which was from the medication, had been going on all the while, but I would never have guessed "Rock and Roll" was Billy.

It came about impromptu, our adopting Billy's war cry. Philip, who was young and irrepressible and under charges for the death of his wife in a speeding accident, was demonstrating how he would greet me if we happened to meet some day in Philadelphia on Market Street. Acting it out, Philip and I stepped boldly toward each other, thrust out right hands, and—

"Yell boozhwaaaah!" Narrel cried. "Yell boozhwaaaah! Kenneth."

That brought down the house. From then on it was the Boozhwaaaah Club, and passing in the hall we would say "boozhwaaaah" under our breath.

We got serious too. Seventy-five feet away was a three-story infirmary for old folk. Some nights a woman would tear us up with her screaming. We pictured her clinging to the window sash, frantic attendants snatching at her gown, while she yelled,

"They're beating me! O my God! Help! Help me!" A few years later, electromagnetic physics would affirm that the full moon affects potatoes and triggers outbursts by emotional cripples, and it was full moon when we first heard her. Still, rumors made us wonder how emotionally stable were the infirmary attendants.

Doctor Eaton had Carter up before a group of student nurses, and he told his other patients about the definite steps being taken for their release; and every week one or two of them were discharged, while I, as in the jail, was seeing no one. So along about the end of the third week, I waylaid Adair in the corridor.

He came around the corner of the front chart room with a brisk wave to Nurse Neglaw. "Good morning, Donaldson." He slowed down as I stepped in with him. "I shall be calling you in after vacation and taking a look at your case."

"But, Doctor, this just waiting around is hard to take."

"I've learned this, Donaldson: Chattahoochee is a very slow place."

"I can see that."

In such wise, after five weeks in jail (dead and buried) and three here (not quite forgotten) there were to be four more. It was impossible not to be bitter. And after Carter went down to the General Wards for having argued with his doctor about medication, each day added to my enthusiasm for a rescue-and-preventive society. All the same, when Narrel came up with a plan to petition the state Supreme Court for writs of habeas corpus, I held off, pending Adair's return. A late arrival had insisted to Narrel that he knew of one neighborhood man who had got out thus. So four of us talked it over between hands of a card game, but only Narrel was ready to wave a red flag in the doctor's face. The next morning, in Narrel's private room, while he stood outside the closed door to signal me to stuff paper and pen into my shirt if housekeeper or attendant showed up, I worked the thing down to a one-page letter addressed to the chief justice. The arguments were that one Narrel Damascus had been committed without proper examination, that he knew right from wrong, and that he had a job waiting.

Narrel gave one-legged Frunk in the wheelchair, who had outside privileges, a dollar to take it on his crutches over to some kid at the diner to mail. We watched from separate windows over the tops of full-blooming azaleas, the unsteady progress of crutches across the block-square green.

We waited uneasy without talking about it. Two weeks went. Then, on a Tuesday, a long envelope from the court came. It was Nurse Neglaw's day off and Narrel got the letter without the attendant's taking notice. The court had granted the writ and set a personal hearing for 9:00 A.M., Monday, the day of Adair's return from vacation.

Immediately I put things in balance. I was under no obligation to wait and under no misapprehension about being let go soon, because, according to the attendants, Adair had released nary a soul through staff in the whole past year. I made out three more petitions.

We felt subdued at the Boozhwaaaah Club. We were haunted with fear that the attendants would learn what we were up to and crack down in some way too terrible to contemplate.

I worried about Narrel's getting to the hearing on time and urged him on Saturday to take it up with the nurse. He said wait until Sunday night. He showed it then to the friendly attendant, who said, "They'll have to let you go."

At breakfast, Narrel was conspicuous in his free-world clothes, even to a tie. Yet no employee commented. Narrel had shaved during the night, courtesy of the attendant, and after breakfast donned his suit coat and sat down to wait. It was forty-four miles to the capital; so at 8:00 he consented to showing the court order to Nurse Neglaw.

I hovered near the door with a push broom.

"I've got to be there in an hour," Narrel insisted. She had him wait while she made a phone call, reporting that Adair would be right over.

Narrel and I took seats widely apart by the front windows. I made ready to shield my face behind a newspaper. The doctor came in, one step ahead of his briefcase. He stood for a long time with the nurse. Then she came out and called, "Mr. Damascus."

I sauntered unobtrusively down the hall and watched from the dimness by the locked bedrooms. I could see Adair flapping his arms while Narrel stood. After Narrel's dismissal, it was fifteen minutes more before the doctor left the building for the day. I met Narrel in his room.

"He won't let me go," Narrel said.

"They can't do this! It's impossible!" I said. "Putting themselves above the Supreme Court!"

Narrel said, "The Clinical Director called the Attorney

General. We can't let this man go like this, and if you let him out we'll not be responsible for what happens. He's dangerous, the Clinical Director said. That's it, Kenneth."

"We can't let them get away with it. Whom can you write?"

Narrel dictated a letter to his union headquarters. By two o'clock I had it boiled down to three pages.

It was surprising that no employee mentioned it and more so when notices came acknowledging the receipt of the other three petitions. It was an unhealthful calm.

Consequently, I felt consternation when summoned to the doctor's office, my throat tightening up as in the jail. It was anger racing.

Adair fussed with some papers, then said, "I've forgotten what you told me. Tell me about your case again."

This was a check, I knew. With a surge of determination I stifled whatever was inside. After two minutes he checked a handwritten page in the chart.

"I've decided to let you go," he said.

This was like LSD, from euthanasia to euphoria in one gulp.

"There is no connection between your other hospitalization and this," he said. "You're not sick, but you couldn't pass staff—not now. I'm going to release you out of state. I can do this without putting you to staff. You do have some friends, don't you?"

"Oh, sure. But I don't know whom I'd ask."

"Let me know."

I walked out ecstatically. Imprisonment was ending. But the dilemma: should I obligate myself to a friend? The answer came while I was looking at the big new shiny leaves on the magnolia across the street. To wait on the court was my option, to rely on the inherent fairness of American jurisprudence. I would dare to ask for that which was rightfully mine—a fair hearing.

But it was a blow to my faith in blindfolded Justice when word came the next week that the other three petitions were denied. No doubt about it, Justice had peeked and liked the carryings-on of the asylum doctors.

Nevertheless, I could still turn to some friend, even though that would amount to their telling me: "It's time for your nap. Don't forget your pill." I spent the day wording the letter in my mind. I did not worry additionally when Scazon, one of us four, was put on heavy medication and Umphrey, another, was transferred to the General Wards. That was Wednesday.

Thursday, after supper, a strange attendant walked up and said, "Get your things."

"What do you mean?" I said.

"Have you some things in your stand? Go get them and come along."

The *Sentinel*s went into a back pocket and the brittle black comb and the yellow pencil into a shirt pocket. I was taken up the back stairs, near the alcove where I had waited the first day with the full weight of all the earth's wrongs on my shoulders. Now I was walking up through the shroud separating two levels of the psychiatric boneyard to face the trip-hammer itself, which pounded woe into mortals. It would pound one so small that he would fit into the minutest niche of conformity that society allows.

My new bedroom was little larger than the one downstairs but was packed with fifteen beds. Mine was in the middle, making me scrape sideways to reach it. This was not far from the open door giving a view of the electroshock machine. "Want to see it?" someone asked. "No thanks," I said.

I dreamed all night of Adair's shaking four writs at me and pointing to the shock machine.

After breakfast the next morning, a dozen of us sat in two rows to have temperature and pulse checked. When a dumpling student nurse removed the thermometer, I said, "How do we stay normal with you around?" She said nothing and walked out, I being the last checked. Then I wondered, would the remark go on the record against me?

For the balance of the day, I mostly kept to myself in apprehensive numbness, walking the corridors for exercise and sitting alone, with not even interest in the papers or a shelf of library books. Two fellows invited me to their room to hear their radio. But I said I needed to walk at that time. One patient, whom I put down at once as a cog in the brainwashing machine, began questioning on Florida politics, then pointing to the rainspouts down the sides of the building, asked: "Know what they are?"

"Sure," I said, "the TV antennas."

Whereupon, he made tracks to report this.

Going through the ritual with the student nurses the second morning, my imagination took off in a heady spiral. What was being prepared for me? or me for what sacrifice? I swallowed a deep breath and held it as long as I could before the soft fingers took my wrist. It worked and my ground waves were normal.

I had not long to wait for revelation. The high priest came around in the intensive-treatment nave each morning. I watched him stop to speak to someone near the archway, then come diagonally across the room. I was suddenly moved to rudeness. I would not stand up.

"Good morning, Donaldson. How are you today?"

"Good morning." Then I looked away. Hatred was consuming me again. This specimen before me—this—this!—who had been going to set me free. I knew I had to grovel to get my freedom, but only a strong beam from my lucky star enabled me to keep a civil tongue.

"I've had a letter from Mrs. Marjorie Donaldson," Adair said. "She wants me to give you electric shock."

That brought me around quickly. I stared the doctor in the eye fiercely.

"I put you down for Monday morning." His voice was cold.

"I don't want them again." I had a strength and calmness from somewhere outside.

"Your mother thinks they would be good for you."

"I can tell you this—you won't give me more than one."

The doctor looked at me in a new way, maybe contemplating total destruction, maybe complete reprieve. "I'll give you a choice. It's either ECT or the General Wards."

"I'll take the General Wards," I said with the alacrity of one jumping off a buzzing platform in the other kind of fun house, "even if it's twenty years."

Then I was left alone. Why would Adair let my mother, three hundred miles away, change the diagnosis and do the prescribing?

A pair of burly khaki-clad guards brought a blue shirt and pinstripe overalls, white and blue, and left me to change while they went looking for my size of shoes.

They took me down the street past the squat dental clinic in the next block. Where we walked, the shadows under the magnolias and live oaks were sharp in the March sun. In the lot behind the firehouse, deep red roses smiled. Beyond and back of the tiny library was a complex of old white stucco three-story buildings. These were the long-term wards, the Mexican jails of the United States.

In three months I had come from the supposedly free streets of Pinellas County to Coventry. I had appealed for justice to many people. I was as important as a fly on a basketball hoop.

(I first read this in 1974. K.D.)

MEDICAL FILE
S.S. _____ 1/25/57

RETURN TO: SOCIAL SERVICE
P.O. BOX 421, Florida State Hospital
Chattahoochee, Florida

Please use back of
paper for additional
information.

SOCIAL HISTORY
Confidential Professional Use Only

Date

NAME OF PATIENT: **Donaldson, Kenneth** # **A-25738** Admitted **1/15/57**
Address before Hospitalization: **Belleaire Village Ct., Largo, Fla.**

1. INFORMANTS: (Names, addresses, relation to patient of those
who fill out this blank.)
    Father—William Thomas Donaldson
        Belleaire Village Ct.
        Largo, Florida

2. REASON FOR ADMISSION: (Why was patient brought to this
Incompetency   hospital? Describe patient's behavior.
5 weeks in Detention   Was patient willing to come? Where
Ward, Pinellas Co. Jail—   was patient taken care of prior to ad-
Treatment unknown   mission here—in hospital? in jail? at
                                    home? If in jail, state how long and
                                    treatment received in jail?)

                                    Has a resentment against his father,
                                    thinking he has been let down
                                    . . .

7. PERSONAL HISTORY:

                                    . . .

(g) Occupation: List all jobs and how long they lasted. Why did patient
    quit jobs or why was he fired? Give reasons for change in jobs and
    anything you know about how he got along with employers and
    fellow workers.

    Cannot list jobs—Was well liked by fellow workers but could not
    hold jobs on account of hallucinations

                                    . . .

68

10. DEVELOPMENT OF MENTAL ILLNESS:

(a) How did patient's illness begin? Give dates of onset and state changes in patient's behavior, habits, ways of talking or expressing self, eating and sleeping. Did patient complain of physical ailments (specify complaints)? Show any trouble with remembering dates, names, places, or events? Show any evidence of hearing or seeing things not evident to others? Show any unusual fears, crying, silly laughter, staring into space, shyness, or unusual intimate relations with strangers? Express any ideas or feeling mistreated, persecuted or influenced by people or things? Develop any difficulty in talking, expressing self? Use any strange words? Was patient over active or under active?

Worrying started illness—thought he was being persecuted and food was being poisoned—Led a natural active life—a good appetite and good sleeper.

(b) Did illness come on gradually over a period of weeks, months, or years? Or come on suddenly?

Grieved at divorce and raising children as he had no way of caring for them.

(c) Had patient been through any recent "shock" or other emotional stress due to financial strain or set-backs, death of loved one, etc? Any talk or attempts to harm self or others? Has patient had previous "nervous break-downs"?

Has had previous nervous breakdowns—
during his college years and dropped out after
2 years. After marriage and children came along,
expenses piled up from sickness in family, and overwork and
worry brought about his breakdowns.

(I first read this in 1974. K. D.)

Florida State Hospital
Chattahoochee, Florida

Gentlemen:

I hereby give permission for the psychiatrists at Florida State Hospital
to administer electroshock to _____ **KENNETH DONALDSON A-25738**
for the treatment of his or her mental condition. I thoroughly under-

stand the risk which it entails, and agree to the administration of such treatment over such period as may be deemed necessary by the psychiatric staff of Florida State Hospital.

WILLIAM T. DONALDSON	FATHER	FEB. 18th
Name	Relationship	Date

Witness: **MARJORIE K. DONALDSON**

RECEIVED
Clinical Director's Office
Florida State Hospital

FEB 19 1957

A.M.   P.M.
7/8/9/10/11/12/1/2/3/4/5/6

(I first read this in 1974. K.D.)

February 12, 1957

In Re: Mr Kenneth Donaldson A-25738

Mrs William T Donaldson
Belleair Village Trailer Court, A Street
Largo, Florida

Dear Mrs Donaldson:

We have your letter regarding your son, Mr Kenneth Donaldson.

He is adjusting quite well to our hospital routine. He is eating and sleeping well, and is cooperative.

We do feel that he is quite ill from a mental point of view, however, and we have received some reports of his previous hospitalization suggesting that his illness is of quite long standing.

At the moment it is our feeling that he should have a course of electroconvulsive treatments. Therefore, we are enclosing a request for your permission in order that we may be able to carry on this procedure.

Yours very truly,

J T BENBOW, M.D.
Clinical Director

CHA:mck
Enc: 1

(I first read this in 1974. K.D.)

March 21, 1957

In Re: Mr. Kenneth Donaldson A-25738

Honorable B. J. Owen
Assistant Attorney General
Tallahassee, Florida

Dear Mr. Owen:

The above named patient was committed to the Florida State Hospital from the County court of Clearwater, in the County of Pinellas. He was admitted January 15, 1957. The pre-admission diagnosis was SCHIZO-PHRENIC REACTION, PARANOID TYPE.

On admission he was found to have a number of delusions of persecution by a group of, what he classified, rich Republicans. He felt that this group had stolen many good ideas which he had recommended for use in Foreign Policy Administration, and in the settlement of various labor problems. He felt that the same group had attempted to, and were still attempting to, poison him by putting chemicals in his food. He had a previous history of mental illness, and was treated for such in New York State during the early 1940s. He has had continual difficulty with job adjustment, and withdrawal from personal relationship has been characteristic of this behavior. Our diagnosis at that time was SCHIZO-PHRENIC REACTION, PARANOID TYPE (PSYCHOTIC).

Since admission he has been seen a number of times in clinical interview, and a detailed social review has been carried out. Detailed neurological and physiological examinations have been performed, as well as our general routine laboratory investigation. His case was last reviewed, and our last examination carried out on March 15. At that time his condition was felt to be unchanged, and he still retained the delusional thinking observed at the time of admission. Our diagnosis has not changed, and we consider this a SCHIZOPHRENIC REACTION, PARANOID TYPE.

Yours very truly,

C. H. ADAIR, M.D.
Examining Psychiatrist
Florida State Hospital

CHA: CK

CHAPTER 6

1957

A Hundred Eyes

A HUNDRED EYES ON THE SECOND AND THIRD FLOOR SUN PORCHES stared down through the wire grilles on the windows, watching me being escorted around the corner of the tiny post office–library to the White Male Department offices. My escorts unlocked a black screen door and turned me over to other guards.

Before I could be seated on one of the straight chairs against the dark wainscoting, a small man in a blue serge suit and rimless glasses came to the middle of a small adjoining room to look out at me.

Clutching the belief that there is good in every man, I went into the farther office to see J. B. O'Connor, M.D. He sat with his back to the small window, late morning sun reflected from the white windowsill to emphasize a pencil moustache in a white face and glistened on pomaded black hair and gold cuff links. His small hand, indicating a chair against the wall at a front corner of the desk, had the Brothers of the Forge ring, anvil on purple stone. That meant that I was starting off with a potential friend, for attendant Shast had shown that all Forgers were not hostile.

He asked a few questions and I started my capsule rundown, but he said, yes, he knew those things, as he had Doctor Adair's report in front of him.

"I'm a student of Christian Science, Doctor," I said.

"You won't have to take any medication as long as you do not cause any trouble on the wards." He turned some pages. "You wrote the Supreme Court."

"I had to do something. I don't belong in an insane asylum."

"You shouldn't have done it that way. Well, I'm going to put you on our best ward and I hope you like it with us."

"Will you let me go soon? Adair said he could let me go out of state without staff. Wouldn't that be quickest?"

"He couldn't do that. But I will give your case some consideration." He took me through the connecting door and introduced me to John Gumanis, M.D.

Gumanis said: "Do you know what day it is?"

"Saturday."

"What day of the month?"

"Twenty-three March 1957."

"You were studying law. What was the name of the school?"

"Blackstone—in Chicago."

"What did you pay for the course?"

"Fifty dollars down—seems like the total was one twenty-five—maybe one fifty."

All this while, a large capped nurse behind Gumanis was pouring pills from large bottles into small bottles and shot-size silver cups.

The guard, "attendant" the doctors called him, who stood in the doorway because there was not room for another chair, then took me down to the cellar to exchange overalls for pants and white shirt; then up past the pool table in the back room, six wooden timbers supporting huge beams, and up fifteen feet of rickety stairs, which were free from the wall, with only a 2×4 railing. The guard let me through another screen door.

If stepping into the jail had been a shock and stepping into the receiving ward hackle-raising, stepping into the General Wards was feeling darkness. I was left standing in a windowless area. I took a step up to a higher level of splintered floor, opposite a point of light. Stooped and wizened men, and fresher arrivals without prison pallor, paraded fitfully back and forth. The window was in an octagonal room, the Belltower, with an old desk and chairs for several khaki-clads, who spat into a three-foot trough lined with galvanized metal on the floor. As calls came over the phone, three of the guards left.

At the noon whistle, one hundred patients, with lots of horseplay, jammed down to dinner. I was held back by a guard at the head of the swaying stairs.

Fifteen minutes later, there was Carter, white hair close-cropped but pink face alight at finding me.

"Those going down were the housemen," he said, "from Ward 1 upstairs too."

Beyond the poolroom below the rickety stairs and past a concrete porch enclosed with cyclone fencing, we went most of the way without guards. On both sides of a hundred-yard-long 10 × 10-foot wooden tunnel, we went single file. "The Tunnel of Shit," Carter said. The deposits spoke for themselves. Through double-hung sash, covered with wire grilles, I saw the street below as we turned. We went down an incline to the uproar and stench of a mess hall with eleven hundred "crazy" men on benches at long wooden tables. The smell was between that of a stable and a torrid-zone open-air butchershop.

The lines wound right and left along the walls to two steam tables. Spotting lettuce, I said, "This is better than the receiving ward." But the ill-smelling tallowy concoction of gravy and sharp bits of white bone on our aluminum trays gave me doubt. I ate cornbread, black-eyed peas, and boiled cabbage. Guards poured one refill for our big aluminum mugs of milk. Before Carter and I could finish, kitchen slaves grabbed trays and banged leftovers into oil drums and threw mugs into a crate on the terrazzo floor. Above it all, guards yelled at one another and cursed patients, occasionally rapping a patient on the side of the head with the aluminum pitchers in which they were collecting the forks and spoons.

Carter and I went back to mission rockers on the sun porch. We watched squirrels run down live oaks and across grass to sun-drenched azaleas. Carter, holding onto the window grille, studied someone getting out of a car at the information booth a block away, near the dental building. He was expecting his brother and sister from Philadelphia.

"They're coming today?" I said.

"They'll be here. I told them about the noise," he said, "and the abuse, the beatings of the old men and the kicking them after they fall."

"But do your letters go?"

"Bull Dean told me the mail went out."

In other ways, too, Carter was coping. He had never been seen by Doctor O'Connor and not been seen by Doctor Gumanis, the pill doctor, since the first day. But Carter was not swallowing his pills: "I roll them back of my lower plate."

"Surely these people can't get away with this," I said, just as I had said to Narrel at the receiving ward. "It's got to end by next week."

A patient, hunkering beside us on a bench, said, "Sure, it's going to stop the second Tuesday next week. Awk, awk, awk. Yahoo!"

The padlocks on the grilles laughed too. My mind vomited.

But I said: "O'Connor is considering my release. Back in Philly I'll make them understand."

After supper I was taken to Ward 7, the third floor of the second building away at right angles from Carter's. Tom Merchant, scratching his bare chest, sat on the edge of my bed. He said, "This place is a miasma of stupidity." I was stretched out in BVDs on the blanket, fresh from shower and shave. Around us on a hundred close-packed beds were the elite among the patients.

Gray-haired Tom, an alcoholic since his divorce, had been locked in only a few days. For six months he had been on the open ward and worked as helper in the little post office. On his last Sunday visit at his brother's, he had borrowed his brother's car, got drunk, and drove into a ditch.

Was he getting psychiatric treatment for drinking?

"I know a lawyer," Tom said, "Orshale in Beetown, who'd get you out for $250. For the first $50 he'll come talk."

There was no way to get the few dollars I had in the bank in Philadelphia and no one I'd care to ask.

"Write Orshale anyway," Tom said. "I'll see he gets it. They're good people in Quincy too—that's where I'm from, the county seat—not like Chattahoochee. They're eight thousand in Quincy. Chattahoochee has eight thousand too, but seven thousand are patients. I know another lawyer—a patient—who wrote himself out. Sent letters through the office and a copy over the fence. But don't divulge anything about yourself. They'll twist it around and use it against you."

He instructed me to write O'Connor for work. I chose outside detail, but Tom said it'd be the kitchen, because I hadn't been there long enough to be trusted outside.

Then the short fellow on the next bed told me his story. He had been a stableboy all his life, coming to Florida every winter. At the close of the Hollywood season, a year ago, he had been driven to Chattahoochee. "I didn't do nothing," he said. "They just put me in a car and brought me here. I didn't see nobody."

I did not sleep well that night. For three days, while it rained, I mostly lay on the bed, thinking, worrying. There were no porches on these buildings. On the third day, after 7:00 P.M. bed check, I was moved to the second floor, Ward 6, where the kitchen workers slept. Relaxed at finally being headed in the right direction ("You can work your way out," these kitchen slaves said each year of their stay) I fell into an exhausted sleep, despite blaring radios and shouting cardplayers. Each time there was a scream, I turned but fell right back to sleep.

Before lights-on, thirty of us were routed out in the shadows from three fifteen-watt bulbs along the ceiling. Someone had hidden the shoes of "Captain," a five-by-five mongoloid. He howled until somebody, screaming curses, flung the shoes back.

Two attendants with flashlights checked us off in a large ledger at the head of the stairs. On Ward 5, we waited in a nervous huddle by the door. Somebody pulled Captain's hair, making him scream, and an attendant hit him so hard in the belly he doubled over. Another patient remarking about brutality got his arm twisted until he too screamed. A third attendant came with a small time book, checked us again, and turned us out like calves from a barn. The back porch was lit now by the stars and the Tunnel of Shit by the ornamental street lamps below. At the mouth of the tunnel, a woman in white checked us off in another ledger.

There were pitchers of fruit juice and hot coffee on the tables and fried eggs and bacon on our trays. I used plenty of ketchup and put both butter and peanut butter on my rolls and plenty of sugar on my oatmeal. One man told me the bacon was made from cadavers and I assured him I had no doubt.

A second group sat down, five dozen men from the open ward and one woman with a cellophane-wrapped cigar in her mouth.

They called her Hobo Babe. She wore a red skirt, a green cardigan over a flowered blouse, a purple-printed kerchief on her head, and a good plastering of pancake makeup. When she left puffing on the cigar, I was momentarily glad I had come to Chattahoochee. No one would tell me, so I guessed she was a night-shift worker from another department.

We cleared the amenities from the tables and I was delegated to dip grits as the noisy multitude wound past. Captain, his long tongue darting in and out, waited with the other slaves in an impatient knot to grab the trays from the last arrivals. Then the lusty attendants routed the raucous army and one could again hear Mis' Brack's little radio at the other end of the barn, blaring country music off the walls. I also mopped some table tops and swept around them. After supper we were checked off in the three ledgers on the way back to the ward.

There were fresh blades in the razors for us. As most everyone undressed after supper, I stretched out in unbuttoned BVDs. Six radios were blasting at one another, four shouting men were playing cards, and one of the mongoloids was screaming because someone had dumped him on the floor and thrown someone else's mattress on his head. Then, asthmatic ninety-pound Pedro started to choke. He and two others, craving companionship nightly, sought the father image in the three attendants, who responded, all in good fun, by twisting arms, knocking heads together, and pulling hair. When Pedro went limp, he was flung onto a bed, anybody's bed.

One midmorning I was surprised to see Umphrey, who had been sent down by Adair before me. Doctor O'Connor had let him off the Back Yard to work in the kitchen. He had been put in with the wild ones as punishment for his part with the writs. He had the news from an attendant, that a regional official of Narrel Damascus's union, out of Atlanta, had pulled up in front of the receiving ward in a Cadillac. That was Tuesday. On Wednesday, the doctors held special staff for Narrel and put him on the street scot-free, which is a record cure for insanity. When Narrel wrote me that he would do something for me, I answered but heard no more.

I spent the next few weeks, before O'Connor would see fit to release me to my proper environment up north, talking to patients and writing letters for them. Everybody talked dirty, especially the attendants in addressing patients. But to placate Umphrey, who did not like rough talk, I substituted "Mother Flickinger." And everybody laughed at everybody else, as long as the one laughed at was a patient, like little Captain thinking with his mouth wide open, words slobbering off his chin.

Mis' Bruce's right-hand man Buddy, who served the "entree" on our steam table, slept next to me. Each night while he prayed for a half hour, his elbows resting on the straight chair between our beds, one of two such chairs on the ward, I wrote a letter to his father about Buddy's promise to drink no more. By the tenth letter, his father came and signed him out. This made the second one I had gotten out. All they needed was someone to write for them. This kind of insanity did not seem so hard to crack, if you approached it with an open mind.

The next one to bring me his problem lived on the open ward, Tommy "Peepee." Besides working in the kitchen, he played the drums, brilliantly too, at the Friday round dances. He was a powerfully built twenty-five-year-old, whose main flaw was a certain stuttering, often having to shake his head to get a word out. He had worked at a nightclub.

"One of the girls in the show asked me to look at her peepee," Tommy said. "Did I do wrong? Do I belong locked up for looking at her peepee? I can play the drums, can't I?" And he drummed with his knuckles on the table and tapped a toe.

I said, "I don't know what your diagnosis is, but I can honestly say that you must be the first one I've talked to who is not a schizophrenic."

The dining room itself wove a clear pattern of the institution's tender loving care. The kitchen might have spotless steam kettles on a red-tile floor, but if a piece of chicken fell in the water of the homemade steam table, or the whole panful fell on the floor, it was served. "If they don't like it, they shouldn't ought've come here," Mis' Bruce said. "And if they want to eat better, let them go to work like us," Buddy said on his last day. However, there were no more than fifty off-ward jobs.

I inherited Buddy's job. But when I ladled out the collection of white bones in a reddish-brown tallow (ten times a week) I had to step back from the lip of the pot. Also, I cleaned out the steam table after supper and kept things in order for each meal, checking the menu posted each day outside the manager's office, a copy of which was sent to the state capital.

"If they're not as they're supposed to be, you tell me," Mis'

Bruce said. Then she went over to sit with Mis' Brack at the other end.

Most helpings were small and the inmates were underweight. At breakfast and supper the menu called for butter. I told Mis' Bruce there wasn't any.

"That's all right," she said.

The next meal, bone stew was substituted for roast beef. I told Mis' Bruce.

"That's all right," she said.

The next day there were dried limas for fresh green vegetable.

"That's all right," she said.

I never reported again. We even went six months without butter, although the menu listed it twice a day.

But she was a good boss, otherwise, sending me around to the employees' cafeteria at 10:00 for a pitcher of good coffee. I snooped in other parts of the kitchen complex and saw unwrapped bread stored on open shelves and eggs left in a crate at room temperature. Denoting progress was the discontinued use of the rings in the walls where inmates were once fastened while they ate.

When I first got to the White Male Department, I had written *The Saturday Evening Post* to learn the fate of my manuscript. Their reply, saying the entire editorial board had read it but decided against using it, I showed to several in the kitchen, so they would believe my story; and Mis' Bruce showed it to Mis' Brack, who took it to the manager. But no one had a comment.

Two other slaves lived on the open ward. One of them had forged his father's name on an eight-dollar check. No charges had been preferred, but he had been locked up eight years for that eight dollars' worth of insanity. In answer to my question, why didn't he run, he said he wanted to wait until O'Connor said he was cured. He never did get cured, dying in Chattahoochee six years later.

A young slave brought me a letter from his aunt in Baltimore, who wanted to take him out. Doctor O'Connor had promised to release him if his aunt requested it. When she did, O'Connor replied. She returned the reply to her nephew. It was worded something like this: "Your nephew is up and about daily, but as for his leaving at this time, he is not quite ready. He needs a little more treatment."

For all the many mental illnesses in Chattahoochee, the most decisive therapy was set in motion when an outsider wrote a doctor, inquiring about one of the patients. The latter would be called down for an interview. This was called letter therapy. The other way of seeing a doctor was for the patient himself to write to the doctor. A typical letter-therapy psychiatric interview would go like this:

DOCTOR: "What ward are you on?"
PATIENT: "Ward six."
DOCTOR: "Are you taking any medication?"
PATIENT: "No."
DOCTOR: "Are you working anyplace?"
PATIENT: "Yes sir, in the kitchen."
DOCTOR: "That'll be all."

In one session of letter therapy, O'Connor told me, "Your mother writes an awful lot."

I was still expecting O'Connor to rule me sane any day. In a further expression of my naïveté, I wrote inquiring about his suggestions for improving state hospitals. I explained that I planned an addition to my book and realizing the difficulty of getting increased appropriations from politicians, I thought my book a good forum for the doctors to reach the public.

Thus, even knowing what this next doctor's call was about, my waiting was, nonetheless, a period of high tension. There was no patient who was not affected, most having to go to the toilet first. It was not a fear of immediate personal injury, rather a fear of the medical treatments which resulted in the grotesque hulks on every ward. At the therapy session, one could count on 120 seconds, during which he would have to answer the three questions, then conduct his defense and make his point.

I sat with fifteen patients for an hour, before the doctor showed up. Above us, above the assorted pipes threaded through the exposed joists, there was a constant creaking from people walking, a Hitchcock setting. Words of Warden Lawes came to mind: "To get the best of a criminal, let him think you believe him."

During this waiting period, usually an ingratiating patient from another ward would park next to you and ask things about your case which you had never discussed at the hospital. In my own case, it was always something pertaining to my parents. This other patient, then, was called in just ahead of you. When you saw the doctor, the conversation, after the three questions, would be about something else, oftentimes trivia, the doctor already having his answer through his "clinical" approach.

This time, though, there was no third party. I was taken into Gumanis's too, which was unusual, he seeing only those on medication. Did they think, from my letter, that I needed Thorazine?

"I have this letter," Gumanis said, pointing with his pipe. "You wrote to O'Connor. It's four pages. What does it mean?"

"Did you read it?" I asked.

"It's long—what do you want?"

I explained about my offering him a chance to reach the public.

"If you can do that, there's nothing the doctors can say." After a pause he said, "You had too many jobs."

Elapsed time was two minutes minus.

On one call, when I tried to make a point, O'Connor replied: "We didn't send for you."

"Why do you continue to hold me? I had a thorough examination in Philadelphia and the doctors gave me a clean bill of health. Down here, in this state, I have had no examination whatsoever, and so I ask you to let me go back north."

"What do you mean, you had no examination!" he said sharply. "You've had a thorough examination and knew nothing about it."

"If I did," I said, assuming he meant the ingratiating patients, "then it must have been by untrained personnel."

"I don't care what you think!" He spun around in his chair to face the window and said, "That'll be all."

At the time, I assumed he meant my examination had been by his informers among the patients. A few years later, I saw that he could have been referring to the "examination" by the committing doctors who did not see me before filing their report.

When I got fed up with his "considering me for staff," I dropped my humbleness and thought of ways to prod him.

One day after the three questions, I said: "I can tell you one thing, Doctor O'Connor—I would rather see my children dead than locked up in here and I bet you feel the same about yours."

"That'll be all." He spun fast that time.

On another call, he said, "If you were a Christian Scientist you wouldn't need any treatment." This was in reply to my repeated complaint about being held without getting any treatment. "But have Philadelphia send me a copy of their findings."

My letter to Travelers Aid was handed back to me in the mess hall.

"Such letters can't go," the attendant said.

"But the doctor told me to write it."

"You can't send it."

"You'd better—or answer to Doctor O'Connor."

It worked that once and a reply came from Philadelphia. O'Connor held up their four-page single-spaced letter in front of me.

"There's nothing in here I didn't know already," he said. "That'll be all."

But O'Connor never told me why he was holding me. I wrote that fact to former employers, begging their help. I wrote old friends and members of the family. But I had made no negotiable friendships in a decade of moving about the country. Finally, John H. Lembcke, old college friend, a certified public accountant in Binghamton, New York, answered.

He had contacted the state hospital up there and they advised his working through the chaplain at Chattahoochee. John wrote me that if there were nothing wrong with me he would see that I got out and if I did need treatment he would see that I got it and was released. The day I got John's letter I was on doctor's call.

There were the three questions, then O'Connor said: "I have this letter from a gentleman in New York, who says you are going to see our chaplain. Have you ever met him?"

"No, I haven't."

"You will enjoy meeting him. That'll be all."

But I did not see the chaplain. Instead, two weeks later this letter came from John:

> I think the thing for you to do is to take a little treatment there or to come up here and take some treatment.

I did not reply to that. If a friend cannot take you at your word, what more is there to do?

No matter how many troubles a man outside has, there are always skirts sashaying and children playing. On Ward 6 we had Persimmon, a short fat redneck, whose "schizophrenia" demanded four years. Its form had been trying to throttle the man stealing his fishing boat. He was the only cardplayer who never got angry.

When the others worked to a certain pitch, he would push the table onto their laps and roar, "I didn't know you cared, love!" Then he would parade the length of the ward in his unbuttoned BVDs with a cigar shimmying in his mouth. He could be light-hearted, because he was one of the few who knew how long his "schizophrenia" would last: four years, it did not matter where, the county said.

My hardest test was tongue-tied and retarded Skootch. His larynx worked backward, I believe. After his frantic pointing and occasional tears of desperation, we were able to convey to his family that he wanted his own clothes for the dances. Our second letter brought his first answer in two years and, a month later, dress shirt, pants, and tie. His gratefulness was never exceeded by any earthquake survivor.

I was not seeking out these people. But when they came to me, I listened and I was finding out that there was little insanity on Ward 6. Some of these people had been locked up for years. All they needed was somebody to listen to them. Al Siebert, author of *Are We Mentally Ill?*, says: "I have found that most people will be fully honest with someone who can listen. The world is full of honest people. What the world needs is more honest listeners."

But there were times when I could not help.

Whenever there was a lull, some attendant or patient would start something. During one brief lull after supper, two huge attendants from another ward burst in and silently beat up a young fat epileptic, who cussed them through swollen lips. Then the patient asked, wasn't I going to do something about it? I pictured Doctor "Stoneheart's" sardonic grimace at being inter-rupted about a housekeeping matter and his issuing an order for my shock treatments. I looked at Rusty, the handsome balding farmer-attendant in charge of the ward, who was rocking furiously with sweat on his face after his own workout with Pedro.

Pedro had been back only a week this time. A twenty-year-old Latin from Tampa, lovable, ingratiating, sharing his coffee with all, he was as robust as a split toothpick. He could talk only when angry; then the most beautifully formed swear words would fall out, but he never cussed Rusty. He would stand for an hour after supper, massaging Rusty's scalp and combing the sparse locks until the sensation of blood-on-the-air-to-a-hyena made Rusty squeeze Pedro until there was no breath left in him and tickle him until he had a choking spell. This would be relieved by having his arm twisted behind his back and a knee carrying two hundred pounds pressed into his spine. Mercifully, an epileptic seizure took away the agony of the asthmatic attack. Then Rusty would toss the surfeited body to some bed to finish its thrashing. After a week of this, I interpreted Pedro's grunts as wanting to go home. Two days after his mother got the picture in my letter, sent through the grapevine, he was signed out.

Most on the ward had all their faculties. Their treatment was doses of total inactivity, such as middle-aged Fortuna was getting for his murder charges, alias, schizophrenia. Twenty years previously, there had been a murder in the office building where he was elevator operator. He knew something about the murder and left the state for thirteen years. When homesickness brought him back, he was promptly jailed, charged with the murder, and rushed to Chattahoochee in a celebrated solution for the local police, despite his angry demands for a trial. Now in the seventh year of the "sentence," I wrote the prosecutor, saying that Fortuna was no longer getting treatment and wanted to be returned for trial. This brought the first reply ever from the prosecutor, who said that Fortuna was ill; and his reply to O'Connor brought Fortuna a doctor's call and the medical explanation that he had not done enough time yet.

Half the men behind the green door had never had so much as an attack of nerves, like Erskine, who owned a liquor store. He had sampled his wares too freely and his family topped off his visit to the old homestead with an icing of Chattahoochee. This was his fifth time. His prayers to his family via my letters were useless. But, as he did not belong in an insane asylum, we sent a letter to attorney Reggie Orshale. I fashioned a blank check for Erskine and he got out that week. Chalk up another cure.

One evening, as I rested after the shower, I heard a neighbor say: "By George, if I didn't have charges, they'd never keep me locked up for a year!" I thought that was a pretty good rule and decided there would be no more Christmases like the one in jail.

Still, December was a long way off from May; so I reactivated my subscriptions to the Philadelphia paper and *Time*. Now began another division of my treatment. The mail went through a dozen hands after leaving the custody of Uncle Sam, starting with the two paid employees of the hospital substation down to the attendant who brought it on the ward. It started with *Time*. In 1957, it reached Florida subscribers on Friday. Mine came

Saturday. Then Sunday. Then Monday, well thumbed and spotted with greasy crumbs. When my indignation reached anger, my hidden helpers started on the newspapers. This part of my "schizophrenia" was to rage unchecked for fifteen years.

Also, my teen-age daughter wrote: "Daddy, I know you are not sick. But why don't you write?" I was writing. Then her letters stopped.

The constant noise tempted me to take Umphrey's invitation. Four of us slaves were sitting on Umphrey's bed, over saltines and jelly. They showed me a "15" key, which opened all doors in the department. It had been fashioned from a spoon handle. They would leave from a screen door on the kitchen porch while the women were busy with early chow. They would be safe in the bushes by daylight.

But it would be tough going that way: no close friends to go to, no money for transportation, and none but institutional clothes, which made one look like a derelict from Mars. Yet those things did not stop me. It was O'Connor's continued promise to give my release some consideration.

I got through another month with my nose buried in a library book or a newspaper. And twice a day, Mis' Bruce took us out in a small enclosure to walk in the bountiful sun with our shirts off. And twice I was called to the office to be told there was a $10 deposit to my account. I did not spend it at the dope stand; it would buy a bus ticket to Philadelphia.

Friday was our big day. In the morning, kitchen men went to the barbershop, walking alone through the tunnel and along the back porch past the poolroom. I always peered through the filthy windows of Occupational Therapy where a handful of patients supposedly "regained" their health by repairing signs and weaving cane footstools; but all I could make out were scraps and uncapped paint cans.

Though the clippers pulled and were hot against the ear, kitchen men were never given an institutional around-the-bowl cut. While I was in the chair, the wallbox phone rang. The end barber took the receiver, with his elbow on the shelf. All work stopped in anticipation of drama unfolding.

"Yes, he's here now," the barber said. "I'm pretty sure when he's had time to think it over, he'll write to his dear old mother." But that kind of psychology always has the opposite effect on me, hardens me against any compromise. I had no doubt it was engineered by the master, Doctor O'Connor.

When we got back to the kitchen, there was the smell of the week: sewer trout and boiled cabbage. But it did not spoil the fun of the round dance afterward. A five-piece band of patients and attendants beat out acceptable tunes and a hundred couples moved around an area somewhat larger than a basketball court. A few characters had out-of-this-world steps. I went back a second time for laughs. Then I pulled myself up short. Why was I laughing at unfortunates and why was I there in the first place? I didn't dance but visited with the women. None were nervous or irrational. Wives were locked away by husbands, mothers separated from young children. One robust white-haired woman, with a master's in sociology, had spent five years on the back wards for some minor infraction of ward rules.

For the movies, the men had two hundred permanent seats in the balcony of the Rec Hall. The women sat under the balcony. The entertainment started in the balcony with wolf whistles, horsing around, and cries from tormented mongoloids. During the picture, the retarded laughed in the wrong places. Wise guys among the criminals made filthy remarks. And, always, the film broke. Then the lights went out, or the sound died, or the reels got interchanged. Once, the film caught fire and we saw it burn in technicolor on the screen. Finally I stopped going and missed the best. A young man took a running dive over the balcony rail and landed on his head on empty folding chairs. He wanted to commit suicide. The next day I was told the doctor sent him home.

On the way back from the Rec Hall, the kitchen bugs had to wait in the poolroom until all the others were locked on their wards. It was like dancing in a compactor. I got over to the side where three grilled windows looked into Ward 3X, sick bay. Carter called out one afternoon. He was there for diabetes. He was tickled to tell me that his sister would be down that month from Philadelphia. But even his ruddy smile did not ease the depression I carried back through the tunnel.

When a card came from California from Umphrey, I remembered his advice: "Don't stay around here. I was born in this part of the country, Kenneth. I left when I grew up. These people are sadists."

By June, I had learned that O'Connor himself was born in the neighborhood, an area with whose residents I had already had too much contact. I had also come to feel that he was not going to put me to staff for examination. Then I made my plans.

But first, there were visitors. In the room in front of the doctors' offices, the wainscoting was painted black and there were venetian blinds. A patient and his mother sat at one of the two small tables. In the old polished chairs, there was a white-haired couple. I was upon them before they looked up—Mother and Dad. She hugged and kissed me.

"Yes, we have seen the doctor," she said, "and he says you are working in the kitchen. That's good—you get enough to eat then?"

But small talk was out. "You're going to sign me out, aren't you?"

"Oh, we can't do that."

"Why not?"

"He says you need a little more treatment," Dad said. "He spoke about shock treatments."

"You wouldn't let him. My God!" I could see the men on the close-packed beds in Marcy. "I've just got over the others. Tell him—go tell him you won't approve."

Dad was back in two minutes. "All right, no shock treatments," he said. But he did not sit down. "We've got to—"

"But you said you were staying all night. Why do you—"

"Come along, Donaldson." Two big attendants were pulling my sleeves.

Mother continued to smile as she waved.

Back in the dining room, I asked Mis' Bruce if she thought O'Connor was on the level. I had to know who was behind the shock business. "Don't you think he can see that I'm not nuts?"

"I couldn't say," Mis' Bruce said.

"You jes' oughtna done it," Mis' Brack said, "or you wouldn't be here."

I asked no more questions and perfected my plans.

Two groups since Umphrey had been caught leaving the kitchen. That way necessitated an accomplice, who might be a blabbermouth. The only sure way was to get outside work and escape from the job. I had to quit the kitchen to get consideration by the doctor for the change. I had to spend three days in midsummer dust, from 7:00 to 5:00, with a thousand fellow sufferers, who did the same every day it didn't rain. It was better than Coney Island—a mere thousand lolling and spitting on three acres. And we had squirrels in the tall pines and we could drool over cars on a small section of the main highway, seen through the trees.

After bed check Sunday, an attendant told me I could start on outside detail in the morning. It was the general maintenance gang, with headquarters in some sheds a half mile downhill by the nine-hole golf course. We serviced the hundreds of landscaped acres and all the buildings where seven thousand were caged under two thousand employees, including twenty doctors (psychiatrists, dentists, and mortician). We did anything somebody else did not do—setting out lawn sprinklers, trimming shrubbery and palms, planting flowers, doing carpentry and plumbing, moving furniture.

For six hours a day, I found serenity in puttering about, deep in the heart of the piney woods. If a person were really disturbed, I can conceive no better therapy than toil in the shadows and smells of forest and lawn. But only the well could get on outside detail. That the so-called sick did not, bit deep into my bosom.

The first day out, "Friend" and I (he was a big farmer with ten words in his vocabulary, who called everybody friend) dug an eight-foot hole, 6×12 across, in the hard soil of the median strip in front of the library.

Before noon Doctor O'Connor came out to watch. He spoke to me: "How are you making out, Donaldson?"

"Fine." I was grinning. "Sure is good to get out of that kitchen." My shirtless back was covered with dust turned mud under the summer sun.

O'Connor turned to the boss, who stood in the shade of a tree: "You're not trying to kill him in one day, I hope."

"Oh," Mr. Zeron said, "he's taking it all right."

So, he was a pretty nice doctor after all, I thought. My digging was carefree.

The six hours flew each day. There were trips in a pickup to the big warehouse; crazy arguments with a railroad man about how to use the saw and square; the doctors' dining room with snowy linen and a bud vase with a rose on each table; and the farm where state road-camp prisoners milked fifty cows in a spotless barn and raised tons of collards for the patients. One day, Mr. Zonker, the big boss, even took me in his car to return some bottles to the stand in the lakeside park and to point out the landscaping, which he had supervised.

The White Male Department got a new supervisor, or "head

housekeeper," on July 1. Gray-haired "Brother" Dean was a foot larger in every way than Dr. O'Connor. There were overnight changes, all improvements but one: on July 2, Hobo Babe came to breakfast in men's clothes. His whole story was that he had been picked off a freight in the local railroad yard and brought to the hospital by the sheriff, who arranged for commitment papers the next day, which is permissible in Florida. Hobo Babe had been only too glad for the free grits. Working in the linen room and acquiring proficiency on the sewing machine, he had for the hell of it made himself a set of women's clothes. July 2 was the death of the best clown in the circus.

TVs were installed which had been lying in the warehouse for a year. Twenty beds were removed from Ward 6 and replaced with new park benches, the outside-white paint still moist. The only objection was that after two programs you had permanent ridges on your behind. The change which came over the ward was spectacular. Horsing around after supper was mostly forgotten and Rusty's hair went uncombed. The TV was turned up loud enough to drown out the radios' mountain music. It was a window to the free world. It kept the attendants entertained—a good example of applying therapy to the right place, for when the inmates were not being agitated, they were reasonable peace-loving men, even the retarded, allowing for a certain little snappishness from being imprisoned and abused for years.

"You know," I said to Zeron over a Coke at a gas station in town, "that's like the application of Christianity in the Menningers' hospitals. They applied love instead of Thorazine and shock treatments and got their patients out in three months. The application of TVs in the White Male Department produced similar results, calming the wards considerably. I say let's follow the further advice of other doctors and apply similar common sense to families of inmates and to judges and country prosecutors where it is also needed. The problem isn't all cured by Thorazine and shocks to the poor souls buried up here."

Another thing I noticed was that those patients with a deep faith—not the religious fanatics—met most day's problems with equanimity, though even a saint would have blown off steam in that slaughterhouse. And under Brother Dean, more opportunities were introduced for attending religious services. Hymn sings were held once a week on the wards in the evening.

It was still hot in Chattahoochee, but up north summer was

past; and if I were to make a break it had better be before the Delaware froze over. I started drawing out my money. As five dollars was the limit each could possess, I had to experiment with hiding places on my person. Shoes were out because they were too obvious, the bed was out because housemen could smell money. It was the difficult part of living like a criminal, getting accustomed to doing things surreptitiously.

Harder yet was keeping my big fat mouth shut. Thus, when integration began in Little Rock, I, on the basis of having enough troubles, was determined not to stir up the turds. But on September 24 when President Eisenhower sent troops into Little Rock, I couldn't just sit there like a mongoloid. Christian heritage advocates teaching by example, not force; however, there was also the necessity of rule by law, lest we have no civilization. When I walked away from the crowd watching the news, I was accosted by an attendant and I answered direct: "The President did the only thing he could." I spoke in all my innocence and gave my reasoning.

Before bedtime, another attendant came over and asked the same thing, maybe in disbelief.

The next morning there were innuendoes on the insulting side. I let it pass. The second morning two khaki-clads stood under the open stairs as I went to breakfast.

"We ought to lynch the son of a bitch," one of them said.

"Yeah, while we've got him right where we want him."

During those days, Snotnose, the Duck, and Beelzebub took up the mother theme. Snotnose, who walked around, and even ate on cold days, with two strings of snot looped together below his nostrils, followed me by the hour, first in the kitchen, then on the ward. He mostly mumbled a senseless original chant but sometimes broke into a song about Mother Machree. He sang well and it was amusing at first. It wore thin after the fortieth day. The Duck, who walked like one, flapping his hands behind him, lived on Ward 1, so could only work on me in the Tunnel of Shit or the poolroom. "He's going to get shock," he would say, waddling up to an attendant in front of me. Beelzebub's method will be shown later. This was brainwashing at its lowest common denominator. At first I laughed at these people, as I recalled Bishop Sheen's description on TV of the sophisticated Chinese brand of brainwashing.

One day after Thanksgiving, Zeron, Friend, and I went deep

into the woods for mistletoe, but I was not quite ready to see "Doctor Bush." By now I had $25 in one pocket and $3 in another. If found, it meant being locked in. Then word went around that there would be an extra shakedown on the return from supper. They stripped us at the foot of the stairs, turning everything inside out. We heard afterward they had hoped to find a knife from the kitchen. When the attendants came to the letter that my bills were in (it was one from my daughter, which I had folded eight times) I looked nonchalantly away.

"What's this?" the attendant asked.

"A letter from my daughter," I said. He handed it back only partly unfolded.

The following day our crew was setting out a strawberry patch in the doctors' garden, north of the women's buildings, close by the state line. When Zeron drove back to the shed for fertilizer, I went down the hill, presumably to answer a call of nature. I walked for a hundred yards, then broke into a run, and, before I was winded, yelled, "Good-by, all you Mother Flickingers!" By then I was deep in the woods of Georgia.

At twilight, a series of vine-covered fences coaxed me to cut across the corner of a plowed field. A bullet whizzed by, six inches from my ear. I made the fence in a half tumble and sliced blindly through the woods and across a paved road into another patch. It was the eve of deer season, but this might also be the substitute for the rope over the tree limb. It was black among the trees. A covey of quail rose under my feet; I almost went up with them. Knowing that wildcats and bears lived about, I sat down on a fallen tree, with a thick piece of branch for a club. Within minutes there was light from a car. I was only in a hundred feet, but one could not see that far from the road through the staggered trees. A door slammed and the car moved off. In ten minutes it was back and went down a road at right angles. It came back again. I hardly breathed. Then the door slammed and it took off. For the balance of the night, I debated whether or not to turn south for Christmas with Mother and Dad.

Shaking the stiffness out of my legs in the chill at daybreak, I knew that Mother would turn me in. Detouring a half mile every time I came upon a farmhouse and avoiding road crossings where attendants usually waited, after hours of sweaty toil, I came out of the bushes only ten feet from a mule. A Negro stood on the other side of the animal filling his pipe. The movement in the bushes had not even excited the ears of the mule. Later I chanced a long stretch on the railroad. The foreman of a section gang told me it was twenty-five miles to a bus. At the next dirt road, I went down to a corner store, buying milk, candy bars, and a pair of khaki pants. I buried the state pants under a tree, took a nap, and decided to try hitchhiking to a bus stop. The first car along was the wagon from the hospital with the assistant supervisor and three young attendants.

After eating my slop, less the stew, I was escorted to the doctor's. Gumanis came out of his office, before O'Connor got back from lunch, and said: "What's the matter with you? You got that far—how come you couldn't make it?"

I told O'Connor I was glad I had been brought back, but I did not say I knew my enemies would not have let me stay free outside anyway. "I'm ready to sweat it out," I said, "and then see my mother before returning to Philadelphia."

Spending the afternoon on Ward 2, I took a shower to cleanse the briar scratches on my legs. Immediately I was called down by Gumanis. "Drop your pants," the doctor ordered, but he was satisfied with my profession of quick healing.

Then I was interviewed by Call Jesstar, the pill pusher, the doctor's right-hand man. Jesstar must have mistaken my anger—anger at the whole deal of Chattahoochee—for hysteria. It was the first time in a year I had been able to sound off to someone in authority. I wound up on the Back Yard after supper. I fell asleep exhausted and did not appreciate how deep I was to find the snake pit to be.

Soon it was Christmas, my second in captivity. I wrote friends that I had stripes on my eyeballs from light coming through bars. I was working as a houseman on Ward 9, the worst, and sleeping on 8, which was cleaner than any on the Front Yard. I had turned down two chances to go back to the kitchen, appreciating the best treatment ever, poor as it was, from Back Yard attendants who rarely got a good houseman.

The drawbacks were many, not counting the loss of extra pieces of meat from the kitchen. There were noises, smells, and confusion, in that order. All day long, attendants tormented patients. I could sit down to read (housemen could sit on the beds, the others had to walk all day or lie under a bed out of the way) but as soon as I began, an attendant would send some idiot to squat beside me and let out a scream. If I chased one away, another would take his place in fifteen minutes. But that was the only way those attendants played with me. When I walked for exercise, I had to be on guard lest an idiot take a poke at my nose unexpectedly. Yet the bugs (some were college men and perfectly sane) appreciated little things like help in tying a shoelace and they remembered and shared their candy from the dope stand. I helped one day on the back end of 9, known as the shitty end, where patients dirtied themselves and their beds daily, threw their stool against the wall, even ate it. Odors were strong. Some patients were scrubbed with floor brooms, which can be gentle in the hands of a gentle man.

On Christmas morning, I sat on a swayback bed, wondering what had happened to the principles of American freedom that would permit the pushing of innocent men back, back, back, until there was no place farther back to push them. I wrote Mother that I forgave her for letting me be subjected to unprintable obscenities and indignities. Her casual reply was that the doctor said I was not quite ready yet. As I read her letter, I thought how charge attendant Gettering on Ward 8 was getting patients ready. He had made his stool on the toilet seat and forced a patient to clean it up, on Christmas. I thought of Christmas Eve, with Gettering beating up ninety-pound Chonty, who was in a straitjacket, while the patients lay on their beds watching.

(I first read this in 1971. K.D.)

TRAVELERS AID SOCIETY OF PHILADELPHIA
Pennsylvania Station—30th Street
Philadelphia 4, Pa.

May 4, 1957

Social Service Department
Florida State Hospital
Chattahoochee, Florida

Re: Donaldson, Kenneth—47—White
G-5 Your Hospital

We are enclosing letters received from this patient. In January, 1956 Mr. Donaldson applied for assistance to establish himself in Philadelphia. We recognized that he was disturbed but had difficulty in arranging proper care. He was known intermittently up to August, 1956 when he returned to Florida where he was hospitalized.

Since November, 1956 we have received letters such as these each month and have forwarded copies to the County Welfare Department in St. Petersburg, Florida. It is obvious that all his hostility is centered on his parents.

We are also enclosing a copy of our reply to the patient. We shall appreciate hearing from you about his progress.

Very sincerely yours,

(Miss) Sarah K. Rosenthal
Case Worker

(Miss) Grace A. Yocom
Case Supervisor

(I first read these in 1974. K.D.)

PROGRESS NOTES
(These are the total entries for 1957.)

3-25-57: Patient appears to be an old paranoid with hospitalization for 3 months at Marcy State Hospital of N.Y. Appears to be in remission at present time. Apparently refuses medication because he belongs to the Christian Science Group. Continue custodial care. Dr. Gumanis/hh

7-23-57: Patient writes continuously letters and states he will write a book about hospitals when he is released from F.S.H. Resides on Wd. #6, and works in General Kitchen. Dr. Gumanis/hh

12-18-57: Patient was returned from escape while working the Horticultural Department. States he is tired of waiting for a release. No injuries except for small abrasion on lower extremities. To Wd. #8. Dr. Gumanis/hh

(I first read this in 1974. K.D.)

December 14, 1957.

Re: Mr. Kenneth Donaldson, A-25738.

Mrs. Wm. Donaldson,
Belleaire Village Court,
Largo, Florida.

Dear Mrs. Donaldson:

This acknowledges receipt of your letter of December 11, and we wish to advise that Mr. Donaldson has shown no basic improvement lately. All attempts to reason with him regarding his stay at the Hospital, or his necessity in keeping in touch with his family, have been futile, so far. He states that he has broken off with all of his relations, including his parents, and he seems unable to realize the lack of logic in such an attitude. He, of course, still does not realize that he has ever been mentally ill, and his judgment continues to be quite poor. He further stated that he did not wish anything sent to him for Christmas, and would not accept it if it did arrive.

In spite of this attitude, though, he seems to enjoy his work on the grounds at the Hospital, is physically in good condition, and he is eating and sleeping well.

Yours very truly,

J. T. Benbow, M.D.,
Clinical Director.

JBO'C:H

IN THE COURTS, 1957

(i)

Supreme Court of the State of Florida   3/12/57

My petition for writ of habeas corpus was denied without a hearing and without calling for papers from the state.

CHAPTER 7

1958

What Cannot Be Undone

> *What was done cannot be undone.... We can remember Auschwitz and beware of listening to the siren song of expediency, beware of abrogating mercy, of setting aside law. Beware of being sheep.*
>
> —SYBILLE BEDFORD

THE BACK SECTION OF WARD 8 WAS CALLED THE SQUAD. IT WAS designed for punishment. Up to three dozen men in overalls sat on backless benches from 7:00 A.M. to 7:00 P.M., with one toilet break in the morning, one in the afternoon. If they failed to contain themselves, they wore full overalls to the dining room. There, a bug, being schooled on the squad for spitting at an attendant, might place a twelve-inch turd in the center of the table to the laughs of the attendants.

One day, a young Jew, Aaron, was let off the squad during the day to "rehabilitate" himself. He was put to work helping me.

On the second day, he complained, "I didn't get my Sunday paper. But my mother's coming today. She'll tell O'Connor."

I was able to sympathize: "They woke me at 2:00 last night to hand me my Friday's *New York Times.*"

After supper, he sent word from the squad with one of the housemen. I was allowed to go see him, my reward for being one of the best workers.

"They cracked my skull," he burst out. "It throbs something awful." As soon as his mother had left, the attendants had worked him over. He made me promise to write his mother, but before I could take down the address, I was hustled off to my own section.

Aaron, a locksmith, had been searched in Miami on suspicion in a robbery and arrested when found with an unlicensed revolver in his car. He had recently moved down from New York City and had failed to license the gun, which he needed for protection in his business. His protests were so vociferous the police said he belonged in Hollywood State Hospital rather than jail. From there, as a "criminal," he was shipped to Chattahoochee.

Doctor Szasz said, "Traditionally, psychiatric hospitals have been jails." And they will never be hospitals as long as there are attendants, so said Dr. John Maurice Grimes (*When Minds Go Wrong*, Devin-Adair: New York, 1954).

I was thinking along these lines, as I sat with a book by Lin Yutang, on a corner bed on Ward 9. It was Don's bed. He was clothes room man and the best worker on the Back Yard. His complete adjustment to warehouse sickness had brought him lenient treatment from the warehousemen. They had pushed the middle beds tightly together on his side of the section, so that after giving them fifteen feet for their rockers on one end, he had ten feet of extra breathing space at his end. As the only window on that side was by his bed, he let me sit there to read.

He was asleep on the next bed when a sudden patch of winter sunshine in the gloom made a zebra pattern from the grille down his cheek and the pillow. He opened his eyes.

"Why don't you move down here?" he said. "The attendants keep the men quiet in this section."

"No need to rock the boat with requests to the office. I should be getting out soon," I said.

"Doctor O'Connor tell you?"

"No."

"When he tells you, you got it made. Me—O'Connor told me

I've got a year yet. Then I'm going back to West Virginia—way up in the hills with my rifle, fifty feet in from the end of the trail—and the first one who shows his face gets it between the eyes. They got me in Miami for armed robbery, but the cops didn't find no gun. They didn't give me no trial."

"Can't you appeal?"

"In this state? At Raiford I complained and they beat the living hell out of me before sending me up here. I was on pills three years. I slept. I'll just lie quiet another year."

Some few got out quicker. One young fellow, recuperating in a straitjacket on the shitty end for lunging over the desk at O'Connor, who had referred to his mother insultingly, got well the next week when his parents got him to court on a bench warrant to face rape charges.

Half of the men on the Back Yard were criminals. Most had good sense like Don. One percent, perhaps, had ever seen a courtroom. All wore housemen's clothes, though some did no more work than hold a dustpan for five minutes each morning.

But for the old men, it was a vacation in the grave. Except for the few days when it was near freezing, they were herded to porch or yard, as being the easiest housekeeping arrangement for the attendants, year in, year out.

"The people sitting in rows along the walls of mental institutions are not the unfortunate victims of 'mental illness,'" Al Siebert said. "They are the unfortunate victims of psychiatry. When viewed through their eyes, it is understandable that some have concluded that the world is a false, hypocritical place and that it is the human race which is 'insane'. "

I tried to tell these things in letters, which I wrote for several of the old men. All they had were soiled scraps of letters from their families, which repeated the formula: "The doctor says you are not quite ready yet." Because the families did not answer, I can only assume that the attendants put those letters in File 13.

The attendants tolerated a few of the bugs, as one tolerates cockroaches in a cold-water flat. One was Billy. I had not noticed him in the general activity of the stockyard, until one cold day he let out a muffled "boozhwaaaah!" on the other side of the section. It was a sort of professional courtesy that only one screamer carried on at a time and, there being so many ready to pop off on Ward 9, Billy had never before stood up for his turn. All he had on was overalls. He was barefoot, even though the thermometer read twenty above in the Tunnel of Shit when we went to dinner. I thought of his mother's sending him up because the doctors in Pinellas County did not know what to do for him. Should I repay her kindnesses to me in the jail by reporting to her that the attendants were not abusing Billy?

A bug who seemed kin to the attendants, thus not drawing their ire, slept on the third bed down from me on Ward 8. At full moon in the middle of the night, he erupted in a shouting, rasping condemnation of God and all else in Heaven. Every fourth expression was "you son of a mother-flicking bitch." It went on for two hours, for two nights, then tapered off. That was Huey-the-Bluey. In the daytime he would wink and, pinch-nosed, sing a ballad from the 1920s.

A few attendants tried to be helpful. One told me, "When you're first locked up, the hospital writes to everyone they have a line on who knows you. Don't put names in your letters."

But other attendants kept up the mild harassment, started the year before. They sent the houseman in overalls, Nutmeg, who squatted in their circle of rockers to get a mouthful of the candy they pilfered from the dope stand packages belonging to the bugs, to ask me, "Don't you know your mother can sign you out when she comes again?"

Holding up the book by Lin Yutang, I said, "It says in here that one fool can ask more questions than seven wise men can answer."

I overheard Nutmeg's report to the circle, while he rubbed his long ears vigorously: "He says that seven wise men are smarter than you SOBs."

Still, it was such as these I had to rely on. I drew out a $2 dope stand card, as we were not supposed to have money on the Back Yard. Besides a coke for Billy, I sent for cigarettes, which brought 15¢ a pack from attendants, enabling me to have a quarter each time I wanted Nutmeg to pass a letter along to an attendant, who for a dime would mail it from his farm in the next county.

Like the beetle I watched, trying to punch its way out of a big drop in the shower, man is supposed to have an adjusting mechanism for correcting mistakes. So, as long as O'Connor would not admit his mistake, I would keep sending letters. In a dozen I wrote: "The remedy applied for blackmail is to lock up the helpless victim," which is practically what had been done to me. The one to Mayor Richardson Dilworth, Philadelphia, brought an instant reply of thanks but no mention of help. The one to United States Sen. Lyndon B. Johnson, then majority leader, was answered by his secretary, who said the Senator was out of town. With no more replies than that, I set a deadline: if the folks did not take me out when they came in summer, that would be it! I would beg no more, even if I never had any more possessions in the balance of my life than the two sweat-soaked letters from my daughter, folded in my cotton pants with a quarter in the corner of one.

Yet, even in these days of incessant agony, there was always a glimpse of a flickering free-world candle. A. B., the hulking attendant who policed the kitchen end of the tunnel, said he could get me back on the steam table.

"Didn't you eat better?" he said.

I refused without giving my reasons. I was too rebellious to go back and face the taunts of kitchenmen all day for my unsuccessful escape attempt. I could not expect promotion again from kitchen to outside detail for another easy chance. Anyway, I would forego the route from the porch off the kitchen. I would find some other way off the wards.

One afternoon, a blond attendant from the Front Yard sat down and gave me a candy bar. I ate it, though I knew it was stolen from that morning's packages.

He said, "I happen to know that Doctor O'Connor is not against releasing you."

Thus cheered, I celebrated by going out to the yard with the bugs to sit with my shirt off. But the dust under the Florida sun, stirred up by the crowd in our small yard, decided me against a repeat.

In May, one evening, twenty-five names were called on Ward 8: "Get your things, you're moving." Four of us said we'd rather stay where we were, as long as we needed some more treatment; however, we were forced to take that bottom step toward a possible release, though I had seen as many get discharged from the Back Yard as the Front.

An attendant took me back the next day to Ward 9 to get my Christmas flannel shirt, which I had drawn as my gift from the state Mental Health Association. The shirt was not there. I turned to assistant supervisor Joe Flake, a stout cigar-smoking executive, who happened to be rocking with the attendants.

"It's gone," I said, "and the only one with a key is the day man here."

The cigar turned with the face, wrapped in a slight smile to study the corner of the room. Helplessly, I demanded action. I got it as the attendant hurried me out the door.

Within hours of my return from the unexpected showdown over the shirt, Ward 1 proved to be anything but a step ahead. All Front Yard attendants became hostile and their stool pigeons, which I soon saw were the nucleus of the brainwashing corps, became intimidating.

Beds were everywhere, two hundred of them, most without room for a chair between. The thirty patients in the housemen's section (two floors above the doctors' offices and visitors' room) were the privileged, mostly criminals who showered the attendants with coffee and cigarettes. Here again, some housemen did not do a lick of work, other than performing dirty tricks.

Ward 1 was as noisy as the Back Yard. Attendants yelled down the stairs, which were shut off only by a wire gate. "Yeah you is," one shouted. Another yelled from the shower room, "I turned the hot water on clear off." "Jeet jet?" all shouted. In between, they managed to torment some bug into a screaming fit.

The results of this were lasting. A report by the American Medical Association, ten years later, said long exposure to noise destroys hearing. Noise also has deleterious effects on heartbeat, temperature, digestion, and respiration, according to James Stewart-Gordon ("We're Poisoning Ourselves with Noise," *Reader's Digest,* February 1970): "Though amazingly resilient in its adaptability to most environmental changes, the body shows no sign of an ability to become conditioned to noise."

One saving grace was that the splintery wood floor was scrubbed twice weekly; and the terrazzo floor of the bathroom and its back-to-back rows of twelve washbasins and ring of cold commodes (seatless) around the walls were hosed down daily.

During the next two weeks, my prison rapidly became hazardous from threats other than of a doctor's putting me on the operating table. They began with nasty cracks behind me in the chow line, pertaining to my family history. I refused to eat with the housemen, going down at the end of the line with the bugs. Thus, sometimes I did not get my four items, though never missing the bone stew. Then the steam table men started giving me smaller servings, and occasionally one even refused to put anything on my tray. The line would back up, with men cursing me, until Mis' Brack came over and dipped out a serving.

After two weeks of hearing threats dropped sotto voce ("We'll strangle him after lights-out," et cetera) and having to duck their "accidentally" inaccurately thrown rubber ball as they played catch when I was in the room, I moved out to sleep with the bugs. Comparatively the bugs were quiet-mouthed, had no radios, and, unless prodded by an attendant, didn't give a damn what the rest of the world was doing, so engrossed with their own misery were they. There were no chairs and the bugs (listed as "sedentary patients") were not allowed on the beds until 7:00 p.m. They sat frozen in any little jog in the walls; they stood immobile along the walls; they rolled under the beds in uneasy dreams, or weariness, when they could not go to the yard because of rain or frost.

Another difference between this place and a "hospital" was that here foul things were scribbled on the walls. The criminals bitched in the chow line; they cursed "A. B." under their breath; and, when he was looking the other way, they rapped some retarded soul across the teeth or behind the ear.

I did not know it at the time, but by voicing objection to what was being done I was indulging in the luxury of cutting my own throat. These attendants, as a matter of fact, believed that what they did to patients and the way they looked at life was normal. Anyone who believed that the hospital (its name being changed in 1958 by the legislature from "asylum" to "hospital") was not operated solely to entertain them for eight hours a day was sick.

Further, crowding of men brings about homosexuality, brutality, and unsociableness, comparable to reactions of animals, pointed out Dr. T. R. VanDellan in his column *How to Keep Well,* June 15, 1970. He quoted from *Medical World News:* "Researchers found that animals crowded together in a laboratory or zoo develop unusual behavior."

On top of all this "milieu therapy," I was now subjected to brainwashing. They put Fidelio, one of the cogs in the system, on the bed next to me. He was a broken-tongued Cuban, whose father had been a doctor in Tampa, thus making him a special favorite of all the doctors. Never having done a day's work in his life, he found Chattahoochee an easier way of life than as a professional cardsharp in the hotels of New York City. He had signed into Chattahoochee, he told me himself, because he could not draw Social Security and had no other retirement benefits.

He started in on me, the first night, berating me in his half-educated but wholly superior manner: "There is no God." Then he laughed nasally, derisively. "Do you think your church cares if you get out?"

I was no fundamentalist, but I was not going to argue with a clown in the brainwashing system. "My belief works for me," was all I said.

The next night, Fidelio said, "The only thing wrong with you is that you are proud."

"What's wrong with that?" I said.

"All you care about is that book of yours."

"Why not?"

"If you'd forget your pride and forget your book, you'd get out."

"Why should I let this place tell me to forget it?"

They hadn't given Fidelio the answer to that. But they had just given me the key to the long term of my imprisonment. There lies the kernel of my story.

Another big man, the Butter-and-Egg man, came on the ward the night I got permission to move away from Fidelio because of his diatribes against the Bible. B & E had a funny shuffle when he stood and a rocking when he sat.

"It's the insane medicine," he explained, the words from his heavy lips coming with more slur than the Pennsylvania Dutch accent of his native Allentown. "I started doing this the day Gumanis put me on Thorazine. I can't stop."

By this time I had done a great deal of thinking. It was July and Mother and Dad were there for the second visit. It mattered less who had put me there, more who was going to get me out. With family news out of the way, I got right down to business: "Are you going to sign me out?"

"That's up to the doctor," Mother said.

"Did you ask him?"

"No."

"Aren't you going to?"

They looked at each other.

"All you have to do," I said, "is tell him you're going to take me out. He can't stop you."

At that moment, Tom Merchant came in to see his attendant sister. I motioned him over and explained to my parents that Tom knew the institution inside out.

"Tell her, Tom," I said, "do I know what I'm talking about?"

"He sure does, Mrs. Donaldson," Tom said. But while he

described Chattahoochee in the very words I had in mind, I was becoming alarmed that the attendants would get angry, but they let Tom finish.

"You can see from that," I said, "that there is no reason for my being here."

Mother walked determinedly into O'Connor's office.

"He says," she said on her return, "that you need a little more treatment."

"I don't need a doctor."

"He says all the doctors and nurses here say you need treatment."

"How does he know? I see him for two minutes—and only when you write. He hasn't seen me at my request since last year in May."

"He says there are twenty doctors here."

"In the whole hospital, yes. But he's the only one I see."

"What about the nurses on the wards?"

"There aren't any nurses!"

"He says you have nurses—and I saw hundreds of them myself, walking around."

"Those are the women's attendants. We've never seen a nurse on our wards. He's lying—he's a lowdown contemptible liar!"

"But, Kenneth, he seems like such a nice man."

I thought: "Yes, that well-scrubbed face and those polished glasses and that Casper Milquetoast expression—the perfect con artist for elderly ladies."

But before I could sound off, Dad said: "You should be big enough to stand a little more treatment. You don't look as though you'd suffered any. He says you will have to take a course of medication before you will be allowed to leave."

"That's ridiculous—I don't need pills. He's wrong when he says I do."

"It won't hurt you to take a few pills."

"That's not the point. If I don't need them, why should I be forced to take them?"

Mother got up. "We've got to leave."

"You're coming back after dinner?"

"No."

So I dragged out my ultimatum: "If you walk out of this room and leave me locked in this God-forsaken hole, I'll never see you again. I'm not fooling. There is absolutely no reason why I should have been sent here in the first place."

I was escorted quickly back to the "pit."

On the stairs, Nutmeg sat pulling up the thousand sheets of a roll of toilet paper, which had dropped behind the stairs. As I stepped over him, he asked, "Did you see your dear old mammy?"

At the Belltower, Snotnose called loudly to someone, who was on the phone, "He needs five hundred Thorazine, four times a day."

Back at my bed, I plopped down and the creak of the springs woke B & E on the floor.

"Your folks?" he said.

"Yeh. I'm going to be punished for refusing something free. I can't leave until I take some medication."

"Won't give in, eh?"

"Never."

"I don't blame you. I wouldn't either, I guess, if they had done me like that." B & E drew up his knees and hugged them to stop his rocking.

I now had plenty of time to contemplate what has been summed up so well in *Constructive Action,* September 1974: "The general hope seems to be that by exposing the patient to a sufficient amount of indignity he will eventually learn that it does not pay to be mentally ill."

Not long after the visit, I retaliated as best I could for my mistreatment ever since the stolen shirt. Attendants were claiming sotto voce that among other things I had sired my brother's child. I would be damned if I'd work for a bunch of foul-mouthed filthy-minded agitators. Besides, they gave me the dirty end of the stick. When razors were put out each morning with fresh blades, housemen shaved first; except that, at my turn, the razor was handed to some local patient. No amount of protesting did any good. There would have been no advantage really, for they were cheap blades, complete with machine-turned burr, like the piston rods at American Locomotive, and the first shavers knocked the burrs off. On the other hand, after a dozen shaves, the blades got tangled in your whiskers. At mail call, attendants would call me from the far end of the ward when there was nothing for me. Or they would come to the top of the stairs and shout my name, as if I were on doctor's call, then tell me I was mistaken.

Other patients suffered likewise. First, they antagonize you till you fight back and then they beat your brains out for fighting.

That is the sum total of the killing-you-with-kindness that I saw in fifteen years at Chattahoochee. I made caustic and cynical comments, in return, on the antecedents and ability of the khaki-clads, and, with B & E, I felt righteously justified on days when the young charge attendant Jason Bennock, black-haired, squat, full-lipped, did his thing. His black eyes opened in earnestness and soft hands turned palms up in front of his chin as he talked. Jason antagonized little miserable Dixie, who was stunted on the left side, dragging the leg and walking on the ankle. Monthly, Dixie would go into an hours-long tailspin, stumbling around, cursing and trying to pick a fight, until he finally dropped flat on his face in a long thrashing seizure, foaming at the mouth. His loving family paid for a sack of goodies for him each day. On days when Jason wanted ice cream, he would shout "Dixie!" until Dixie would grab for his sack and throw it on the floor, leaving a smug Jason to pick up the ice cream and gobble it down. On Dixie's passive days, Jason might chase him around, with ankle bone pounding on the splintered floor, and then choke him out for cursing his better. That still left the attendants free to sit back giggling, joking, and gulping goodies.

Yet Jason was one of the better ones, quite personable; and, because his aunt was an RN, he knew just what was good for his charges.

I added it all up and quit working for the sadists. Then for a while, they laid off me.

I sat with the unemployed on the porch. Some days, the bugs filled the porch's 100 × 8 feet from 7:00 A.M. to 7:00 P.M., except for meals and toilet. Each ward was a duplicate of the Chattahoochee master plan. There were screamers, sleepers on floor and bench, singers, arguers, and catatonics whose stretched-out legs were insensible to the constant traffic of busy feet that often stepped without looking.

One rainy day, I picked a group of empty rockers near the door. A sudden clomping and cursing rushed out, followed by an attendant's yelling, "I heerd you. You better git you ass along." Then Jason called, "Where's my cup, Dixie?"

The next thing to bring me out of my reveries of Philadelphia was Rangy Tizella's falling flat back and bouncing his head on the floor. At night, in a seizure, Rangy would walk to some distant bed, shove the sleeper onto the floor, and get under the covers.

That day on the porch, I got *Time, The New York Times,* and three Philadelphia *Bulletins*, enough, by reading through recipes and Dear Abby, to keep me beyond prison walls all day, had not Snotnose sat opposite to chant "Mother Macree." No sooner did I move than Cannonball, fleshy native of Tobacco Road with a clean-shaven billiard ball on top, sat down and asked, "Are you going home with your dear old mother when she comes next summer?"

To get money for newspapers and magazines, I rolled cigarettes after supper, astraddle the bed. One got a machine in a 79¢ deal at the dope stand and the men furnished their state tobacco. At five cents a pack, I deposited $20 in the office, besides keeping up my subscriptions, buying coffee and some clothes, the latter intended for my second unscheduled appointment with Doctor Bush. While I rolled, Smokey, an always smiling bug, watched with his tongue hanging out. His family furnished him tailor-mades, but he shared them before 10:00 A.M., then pleaded with me: "Cig, cig." In mock protest I drove him off, then always gave him one more.

"Thank, thank," he would say.

On one rainy Sunday, B & E raised himself on his elbow on the floor, as I was reading my mail.

"New Jersey will take me back," I said. "They told me to have my ward doctor complete the arrangements."

"You think Chattahoochee did it?"

"I wrote two letters to Governor Robert Meyner and he told the head of hospitals to take me back."

"I bet you'd walk."

"Or muleback—any way to get out of Florida."

"They might fly you."

"It would be fun by helicopter. To see all the green countryside again."

"That's my idea," Sedge Wicks said from down beside the next bed. "It was my idea to have something in between the automobile and the big planes. I've sent a bill to Superintendent Rogers to collect for me. I don't care how many they make—just so's I get the royalties."

This was the first time Sedge had spoken to either of us. It was natural to reason with him. I said, "Usually more than one person gets an idea for an invention. It's like television. The first one to patent it owns it."

"But the patent is mine because I thought of it first." Sedge was not angry, for the superintendent would collect, he knew. "It's like my time before here. I sent a bill to Doctor O'Connor for every hour they held me, at the rate I was earning when I was kidnapped. This time I'm sending him a bill every week."

"You expect to collect?"

"Yes. When I was signed out the first time, I went into Farris Bryant's office—he's governor now—and demanded they lock up the ones who brought me up here."

"And what did he do?" B & E asked.

"They sent me right back."

"How'd they ever let you out in the first place?"

"I told my wife how they beat me up—blacked both eyes, knocked out teeth, and choked me out on the Back Yard—just because I wanted to see O'Connor about arresting my kidnappers."

On frosty mornings, it was pleasant to sit in the back window with my shirt off, the grille letting in diamonds of sun, two inches across. From the mile-wide valley below, a bit of peace rose from virgin forest. I sometimes worked on short stories here, sharpening an old hobby.

Beelzebub, which was the name I gave him later, came up to the window the day he was locked in for slipping ExLax to a criminal. Beelzebub was a fat-headed red-faced loud-mouthed barrel-chested "idiot" of less than average height. His face and chest were dripping sweat from doing push-ups, with his feet on the footrail of a bed, his hands on the floor. He had been an assistant trainer for a major-league baseball team. Later I looked for muscles under his graying blond butch haircut; they did indeed roll down the back of his bull neck, or was it rolls of fat?

He offered the glad hand of Forge fellowship. He questioned me about my past and threw off homilies about dear old mothers. He saw a parallel: "I too turned to Christian Science once," he said. "But all religions are wanting. Do you think God can get you out of here?" He asked it every day.

"That is not why I study Christian Science," I said.

"What you should do is get into politics in Tallahassee. I know a man in the governor's office. I used to caddy for him when he came up for golf. He'd take you on tomorrow, if you'd make up with O'Connor and your mother."

"I won't crawl for anybody. I wouldn't stay in Florida one second if not shackled."

"That kind of talk won't get you anywhere."

"Then I'll take it up with my God."

At that, he threw up his fat hands and walked out.

A bus accident, while with his team, had put him in Chattahoochee with a head injury and his mind did not track right. I put it down, at first, to paranoia resulting from the injury; then I began to see there was something wrong with his basic attitude. No matter what the subject, he would turn it around to belittle my religion, my politics, my morality. I tolerated him as a necessary adjunct of an asylum, until he started in on my mother, when I would pick him up on the least flaw in his reasoning and persist until he ran from the room.

"You go down to supper late," he said one day. "Would you be willing to wait until the end of the line and see that all the stragglers were rounded up? It would be a big help to the attendants."

"I wouldn't raise a hand to help any of them," I said. "Just last week on dope-stand run, they shut the door in my face and said no more could go. The same today on library run. You expect me to help such mother-flickingers?"

"But you'd help Brother Dean, wouldn't you? He's endeavoring to improve the patient's lot. He's shorthanded right now."

"He's probably no different from the rest."

Another day, Beelzebub came with the request that I watch certain attendants on the evening shift and report when they took naps in the linen room, saying: "Brother Dean wants to break this kind of thing up. Nobody will know you were connected with it."

"My family never taught me to carry out underhanded schemes."

"But you want to see a better grade of attendant on the job, don't you?"

I was the one to walk away then, for Beelzebub, an erstwhile musician's union organizer, was helping the attendants to organize their first union. He was ingratiating himself with those very attendants. He was buying them cigars, massaging them in the linen room (massaging was also against the rules) and standing guard to warn sleepers, should the night supervisor happen along off schedule.

He tried another angle, bringing around a typed set of rules for the ideal attendant, such as: "The night shift should wear crepe-soled shoes" (in Chattahoochee, on every night, attendants in hard heels used one of the "lames" for a football, chasing him at all hours, around and under the sleeping patients, the lame all the time screaming bloody murder); and "Attendants should talk quietly after lights-out" (in Chattahoochee, they pulled a chair up to the window beside your bed, at 2:00 A.M., and carried on a long-winded conversation with someone outside the cafeteria a half block away). At Beelzebub's request, I marked the errors in the typing, but I wanted no other part in his dubious schemes.

Things I had early mentioned to Beelzebub in casual reminiscing—I had nothing to hide—were flung back ad nauseam by the attendants. But mostly they harped on "pore old mother," at the foot of the stairs, the bend in the tunnel. Over my head, while they poured milk, one said, "Maybe his mother will sign him out for Christmas." To this day, I can't see how my deciding against being signed out by someone who thought I was sick made me sick.

Grandma was a more interesting big shot. His sandy red hair had traveled the world, waved at stars in show business and assorted royalty in the South Pacific, even blown in the wind behind the Iron Curtain. On my first night on Ward 1, Grandma came smiling and offering a job at $1,000 a week as legal advisor for the TV show he was scripting. One week we would interview inmates at a prison in Atlanta, the next at an orphanage in Harrisburg, and so on around the state capitals.

But Grandma seemed more preoccupied with "curing" me. He said, "You're too mild. Say 'Jesus!' " Then he looked down. He was a droopy old woman with his shirt off, but not in voice, which dramatics had trained to a commanding pitch. "Say 'Christ!' " he said, looking up with his stage smile.

He had come to Chattahoochee after a series of dubious checks in Miami.

He explained: "They held me in jail on a postdated check—for only fifty dollars. Imagine! I got a heart attack and asked to be sent up here a few weeks. It's been paid off, but O'Connor told me at staff he would never let me go."

"What day is it?" a tall thin patient asked me in the noon crunch in the poolroom.

"Friday," I said, noting the two quarts of bone stew and tobacco juice lavished on the white shirt.

"Is there a dance today?"

"Yes—but your shirt!"

"Do we get shirts today?"

"On Thursday."

"What day is this?"

"Friday."

"I forget. See these?" He rubbed the two holes in his slanting forehead and smoothed the receding brown hair. "I'm an architect. My wife had them do this to me. Do you think I'll ever go back to work? What day did you say it is? Thursday?"

"Friday."

"My name's Hobson. You don't mind if I ask you questions, do you? I need a friend in here."

"Not at all," I said.

I thought of Hobson as I read this in *Constructive Action*, September 1974: "In 1938, Egas Moniz, a Portuguese physician, developed lobotomy to deal with aberrant behavior. The operation was so effective in calming persons, removing anxieties that it became the 'in' operation of cafe society. Physicians did the operation in their office. One physician alone did 1,500 of them. Lobotomies calmed persons down at the expense of their imaginations and turned them into vegetables. Still Egas Moniz was awarded the 1955 Nobel Prize in medicine for his great discovery."

Just before I had left the Back Yard, a visiting houseman from the Front Yard chased Cannonball away from the end bed where he was singing crazily while I tried to digest the *Times*. "You ought to talk to the attendants," the visitor said.

"Them? Never!" I said.

"You could give the doctor a chance to learn from your case."

"That's ridiculous. I'm not sick."

"If you weren't sick, you wouldn't be here."

"You're the one's sick," I said. "I've wondered up to now where the doctor got his information from."

An inkling of something sinister came to me then. As *Constructive Action* puts it: for workers in the psychiatric field, "the detection and elimination of mental illness is much more important than such things as human rights, civil rights, and constitutional protections."

However, though the warning had been given me, acceptance of the fact that anyone could think I was sick in 1958 was beyond me. I did know that the future in Chattahoochee could be unhealthful. As my stay approached the two-year mark, I was canvassing all the possibilities, short of committing mayhem on a guard to get his keys. Doctor O'Connor sent no more than a handful to staff each year, with only half of them passing. (Note: A Florida newspaper reported that Judge White, from one county alone, had sent three hundred to Chattahoochee the year he sent me.) That left families and friends, and there just did not happen to be enough families anxious to contest the usual letters of Doctor O'Connor: . . . as for leaving now, your son/husband/nephew is not quite ready yet. He needs a little more treatment.

For my friend on the squad, treatment had meant a cracked skull while he sat twelve daylight hours in a straitjacket with two toilet breaks. For others on the Back Yard, it meant a broken arm from being knocked down in the shower, which the attendant would put down as "accidental fall."

For some, treatment meant the wrong medication. Pills were passed out as you went through the chow line, and the pillpusher would often say, "We're out of your kind—what color do you want tonight?"

Treatment meant letter therapy; and dosage of your chow to burn out your sex drive; and ego-destroying remarks hammered into your noggin through the foul vocabulary of Tobacco Road.

A full staff of doctors on my case, O'Connor had told Mother, and innumerable nurses.

The attendants drove the bugs like cattle to and from the yard, to the holding pen of the poolroom, and through the chute of the Tunnel of Shit. On the day in 1957 when the Russians put up their first Sputnik, attendants collected on the back porch after supper with proof for me from the Bible and their Sunday school lessons that no such thing had happened.

Anyway, the problem had to be faced. If one's mother refuses to believe the simple truth, if former employers refuse to honor a letter from the bughouse, and if one can't talk to the attendants. . . .

So, I asked Doctor O'Connor, the next time he called me down after receiving a letter from mother: "If you can't put me to staff, Doctor, would you let someone up north sign me out?"

"Certainly," O'Connor said, "I'll let anyone up there sign you out."

"Would a lawyer do?"

"That would be acceptable."

The first one I tried was that grand old gentleman, Philadelphia lawyer McSorley. He accepted the case, going to work at once.

(I first read this in 1974. K.D.)

Kenneth Donaldson A-25738

PROGRESS NOTES

(This is the total of entries for 1958. K.D.)

9- 2-58:   Patient is a 51-year-old paranoid who again requested that he
be released. Treated at Marcy Hospital of N.Y. with ECT.
During interview overtalkative, delusional, well oriented in all
spheres. States he is a native of Philadelphia and would like to
obtain a position in the above city. Psychological examination
ordered for our files. Dr. Gumanis/hh

12-11-58:   Resides on Wd. #1, no work. Writing short stories complaining constantly about his N.Y. papers. States the attendants
are delaying his papers, appears paranoid and delusional to
writer. Continue custodial care. Psychological examination
not satisfactory. Dr. Gumanis/hh

(N.B. No psychological examination was given Donaldson in 1958. K.D.)

(I first read this in 1974. K.D.)

Largo, Florida
25th Feb. 1958

Dr. O'Connor
Dear Sir—
    Illness has prevented our writing and inquiring about our son
Kenneth Donaldson. Lately we have received several letters that seemed
to have a more favorable trend. He has also asked for papers, books, etc.
    His daughter will be married this coming Saturday in Arizona and
she too received a very nice letter from her Dad, which shows some
improvement.
    Would appreciate a reply as to Kenneth's condition. Thanking you,
we are,

Very truly yours,
MR. AND MRS. WM. DONALDSON
Belleair Village Ct.
Largo, Florida

(I first read this in 1974. K.D.)

June 26, 1958.

Re Mr. Kenneth Donaldson, A-25738.

Mrs. Wm. Donaldson,
Belleair Village Court,
Largo, Florida.

Dear Mrs. Donaldson:

This acknowledges receipt of your letter of June 23, and we wish to advise that there has been no basic change in Kenneth's condition lately. His physical condition remains satisfactory; he is comfortable, and he is eating and sleeping well. His mental condition is still characterized by a rigidity of personality and expression of delusional ideas, and a feeling that he has been persecuted. He is still inclined to write complaining letters to various important people and he still feels that he is going to write a long successful book exposing the treatment of mental patients both at home and in hospitals.

In spite of such thinking, though, he tells us today that he would be pleased to see you at the time of your anticipated visit next month.
Yours very truly,

J.T. BENBOW, M.D.
Clinical Director.

JBO'C:H

CHAPTER 8

1959

Faceless Wraiths

THE YEAR BEGAN LAUGHABLY, IN A WAY. ON NEW YEAR'S DAY, WE were squeezed, six to the bench, with criminals teasing me in holiday camaraderie, to watch the Oklahoma-Syracuse game from the Orange Bowl. Five plays into the first quarter, Jason Bennock came and flipped the picture to LSU-Clemson in the Sugar Bowl. Most of us left. After Jason went back to his little alcove at the top of the stairs, a criminal got Miami again. I smiled from the porch, seeing Dixie get up. Much as he hated Jason, he hated criminals more, for their goosing him and pounding him on his deformed left arm; so he summoned Jason to the TV.

My smile lasted only a moment, then my thoughts raced like the squirrels in the live oaks. It was always like that when I watched the boob tube. First it had been the Christian Science program switched off by the attendants as soon as I faced the set; then even their beloved cowboy pictures were turned back and forth for my benefit. All right! I didn't need their TV. Not once again, until I got out of that infernal hole, would I watch TV. One good resolution deserved another. So, to further my recuperation, why not eliminate the daily razor hassle? I'd go down to the barbershop once a week with the subdued bugs—ragged blades, hazing phone calls, and all.

To counteract my new syndrome, the left-handed tea-leaf readers shut off my only lifeline—my mail. But it was some time before I was sure, because my newspapers kept coming, albeit by skips and jerks.

"There's been no answer to any letter," I told Grandma one spring day in the yard, "since O'Connor let the lawyer take my case."

"I wouldn't want you to repeat this," Grandma said, chasing a fly from his bare great-grandmotherly chest, "Gumanis told me himself. Now that O'Connor is Clinical Director, Joe Flake is the real boss of White Male. What letters he wants to go, go. He has a meeting with O'Connor every morning."

"But O'Connor gave me permission himself."

"You don't try to send letters through the office, do you? I'll get them out for fifteen cents."

"I can't believe such a place could exist in America."

"It's the fee system. Thirty-five dollars a head to the sheriff's department for each one they send up."

"But I'm no criminal to be sent up and forgotten!"

"The criminals get out."

The next enlightenment came on a Saturday at ten past five, when Ward 1, the last in line, was bunched at the top of the stairs. There was a yell from the Bell Tower below: "Kenneth Donaldson! Visitors!" Two khaki-clads hurried up and urged me to follow on the run. It was a joke, I knew, for all day the calls from the marcelled blond Gettering had tormented me.

"But I'm not going without supper," I protested. "It's nobody anyway."

Talk like this in front of the bugs! "You better git you ass along or you're going to the squad right this minute!"

Next it was Joe Flake making a sugary introduction: "You know Father Browncollar, our chaplain?"

The old man in clerical garb extended his hand.

"No, I don't know you," I said and drew back.

"Why, I was here to see you two years ago. Don't you remember?" he said.

"Yes, I remember. You never came near me."

"But I want to help you."

I walked to the door and the two attendants took me to the dining room. The meat was gone, but B & E had saved his for me, two hot dogs. Upstairs, talking about the Honorable Father, B & E said, "I'd rather make my confession to Boogerisch."

The goldfish bowl we lived in was always charged. I was passing the little office, going from bed to porch with the Christian Science textbook, and overheard the following:

Jason: "The bastard reads an awful lot."
Beelzebub: "He's reading religion now. He never had religion before. Suddenly the son of a bitch—"
Gettering: "The mammyjammer's got it now, I'll swear by the great catfish."

Though burning, I had to smile to myself. "Anyway, you can't cry all day," I kept saying. And there were momentary reliefs, like when little old Trancie brought back the twenty dollars in a coin purse, which I had lost while hunkering on the toilet. I had been hunkering ever since the second dose of Chattahoochee rot (ringworm). The first dose had hit my testicles. In the dressing room after supper, the attendant painted me with a green solution with twice the potential of horse liniment. I barely staggered widespread to the third floor where I could neither stand, sit, nor lie for fifteen minutes. With the second attack, lower down, I spoiled the attendants' pleasure by refusing the green stuff. From then on I hunkered.

There were always new long-lived annoyances to cope with too. Every scrap of writing paper was taken from us one afternoon without warning. This rule lasted a whole year, though we were given paper for two letters a week to be written under supervision of the attendants. But after supper that day of the shakedown, a patient sold me a hundred-sheet box of good bond paper. I carried it inside my blue shirt for two days, before trusting it inside a magazine under my mattress. Fortunately, there was always an alert from some patient in the brainwashing corps, who, though he spied on his fellow patients, loved them more than O'Connor & Co. On the days of an alert, the paper was in my shirt. When the shakedown was in the yard, the paper was under the mattress.

The next time Mother wrote, which was infrequent now, I argued with Gumanis about the loss of the paper. He said there was plenty of work to do around the hospital, if I wanted to keep busy.

"I wouldn't work for these misbegotten people again," I said, "after the way they've done me."

"I have to put up with the same thing."

"But in your position they can't do the things they do to us."

"That's true," Gumanis said, really surprising me.

We were soon to test whether his sympathy was more than skin deep.

While 2:00 A.M. was the most frightening hour, when attendants chose to chase screaming patients around the ward, right after supper was the most disgusting, when attendants had nothing to do. Four nights a week, there was only one supervisor on duty. He made only one well-timed round of the ten wards and the flattop (jail) down the hill. Otherwise, the attendants had things their own way and their way was to take their entertainment out of the hides of patients.

The four evening attendants had to sit in the back section of Ward 1, which was a half block from the television. They were rocking placidly one Sunday, waiting to think of something. One reached for a pillow on a nearby bed and idly threw it at an old man already asleep. The others had to try too and like all circuses the act worked up to a climax. They were not satisfied throwing pillows far and wide, they must pull them from under sleepers and beat full force on these humble heads. It was all in fun, for the hardest blow with a sack of cotton was not liable to break a cheekbone. Nevertheless, toothless Old Tom, with tobacco juice down his BVDs, who had lost one eye since I first saw him at the dental clinic, tired of it after three times composing himself for sleep. Foolishly, like any old idiot would, he cursed his annoyers. They liked that. They ganged up on him. When he picked himself up off the floor, he grabbed wildly for a pillow and almost toppled over flinging it in the general direction of the rockers. What glee! A 240-pound Mr. Peccler punched old one-eye in the ear and drew blood. That was nothing so special, the others could do the same, and more easily too, for the other old men who got bloodied were lying down.

The cries of pain brought us running from the next room. Did we intervene? The price at night was the linen closet where attendants gave treatment, cracked skulls, broke arms. Still it was too much to stomach and encouraged by Gumanis's feeling, I reported it next morning to Mr. Dean, and B & E and Sedge Wicks backed me up. Another patient reported it straight to Gumanis. The total result of protesting was that no attendant would speak to me for six months.

Conversation was hard to come by. Grandma and Beelzebub were long gone to the best ward as housemen, coming to the yard in starched white shirts, afternoons only. So, with Carter having high blood pressure besides diabetes and not likely to get off Ward 3X, sick bay, I would walk with B & E for an hour on one of the terraces, which were wide enough for two if you stepped over feet in passing each bench. The few times Carter came out, we talked only about our leaving. I wrote letters to his sister, after medication made his hands too shaky. "Look," he said, pulling a handful of state paper from inside his shirt, "from the night attendant." I wrote the letters behind my newspapers and he carried them inside his shirt. For most of my own letters, I used wrappers from my newspapers, even getting a reply to one from the clerk to Chief Justice Earl Warren, Washington, saying there was no legal point for the justice to rule on.

But while I waited for someone to see the sense in my pleas, I could do more than write short stories. Having sat on the splintery floor long enough to develop callouses, I began planning my book. Whether fiction or nonfiction, the form would be the same. I would risk attendants' getting it in a shakedown. So far, my few papers had gone uninspected, filed between pages of a magazine under the mattress. Everything else I owned (toothbrush, paste, needle) were in a cigarbox beside the magazine. Sitting on the floor, I was almost out of sight and less liable to draw an attendant's slurs. I noticed that anything a patient could do out of sight was "permissible." By keeping away from argumentative patients, I did not attract attention. And after a couple of years of listening to constant screaming and cursing, my ears were able to shut out enough to let me get the book under way. I made eight-page composition books of brown newspaper wrappers, torn and folded to size. They wore down a pencil like butter on a sidewalk, but I was getting ideas whipped into shape. I used up a thousand pages over the years with endless rewriting, without a single page falling to other eyes.

As I was recording the story of so many others, I realized how easy it was to get locked up and stay locked up. In the free world all that was needed was someone to point his finger at you and say he was afraid of you. Even in here, the doctor judged your case not by what he heard from you but rather by scuttlebutt from an assistant pill pusher.

I was suffering from what today I call "supplemental insanity," something added from the outside. It rested partly on my mother's naïve reports to the hospital (which I did not read until 1974) but mostly on the offhand interpretations of the doctors (most of which, also, I did not read until 1974). At that time, 1959, I had no idea that the staff could paint my "illness" in quite such colorful words. These are what the American Psychiatric Association must have been swayed by, when they said in an *amicus curiae* brief in the Supreme Court of the United States (*O'Connor* v. *Donaldson,* No. 74–8, 1974): ". . . Like Kenneth Donaldson, there are many thousands of people throughout the country who [are] suffering from serious mental illness. . . ." Like Kenneth Donaldson, then, are thousands suffering from supplemental insanity?

The less serious mental illnesses, Carter kept me posted on from sick bay, which was a clearinghouse for scuttlebutt. They were substrains of schizophrenia, such as "being uncooperative" (refusing to buy an attendant a pack of cigarettes), "being emotionally volatile" (telling an attendant to go to hell when he accused you of having sexual relations with your mother), and "having hallucinations" (saying an attendant broke your arm when the report says you fell). Carter was allergic to these minor manifestations too; he could not stomach them. "You know one-eyed Tom," he said angrily. "The night attendant choked him out because the dressing pulled loose from his ear."

In an editorial on my case, *The New York Times* said (November 12, 1974):

> There are dark corners in America where people are trampled, broken and forgotten. The saddest of these—and the most demeaning to our society—are those institutions, paid for and run by the public, where people are stashed away for the safety and convenience of the rest of us and then left to rot untouched by the collective conscience of the community. Attica and Soledad turned flickering attention toward the prisoners; but few have cared to look at those huddled in the rotten crannies of America's public mental institutions.

On the lecture circuit now, I am often asked how mental illness could be handled without use of involuntary commitments.

My answer always is, "Name me one case that can't be handled under other laws."

Dr. Walter Fox, of the Georgia Mental Health Institute, and past president of the association of superintendents of state hospitals, who was an expert witness at my later trial, said, "Ninety-five percent do not belong locked up in these state hospitals."

Violent people need to be restrained, yes. Criminals belong in prisons, yes. But the retarded, the aged who are not senile, and the true schizophrenics (not those erroneously labeled) ought not to be locked up against their will.

Take Smokey, for instance. He dressed and bathed himself, and kept posted on all going on around him. He was always good-natured. To protect whom was he locked up? Furthermore, Smokey had better control of his emotions than many doctors and attendants guarding him.

I never looked at Smokey, or little asthmatic Pedro, without recalling a mother I came upon one day in my canvassing for painting and carpentry in Florida. She was sitting on her front-porch steps with her eight-year-old retarded boy.

"What should I do?" she said. "If I keep him at home, he'll destroy life for the rest of the family, our doctor says."

I had read that retardates should be locked up with their peers, so they could live happily without feeling inferior. I wished I could have told her about Dixie hobbling about the ward with his ankle bone pounding on the floor, with Jason in full pursuit.

The United Nations gives the best answer in their resolution 2856 (XXVI), "Declaration of the Rights of Mentally Retarded Persons":

> . . . Whenever possible, the mentally retarded person shall live with his own family or with foster parents and participate in different forms of community life. The family with which he lives should receive assistance. If care in an institution becomes necessary, it should be provided in surroundings and other circumstances as close as possible to those of normal life.

Why can't the richest nation in the world provide that?

One of the smallest nations has been doing just that for some of its mental patients for nearly a thousand years. In Gheel, a farm town in the Flemish-speaking region of Belgium, the townspeople have been caring for the mentally ill in their homes. Of 22,000 inhabitants, 2,400 are men, women, and children who have been judged mentally ill.

"Instead of being locked up in hospital wards, these patients live as members of families in the neat brick homes of Gheel citizens," stated an article in *Look,* May 23, 1961. "They work in the fields, help with household chores, take care of the babies.

"They arrive at a small receiving hospital, where the staff of four psychiatrists can observe them for a few days. Based on their past history and behavior, a decision is made whether they can be boarded out with a Gheel family. Those who are not suitable because of extreme illness—less than 10 percent—are either kept in the hospital until they can be transferred to foster-family care or sent to other hospitals in Belgium."

These defectives in Gheel have full run of the town. If able, they work five minutes a day or forty hours a week for grocer and farmer or keep house and watch the children. They save part of their earnings, and twice a year some of them charter buses for outings to a fair, museum, or seaport.

Some patients have lived there all their lives. And when the foster parents die, the patient is taken in by the parents' children. Each patient is a full member of the family. A New York businessman visiting there, John D. J. Moore, reported that it is a favorite joke of the Gheelois people to say, "You visitors can't tell us from our patients."

Dr. Matthew P. Dumont, who visited there in 1960, as reported by *Science Digest,* May 1962, said: "I have seen coffee served in a cafe with as much deference to actively hallucinating psychotics as to anyone else. . . . I never saw any revulsion or fear displayed toward patients, although many of them act in a bizarre fashion. About a half-dozen incidents of violence have occurred in the past twenty-five years, two of which resulted in fatalities."

It is interesting to note that the Chinese, before their modern revolution, had no insane asylums. The mentally ill roamed freely through the country. They were respected and cared for by everyone.

There is a growing trend in the United States to place the mentally ill in foster homes rather than huge state institutions. One factor working against this trend is the public's fear, because of unfamiliarity with the true nature of the mentally ill. Primarily, many of our mentally ill are institutionalized away from population centers. Then, too, a few years in a place like Chattahoochee would make even St. Peter at times appear snappish and psychotic.

While I was in Chattahoochee, I did what you would have done too, to alleviate the retardates' condition. When Smokey came up to me one frosty morning while I was soaking up the sun in a back window with my shirt off, I took time from working on a short story to write a letter home for him.

"You say cigarettes," I said. "Don't you get your pack every day?"

Nodding, he pulled a half-empty pack of tailor-mades from the pocket of his blue shirt. Then he said, "Tie." He did a couple of dance steps. "Tie, tie."

Boogerisch hurried over, as if incensed that any favorite of the attendants (a favorite because of free cigarettes in the morning) should be friendly with me.

He lit into Smokey: "You good-for-nothing mammyjammer, don't you know your family doesn't want you? I saw your chart downstairs. Your father has no use for you. If you hadn't killed your mother—"

Smokey bit his lip and turned his head as tears poured down.

"I was told," I said to Boogerisch, "that the Forgers didn't have a Mephistopheles anymore, but you are the original Beelzebub."

After Beelzebub left, Smokey said, "Works, works."

"I know," I said. "Your daddy works. There's no one home anymore, since your mother died."

There was a wet smile. "Thank, thank."

My plans were not to stay in Chattahoochee until I got broken. I was hiding money for a possible second escape. I let ex-navy-man Goran catch me threading five dollars into the knit piece at the bottom of my leather jacket. But he could be trusted not to mention "Doctor Bush." He showed me how to construct a code for my hottest notes. I first translated mine into Esperanto, then into code, which I figured would take the brainwashing corps 115 years to figure out, if it fell into their hands.

Goran showed me, too, how fear was spread also among the women. His girl friend's letter to Tallahassee, mailed over the fence, had come back to her doctor's desk. It had been unsigned, but the suspects had been narrowed down to five on her ward and

all five were in danger of the shock machine. Goran brought a copy
back from the dance:

> They have, on Wards 30-31-32, what they call the "pens" . . .
> wire cages, enclosed with guard wire, approx. 6′×6′ . . . bare of any
> furniture . . . cement floors. These cages do not provide *any* bath-
> room facilities whatsoever.
>
> White female patients are stripped of all clothing and placed in
> these cages, usually for punishment purposes and left there, naked,
> for hours and even days.
>
> These cages also have an immoral factor, in that . . . the naked
> occupant may be viewed by the trash collector, plumber, or any
> man coming to the "back buildings. . . ."

I was becoming so incensed at it all that I began showing my
"schizophrenia." I would say as I passed attendants, in the very
style they used, doing it behind their backs, "No pile of shit's so big
it can't be moved." And with Grandma I explored ways to get
things corrected, rather than escaping the sinking ship and leaving
wounded comrades to the psychiatric sharks.

"But if you do get ready," Grandma said, "you can always go
over the fence. See, a *Reader's Digest* rolled up and poked in the
fence makes a step. Three of them and you're out of this world."

"One could get out anytime he makes up his mind. They even
made it from Alcatraz," I said. "Stopping escapees is like stopping
criminals in the free world. You couldn't stop all of them—there
wouldn't be time for anything else. By the way, don't you think if
criminals had something else in their heads, say, if they could read
better—don't you think it might give them a different outlook?"

"I've been trying to start up a class—with noncharge patients
too. Gumanis okayed it, the drawback is O'Connor."

"Getting back to escaping—I learned from a wise man, a
person will always manage to do what he wants the most. And
today the most important thing is to beat this thing the right way
and see that O'Connor gets his."

"A bullet in the back of—"

I laughed. "We've got to make people listen. If I ran, I don't
think they would. And I've come so close to getting out I'd like to
try a little longer."

"You never did tell me exactly what got you into this. You're
not the criminal type."

"You'd never know it from the attendants. Really, though, the only thing wrong with me is that it took forty-eight years to grow up, that is, to find my path through life. When I finally got past all the postponements, others thought I had lost my way and so they locked me up until I should go back to carpentry and silence. That constitutes my disease."

"Call Jesstar says it was drink and women."

"That and calling me a homo."

"There are some people," Grandma said, looking his very wisest and stroking his chest, "who are bisexual. Maybe you are. I am. It's nothing to be ashamed of. Gumanis says the same."

By the middle of summer, I was pretty much alone with the manuscript and a variety of grammars from the library. As for the new patients, they all had the same story; so, when I saw a man under a tree, who looked like Narrel Damascus, I did not check. But after dinner Grandma told me Narrel wanted to talk.

"Serves him right—being back," I said.

"But it wouldn't hurt to find out what he's got to say," Grandma said.

So I listened to Narrel: "I wrote you, Kenneth."

"One letter."

"No, three. The other two came back with a note that you were no longer here."

Soon, Narrel, Grandma, and I composed an open letter to the Committee in Charge of State Institutions. We sent copies to six newspapers. All were signed by forty men; we stopped the collection of signatures when the yard foreman became suspicious. As we heard from none of them, I stuck my neck out and sent a copy from memory to a woman who lobbied in Tallahassee for patients' rights. She carried our petition to the committee.

The letter made the following point:

> We suggest that a team of quality doctors of good character, perhaps three in number, be sent in here to process for discharge the backlog of hundreds of patients who are being held without treatment, some at the whim of a relative or an official, some illegally from out of state, some hiding out to beat a court rap. In two years at the most, sooner if more doctors are employed, they should be able to lower the permanent case load by 200 to 500 in our one department alone. Three doctors at $25–40,000 a year would cost $75–120,000 a year. Balance this against ... maintenance of 100 patients at a mere $4 a day, which adds up to $146,000 for one year.

We got no reply from Tallahassee.

My main interruption in a plodding summer was a call by Gumanis. "What ward are you on . . . ?" he asked.

Then I interrupted, "How is my transfer coming to New Jersey? I wrote you about it nine months ago?"

"Doctor Rogers wrote them that you were a resident of Florida."

"But that's not so."

"Your commitment papers—and I read them myself—say you lived in Florida for four years. Rogers says there is nothing he can do and New Jersey has dropped the matter."

"But—"

"I called you on another matter. I have a letter from a Mrs. Donaldson—that's your mother?—she refers to you as her son. She will be here week after next to visit."

"I shall write and tell her not to come and I am requesting you to tell her not to come all the way up here in this heat for nothing."

"Whatever is the matter?"

But I was not going to tell him my personal feelings. As I have said before, I had had no fight with my parents and I was not angry because they thought I was sick. That was their privilege; however, I am appalled at the things they wrote the hospital about me (which I did not read until 1974). They said such things as that I went to pieces at my divorce and that I "resented" my father. I was overwhelmed that, visiting with me, they could not see me as I was but rather saw what they feared and what the doctor had painted. It was a matter of highest principle to me to clear my name totally and wipe away the shadow cast on my children's lives and our relationship.

What I saw in fifteen years in Chattahoochee, of how psychiatrists continually destroyed the love of a parent for a child, condemns psychiatry beyond redemption. I am not being maudlin about this; a fifty-one-year-old man (as I was then) does not always sentimentalize mother love. There are crimes that are equally bad, but there is no crime that is worse than stepping between child and parents, poisoning the latter's love with sophisms. What compounds the crime is the use of coercion, holding one until he stops protesting, until the flying against the window stops, like an exhausted insect in a locked attic. I lived with perhaps ten thousand men over the years in Chattahoochee. I saw many of them die, like the four this book is dedicated to, broken against the dirty pane. They died with a love snuffed out by the abuse of psychiatry. When students ask me what stands out in my Chattahoochee experience, my answer is "the needlessness of the whole thing, the incredible viciousness toward people who are given a chance to buzz endlessly against the windowpane because someone imagines it is doing them good."

But my wishes did not keep Call Jesstar, two weeks later, from finding me in a far corner of the yard. He moved in like a dogcatcher with a net. "Why didn't you answer?"

"I can't understand you people," I said, "the way you form the words down in your throats."

"Never mind that. Come along. You've got visitors."

"I'm not going."

"Oh, yes you are. Do you want me to call for help?"

"I told Doctor Gumanis I'm not seeing this visitor."

"You better git you ass along and let Gumanis decide if you're going or not going to."

I refused the entreaties of two other attendants to budge farther than the dressing room. Jesstar talked to Gumanis, then me, then Nurse Park. She emerged from Gumanis's office and said to one attendant, "I never saw a woman so broke up."

Going to supper in the tunnel, Snotnose kept bugging me. "The rabbi says if one would always honor his aged parents, he would make out all right."

"Get away from me, you constipated Jew!" I snarled.

"Oh, if I could only shit," he moaned.

I was about to help him by knocking it out of him, when he saw the expression on my face and ran. I cursed out the window: "Goddam my mother! Goddam her!"

"What did you say?" B & E asked.

"I'm sorry I said it," I told B & E. I silently added, "God, I didn't mean it."

But there were other things to think about. One oppressively hot day, an attendant was saying, "It looks like we might get a shower of rain," as we were suddenly rounded up. We were watching the Back Yard go up the hill first. There were catcalls and curses at individuals. Cannonball was on the Back Yard again and greeted his former buddies with well-rounded oaths. There was Billy, barefoot, in ragged overalls, whose mother had entrusted him to the expertise of Chattahoochee.

"Isn't that a pitiful sight?" Narrel asked. "If the people outside could see those men, something would get done in a hurry. Look at that tall one with his overalls in shreds. Who could say looking at him that he's insane? How does anyone know? And the few staff who have training are leaving fast. Did you hear that the student nurses have left? It isn't an accredited hospital anymore."

The clouds turned away and we did not follow the Back Yard in. The heat held to the ground. Cicadas in the live oaks and redheaded woodpeckers in the thin pines were drumming it up. Carter and I were surprised by a small mob approaching. Dr. John Gumanis himself, in red-orange shirt, was at the eye of the disturbance, his first venture to the yard. Attendants funneled patients selectively up to the master. Snotnose had a bouquet of weeds, which the great one smiled at, and a new attendant said, "They smell gooder 'n snuff."

"Here's your chance," Carter said.

"I'm not going to beg," I said testily. "I wrote both him and O'Connor and neither one has ever called me since May 1957, in answer to my letters."

"Hi, Carter," Gumanis said cheerfully. "I'm glad Mis' Park has you out in the sun." Turning, he said, "Hello, Donaldson, I don't know what you're doing, sitting out here."

"Why don't you just put me on a bus and let me go back to Pennsylvania, Doctor?" I said, tongue in cheek.

Gumanis's slicked black hair and serious brows, and the way he put his pipe in and out of his mouth, marked him a professional. "When did you go to the psychologist last?"

"I haven't seen one in Florida," I said.

"I'll send you tomorrow. Call Jesstar, you see he gets up there in the morning."

The office of Mr. Julian Davis, head psychologist, whose father had been the city of Chattahoochee's only general practitioner, was in the front wing of the receiving ward. The walk up the street, in the hush of an idyllic southern morning, continued my feeling of clouded satisfaction, like finding a four-leaf clover after spending two years on your hands and knees doing nothing else. Now, with the four-leaf clover in my hand, no one was going to ease me out either, before things got talked through, and there was an arrival at some understanding. Nor was it the psychologist's fault that we were herded out to the yard in the morning and back at night like cattle. He, being a professional man like those in Philadelphia, would readily see the injustice of holding me for two years in pasture.

His door was open and the receptionist in the lobby had me taken in before he appeared from a connecting office. Thin sandy hair topped a tall frail man, who limped on one deformed foot.

He smiled but there was no humor as we went over the high points of my case, which was now like reciting the multiplication tables.

When I expressed displeasure that Chattahoochee was giving me the grand shuffle over my transfer to New Jersey, Davis said: "I understand these things. My first job here was to arrange out-of-state transfers."

"Would you see what you could do for me then?"

He made no comment and proceeded with some tests: ink blot, word association, numbers. He asked about my reading habits, which called for an explanation of my refusal to read Florida newspapers: "I have nothing against the papers themselves. It's because of my nasty treatment. There is no excuse for what has been done. I want no part of anything Florida."

Before leaving, I pointed out that hospitals in Kansas and some in New York got patients out in an average of ninety days. He had no answer to why Chattahoochee took longer.

At the end, he was very polite, escorting me into the hall. I was nearly to the lobby, where the attendant waited, when Mr. Davis called down the length of the hall: "Mr. Donaldson? You couldn't really expect our state papers to be of the same quality as *The New York Times,* could you?"

"But I didn't put it that way," I wanted to protest, but Davis had ducked into an office.

I kept my perplexities to myself, off in a corner of the yard. Its three acres were obnoxious to most, including the housemen, who enjoyed lying on their beds, but it was the principal blessing I had. Lying, with shirt off, in the early subtropical sun, was a balm through the pores of my back to counteract the Chinese water-drops on my skull. It might seem that ants—red, brown, black, large and small—were about to take over the place and it might have been necessary to spread your blue shirt over the sandburs, but it was genuine pleasure after the sunbath to lie in the shade and stare way up past the tips of the high pines, so dark against the brilliant sky. My thoughts took wing to Philadelphia, to future reunions with the children, to the early days of marriage and working on the house in Auburn. I was no different in the yard than I had been on construction jobs. Only a chain-link fence separated me from the other world. Visitors could look out of their cars and see the world of make-believe—five hundred men cooped up like animals, to be smiled at by the knowing. We were schoolteachers, lawyers, saloonkeepers, doctors, grocers, farmers, all restrained because the world was afraid of us. We had supplemental insanity.

In the morning under the trees, with strength renewed, I knew they couldn't keep up the farce much longer. But when we cued up for the monthly weigh-in, after supper, and the gray-haired attendant bellowed, "Kenneth Donaldson! You're out of place," before he discovered he had been peering over his glasses at the list upside down, I realized the enormity of ending the farce. These were our only contacts with the free world, these Tobacco Roaders who saw their charges in reverse order.

And there were also the ones who did go home on furlough. There was a thunderstorm, with rain gusting onto the few bugs refusing to move. I pulled down the lower sashes. Hettaway, who shuffled unsteadily and swayed from his medication, had his elbow on the sill. I pulled easily but the sash dropped suddenly and touched his elbow. I apologized and walked away. Something landed on my shoulders and, yanking out a handful of my hair, felled me like a tree. My forehead bounced off the corner of a bench and smack dab on the floor, a la Rangy Tizella. The force scurried back to its bench, from which it had jumped. I stared at it wordlessly. There was no blood, so I sat down with my papers. Within minutes, though, one eye blurred and a painless lump raised on my forehead. I asked to be taken down to have the dust rinsed out with boric acid. The "professional" unearthed a colorless liquid from the cabinets, which he insisted on dropping into both eyes. The attendant made me grope up the last flight of stairs alone, sightless, and for a week my pupils were out of focus. The day after the incident, Dr. John Gumanis furloughed the bushwacker to his mother in the neighborhood.

"I should have blacked the jammer's eyes," I told B & E, "but I wasn't hurt, really, and I felt sorry, sort of, for him."

Assuming that was the end of the excitement for that year, I settled down to wait. Believing that my letters through the grapevine must some day result in my transfer to New Jersey, where they would see that I was sane, I waited with some forbearance. While I waited I was summoned for a surprise visitor, but I was not given starched and pressed clothes, as the neighborhood bugs were.

It was my sister-in-law Irene.

"Do you think I'm mentally ill?" I asked.

"No," she said.

"Do you think I belong with a bunch of hardened criminals and retarded men who can't contain their bodily functions?"

She looked away. A little more description would be convincing, I thought. "The attendants choke a person into insanity. They wrap their arms around a guy's throat." I threw my left arm as tightly as I could across the front of my neck. "Then they squeeze until you stop breathing. It is called a 'little more treatment.' "

She put her arms in her coat. "I've got to get moving if I make Clearwater before dark."

Suddenly, my love for her as a sister prevented my embarrassing her in front of the lecherous guards, with the lie about my fathering her child. "I can't tell you what they say about you and me."

"What do they say?" Her expression conveyed what she was now convinced of, my paranoia.

"You could sign me out," I tried.

"But I would have to ask Mother first."

"I understand. But, really, I'm no different than when we lived in Syracuse. You know I couldn't change. Then you'll stop on the way back?"

"Oh, I couldn't do that—I'm going back a different route."

That terminal slap of aloof kindness knocked my thoughts back onto themselves. I could see that from being normal at the receiving ward I had deteriorated to the appearance of anything but. I was a "sick" person who refused to ask attendants for anything. What I couldn't do for myself, or get a patient to bring for a dime, I did without. I had stopped going shopping myself, in order to frustrate the attendants' cutting me off at the door.

The attendants too had changed, for the worse. In their frenzy to get organized for better hours and pay, they did not notice the swelling discontent resulting from the smaller portions in the mess hall and the resentment over the weekly shakedowns. Jason was determined to find somebody guilty of something. They would turn things topsy-turvy for a butcher knife supposedly brought in by a quiet criminal, who refused to supply goodies to Jason and Gettering. Then it would be in retaliation for Dixie's cursing all attendants during a seizure. So it gave utmost satisfaction to B & E, Grandma, and me to see attendants going about in twos late at night, with backs to the wall, after they realized that the increasing grumbling was directed toward them by the very ones who shared coffee during daylight hours.

It was then that the Tampa *Tribune* struck a timely chord with its front-page story of mistreatment at Raiford State Penitentiary. The NAACP was behind a demand there for an investigation by the legislature. That set all the literate inmates of the White Male Department to writing to the *Tribune* for a parallel investigation.

During this excitement, a discouraging letter came from lawyer McSorley, via Mrs. Stronth in Arizona. It said: "I have been trying to reach you for a year. I have received each of your numbered letters, but I know that you did not get my replies. I must advise you, that the only thing left is for you to get a lawyer down there." But that was almost academic, now that the *Tribune* might be won over for the faceless wraiths of Chattahoochee.

(I first read this in 1974. K.D.)

PROGRESS NOTES

3-12-59: Patient today is complaining that a certain friend in Tucson Arizona is not receiving his letters. There are no changes in his mental condition he still is delusional and paranoid. Believes his letters to his daughter are not mailed, and he is not mentally ill, judgment and insight defective, continue custodial care. Dr. Gumanis/ep

5-22-59: Patient today asked that a registered letter be mailed to his sister in Arizona, he had a $1.00, enclosed. the matter was brought to Dr. O'Connor's attention and it was decided that it be send by ordinary mail no changes in mental condition, refuses to take any type of medication, states he is not sick, judgment and insight grossly impaired. Dr. Gumanis/hh

132

(I first read this in 1974. K.D.)

PSYCHOLOGICAL EXAMINATION

Kenneth Donaldson, A-25738   Age: 51*
Date Examination: 9-19-59*   Educ: 1½ years
Referred by: Dr. Gumanis   Syracuse Univ.

* (Age and date have been corrected. K.D.)

SUMMARY AND CONCLUSIONS:
Psychological evaluation reveals that this man's thinking is essentially paranoid. He has many rather poorly systematized delusions. He believes that people are continually talking about him not only telling things that are not true but telling obscene stories about him. The Rorschach record includes associations which point up some homosexual tendencies which is in agreement with the MMPI in showing a strong feminine orientation. Also it is noted that the paranoia and the psychopathic deviant are significantly beyond the normal range of the MMPI profile. The test record suggests that this patient is actively psychotic suffering from a paranoid psychosis which is probably schizophrenic in nature.

TESTS:
Rorschach
As-a-Person

ATTITUDE AND PSYCHOLOGICAL CHARACTERISTICS:
On entering the examination room the patient stated in forthright manner that he did not appreciate the treatment he had received since being here. He does not believe that it was necessary for him to come here and he believes that since he has been here he has been discriminated against because he wrote a letter to the Supreme Court and because he is a Yankee. Mr. Donaldson maintains that certain persons he did not identify in Pennsylvania tried to blackmail him over the fact that he had had a previous mental hospitalization. He says that he wrote a book about this blackmail and sent it to *The Saturday Evening Post*. Several days later he was picked up by the authorities without explanation and briefly interviewed by some physicians who walked through the jail. He is very insistent that he be released from the hospital.

JCD:sb

(I first read this in 1974. K.D.)

FLORIDA STATE HOSPITAL

May 18, 1959

Re: Mr. Kenneth Donaldson, A-25738

Mr. and Mrs. William Donaldson
Belleaire Village Court
Largo, Florida

Dear Mr. and Mrs. Donaldson:

This acknowledges receipt of your letter of May 14 and we wish to advise that Kenneth has shown no basic improvement lately. He still possesses abnormal ideas and still believes that he is being persecuted. He also still doesn't realize he has ever been mentally ill and his judgment continues to be poor. In addition, he makes no effort to engage in any occupation here, and his only interest is in obtaining his immediate release.

However, he is physically comfortable, is eating and sleeping well, and is up and about every day.

Yours very truly,

J. T. Benbow, M.D.
Clinical Director

JBO'C:da

CHAPTER 9

1960

Right to Treatment

DAY FOLLOWED MONOTONOUS DAY. FROM SEVEN TO FIVE I SAT IN THE dust of the yard or in a back window or on the porch.

From the window there were suggestions of blue branches in the sun-drenched pines crowding out of the valley a mile away. From a sawmill hidden in haze, a straight plume of smoke cut the horizon, which was as level as a line on the map of Texas.

A quarter-mile below the grilled window of Ward 1, this vast solemnity was cut harmlessly by the school bus and the morning train. The interstate motorist could look up through breaks in the trees, at picturesque white buildings behind chain-link fence, and feel thankful that there was this place for the impossibles.

I noticed the smoke from the sawmill across the valley was diluted by the bright sky. My best plans for three years were like the smoke. But I was still determined to find a way to tell the man feeding logs to the sawmill and the motorist tramping the gas pedal to New Orleans that my flesh and blood differed from theirs only in their possibility of pursuing freedom.

Sixty-eight hundred of us cried out every day. And nobody

wanted to go home more than Nutmeg. His father had beaten him and tied him to a tree, but that was preferable to working for cigarette butts from the attendants. Tattletale to the attendants and schemer though he was, I still tried to help him, for even the most far-out character on the Back Yard was a restless panther in his cage.

"Call Jesstar's back," Nutmeg began. "Had the flu."

"At least he got good treatment out there," I said. "Thirteen hundred men in here—half of them on their backs—and one callous doctor."

"You mean Doctor Gumanis? He's a fine doctor. He told me this morning I could go home if my father'd take me. Write for me, will you?"

"I wrote last week and he said he didn't want you."

"But Gumanis said I could. I want to go so bad. I'd do a job of work for my daddy now. You can write gooder'n Gettering."

"All right. If you can get the paper."

In two minutes Nutmeg was back, saying, "Call gave it me. He said he likes your style. He's going to take another man out— you know, tend the garden, feed the pigs, cut wood. He'd like to take you this time."

"How about the man last year?"

"Call had to bring him back in eleven months."

"So he wasted his year."

"Call says you'd make it."

"I don't want the help of any of the bastards."

"Your mother don't want you. Oh—Doctor Bush."

We were interrupted by my call to Gumanis's.

"What ward are you on?" he asked, et cetera. "Your mother wrote. That'll be all."

The guard got off his chair.

"Do you have time for a question?" I asked Gumanis.

"Sure."

"How'd I do with the psychologist? It's nine months."

"You didn't pass. I knew you wouldn't."

"It doesn't make much difference what these farmers think of me. The doctors up north know I'm not sick."

"Davis says you have hallucinations."

Who cared what Davis thought! I'd still get somebody out there to listen. Peter W. Rodino, Jr., Congressman from Newark, did. He wrote the hospital: "Please advise as to the nature of the proceedings by which Mr. Donaldson was committed, and, further, what steps are necessary to arrange his transfer."

Gumanis called me down and told me: "I wrote him that the doctors here would work out your case to your best advantage and that you were a four-year resident of Florida."

I fumed for many days. I was still hot when Chegg, one of the many criminals who had never seen a courtroom, asked my help. He was a nightclub bouncer and pimp from Miami, doing time for alleged rape. One of the night women had fixed him when he held back a fair share of the spoils off a glittering foreigner.

"Do you know why I'm so thick with the attendants?" Chegg said. "When I play up to somebody, I want something. These shitheads would have been a joy on the strip. I've studied you, Donaldson. I've got a plan. You know law. You help me and I'll give you a tip. You write me four writs and I'll give them to Bull Dean with a dollar for a notary."

"It won't work. That's why I'm still here."

"This is different. Dean takes them to Gumanis. Gumanis goes up to O'Connor. They put me to staff and I pass."

"They'd throw me on the squad."

"I'll copy them in my own hand."

That same week, there was light through a second chink. There was a front-page item in *The New York Times* about a new theory advanced (in the *Journal of the American Bar Association,* May 1960) by Brooklyn attorney/medical doctor Morton Birnbaum for the benefit of unjustly held inmates in "mental prisons." He called it the "Right to Treatment." Either the inmate should get treatment or be set free, especially so if no treatment was called for.

I wrote him on May 28: ". . . I hope you are moved to do something . . . I tell my own story, but only because I can tell it better than someone else's. . . . I have been in the presence of doctors here for a total of only about 2½ hours in 3½ years. Taking out 1½ hours (dentist, 'psychologist,' admission day and transfer day) there is left one hour spread over 3½ years . . . for what the doctors call 'psychiatric treatment. . . .' "

Doctor Birnbaum's reply enclosed a copy of the bar journal's article and suggested "you use this article as the basis for an application for a writ of habeas corpus addressed to the Florida

Supreme Court. More than this advice I cannot give you as I am not a member of the Florida Bar."

While I was thinking it over, Chegg reported: "Because of the writs, Gumanis is putting me to staff in six months. Said I'd be home by Christmas."

Still knowing it might lead to complications, I was unwilling to wait longer. I decided to force the issue, basing my argument on the dual premises of fraud and the Right to Treatment. "It is a situation beyond my control," my brief stated.

But I would not be satisfied with a leisurely six-month extension of my "sentence." It was not some subservient law-breaker these people were dealing with in my case. If Doctor Birnbaum thought I had a case, then I would put it all on the line in the hope that the state of Florida did not operate wholly through fraud. Besides the four copies to Brother Dean with the dollar, I put one over the fence for fifteen cents, asking the chief justice if he did not receive the other four copies within ten days to please grant the writ.

I did not tell B & E about the fifth. As it was, he pointed out that the four others might lead to three more years. "I thought you were up to some such thing," he said.

There is no copy of this petition on file with the Florida Supreme Court today. My papers of those years are largely destroyed. But Doctor Birnbaum filed a duplicate for me with the United States Supreme Court as No. 244 Misc. (364 U.S. 808). Incidentally, I was unable to get a copy of No. 244 by mail. It was only when I went to the court in person on December 18, 1974, that I got a copy.

My brief was based on the Right to Treatment (because I was getting no treatment and because I needed no treatment, I was entitled to my freedom) and based on fraud (because the statements on my commitment papers were uniformly untrue).

After the petitions were on their way, I woke to the least sound all night, not unaware that the gestapo could have me on the shitty end of Nine before daybreak, as punishment for the four writs. But, when I got through breakfast in the usual routine, I knew that the worst would not happen before ten days.

Then there was scary news of another sort. May 15 had been our first day in the yard since September 15. When the results of the first annual visit of a mobile X-ray unit were announced, we learned of the incidence of TB in four patients and one attendant in the White Male Department alone, the attendant and one patient being on my ward.

On the eleventh day, the writ arrived in my mail. It was dated July 19, a Tuesday. I had now scored for the second time. I could hardly contain myself to whispers as I read to B & E and Grandma: "The hospital was 'hereby commanded to make return to this Writ instanter, showing the lawful cause and authority for the detention of the petitioner.' Now," I said, "we'll see what they are going to tell the court."

On Thursday, still mystified at not being called by Gumanis, I was waltzed up to the psychologist, Davis. I would play it by ear.

"Doctor O'Connor," Davis began, "asked me to have a chat with you."

"Before we start anything," I said, "I would like to get one thing straight. It was nine months after I saw you, that I saw Gumanis again, and when I asked how I did on the tests he said you said I had hallucinations. Just what hallucinations did I have?"

"I don't remember. Let me go check." He left me alone for five minutes, then reported, "There is nothing in your record about hallucinations."

Here was proof Gumanis had lied, so I thought.

"Shall we proceed to take some tests, Mr. Donaldson?"

"I'd rather not. I don't need any tests. There was nothing wrong with me when I came to Florida and there is nothing wrong with me today. You can't tell anyone that I'm out of my head—you just said there were no hallucinations. Then why are you holding me? Why didn't Chattahoochee let my home state of New Jersey take me?"

"I'm sure no one in Chattahoochee would want to keep you if you were eligible for transfer."

"But that's just what they are doing."

"I know better because that was my first job and if you are entitled to one you'll get it."

"But somebody lied and—"

"Nobody at Chattahoochee lied about you—least of all a doctor!"

"Anyway, it's academic," I said. Then, foolishly, like old Tom throwing a pillow, I pounded lightly on the desk (though still *pounded*) and said, "The court will free me and then I'll bring suit for damages. So let's skip the tests and wait on the court."

"What kind of treatment do you think you should have, if you were to have some treatment?"

This was dangerous ground for me, in the event the court let me down. "There is no point in making a hypothetical choice."

"But you told the court you wanted your release because you were getting no treatment, didn't you?"

"I don't want any."

"Oh, I see." Davis shuffled his papers. "Tell me about this matter of the slander."

This was an area I wanted to avoid. No answer would mean I was evasive and every item I did give would lead to one more question until they had enough to hang me. Yet this story had passed muster in Los Angeles by an attorney, a psychiatrist, and the FBI, and in Philadelphia by eight doctors in the psychiatric clinic. I kept my facts to a minimum, saying that a filthy campaign of slander about sex had grown up about me.

"You mean to say," Davis asked, incredulous, "it followed you all over the country?"

"Yes."

"And it started in Arizona?"

"Yes."

"Why there's no one in Arizona who's even known in the rest of the country!"

This seemed a safe and irrelevant thing to talk about. I named both senators as examples of well-known Arizonans: Carl Hayden, president pro tempore of the United States Senate, and Barry Goldwater; though I quickly added that they did not know me.

It is interesting to note, in comparing the above report with that in the hospital files (see end of chapter) that a college professor with a Ph.D. in psychology, who has done graduate work and taught at three universities, told me he doubted that the raw material from my tests would show, to a well-trained psychologist, that I was sick. Just because one's answers do not fall within the average range of answers does not make one mentally ill. The wire services, several years back, carried a story of a research project in which raw material from one patient's tests was given to several-score psychologists for evaluation. The psychologists came up with almost as many different results, from psychotic to sane.

Or, as B & E said when I walked back into Ward 1, "It only takes a stroke of the pen to seal your doom."

The record shows phone calls and letters between Tallahassee and Chattahoochee.   What surprised me, at the time, was that no employee in White Male talked about the case. It seemed to be in limbo; however, tension was mounting in B & E, Grandma, and me. But as often happened, the scuttlebutt brought us a diversion.

It was B & E's telling us: "Gettering got his last night." He was working the Back Yard again and Goran, who had been transferred for having $25 in Jason's weekly shakedown, evened some scores. "Goran snuck up in back of him and let him have it with the fire-hose nozzle. I bet it weighs fifty pounds."

"Is he alive?"

"Gettering? Four stitches, that's all."

"More's the pity." Grandma sighed.

The next excitement was the highlight of my Chattahoochee career. On Tuesday morning, July 26, two attendants rushed up to where I was writing, on the floor between the beds. Just in time, I had seen them out the corner of my eye and slipped the manuscript between the pages of a magazine. I froze inside. Why two attendants?

"Hurry," they both said. "Get your ass along fast."

It was reflexive to ask where.

"No time for questions. Quick."

As I pushed the magazine and pocket dictionary under the mattress, the attendants were already twenty feet away. They looked back and motioned for speed. It being past the hour for doctor's call, I must be going to the Back Yard. My papers would be destroyed if I left them, and so I turned for them. The attendants came back angry.

Oh, well, I'd squeeze one last drop of pleasure from the scene: I detoured three feet to the water cooler. They glared.

"Gumanis's waiting," they said.

"I know what it's all about," I said, relieved. "I've waited all these years for him, now let him wait."

As I came off the rickety stairs in the poolroom, the attendants had the door open. Gumanis was standing in the middle of the dressing room. He darted back into his office, the larger one now. The other patients did not dare speak to me. They had been waiting two hours.

Like a maître d', the doctor saw that I was seated, then closed both doors himself, leaving one guard inside. Gumanis took a stand behind his desk, pipe in mouth. I bit my lower lip, for he was hot enough to blow smoke rings from the cold pipe.

"You did this?" he asked, his voice very high-pitched, tapping his pipe on the paper on his desk. "You got this writ?"

"Yes," I said, as he laid the pipe on the paper.

"Why?" Incredibly, his voice rose higher.

"Because I want out."

He paced behind the desk. Stopping, he asked, "How did you do it?"

"I gave four copies to Dean to mail—with a dollar to have them notarized."

"I don't believe you." Gumanis was shouting.

"But I did." I was looking for froth at the corners of his mouth.

"And he took them?"

"Yes."

"No! He couldn't do it!"

"Yes, he did."

"He couldn't!" Gumanis pounded the desk, and I bit on my lip again to keep from laughing. He walked some more. After a while, he sat down and pulled a card out of his three-by-five desk file.

In a normal voice he asked: "What ward are you on?"

"Ward 1," I answered soberly, as he wrote on the card.

"Are you taking any medication?"

"No."

"Are you working anyplace?"

"No."

Gumanis waved the guard to take me out.

Two days later, I received from the attorney general's office the respondent's reply to the writ. I was shocked. Doctor O'Connor, as Clinical Director, said I had a "mental disorder which is often found to be chronic and very severe. . . . Most recent psychological examinations reveal that delusional content continues to be in evidence and that a certain senator from Arizona is responsible for the nasty stories being told on him. . . ."

The above is the nub of the entire "medical" case against me.

The respondent's brief included copies of my commitment papers (which I was seeing for the first time) which stated that on December 13, 1956 (which was my third lonely day in the Pinellas County Jail) a sanity committee, appointed by Judge White, consisting of two doctors and one deputy sheriff, had "examined

[me] thoroughly both physically and mentally" and found me to be a "schizophrenic paranoiac who was seeing and hearing things and was possibly dangerous to the people of the state." The commitment papers included the information that I had lived in Florida for four years prior to my commitment.

Part II of the respondent's brief (see end of chapter) is the basis for fifteen succeeding court decisions in my case. It was the defense of *res adjudicata*, relying on an earlier decision. This same court had been intimidated by the hospital in the case of Narrel Damascus. If you let this man out, the clinical director had warned of Narrel, we will not be responsible for what happens. Then the court had refused to grant habeas corpus to me in 1957. So that was it, final, for the next decade.

I sent off a rebuttal to the court the next day, via the grapevine. I felt certain that Chief Justice Elwyn Thomas, who had believed my petition, would also believe my rebuttal. Of course, it would be my word against Doctor O'Connor's, but anybody would be able to see that I knew what I was talking about.

B & E showed me the news that the state Supreme Court would be on vacation until September. Also, Attorney Birnbaum wrote that he had put a copy of my petition for habeas corpus on file with the United States Supreme Court. This would be insurance for any failure of the state court to do its duty. So, in rapturous entr'acte, I reared back with vigor to wear down a pencil a day on the rough brown pages of my workbooks.

There were no vaporous emanations from the miasma downstairs, no parlaying of rumors about my forefathers, but there were bad dreams of punishment by the gods up the street. The judge could see that there was something wrong. But would he understand the doctors' dodging? Could any outsider expect the inmate to be more accurate than the keeper? There was the sultriness of doubt in the southern August.

On September 15, the mailman hurried up to Ward 1. Jason sent Dixie on the run for me. I opened the letter in front of the attendants but waited till I got to the bed to read:

... the writ of habeas corpus is discharged.

I hadn't believed there could be such cruelty in the United States.

But to be sure, I checked through the grapevine with the court, and the clerk informed me that my rebuttal had not been received. I did not doubt the privilege-card patient, who had put it in the substation letter drop with sufficient postage affixed. Then all the papers I had on the case, which I mailed similarly to Mr. Birnbaum in New York at his request, never showed up in New York. All the demands for an investigation of the hospital's mail-handling to the postal authorities and the court could not make them listen to one who "was seeing and hearing things and was possibly dangerous. . . ."

It is important to underline what the courts and doctors did in 1960. Looking back to the early decisions by the Florida Supreme Court, Dr. John P. Spiegel, president of the American Psychiatric Association, pointed out (*Psychiatric News,* October 16, 1974):

> . . . in the course of the patient's stay at the hospital, Donaldson had brought [19] different legal petitions before state and federal courts requesting release, and protesting the conditions of his confinement and lack of treatment. All of these were denied or refused by the courts. "If none of these judges, wise in the law, can be guilty of ignoring Donaldson's civil rights, then how can psychiatrists who must rely on the courts' wisdom and authority in their own domain be accused of acting maliciously, knowingly, or in bad faith concerning Donaldson?" Dr. Spiegel asked.

Thus the doctors today point to the original preconceived notions of the Chattahoochee doctors, which were accepted by the courts as fact without weighing evidence in open court, as both defense of themselves and proof of my illness.

I coasted for a couple of weeks. Then, on the first Tuesday in October, B & E was sitting with me on the floor. I was checking my notebooks of short stories, which had been taken in the super shakedown in April 1959 and just been returned.

"Are they all there, really?" B & E asked.

"It looks that way," I said. "Not a page out of order."

"Well, I'll be going. You'll want to get some work done this morning," he said. In a few minutes he was back with the Tampa *Tribune.* On the front page was a piece about the Supreme Court's having turned down some nine hundred cases at the opening session in Washington.

"Mine's got to be in the thirteen they'll hear," I said. But the one thin sheet of paper came at the end of the week. Mine was among the nine hundred.

As I look back, the doctor probably thought to buy insurance against writs by letting me write stories.

While I thought about my next moves, I watched for any openings. Catching Jason smiling one day, I said: "No pile of shit's so big it can't be moved."

Jason's face flushed and his eyes popped. I had him impaled. "Why don't you do something about it then, except talk?" he snapped.

"I have," I said, self-satisfied.

In fact, all of us were doing something. We rallied behind Narrel to bombard the governor to investigate Chattahoochee. Narrel had collected signed statements from each patient who had been tortured. He brought young Jackbrace over to my bed to tell how he had been tied, spread-eagled, on the bed.

"And you mean they actually jumped up and down on you?" I asked.

Jackbrace showed the mark where his belt buckle had cut in.

"Why didn't you report it?" I demanded.

"To who?"

But there were better moments sprinkled about. Grandma came rushing over on a Sunday morning.

"O'Connor did it!" he said. "Shot himself—during the night. I knew he would."

I made him repeat it. By then the whole ward was abuzz, with figures darting from the attendants' station in all directions.

On Monday at 9:00 A.M., Doctor O'Connor came to work as usual. Supervisors and all were disappointed.

The reaction was all the worse, because the men were restless with nervous energy. Here it was the first week in December and no one had been to the yard since October 1, not even ballplayers. The attendants, believing they were on top of the situation, bore down all the more. Two dollars were taken from a letter to Pedro from his mother, though he got the letter. I overheard Gettering: "Donaldson is one of the mammyjammers we're going to get." I didn't mind, for it took attention away from Narrel. I was called down on package run, standing around for an hour, with no package for me after all. The barber took a chunk out of my ear with the clippers. And Jason and Gettering were tearing up and scattering everybody's possessions.

In a night of unrest, one criminal hanged himself in the

Flattop and one got out a window from Ward 1. And Sedge yelled out the window at midnight: "You go down to Tallahassee and tell them to come after me."

I thought Sedge was hopelessly funny. I can look back and see he was a tower of strength. From the very heart of a conflagration of noise and brutality, he still had faith that some decent person would listen.

"The jokers are wild," Call Jesstar reported Doctor Gumanis as saying. Our letters brought orders from Tallahassee to close the Flattop. Most of the men came to Ward 1. They told how attendants in the Flattop kept disturbed men awake all night, withheld medication, disclosed the contents of letters the inmates never got, and even threw chicken and bread on the floor, which one had to pick up or go hungry. One man had the fire hose turned on him full force in his cell, three nights in a row. The third night he killed himself. Brother Dean finally prevailed on Gumanis to go talk to the men. For all the good it did, the night after his visit, two more suicided.

Punishment in the name of compassionate medicine.

Carter, who was critical of the attendants' eating all the soup and drinking all the juice intended for the men on sick bay, took a turn for the worse and called me over to the grilled window between sick bay and the poolroom.

"I can hardly stand up, Ken," he said. "Write my sister in Philly. They're doing something to me. I saw them put something in the needle. It wasn't for diabetes."

The new permanent furrows in my brow deepened. Was Carter imagining? Just as he had always stood up for Gumanis, when the rest of us knew the attendants couldn't get away with any more than Gumanis approved of, was Carter wrong again?

"Why don't you tell Gumanis?" I asked.

"They won't let me. I don't even see Mis' Park."

A week later he called me to write again. There was gray in the formerly red face. No replies came to the letters. Eventually, the nurse, in a routine check, learned that he was getting the wrong medication, enough to kill an ox. But he never snapped back. He was withered, stooped, ashen, trembling.

I felt terrible inside. Each of us stood alone, helpless to save ourselves or a friend. It was horror of my total inability to help him that made me avoid the window, but Carter insisted on telling me another story:

"You know Cannonball—the bald-headed chicken plucker.

He had a heart attack. Gumanis let him up in a wheelchair. The attendants pushed him under an ice-cold shower. He died in an hour."

Of what value to the world would Cannonball have been, had he lived? Of what value was I to the world? Were all seven thousand persons, gathered helter-skelter from around the state— were we all beyond the point of no return? I never slept easy again in Chattahoochee, if I ever had.

In the dining room, spots of mold, as big as a silver dollar, went through several slices of bread. The old patient who cut and served the butter, and who never washed his hands, went to the TB ward. When tension got too much, little snaggled Dixie jumped off his chair and bit in the seat of the pants the attendant who was beating on someone with a pitcher.

With it all, sometimes I could not understand the reactions of some patients.

"The patients and the attendants average out the same, don't you think?" Grandma asked, with water rolling off his amusing figure in the shower. "In your book, Ken, tell what is being done for the patients. To start with—a roof and a bed and three squares—"

"Not three squares," I said.

"But there really is no difference between them, only some patients go to extremes."

"And the attendants?" More than the water was warming me up. All I could see was blood: blood on a man spread-eagled on a bed; blood on a ninety-eight-pounder in a straitjacket; blood on an old man's ear. And a naked woman in a cage. I rinsed off quickly and got out of the shower.

The rest of us kept bombarding the Tampa *Tribune*. Finally, some of our letters appeared on the front page. They told it all. I liked this one: "You could read a newspaper held six inches under the surface of the milk."

Superintendent Rogers allowed a *Tribune* reporter to see one ward of bedridden men, Ward 10. The story told of "the stench of urine," the lack of equipment, the shortage of nurses. The public demanded an investigation.

That same week, Narrel introduced Happotine: "He just came up from the Flattop, Ken. I told him he could trust you."

Happotine refused to shake hands. He refused to say anything. Narrel said wait. Happotine was not a beast. His crimes were armed robbery and safecracking. He came back the third day and studied me, with narrowed eyes withdrawn in his fine-lined prison pallor. The fourth day he told me he had been in prisons and asylums all over the country.

"I led riots in Missouri and West Virginia," he said. "This place is ripe."

"These men won't stick together," I said. "They go all which ways."

"Give me six men—that's all I need."

"Innocent men would get killed."

"You've got to shake this state up."

Narrel advocated caution too. At least two attendants would get killed initially, if we tore the place up.

"So what?" Happotine said. "Many an innocent man died at the Bastille."

But after riots, after the broken bones are mended, public indignation gives way to the gray mold of indifference again. If we could accomplish a legal victory, then there would be enough legal antibiotics to keep things pure. The men listened to Narrel and me.

(I first read this in 1974. K.D.)

TRAVELERS AID SOCIETY OF PHILADELPHIA
Pennsylvania Station—30th Street
Philadelphia 4, Pa.

March 1, 1960

J. T. Benbow, M.D.
Clinical Director
Florida State Hospital
Chattahoochee, Florida   Re: DONALDSON, Kenneth
                                                  A-25738

Dear Doctor Benbow:

In 1957 we forwarded you copies of letters sent us by Mr. Donaldson—protesting his confinement in your hospital.

This is just to advise you that we have received further communication of a similar nature from him. We are filing them in our record. If by any chance you should want copies please advise us. We are not replying to Mr. Donaldson.

Sincerely,

(Miss)   Grace A. Yocom
Case Supervisor

GAY/mg

(This was the wording of the law
at about the time I got my writ. K.D.)

FLORIDA STATUTES

Chapter 79.01   APPLICATION AND WRIT.—

    Whenever any person detained in custody, whether charged with a criminal offense or not, shall, by himself or by some other person in his behalf apply to the Supreme Court of the state or to any justice thereof, or to any circuit judge, in vacation or in term time, for a writ of habeas corpus, and shall show by affidavit or evidence probable cause to believe that he is detained in custody without lawful authority, the court, the justice or judge to whom such application shall be made forthwith shall grant the writ, signed by himself, directed to the person in whose custody the applicant is detained, and returnable immediately before such court, justice or judge, or any of said courts, justices or judges as the writ issued may direct.

(I first read this in 1974. K.D.)

PSYCHOLOGICAL EXAMINATION

Kenneth Donaldson, A-25738   Age: 52
Date Examined: 7-28-60   Educ: 1½ years
Referred By: Dr. Gumanis   Syracuse Univ.

SUMMARY AND CONCLUSIONS:
This patient was originally tested on 9-19-59,* at which time it was felt that his thinking was paranoid.
The present testing shows no significant change from the earlier findings. While many of his responses tend to be of good form quality, some of the content is bizarre and reflects a deteriorated logic.
Delusional content continues to be in evidence, essentially as described at the time of the previous tests with the exception that in 1959 certain unidentified persons in Pennsylvania were responsible for the nasty stories being told on him. Now he alleges that a certain senator from Arizona is responsible.

* **Corrected. K.D.**

TESTS:
Rorschach

ATTITUDE AND PSYCHOLOGICAL CHARACTERISTICS

Mr. Donaldson stated that the person who did the previous psychological examination on him was either incompetent or dishonest. He based the statement on being told that the report stated he experienced hallucinations. Actually, the only reference to hallucinations was on his commitment papers. Mr. Donaldson again told about the book he has written, the deplorable treatment he has received, and the way people have talked about him everywhere he has been.

JCD/fd

FLORIDA STATE HOSPITAL
CHATTAHOOCHEE

July 30, 1960

Re: Kenneth Donaldson, A-25738

Honorable B. J. Owens,
Assistant Attorney General,
State Capital
Tallahassee,
Florida

Dear Mr. Owens:

The following is a report on Kenneth Donaldson who was committed to this Hospital on January 3, 1957 by the Pinellas Court at Clearwater, Florida and was admitted to Florida State Hospital on January 15, 1957. Recent psychiatric interviews in this Hospital indicate the presence of a mental disorder which is often found to be chronic and very severe. At the present time it is our opinion that Mr. Donaldson possesses extremely defective insight and judgment and he expresses false perceptions and paranoid ideas. Most recent psychological examinations reveal that delusional content continues to be in evidence and that a certain Senator from Arizona is responsible for the nasty stories being told on him. Our diagnosis remains the same, namely Schizophrenic Reaction, Paranoid Type with a poor prognosis. In conclusion we wish to advise that this patient is still psychotic and requires further hospitalization.

If further information is desired, please so advise and this will be furnished at once.

Yours very truly,

J. B. O'CONNOR, M.D.
Clinical Director

JG:mt

(I first read this in 1974. K.D.)

PROGRESS NOTES

(This is the 1960 Progress Note from my hospital file. K.D.)

10-18-60:   No changes mentally, continue care on the wards.
Dr. Gumanis:jwl

IN THE COURTS, 1960

(ii)

Supreme Court of the State of Florida   7/19/60

Upon my petition, the Supreme Court of Florida granted a writ of habeas corpus on July 19, 1960.

My argument was: "I. . . . Petitioner is . . . receiving no treatment . . . seldom sees a doctor . . . (and) II. . . . Petitioner was illegally committed to said hospital . . . doctors of said hospital have refused petitioner a sanity hearing . . ."

The state's response was based on copies of my commitment papers (which contained only one accurate thing: the spelling of my name) and a fraudulent report of what I had said to the psychologist Davis. My rebuttal never reached the court, presumably being stolen from the U.S. mails in Chattahoochee. Without giving me a hearing in person, the court quashed the writ on September 14, 1960.

(iii)

Supreme Court of the United States   No. 364 U.S. 808
7/6/60

Upon my petition, filed by Morton Birnbaum, M.D., LL.B., the Supreme Court of the United States denied habeas corpus, the first day of October Term, without a hearing and without calling for papers from the state.

CHAPTER 10

1961

Pale in the Fy-uss

MEMORIES, WHEN THERE WAS A QUIET MOMENT FOR THEM MIDST THE dust of the yard, were poignant. One regular recollection was from my youth, a cartoon showing two inmates inside the fence of a lunatic asylum. Looking out, one said to the other, "It's the ones outside who are crazy."

It was funny then; it was a different story now.

But that was 1961, you say. Is this book necessary in 1976? Since 1961 there have been innumerable investigations; state after state has passed new laws; and doctors have published libraries of books telling how to cure these people. I don't argue with the doctors' searching for new methods of healing. The "healing," however, ought not be forced on those who aren't sick. Nor am I against more humanitarian laws; however, as in the 1960s, the courts today do not enforce the laws we already have concerning commitment and patients' rights.

In 1961, patients continued to die in Chattahoochee. Buried, too, was the doctors' recognition that their neglect had saved the wretches another year of misery. For those who lived, without getting TB or without being crippled by wrong medication (as was my friend Carter), there were periods of hope, occasions in the middle of the night when there were no screams, no sickening thumps from bodies being broken. A few of the old-timers took heart. Ninety-pound Chonty, who had never stopped his dreary retaliatory threats since being beaten up in a straitjacket that Christmas Eve on the Back Yard, took time to sniff the mental atmosphere. He raised his head a little and the look of expecting a blow across the face seemed to float away with the freshet coming through the ward. Newly installed Governor Farris Bryant said there should be an investigation of Chattahoochee to put an end to the rumors and see what should be done. Hopes built to the skies. A feeling of bravado took some. Persimmon hit A.B. in the face for unnecessarily roughing up little Dixie in the tunnel; but nobody stepped in to help Persimmon when five attendants rushed out of the mess hall and splattered him all over the Tunnel of Shit. He just stayed there in one lump, unguarded, crying, until patients pulled him back to the ward after their meal.

Why were these people locked up in the first place?

Al Siebert has said: "It would be more honest to say, 'We're locking you up because we don't like what you're doing.' We can and should take action against someone who has lost control of himself and is intruding into the lives and minds of others. This holds for children and adults. But when we take action against a person because of our guesses and fears about what he *might* do then we are the ones out of control and we are intruding into his life."

Doctor Szasz has written: ". . . The advocates of involuntary mental hospitalization raise the second justification: protection of the public. This, of course, is a legitimate interest. But following in the libertarian tradition, I hold that a person should be deprived of his liberty only if he is proved guilty of breaking the law. No one should be deprived of his freedom for the sake of his 'mental health.' "

The report of the American Psychiatric Association on the "Clinical Aspects of the Violent Individual," July 1974, said:

> *"Dangerousness" is neither a psychiatric nor a medical "diagnosis."*
>
> Despite various attempts at classification there exists no adequate typology of violent persons. . . . The clinician should not regard the prevention of future violence as within his proven capability. . . .

> Neither psychiatrists nor anyone else have reliably demon-
> strated an ability to predict future violence or "dangerousness." . . .
> In summary, the state of the art regarding predictions of
> violence is very unsatisfactory.

With all the improved atmosphere on the wards in early 1961,
the mental illness that we were still being treated for was letter
writing. The Brothers of the Sheet clamped down on our incoming
mail, more and more of it never showing up for the patients. And
Jason Bennock had a duty to see that the "mentally disturbed" in
his charge did not forget whose patients they were. He accomplished this by repeated shakedowns of the letter writers.

How then to get outsiders, who could take action, to believe
what we told about our circumstances. The courts would not give
us a chance to testify and produce witnesses. Riot, then, or what? A
feminist civil-rights lawyer, Florynce Kennedy, told Doctor
Birnbaum: "Unless they openly and forcefully protest as have
blacks, prisoners, homosexuals, etc., the involuntarily committed
will not receive their just due." Patient Happotine and others
urged that same thing on Ward 1 in 1961. Narrel and I thought
the slower legal way was better.

Narrel and I thought we had won when we looked down from
the porch one morning, at a quarter to nine, and saw young lawyer
John Parker and his secretary, a stunning brunette, get out of his
car and go into the offices below us. Gumanis was frantically
phoning O'Connor for directions. Parker, hired by the Committee
on State Institutions, of the Florida Legislative Council, blew the
whistle. He had the names, smuggled out, of patients who wanted
to talk.

Gettering, who happened to be in the dressing room when
Parker walked in, was telling Jason about Gumanis: "The
mammyjammer looked pale in the fy-uss."

Jason's fingers waved out in happy excitement and his eyes
flashed. "We might get a raise out of the deal."

"In that case, I hope the mammyjammers win."

I was second to be called, after Narrel, who had taken down a
copy of his dossier. When he came back, he told me, "I told him to
listen carefully to what you have to say."

But Happotine said, with the knowledge that had come with
the hard deep lines in his white face, that it was all a sop to keep us
quiet until they could get the ringleaders moved. To that, Narrel
said, "Here's a signed statement—here's Parker's signature. That's

proof our testimony will be held confidential."

"Okay, I'll go down," Happotine said.

It was hard to believe that here I was, going down to spill the beans; as hard, really, as once believing I was spending the night in the hole of the Clearwater jail. Faced with it, there was so little time to cover four years and so much depended on saying things right.

"You'll have to excuse me, I'm a little nervous. This is quite a thing for us," I said.

"I can understand that," Mr. Parker said. "Just take your time. Miss Brickar and I are having our morning coffee. Would you have one with us?"

"No thanks." As they sipped, I said, "I prepared a statement, which I was going to read. But there's just the two of you—I'll give you a copy. But there's one point I would like to emphasize. Mental hazing—oral hazing—is just as hard to take as the physical kind. Maybe it intimidates more."

"Make a note of that, Miss Brickar: 'Mental hazing is just as destructive as physical hazing.'"

A couple of years later, I read what Doctor Szasz said about it:

> . . . a person who has been attacked, violated, and abused—especially over a long period of time—has, in fact, been *doubly* abused. First, by the act itself. Second, by the changes in his personality, in his inner self, wrought by his submissive position vis-à-vis his exploiters. While the first violation is obvious, the second is not, and often eludes attention. Yet, of the two, it is probably the more important, for its consequences are more lasting. . . .

Next I told the investigators, "You'll hear quite a bit about the cruelty from those who suffered it. I'd like to point out a few things." In my intense anger at that time, I made broad generalizations about the doctors. "Even if they had a work load they could handle, they are facetious, especially O'Connor, who sets the pattern, and they are indifferent and arrogant. When they talk to a patient and they hear a word they've seen on textbook page 14, right away that's the poor guy's disease. They've got a patient for each page. There's just no sense to the whole thing. Most of us on the wards are as sane as anyone in Tallahassee. What we need first of all is doctors who know what they are talking about when they talk about mental illness and who can tell a sane man when they see one."

"I'll put special emphasis on that in my questioning, Kenneth," Parker said. "I am already amazed at the caliber of the people they have locked up in here."

Overnight, things progressed. There was a full strip of bacon with the powdered eggs next morning at our breakfast. In fact, conditions improved to the point where there were no more chokings reported, except on sick bay and on Ward 9 where the patients lacked physical or mental strength to protect their inalienable rights.

The only true miracle that happened in my fifteen years in Chattahoochee was the arrival of an impressive man in a gray suit, gray head six inches above everyone else's, standing with a clipboard on Ward 1. With two of his assistants and three attendants, they made a loose circle near the shower room door. Grandma said it must be Representative S. Chesterfield Smith, chairman of the Committee on State Institutions.

"On the ward?" I said. "It can't be!"

The group was waiting for Narrel, who came in in his civilian clothes. He handed the tall man a pack of about a hundred sheets of paper. In twenty minutes, Narrel broke away and came over to us.

"He wants to see you," Narrel told me. "Show him the statement we drew up. He asked to see it."

I stood quiet as Smith read the two pages, signed by five of us. In it we had shown again how the state could save money by sending in good doctors.

"These men aren't nuts," I said.

"I can see that," Mr. Smith said. "I like your idea of a review board. Who would appoint them—the governor or the legislature?"

"Makes no difference so long as they were not connected with the hospital. Any group of people—a shoemaker, a grocer, preacher, even an outside doctor, with not more than one from any one vocation—could tell from the facts what is right. Do you know that only a handful of patients were sent to staff all last year? Why is that? Get us some better doctors or get us a review board, Mr. Smith."

"I'll do what I can, Mr. Donaldson. The gentlemen in Tallahassee are rather set in their ways, you know."

Grandma was not called. Happotine was afraid to talk to Mr. Smith; nevertheless, because of his record the hospital thought he was the ringleader for this investigation and they discharged him.

He was sent to a downstate jail to be held on a minor charge pending against him.

Narrel argued against singling out any attendants for censure. "They're just caught up in the system," he said. "Most of them are all right if they're shown the right way."

The same week that S. Chesterfield Smith was on the ward, a Spanish-speaking doctor came to assist Gumanis. Narrel talked Spanish to him, was presented to staff and discharged. A dozen others were released to the courts. Then the extra doctor was taken away, leaving one doctor for thirteen hundred men just as there had been for eighteen months.

When the legislative committee filed its report, the newspapers summed up their recommendations, some of which mirrored our ideas. But what bothered us was their stating: "The Committee feels that an investigation as to the truth or falsity of particular statements and particular acts is more properly a function of the executive department than of the legislative, and hence has made all portions of its records and files available to the Governor's office for such further detailed investigation by the administrative branch as it may find justified."

To that extent, it meant that the men on the wards had been doublecrossed, having their confidences made available to all politicians.

"We've got a life sentence," Grandma said.

A few days later, I was skimming my newspapers on the porch, right after mail call, in the midst of my morning's work on this book, when Smokey called my attention to an excited group of patients. They were following Mr. Parker and his secretary through the ward. The ward men were griping about the food. Grandma, in the forefront, with his nylon "staff shirt" draped over his shoulders and held closed by two buttons over his breast, grabbed my arm.

"Tell them," Grandma said, "to go through the chow line one time."

"Yes, it wouldn't be a complete investigation without that," I said.

"All right," Parker said, "we will. I know Maude here is game. We came over unexpectedly this morning—it will give us a good chance."

Still we hardly believed it and watched excitedly from the mouth of the T.O.S. as they wound their way toward the steam table among the hundred men ahead of us.

B & E said, "I only hope she doesn't pass out in there."

The two were escorted to the milk table, reserved for a few of the old men who got a mug of milk at each meal. She looked up as I was marching along with my tray and called over: "I know what you mean."

"She's actually eating the stinking stuff," I said to B & E.

The next day for dinner we got steaks as big as a Bible, not the best and cut thin, but nicely browned and chewable. For dessert there was ice cream, big gobs of it, made right there in that building that morning. For supper, besides sliced beef and fresh tomatoes, there was vanilla pudding dipped onto a slice of apple pie. The next day there was marble cake with four-ounce packages of ice cream. For two months we had fruit jello, pork chops, good hash, free-world stew, chocolate cake, lemon cake, molasses cake.

To that extent, it was not a snow job.

Then, surprise of surprises: Doctor O'Connor came up on the ward.

"It's the first time any doctor walked in our rat warren," I said to Grandma.

I went away as O'Connor approached, but Grandma urged me to talk. "He says he wants to do what he can until the legislature acts. Show him that outline."

So I got it from the *House Beautiful* under my mattress and O'Connor led the way to the porch, as patients scattered from the door.

"What is it?" he asked.

"An outline covering the last five years before I was locked up," I said. "At the least, I am entitled to go back to a hospital in my own state."

"Let me see your list. I will give it my consideration."

Then, week followed week with no word from O'Connor. So I wrote Superintendent Rogers that I was going to ask the Supreme Court to return me to New Jersey unless he did something. That resulted in my being fox-trotted up to the psychologist's, only this time not to Davis. I flatly refused to see Davis again, pointing to the "interpretations" sent to the court the previous year.

I have appended the report by Mr. Sam Cunningham. I want to comment on two of his clinical observations. He was amused at my difficulty in reading back my code. There were several reasons for this. It was a totally different script, unlike anything my eyes were accustomed to. I had never found it necessary to read back any of it. I had not used it for better than a year, instead sending my notes out via the grapevine to friends. And last, I stalled, not wanting to read back the names of attendants to Mr. Cunningham.

The other remark of his, that the code "somehow concerned 'toilet paper,'" can be traced to his only half listening and then only half remembering the half he had listened to. I had explained that some patients wrote letters to the Supreme Court on toilet paper, during the time we were not allowed to have paper on the wards. That was when I started carrying my coded notes in a five-cent spiral-bound notebook in my shirt pocket. Cunningham thought it funny that I worried about someone stealing my notes and cashing in on them. I had explained very carefully that it was only to protect myself from punishment, if the notes got read in a shakedown.

In 1961 I thought that the falsities by the staff about me were deliberate pernicious lies. It was some years before I accepted the fact that *some* of their errors were not lies but merely expressions of their *honest* beliefs. This is what hundreds of professional people today are calling a *sickness* of the mental health establishment. In Chattahoochee, the psychologists parroted the psychiatrists. The psychiatrists parroted the commitment papers. The Social Service Director, Ronald O. Pickens, when asked by Doctor Gumanis to look into my claims, "reviewed the medical record of the above named" (meaning Donaldson) and decided "that no residence investigation is indicated." Doctor Rogers called for a report from Doctor O'Connor. O'Connor parroted the psychological report, with a few embroideries of his own: ". . . On admission to this Hospital, examinations showed this patient to express delusions of persecution, for which he blamed rich Republicans. He thought they had stolen many of his good ideas. . . . He also felt they had attempted to poison him by putting chemicals in his food. . . . He believes at times that his letters are not mailed, and that letters are withheld from him, and that people are stealing his short stories, which he feels are valuable. . . ."

As O'Connor, Rogers, and the chief justice did nothing more, I wrote to the governor. Sedge Wicks knew Farris Bryant personally and told me he was an all-right guy. In reading my file in 1974, I see that the governor asked Rogers for a report. He got a copy of the "form letter" from O'Connor.

Next, I asked the governor for his personal intervention to get my release to New Jersey. I received the following reply:

Dear Mr. Donaldson:

Thank you for your letter of July 11, 1961, relative to the problems you are faced with as a patient at the Florida State Hospital.

I am asking Dr. Rogers to assign a member of his staff to discuss your case with you.

Sincerely,
FARRIS BRYANT

Governor

Here was an honest man trying to get something straightened out. Here is how the bureaucrats fixed that idea. At the bottom of the above letter is a note (which was not on my copy in 1961) saying: "We are in receipt of a very lengthy letter from Kenneth Donaldson which bears out exactly the memorandum given to us June 12, 1961, by Dr. J. B. O'Connor. Sincerely, Mal Ogden, Administrative Assistant."

I often wonder if all these good people ever felt that their performances were akin to this observation on historians in *The Education of Henry Adams* (Chapter XXV): "Historians undertake to arrange sequences—called stories, or histories—assuming in silence a relation of cause and effect. These assumptions hidden in the depths of dusty libraries, have been astounding, but commonly unconscious and childlike; so much so, that if any captious critic were to drag them to light, historians would probably reply, with one voice, that they had never supposed themselves required to know what they were talking about."

As nothing ever developed to help me after the pleas by Congressman Rodino and Governor Bryant, and as my follow-up letters went unanswered, is it any wonder that I thought there must be something sinister about the "sound barrier" I could never quite penetrate?

What was one to think? I had been locked up now for four years. Every day, I was being told by those around me, by the attendants and fellow patients, that I was not sick and did not belong locked up. Every week, I sent those facts through the grapevine to some friend up north, some elected official in Florida, or some editor, lawyer, or judge. I knew that many of these people wrote to the hospital inquiring about me. Then they would almost invariably fail to reply to my further entreaties to investigate my detention. I had no idea then why the doctors were turning these people away from me, any more than I knew why they had reported to the Supreme Court something I had not said. In my intense indignation at the time, I was certain they were lying. But there exists the possibility they had not even listened to what I said. Furthermore, no doctor yet had told me to my face in what way I was mentally ill or for what reason I was being held, other than: "You must have done something or you wouldn't be here."

An example of how the doctors extrapolated the symptoms from my commitment papers into more bizarre psychoses on their reports is Gumanis's one-page report, July 27, after he had been assigned to talk to me. It carried this further charming message to Doctor O'Connor: "When this writer tried to explain the situation, he [Donaldson] showed no reasoning and continued to be delusional." How he got all that tucked into the interview, after asking me the three questions and chanting, "That'll be all," I haven't yet been able to figure out.

It was during one of my three-question therapy sessions in those early years that I had complained about being held without getting any treatment. In reply, Gumanis pulled my card out of the three-by-five file and reading off the dates (about seven) said they had been "psychiatric treatment." One of the dates was when he had told me to "drop your pants," the day I had been brought back from the woods.

The fact that we weren't satisfied just to sit there and take our treatment finally aroused the bureaucrats in Tallahassee to ask Doctor Rogers: "What do you want, doctors or buildings?"

Despite the fact that our letters from the wards had shown how money could be saved by hiring good doctors for Chattahoochee and getting patients out, Rogers asked for new buildings.

There followed an interlude of hope, starting with a letter from an Ed Tuber, Post Office Box 357, West Palm Beach: "Hi, Ken, I've gone underground. This is from one of the Boozhwaaaah Club. I have a job here. My union boss lives here. I've taken this box so you can send me things safely. As soon as you get back to Philadelphia I'll forward them."

I had kept copies of all the papers in my case, after having sent out the originals via the grapevine to friends. So, now I felt relieved to have a safe place for everything and I cleared the decks, sending all to Ed Tuber (Damascus). Ed acknowledged receipt of the papers. Then there was silence. But I did not worry. He had proved himself. His promise to get me out was enough.

Nevertheless, it was good to have attendants break my vigil beside the hourglass by screaming: "Visitors! Nonnon Allson! Nonnon Allson!" At a far point in the yard, sitting against a tree, I looked up, decided it wasn't for me, and went on with the book.

From twenty feet, B & E said, "They're calling you, Ken."

"Maybe it's that lying preacher again."

I was taken first to the barbershop for a shave, then to the clothes room for a clean white shirt.

The golden June afternoon had not penetrated the quaint charm of the visitor's room. My grandmother used to pull the shades against the summer like this. I made out two people. A round-faced man in a dark suit was rising from one of the small tables. I was ushered to that table. The man shook hands.

"I've been waiting to meet you," he said. "I'm Doctor Birnbaum."

"Oh!" I squeezed the hand.

"You look fine. I'm surprised that you keep up so well in such an atmosphere."

"Well, it's no credit to my hosts."

"I can believe that. Didn't the investigation do any good?"

"There's improvement. But no heads rolled. You'd never believe that human beings could be so despicable. You'd—"

"Keep your voice down. They're watching you. What I wanted to tell you is that I have a similar case in New York. This man has been locked up for twenty years. He was sick when he was put away, but he's all right now. The case has been in the courts for six years. I've had it from New York to Albany and then back to New York. All I want is somebody to hear the man's story. At last, I got it before a jury. I had it won—I could tell by the way the jury was following me. Then for a clincher, I showed proof that the doctor had been lying. Right there I lost. I saw the change come over their faces. People won't believe that a doctor would lie. You can't say it in court. What these doctors do is copy over from one year to the next whatever is on one's commitment papers. But nobody will believe that. So now I'm starting all over again. What I would like to do is combine your case with the one in New York. That way both would be stronger. Do you have any objection? Would you consent to that?"

"Would I? Man!" Here was the end of the rainbow on a silver platter.

"But bear in mind, Kenneth, that we can't beat the doctors. The most we can hope for is to free you."

"Then I'll finish the job myself—with my book. I'm mad enough to do the job."

"I know you can. You got a writ of habeas corpus where I couldn't. That's one reason I wanted to meet you."

That night, sitting on the plastic chair beside my bed in an eight-bed pen in the new three-story building, I surveyed the present and the future. Around me were comfortable beds and a three-drawer stand between each pair. The walls were pleasant pastels. But there were no windows on the building's ends, east and west, and there were overhangs on the sides to keep out the sun. Into this structure had gone the best psychiatric and architectural planning. Gone were bars, replaced by stainless-steel screens. But, for me, a good sunbath in an open window outweighed all the modernization. Or, as Doctor Birnbaum said, "A bureaucrat is never wrong." If a bureaucrat approved it, it was the best building in the world.

I still thought, in 1961, that a bureaucrat was sometimes right. I thought if I kept telling them that I had not been driven insane but only driven to an insane asylum and that I had looked up at insanity from the bottom of the snake pit and found it to be nothing more than a label from the clinic, that then, finally, someone would believe me. Of labeling, Judge David L. Bazelon has written in *Freedom*, July–August 1974: "What became more and more apparent was that these terms [used in psychiatric labeling] did not rest on disciplined investigation with facts and reasoning as required for the fulfillment of *Durham* [which was Bazelon's ruling exculpating a criminal whose unlawful act resulted from mental illness]. I regret to say they were largely used to cover up the lack of relevance, knowledge and certainties in the practice of institutional psychiatry."

But if the courts of Florida did not listen and others did no more than make a report, was there a way out? "All barriers can be melted through discovery of fact concerning them and communication of such findings to the professions and the public." That was written by Robert S. Shaw, M.D., in *National Health Federation Bulletin*, December 1972. I knew that instinctively in 1961. I would do it through my book. But to get anyone to listen to the book, I had to be outside the green door.

Committee on State Institutions, Florida Legislative Council:

"FINAL REPORT OF GENERAL FINDINGS OF COMMITTEE ON STATE INSTITUTIONS RELATING TO CONDITIONS AT FLORIDA STATE HOSPITAL AND ALLEGED MISTREATMENT OF PATIENTS, MAY 1, 1961"

. . . Some attendants have misused their responsibility . . . buildings of the White Male Department . . . are in a state of complete obsolescence. These facilities were erected for use as an arsenal prior to Florida's admission to the Union in 1834. . . . Criminal patients, sexual psychopaths, elderly feeble and helpless patients and teen-age boys are bunched together in crowded wards . . . the wards are maintained more as detention wards for inmates than they are as hospital wards for the sick. . . .

The major complaints of both patients and attendants include briefly: Choking, beating and teasing of patients, stealing packages, loss of mail, the use of punitive wards such as the squad which existed until a few months ago, prolonged confinement in solitary "strip cells" and the lack of medical treatment and occupational therapy. . . .

. . . It has been common practice for years for attendants to "choke down" disturbed patients for the purpose of subduing them . . . leaves the door wide open for an unscrupulous attendant to "choke a patient completely out" for any cause whatsoever. . . . Teasing of patients is a form of mental cruelty which can be more brutal than an actual beating. . . .

During the interview, a number of non-charge patients expressed feeling of total despair of ever being released from the institution. . . .

The attendant is the key to the patient's welfare. He lives with the patients eight hours a day, knows when patients are upset, and when they are contented, and their change of behavior. However, he is not a means of communication with the doctor who does not have adequate time to devote to each patient. . . . One of the most frequently heard complaints of patients is that of not having received treatment or of not having seen a doctor for periods ranging from as high as six months to two or more years. . . .

Morale, in general, among the attendants is low. There appears to be wide-spread dissatisfaction and unrest because attendants feel they are receiving only bare subsistence wages which range from a minimum of $165.00 per month to a maximum of $192.00. . . .

During the interviews and while filling out the questionaires, many of the attendants manifested considerable outward fear . . . of possible repercussions on the job or the loss of employment . . . some attendants . . . can neither read nor write and many others [are] ill-equipped to adequately administer their responsibilities in the care and treatment of patients. . . .

(I first read this in 1974. K.D.)

PSYCHOLOGICAL EXAMINATION

Kenneth Donaldson, A-25738
Date examined: 6-1-61   Age: 53
Referred by: Dr. Gumanis   Educ: 1½ yrs. college

SUMMARY AND CONCLUSIONS:

This patient has been tested on two previous occasions. He was first seen on 9-19-59,* at which time it was felt that his thinking was paranoid. He was next seen on 7-28-60, and the testing at that time showed "no significant change from the earlier testing."

Present test data fail to show any undue disturbance of association or visual-motor incoordination. His drawings of persons are sketchy and non-contributory. His Rorschach responses are generally of acceptable form quality but some of their content tends to be bizarre. The overall impression gleaned from this test is that he is an emotionally volatile and overly suspicious type individual who is currently rather depressed. It is possible that he would show more deviant test results were he not so guarded and so familiar with the tests.

The impressions one receives regarding the subject's mental status is more definite when clinical observation alone is used to evaluate him. He tells a long and rather involved account of how certain unidentified persons have supposedly harassed him for years. These persons have, according to him, continued this up to the present and he has written a book concerning this. He has also taken notes regarding observations made during his hospitalization, and has written these in some type of "code" unfamiliar to this examiner and evidently none too well known by the patient himself. He was asked to read some of this "code" and was only able to decipher a few words within several minutes. It seems that whatever was written somehow concerned "toilet paper." When judged in the light of a combination of behavior, current beliefs, and test results, this examiner feels that the patient remains incompetent.

TESTS:
Rorschach/Word Association Test/Draw-a-Person/Bender Gestalt/TAT

ATTITUDE AND PSYCHOLOGICAL CHARACTERISTICS:

The patient was oriented and reasonably alert. He denied hallucinations. He discussed the results of prior testing done here and it was obvious that he has seen copies of at least the results of 7-28-60. He was firm in his conviction that he has not been treated fairly by Mr. Davis or Dr. Gumanis.

SC:fd

* Corrected date. K.D.

CHAPTER 11

1962

Science with the Fiction

ON WARD 7, NEW YEAR'S DAY WAS LIKE A SATURDAY. ONE attendant covered both ends of the ward. There was no dental run, no drive to the yard, no Occupational Therapy. Half the men were asleep on their beds. Rather than working on my book, I was lying back, trying to reach some balance in my plans.

All I was seeking was an unbiased investigation of the facts by an outsider. I had never been found nuts by any doctor in an examination outside the walls of a state institution. And it still seemed possible to get one outsider to accept that fact.

A houseman from the other end, a new man, broke into my thoughts: "Off your bed, man. The doctor's on the ward."

B & E went into the aisle. The doctor came straight to me, alone now in the pen. I got up and we stood, backs to the windows.

"How're you doing, Donaldson?" Gumanis's fleshy lips were quite pink.

"I'm surprised I haven't heard from New Jersey—from one of the sanatoriums," I said.

"I couldn't let you go there."

"But you let me write Doctor Birnbaum and he telephoned and got the rates, and you told me to write them."

"I couldn't let those letters go."

I strongly felt he wanted to help me. Yet why had he lied, telling me I could go to a private sanatorium? Was someone higher up countermanding his orders? I learned later that even his letters carried only his initials, below the signature of the clinical director.

Then Gumanis said, "Have one of your children write me. I'll let any of them sign you out."

"How come, then, you wouldn't let me send the money for my older son to come get me when he got out of the navy?"

"I couldn't authorize that much."

"But you could have recommended it to Doctor Rogers."

"Ask your children to write me."

"They wouldn't believe me now. You write for other patients. Would you write them?"

"Why don't you go back with your mother?"

"I couldn't trust her judgment again. I would have let my parents sign me out when I was first here, but not now." I could not forgive their allowing me to be locked up for five years.

Nevertheless, I did get three letters off that day to the children. Some months later I again wrote my daughter, who was married. In October she inquired of the hospital:

> He writes that he isn't sick, so then I wonder what he is doing in the hospital . . . please tell me the facts.

On October 22, 1962, Doctor O'Connor replied:

> He is suffering from a nervous disorder, namely, Schizophrenic Reaction Paranoid Type with a guarded prognosis. If he is released supervision will be required.

Can you picture a young married couple signing a stranger out of the asylum who is liable to run amok with a hatchet?

As for Gumanis, while he was saying one thing to my face: "The only thing wrong with you, Donaldson, is that you are stubborn," here is a Progress Note he put in my file, which is representative of the year:

> 4-3-62: Resides on ward #8 [*sic*], shows no particular changes mentally, he is still delusional and paranoid with impaired judg-

ment. He has no other object in life than his transfer to New Jersey State. Still persists he is a New Jersey resident and refuses to submit to injustice. Continue custodial care. Dr. Gumanis; ml

In those early years, I did not know where to pinpoint the blame. Now, studying the hospital documentation as I write this, I see that the blame for my continued detention could be divided equally between the staff's "deceit and trickery" and their retaliation for my writs. Illustrative of both is their handling of my Social Security money.

A year previously, without assistance from the hospital, I had myself applied for benefits, with a request that payments be sent to my lawyer McSorley in Philadelphia to be administered for the education of my children. Instead, when the Social Security Administration turned my checks over to Rogers, as my guardian, I wrote him. Then followed the great Chattahoochee silence.

The first report to me was given orally by an attendant in the yard. A credit of $104 had been made to my account. This first payment was for several months. A month later I got another $26. But how much more was going to "city hall?"

My further letters of protest to Baltimore, Tallahassee, and the Chattahoochee front office, about giving my money to the hospital, went unheeded until George Preepuss's preferential treatment angered many of us on Ward 7.

"I just heard Preepuss tell Beelzebub," B & E said, "that O'Connor refunded every cent of his Social Security money. Fifteen hundred dollars."

I was incensed. "What's fair for one is fair for all!"

Preepuss had escaped from an asylum in Ohio, where he had bugged out for murder, and had come to Florida with the sole purpose of killing his wife, which he did, then bugging out again to escape the chair. Here he earned favors by doing Gumanis's brainwashing. With his returned money, he bought a deluxe electric razor, an expensive radio, and expensive clothes for wearing on the ward. Many other inmates, bona fide residents of Florida, who owned real estate, automobiles, and pleasure boats, paid nary a cent from their Social Security, so they told me. Most had their checks go directly home, but in some cases like Preepuss's, the hospital received the checks, other patients told me, holding them solely for the patient's personal use.

"... My kids couldn't go to college because Chattahoochee

needed my money for maintenance," I protested to Social Security in Tallahassee, with a copy to the hospital treasurer.

The next day, I was summoned by the administrative assistant to the superintendent, Mr. Paalsgraaf, a short, mild man. Paalsgraaf tried to be pleasant.

"Your check," he said quietly, "is $101 a month. Of that, Chattahoochee takes $75 for maintenance."

"My God!" I said. "That's the worst mammyjamming thing I've heard since I've been here. You can't—"

Mr. Paalsgraaf flew out of his chair behind the desk. "I'm insulted. I'm insulted to have any patient talk to me the way you are. I won't—"

"You're insulted? I'm the one's insulted!"

"Attendant! Attendant!"

The next month, they took $80 from my check.

Also, I was still marked as fair game, one year since the legislative investigation, for deviltry by the attendants. They kept me from the dope stand and library, closing the door in my face. They invented foul stories about me. I felt I could take no more without exploding. Something had to be done quickly. When the state Supreme Court turned me down again, I wrote to Doctor Rogers, saying: ". . . I am sending one last letter to you in the hope that I shall be able to break through official lethargy or city-hall skulduggery (whichever it may be) and reach an intelligent solution to my case."

Rogers happened to come through the ward that week, showing the new building to some visitors. I interrupted his smooth progress and he had the decency to hold back and talk. What doctor did I want to see?

"Anybody but Gumanis," I said.

In the latter part of 1961, the hospital had hired six new doctors. We called them "banana-boat quacks." Two of them had been sent down to learn the O'Connor system under Gumanis. One, Doctor Char, became the medicine supervisor. While he was not my doctor and I was not taking medicine, he had called each man in the department down to get acquainted. After our first meeting the previous year, I wrote him, but he did not call me again. Then on the morning after Rogers walked through the ward, I was on call to see Char for a second time.

I sat in the dressing room for an hour, alone, while Char was closeted with Gumanis. Then Gumanis went up the street.

"You have been 'seek' all your life," were Char's first words to me. "You have spent half your life in state hospitals."

I let that pass, figuring the reasonableness of my story would discount whatever Gumanis had told him. I took some notes from my shirt pocket, which I had jotted down during a restless night. I brought up the first point: "Why should Florida hold me when my home state offered to take me back?"

"What have you got there?" Char asked excitedly, grabbing the small piece of paper. "I can read. I can read. You think you have to read them to me?" His bushy black brows pushed over the tops of his glasses.

"No, no. They are only notes so I wouldn't forget something."

Char read aloud: "last letter, 1957" and "have place to go." His face was triumphant. He gloated, "See, you don't make sense. You can't even write a complete sentence."

I gave up. Another morning wasted. But Char was too excited to restrain himself. Opening my chart to my letter, he said, "See—here—you say you saw me seventeen times. You're seek when you say something like that."

"I have a copy of the letter. Show me where I said that." Pointing it out, he read aloud: " '... when you saw me on seventeenth instant.' That means you thought you saw me seventeen times. So you see for yourself."

"Oh, my God!" I thought. "What have I drawn this hand?" But I kept from laughing, feeling that such a jerk I should be able to find some way to lead.

"In English," I said politely, "that means the current month. That meant the seventeenth of February, the month I wrote it."

"I know what it means," he snapped. "You don't have to tell me. You are seek. Besides, why do you save your letters? What good are they to you?"

Still hoping to salvage something, I said, "Tell me one way in which I am mentally ill."

"I cannot do that. It would take too long. I have tried to explain it to some of the others. I have spent hours—it is a waste of time."

But there was kindness in his voice too. I felt it worth another try: "Look at it this way then. I sleep and eat regularly. I have no crazy ideas. I don't bother people. I'm not nervous. Name just one way in which I am sick."

"I can't."

"Just one way."

"You are seek."

At that moment Gumanis and another new doctor, Fernandez, came in to get Char off the hook.

"Tell me about this book you are writing," said Fernandez. "Have you written one before?"

"One—just before I was locked up—but it was not published."

"I am going to put you to staff next week," Gumanis said.

There is no Progress Note for that interview. But one from the previous year could well serve in its place:

8/30/61. Patient was interviewed today. He had a lengthy (5 pages) letter which was discussed in details. Well written at the beginning of it was becoming disorganized and at the end showed full paranoid content against masons, KKK etc and centering all of his ideation about the fact that he was a "hard-shelled yankee." Patient has absolutely no insight and believed that because he "ate well, sleep good, is not violent to others," etc. should be released from the Hospital. He even denied being mentally ill in the past when he had to be Hospitalized in N.Y. and given a series of E.C.T. Possibility of taking medication was discussed but patient refused and asked no to be "forced to him". He was explained that unless he was convinced of his being mentally ill would probably be of little benefit in his particular case. Possibility of out of state discharge was discussed (two daughters living in Arizona) and patient accepted it. Dr. Char: jwl

Next came a psychological testing by Mr. Cunningham. There was a friendly and perceptive look behind his glasses. It gave the impression of his trying to understand. Here again, I had the feeling I could trust the interviewer and I answered all his questions without reservation; however, I refused to take any tests.

I said, "If you don't know by now, after all those tests I took last summer, whether I'm sane or insane, you never will."

"Don't you want to know if you're a little more sane than last year?"

"That's ridiculous. I wasn't any crazier then than I am now."

"Why did you refuse to see Mr. Davis?"

I told again about the signed statement to the state Supreme Court. Then, while Cunningham took notes, I went over again what I thought had caused my commitment. I maintained there had been a misunderstanding.

At the end I said, "What do you think my chances are?"

"You tell the staff what you've told me and you'll do all right."

Here is what Cunningham put in my file:

Date examined: 4-3-62
SUMMARY AND CONCLUSION:
This patient ... has been found to be emotionally volatile, overly suspicious, depressed, and paranoid. The subject stated that he did not wish to take any tests at this time.... He was willing to talk, however, and expressed the same beliefs that he has maintained for approximately the past ten years....

Then up until staff, which was scheduled for Friday week, I racked my brains for some way to dramatize the case. I settled for a condensed statement of the case, making a dozen copies on looseleaf paper.

Come Friday, I had twenty minutes to study the attractiveness of the lobby of the receiving building, through which I had been hurried one other sunny day, exactly five years, two months, and twenty-two days before. I was sitting in a comfortable chair in the hall with two attendants waiting across the lobby on a sofa. Potted palms nodded lazily by the open windows. A transferee from Raiford had gone into the staff room ahead of me.

One attendant, nodding in my direction, said, "It hain't, is it?"

"Yea you is," retorted the other.

"Jeet jet?" said the first.

Then I had to watch a deputy sheriff from downstate escort another sheep to the far side of the green door. It added repugnance to my tension. I was nervous from hope that it was not all cut and dried, and from righteous indignation that a sane man must go through such a performance. When Gumanis opened the door opposite me, my last thought was, "My mother may think I'm crazy, but I'll face these doctors in a way that would make her proud."

Gumanis seated me in a mahogany armchair beside him at the end of a long table. There were twenty others, including one woman at the far end with Cunningham.

Addressing the table, Gumanis said, "This is Kenneth Donaldson." Turning, he said, "Tell them your story, Donaldson."

I opened a Manila folder and took out the handwritten two-page statements. To Gumanis I said, "May I be allowed to read a statement?"

He got permission from Superintendent Rogers and passed along the copies, although only four doctors took one. Rogers, whose dignity would have graced any boardroom, declined with a smile.

I read calmly: ". . . There have been some heated differences of opinion during my stay here . . . but on mature reflection I pass over those things to more important ones. You have had five years to experiment on me and observe -me; and certain facts remain. . . ." I emphasized that I had not been sick when I came to Florida and that the sanity committee had not seen me before pronouncing me crazy. " 'The *fact* has always been for the [scientist] the one ultimate thing from which there is no appeal, and in the face of which the only possible attitude is a humility almost religious.' " (The quotation is from Stuart Chase, *The Tyranny of Words*.)

In what I thought was an attempt to blacken my character, Doctor O'Connor asked, "Isn't it true that you were in jail for three years before you were committed?"

"No, that isn't so," I said strongly.

Then, in turn, O'Connor called for questions around the table. I saw that Mr. Davis, head psychologist, was not present. That meant one less negative influence. Three or four of the staff had questions on minor details, like where had I worked in Los Angeles and how many children I had.

Then one young doctor asked, "What would you say was the reason for your being here so long?"

I had felt they were going to ask that and I had been considering my answer every hour of the past week.

"The stupidity and indifference of the doctors," I said without waiting.

On it hung my mental integrity, which was more important than an immediate ticket to freedom. It brought only some guarded smiles.

The last question was O'Connor's, "Where is your home in New Jersey?"

"Wherever I choose to hang my hat."

"Oh, I see." O'Connor smiled.

Then I got the sudden inspiration to ask the doctors point-blank why they were holding me. Their politeness and their absence of questions about my supposed illness led me to believe that they had accepted my written statement as true.

I turned to O'Connor for permission to ask this question: "If there is nothing wrong with me, which you doctors seem to admit, is there any reason why you cannot let me go immediately?"

"It's unfair to put it that way," O'Connor said, pouting.

Their complete answer, appended at the end of this chapter as the staff report, together with the psychologist's report, above, is a perfect example of what I call "supplemental insanity." Remember, only three of the nine doctors present, plus Cunningham, had ever seen me before I stepped through the staff-room door for a fifteen-minute hearing.

As soon as I got back to the ward, Gurtrim Wormen, a flat-faced and bulbous-nosed deputy sheriff who slept in Grandma's pen at my back, was called to the superintendent's office. Wormen was being held on criminal homosexual charges. On the ward, every evening, he wrestled the pants off several young men. He returned from the front office in thirty minutes and, standing near me, engaged a neighbor in conversation across the center aisle.

"He wants to hang his hat up there. New Jersey. He's a real lawyer—briefs and all that."

"Indeed!" said the neighbor.

"He thinks he's a hero."

"Really!"

Thus did Gurtrim reveal that somebody above Gumanis was behind part of my harassment. The usual variety of brainwashing in a state institution, as Goffman shows in *Asylums,* consists of lies spread through the wards by the department doctor. And it can be quite effective, I had learned. After the lies have been mangled and multiplied, and flung back at you by a hundred others, you've been bugged, brother!

My *Jersey Journal* (February 28, 1962) happened to run an article on Chinese brainwashing. I saw that it had parallels to what was being done to me. First, the Chinese subjected the prisoner to an emotional assault and continuous interrogation, coupled with tortures, real and threatened. This corresponded to steady questioning by the "rats," the foul stories by the barbers and attendants, and life on the Back Yard plus hints of electroconvulsive therapy and medication. Second, the Chinese gave a period of leniency. A several-months respite before I went to staff corresponded to this. Third, the Chinese asked the prisoner to "confess."

This corresponded to my "opportunity" at staff. Fourth, the Chinese gave "reeducation." As I had failed in the third stage, my captors were starting all over again at point one.

Life on the wards continued its wild fluctuations. Beelzebub put a spoonful of honey into a two-ounce bottle of water and sold it to asthmatic Pedro for one dollar, guaranteeing that a spoonful twice a day would make a Charles Atlas. Pedro had doubts after three weeks of two bottles a week. With gestures, he conveyed the problem to me. Pedro bought no more elixir and Beelzebub told lies to Brother Dean to get Pedro moved. I advised Pedro's mother via the grapevine. Within three days, an order came from the doctor to reinstate Pedro. Beelzebub, demoted to the old wards, shouted revenge at me.

Two days later, mangled Dixie came clomping toward where I was writing propped against a tree. He cursed me out, then without warning aimed a vicious kick at my head, but missed as his twisted left leg crumpled. Thereafter, other inmates and some attendants took up the cursing. On every side, some of the toughest criminals in the state (who were in Chattahoochee for a "rest cure") began to make threats ("We'll break his goddamned legs," et cetera). It was not done to my face, but was a steady dribble of sulphuric acid. These criminals and attendants, largely semiliterate, had all the time in the world to lie around and look for ways to antagonize the "albino."

One day, as I walked down the center aisle, one brainwasher called across the ward to another, "The doctor says the only thing to do is to burn him out." Within days, I noticed some new medication in my food, which caused me to break out in heavy sweats. To an outsider this seems farfetched, for many have told me so. I appealed to Superintendent Rogers, via the grapevine, for help. As the medication continued, I believed then that he approved of it. From the file, I have learned that he merely thought I was nuts.

On the other side of the coin, any analysis of Chattahoochee must include the fact that any attendant, as well as some patients, could get a handful of any kind of pills. I witnessed this myself later, in helping attendants dispense medication. About that time, the newspapers also were telling how inmates controlled all medication at Raiford Prison, including even narcotics. Showing that things have not changed much, here is an item from *Our Town*, New York City, December 6, 1974:

The following is ... an exclusive interview with a former aide at Manhattan State Mental Hospital. ... Medication is distributed by the aides. According to this source, one could give whatever quantity of medication they desire.

From time to time, I kept such things as Postum and powdered milk in plastic containers in the bedside stand. From my physical reactions, I could only deduce that something was maliciously mixed into them when we were in the yard. Other patients experienced the same. All we could do was discontinue our use.

The medicines themselves worked on the sex glands, literally burning a person up. The gonads puffed up, then shrank tight; the breasts swelled, then softened; body hair spurted sporadically; and there were shortness of breath and pain under the breastbone after physical exertion.

Nor could one escape it by giving up the little things which eased the horror of asylum days, for one got it in the mess hall—this in addition to the thrice-weekly dosage of everyone's chow, which seemed apparent from our instantaneous torpor. It could be done by the attendants' spiking the beverage, as they filled the pitchers in a back room. So my pals and I stopped taking seconds. It could be done on the steam table, where the trays moved along the inside, allowing a server to drop a powder into the fourth tray from the end for the fourth man in line. And sometimes, there were trays already made up, sitting on the top of the glass, which the attendant in charge would pass out as he wished.

Although Doctor Gumanis had never called me down to say how staff had come out, a second letter had come to me from the governor, stating that further consideration would be given by the staff of doctors as soon as my condition improved. That left no choice but to keep petitioning the courts. About the time of my appearance at staff, the state Supreme Court turned me down again. Then shortly after staff, Judge G. Harrold Carswell, United States District Court, in Tallahassee, told me for the second time that federal courts could not take cases involving mental illness, even though my petitions kept showing that my case concerned not mental illness but fraud.

I realized by this time that a northern judge would be more apt to see my plight. Thus, as was my right as a citizen of New

Jersey, I filed in the Third Circuit, United States Court of Appeals. The chief justice of the Third Circuit returned the brief with a notation to file it in the Fifth Circuit, which includes Florida.

Instead, which was also my right, I petitioned the Supreme Court of the United States, for the second time. It was put on the docket as #212 Misc., October Term, 1962 (371 U.S. 806). On August 10, I filed a supplemental brief, entitled, "Added Statement":

> I. The original petition in this case left my hands in April 1962. Since that time I have been poisoned persistently by medicine being added surreptitiously to my food which has done irreparable harm. . . .

There was no question in my mind about the clerk's looking at it askance. But that was not the primary factor with me. If I were destined to go down the drain, at least (by God!) I'd have all the facts on record. When the clerk failed to acknowledge the Added Statement, I sent a duplicate. This he returned with notice that it could not be filed. (I fumed on the ward in 1962. In 1974, on December 18, at the Supreme Court, I found the original statement, folded over, with a red rubberband around it, in the manila folder for case No. 212. Thus, some bureaucrat had defied his boss to keep that part of the record intact.) On the first day of the October Term, the court declined to hear my plea, along with a thousand others.

While I was waiting on the courts, Grandma asked one day, "Have you heard from Narrel?"

"Not since last summer," I said.

"Maybe he ran out on us again."

"He must be sick. I'll write the sheriff." When the sheriff did not reply, after some weeks I wrote the chief of police. An immediate reply said, "Narrel Damascus dropped dead on the job last Thanksgiving week."

"That's only six months after he left here," I said.

A request for his widow's address, as I wanted my papers forwarded, brought this further reply from the police: "Mr. Damascus's widow says that she destroyed all his papers. She has since moved and left no forwarding address."

"That stinks, doesn't it?" I said.

"Here's a piece," Grandma said, "that I clipped from the

Tribune a couple of weeks ago. It says that a Mrs. Rose Damascus, native of Tampa, was found shot to death in her furnished room. No motive is known for the shooting."

With Narrel gone, who was there to help us?

Could we expect help from a relative? The following from my younger son was typical of many relatives' reactions: "Take it up with your doctor. . . . Don't you have an investigating committee in your state?"

As for looking to the courts for help, besides my own experience, other people have shown the hopelessness there. And Doctor Birnbaum says that most courts and civil rights organizations go all out to see that criminals get habeas corpus, but toward mental patients they are "sanist."

In my case, that left only the hope that one of the hospital doctors might help me. Unfortunately, the one who had shown the most sympathy for me, Doctor Rogers, was at that moment volunteering damaging material to Tallahassee. Violating his own rule of confidentiality of the patient's record, Rogers wrote Mr. Mal Ogden, administrative assistant to the governor:

> I thought you would be interested in the attached letter I received from Kenneth Donaldson since you frequently receive letters from him. . . .
>
> This is the first time to my knowledge that he has expressed delusions such as stated in this letter which had reference to chemicals being added to his food.
>
> We received a letter from his parents recently inquiring about him, stating they had received two letters from him recently and referring to the fact that they were not pleasant letters.

Assuming for the moment that there was no ulterior motive of wanting to poison the thoughts of anyone in the governor's office who might be willing to look into my case, and assuming further that there was an overpowering reason for breaking the hospital's rule of confidentiality, what have we then except Rogers's compulsion to prove to the nonmedical world that hospital doctors are infallible?

In an effort to counteract all the letters from inmates, broadcast throughout the state, Rogers allowed the *Times-Union* to send a reporter and a photographer to do a piece for its Sunday supplement.

As illustrative of the need for such a large human warehouse, Doctor Rogers took the men to the round dance in "Lunacy" Hall. The newsmen were captivated by the fanciful steps of the Mad Russian, as he was called on the wards, an impecunious immigrant who had hocked his employer's tools for fifty dollars and been sent up for treatment. Gumanis took him off pills after three months. The Mad Russian was shining for the cameraman. His sunny disposition just would not be suppressed. He let go his partner's hand at each end of the dance floor, assumed a crouch and sprang twirling to land beside her other hand.

"He thinks he's on the Bolshoi stage," Superintendent Rogers said, offering a most acute scientific diagnosis.

The *Times-Union* reported it just like that, science with the fiction.

(I first read this in 1974. K.D.)

Mr. Kenneth Donaldson A-25738
GENERAL STAFF CONFERENCE:
April 6, 1962

Doctor Gumanis:
SUMMARY: This is the case of Kenneth Donaldson, white male, age 54, who was committed from Pinellas County on January 3, 1957, and admitted to Florida State Hospital on January 15, 1957.

Past history indicates he was born in Erie, Pennsylvania, on May 1, 1906, and had lived in Florida four years prior to his commitment. [**I was born May 22, 1908, and had never been a legal resident of Florida. It was my parents who lived in the state for four years. This is the kind of factual error the doctors refused to correct, insisting that I was out of touch with reality— one of their definitions of insanity.**] His occupation is listed as painter and carpenter. He was hospitalized at the Marcy State Hospital in New York during 1943 for a period of three months and received ECT. He was diagnosed Dementia Praecox, Paranoid Type.

On the Receiving Service in Florida State Hospital, he was delusional and paranoid, with defective insight and judgment. He believed that the Republicans had stolen many of his good ideas which he had recommended to the Foreign Police [*sic*] Association. He also felt that they had attempted to poison him by putting chemicals in his food.

On the General Wards he refuses his medication, and spends most of his time writing letters to various officials and demanding his transfer to a New Jersey or a Pennsylvania State Hospital. Otherwise, he is cooperative and has caused no other trouble.

Doctor Gumanis: He is being presented today for evaulation and further disposition of his case. He refuses to be furloughed to his parents and definitely does not answer any of their letters.

POST STAFF DICTATION: The summary is as given. Kenneth Donaldson has been ill for the last fifteen years. He was hospitalized in the Marcy State Hospital in New York during 1943 for a period of three months and received ECT, and when released was on convalescent status. On admission here he was still delusional and paranoid, insight and judgment defective, expressed ideas of reference and other delusions. He spends most of his time writing letters to various officials, and I believe he enjoys doing this. The writer believes patient is still psychotic and should remain in the hospital.

Mr. Cunningham: I believe this patient still has a paranoid psychosis and should remain here.

Doctor Ojeda: I agree with the examiner. I am of the opinion that efforts should be made in order to treat this patient with some intensive treatment and medication.

Doctor Fernandez: I agree.

Doctor Erdag: I agree that this patient needs treatment, although he refuses it. He should remain here.

Doctor Mussa: I agree.

Doctor Rich: I agree with Doctor Gumanis.

Doctor Hanenson: I agree with the examiner.

Doctor Rogers: I agree.
Doctor O'Connor: I agree.
CONSENSUS OF OPINION: HOLD.
DIAGNOSIS: SCHIZOPHRENIC REACTION, PARANOID TYPE.

IN THE COURTS, 1962

(iv)

Supreme Court of the State of Florida   March 1962

My petition for writ of habeas corpus was denied without a hearing and without calling for papers from the state.

(v)

U.S. District Court, Northern District of Florida   April 1962

My petition for writ of habeas corpus was denied without a hearing and without calling for papers from the state.

The United States Court of Appeals, Third Circuit, returned my petition (same petition as above) with instructions to file in the Fifth Circuit.

(vi)

Supreme Court of the United States   No. 371 U.S. 806
                                                      4/23/62

My petition for writ of habeas corpus was denied on the first day of October Term, without a hearing and without calling for papers from the state.

CHAPTER 12

1963

". . . a heap of ruins." Job

PREEPUSS, THE WINNINGEST POKER PLAYER, CAME FORTY MILES PER hour down the center aisle and into his pen at the end of the ward across the aisle from where B & E and I were standing. At thirty per, came the little Greek and grabbed Preepuss off the bed. So far, the only sound had been the whoosh as they went by. Preepuss managed to push his opponent back about five feet. Both were featherweights, but Preepuss had twenty years on the Greek, whose narrow brown face was crossed with tight creases. But the Greek swung an uppercut and stepped deftly aside, letting Preepuss fall flat on his face like a frozen log. It was then we saw the coffee jar in the Greek's fist.

No one had tackled Preepuss before. Because of his pull with Gumanis, fighting with him meant punishment. But the Greek, in losing a large sum, had become incensed at the odd way the winning cards kept repeating.

The evening attendant, J. Billings, a mighty hog caller, watching from the dayroom, dispatched his particular tool in the ward system to investigate. This was Frederick Leccatt, armed robber, convicted rapist, and two-time assaulter of police officers. He chased the Greek into Billings's arms. Billings held the struggling, screaming man at arm's length while the two-hundred-pound convict beat him. Then the attendant dropped the body and the goon jumped up and down on it to prepare it for the operating table.

Our protests to the evening supervisor and the doctor resulted in the transfer of Billings to another ward.

A small victory but larger defeats. I was going through a physical change. Like all my friends on the wards, we were wasting away. Like a hundred thousand others in state warehouses across the nation, we were all dying.

One-third of all the men and women "admitted for the first time to a psychiatric institution died within that institution within three years ... 19%, almost one out of every five inpatients, were separated from a psychiatric institution by death." Thus spoke Prof. Edward S. Sulzer, University of Minnesota, at the second national convention of the American Conference of Therapeutic Selfhelp Clubs, on June 22, 1962.

Sufficient to cause these premature deaths, not counting the deficient food and the TB-inducing confinement, was stress. Noise, fatigue, fear, frustration were victors on the wards. But *"no matter what the stress, the same type of internal wreckage resulted,"* reports Dr. Hans Selye ("How to Avoid Harmful Stress," *Reader's Digest,* July 1970). He found that in rats, "Blood pressure and blood sugar rise, stomach acid increases, arteries tighten. ... In animals under emotional stress, fats are drawn from body deposits, emptied into the blood and deposited along artery walls. Presumably, the same thing happens in man, producing those top killers, atherosclerosis and coronary-artery disease."

To stop my downhill slide, I would have to get out soon. To get out, I would have to change my way of fighting. The hardest inner struggle the fifteen years gave me was in turning my life around and carrying on a covert fight. How far should one stoop to win? It was a temptation to fight fire with fire. But it was more important, it was vitally important to hold onto some of the virtues of the free-world people I respected. I refused to play it dirty. You won't find a lie from my hands in this book. This was one war that I painfully decided could not be fought any other way.

Those of us who did live through those darker years were stubborn men, too stubborn to say "die." Without stubbornness, the body literally lies down and gives up the ghost. It happened before our eyes. Laughter helped us too. We kept our sanity by laughing at our oppressors; though more and more we learned to pull our horns in and to confine our innocent horseplay among ourselves and confine our not-so-innocent aspersions on the khaki-clads to the remoter corners of the yard. For a rare few of us, the absence of "prescribed" medication meant our chance for survival. Also, to Christian Science I give full credit for my pulling through. I had a peace of mind that no outside force could change.

Several astute people have added one more thing: my fierce determination to write this book.

In 1963, on the wards, we couldn't keep all those things in mind. We lived from one hour to the next. My friends now understand why I can't visit a zoo with pleasure. In Chattahoochee we lived in aimless pacing *plus* stress.

As the periods shortened between my days of excessive weakness, I took up my Bible and, for the first time since I had been turned around by Odessa Stronth, I read the 91st Psalm. "He that dwelleth in the secret place of the most High shall abide under the shadow of the Almighty." It carried me, though I stopped on the landings for a breath, up the three flights of stairs without a whimper.

Doctor Sulzer had said: "Now, one might ask, is it not better for a person to be thought of as mentally ill in our society than to be thought of as a criminal. I would raise very serious doubts about that. In criminal law in this country, there are many safeguards afforded the individual who is accused of committing a crime. On the whole, the very same safeguards are *not* afforded to the person accused of being mentally ill. . . . Our true second-class citizen is the psychiatric patient."

Many of the criminals in Chattahoochee were not there from personal choice. I respect them for that.

Some were on the wards because of uncritical public and official reaction to bizarre crimes. One typical story says: "'This is one of the most brutal crimes on record here,' a senior police official said. "It must have been carried out by mentally deranged persons.'" That is from United Press International wires on December 27, 1974. There would be a similar story to be found every day from January to December. And over and over again, we would see vicious criminals taking as their successful defense the public's horrified reaction to the crimes—the defense of insanity.

Some criminals were on the wards because of borderline doubt by judges and prosecutors. The judge, David L. Bazelon, who tried to resolve this problem in his famous *Durham* rule, has this to say about it. He writes (*Freedom,* July–August 1974): "The experiment undertaken by my court in its 1954 decision in *Durham* v. *United States* is a real lesson in this regard. That case involved formulation of a new test of criminal responsibility: it held that an accused is not criminally responsible, if his unlawful act was the product of a mental disease or defect. *Durham*'s purpose was to grant the psychiatrist his hundred-year-old request to be allowed to tell what he knows and (just as importantly) what he does *not know* about the phenomenon of human behavior—rather than face demands for conclusions resting on ethical, moral and legal considerations." But it has not worked, Bazelon said, because the psychiatrists have got lost in a forest of meaningless terms. "In 1970 I commended the behavioral scientists for caring about people in distress but I warned them of the dangers in playing wizard to society's problem for which they had no expertise. The issue was not whether the behavioral scientists were good, but what they were good at!"

John Irwin, Ph.D., a San Francisco State College professor and ex-convict, said (*Christian Science Monitor,* July 19, 1971): "It is necessary to return to a focus on crime, not the man. We don't have sick people, but rather people who commit criminal acts. They don't differ significantly from a random sample of the population."

That thinking was subscribed to by many of the criminals on my wards. That is why they were "criminals" while the rest of us were "patients."

Altogether, criminals comprised about one-third of my wards. Among them was a small group who used the state hospital to make a mockery of justice. They were the recidivists, the bank robbers, assaulters of police, mobsters. Their crimes were not cured by Doctor Gumanis's pills; however, because they were not psychotic, the doctors released them. Back downstate, or up in New York City or Chicago, if they happened to be picked up in another crime, they could not be prosecuted because they had a record of incompetency. This is one of several revolving-door situations in our state hospital and prison systems where it would be interesting to study the application of a new recommendation for barring psychiatric testimony in the courtroom. This was broached in an article in *California Law Review* by lawyers Ennis and Litwack, 1974. It states that "psychiatrists have bitten off more than they can chew. . . . Human behavior is difficult to understand and, at present, impossible to predict. Subject to constitutional limitations, the decision to deprive another human of liberty is not a psychiatric judgment but a social judgment."

Another group of criminals who were making a mockery of justice were the professed homosexuals. They seemed to rate an automatic ticket to the hospital in Florida, although few of the ones I met on the wards had committed crimes of violence. Their most striking characteristic was a lack of truthfulness. It seemed necessary for them to lie about such mundane things as the time of day.

I talked about these things, one time, with Grandma, who was a gifted and intelligent soul. I had been voicing my annoyance with the homo-wrestlers, who held the "sound stage" from 6:00 to 8:00 every evening. Gurtrim Wormen would go down the line of his harem, noisily wrestling the pants off each, until his black moustache glistened with sweat.

Wormen had been declared incompetent after having hijacked furniture and, with unnamed parties, opened a furniture store one block from the jail.

"Maybe Wormen slept with the sheriff," I said to Grandma.

"That would not be unheard of," Grandma said. "You know many men are bisexual. I am."

"Does that make them incompetent?"

"No—and they are entitled to their rights just the same as anyone else. Even Gumanis says that." Grandma pulled a page of *Time* from one of the constantly worked-over piles on his bed. "I've been saving this to show you. The *M'Naghten* rule, telling right from wrong, has been supplanted by the *Durham* rule: 'a prisoner should not be held culpable if his unlawful act is the product of a mental disease or defect.' So you see, under modern diagnosing, Gurtrim is entitled to come up here rather than go to jail."

"The latrine gossip is that Wormen split the furniture profit three ways with the chief of police and the sheriff. To get him out of circulation until things cooled, the state's attorney put him in Chattahoochee on homo charges. Which rule does that come under?" I demanded.

"It's not wrong to be bisexual."

Grandma's views anticipated the American Psychiatric Asso-

ciation's vote in 1974 that homosexuality was not a mental disease
and that no person should be committed to a mental institution
simply because of homosexuality.

Grandma reached under his mattress and pulled out a
diagram. "This is an octopus. This is also the state of Florida. It
reaches into every corner of the state. It funnels enough men here
every year to give some politicians a good living. Take my case.
Should I be locked up in Chattahoochee for seven years because I
had a heart attack in jail and asked to come here for a rest? Or
because I'm bisexual? But that's no crime in England. And it has
been practiced and enjoyed in Greece and Egypt—way before
biblical times." Grandma's words spouted. "And that big boob,
Billings, laughing because Nassy and Gurtrim bought a jar of
vaseline at the dope stand. 'Weddin' jelly,' he called it."

The pressures of confinement were working on the attendants
too. I was beginning to see the wisdom in Narrel Damascus's
saying not to single out attendants for blame, when I read Doctor
Irwin's words: "If we had a less brutal system, the guards' behavior
would be different. Even Christian monks would behave the same
cruel way as guards if you erected a system which necessarily treats
the client as a person without rights or dignity and will only grant
him privileges if he becomes a compliant, sniveling being. You
turn him into a hostile hating person. . . ."

Guards, criminals, "patients," in state prison or state hospital,
all were haters. And as mental illness has been shown to be
contagious, so it was spilling over onto the doctors too. Doctors
Gumanis and O'Connor were haters as well.

This hatred was making me do drastic things. Hatred in
retaliation of the barbers' hazing, for one thing, made me decide
not to go to the barbershop again. Tediously, for several years, I
clipped my hair (four hairs at a time) with nail clippers on the
ward.

As always, there was some palliative. About this time, the
Tampa *Tribune* was printing a four-column picture of the "Bloomer
Girl" (Mrs. Nell Foster Rogers) in her knickers and tennis shoes.
They called her a one-man lobby at the annual legislative session.
For ten years she had been working for better laws to protect the
rights of the *patients* in the state's institutions.

B & E hurried over to show it to me. Grandma joined in,
"Now you write her again, Kenneth."

I said, "They mean all right, but they all turn out the same."

"There are exceptions," Grandma said. "See, here she gives the average outsider's view of a patient." Grandma read: " 'Of course, the humane thing is to put him someplace and do something for him. And if we taxpayers are too poor to provide better, at least we rest in the knowledge we are doing all in our power to help these unfortunates.' "

Nonetheless I wrote, and surprisingly the Bloomer Girl replied, telling me that a lawyer downstate, Basil H. Pollitt, would get in touch.

During the following week, the new ward boss, Yillabar, a big man with pink skull showing through very thin brown, was making the rounds to get acquainted.

"How's your book coming?" he said.

"Slow," I said.

"I noticed you're not writing so much these last two weeks. You've got good learning, Kenneth—I don't see why they keep you here."

"If I could just get somebody outside to believe that," I said.

Then a letter came from lawyer Pollitt, Miami. Yillabar, watching the lines ease between my eyes, said, "Good news?"

"Looks like I've got a lawyer."

Mailman Airtrane said, "There's one guy deserves a break. Can you figure it, Yill?"

Pollitt, in response to the Bloomer Girl's urging, was putting my case before the state Supreme Court. The only fee would be twenty dollars for filing, which I sent in two payments through my private mail, together with the requested complete outline of my case.

Three pleasant weeks followed, that is, pleasant for an insane asylum. Each morning I would carry my manuscript to the yard between the pages of a newspaper inside my shirt, and after walking with B & E for an hour before the dust was dry from the dew, I would go to work on one of the benches tipped against the fence, as far from the buildings as I could. One day, I was narrating the tale of murder in a small Negro home in Walterboro, South Carolina, which I had come upon in my canvassing. I was again on the front porch, looking through the screen at the mother wiping her eyes on her flowered apron as she told of a deputy sheriff breaking through the screen door, knocking her down without provocation, then shooting her boy.

Now, something new was being added, an interruption directly behind me, breathing down my shoulder. A young curly-haired attendant said contemptuously, "What you doing—writing about niggers?"

I said, "I didn't know you could read."

"No wonder they got you locked in—writing about niggers!"

In three weeks a large Manila envelope came from the attorney general in Tallahassee: "Your lawyer has withdrawn from your case, and so I am sending you the papers, which he says are of no value to him." There was a copy of the state's response to my 1960 petition and copies of the statutes on commitments. The latter was pure gold. But my blood pressure was already up.

"This really stinks," I said.

"I know the breed," Grandma said. "It's the octopus—the whole state."

Then a letter from Pollitt made me think Grandma was right. It said, quoted from memory: "You said no doctor saw you and that you did not have an attorney before you were committed, whereas the state's brief shows the direct opposite. I certainly am not going to waste my time trying to represent someone who cannot be truthful. Please do not send me any more money. I am returning the ten dollars to your daughter."

I was still seething when I found myself being escorted up the street. One's heart was up the throat at times like this. Was I going for shock at the receiving ward? No, we turned into the "hospital." Surgery? Lobotomy?

A registered nurse led me to a small colonial parlor with white woodwork and dark shiny desk.

Doctor O'Connor came in. As soon as we were alone, he got up and reached across the desk to shake hands. I was so relieved after expecting shock treatments that Satan himself looked like a blood brother.

"Please be seated," he said. "I have a communication from a Mr. Basil H. Pollitt, a lawyer, who says you asked him to represent you, and he has notified you that under the state laws he is not allowed to do so, and he says that you are sending him money and that if I cannot stop you from sending him money he will take action through the courts to stop you. Is this true, Mr. Donaldson?"

"Why that good-for-nothing!"

Then O'Connor quizzed me on the details.

"I'll tell him just what you said."

And I see from the hospital record that he did, this one time, report it honestly.

Parting, the spotless doctor rose again and reached across and shook hands.

Back on the ward, I told Grandma that I felt like washing my hands every five minutes.

"It's the octopus," Grandma said.

"I bet O'Connor's laughing now. They really are sharp—turning a guy against the first person who steps in to help."

But Grandma made the correct observation: "He wasn't much help when he wrote that letter."

It sums up as one more example of sanism. Outsiders, even those who should know better, like Pollitt who was once a patient, these outsiders simply would not take a patient's word against the typed page of the record.

There continued to be similar reactions, no matter in what direction my letters turned. The postal inspector in Atlanta returned my letters to the hospital with this remark: "If you would care to comment as to the reliability of Mr. Donaldson's complaint. ..." The hospital's reply spoke of their "expenditure of a considerable amount of time investigating all of his frequent and multiple complaints." Would typing a two-page letter be a considerable amount?

For Mr. Terry C. Lee, Coordinator of State Institutions, who promised both the Bloomer Girl and the Senate Committee on State Institutions to make a thorough investigation of my claims of out-of-state citizenship, the hospital itself conducted the whole investigation, to the considerable amount of a standardized two-page letter: "... The papers stated he had been a resident of Florida for four years ... [and] he will require hospital care for an indefinite time."

While I did not read the above correspondence until 1974, I surmised correctly, in 1963, what was going on. On the wards we said the hospital was lying. Doctor Birnbaum told me later, it was the workings of bureaucracy. When we finally were to get my case in court, the jury would make the correct evaluation.

Little of this frustration happened to patients from the neighborhood. In weekly visits their families could see how things stood. The doctor had to admit these men recovered quickly and he let them be signed out. But for B & E, Carter, Grandma, and me, it seemed hopeless, finding a way out from behind a life sentence; until on May 22 a remarkable happening changed things. The newspapers reported four new laws, which had been guided through the legislature by a representative from Jacksonville, the Hon. George B. Stallings, Jr., benefiting inmates of state institutions. Several criminals got out overnight, after their families hired new lawyers.

One of the new laws provided for a writ of habeas corpus for any patient, either on his own petition or someone else's, who had been committed through fraud. In a petition dated May 23, I addressed the Gadsden County Court, Quincy. Hearing nothing from them, on August 15 I petitioned the Circuit Court, in Quincy, pointing out that I was too poor to get a lawyer and that the bar association in Tallahassee had ignored three letters from me. I provided an honest recital of the fraudulent acts in my case, the identical simple recital of the facts which I used in every petition from the first to the last. On August 28 the Circuit Court ruled there was "a lack of any right on the part of the Petitioner for a discharge from the Florida State Hospital." How would they know that, without considering my proof in open court?

Still, on Ward 7, we thought there must be a judge in Florida who would listen. So I petitioned the District Court of Appeal, then the Supreme Court. Results were the same in every court.

But hope, even for the lowest of men, even for the victims of Auschwitz, has nine lives. Even in the darkness of Ward 7, hope dared to show again. On the letters page of the *Post-Standard* was one in memory of William Moore, founder of the American Conference of Therapeutic Selfhelp Clubs (ACT). It was signed by Shirley Burghard, R.N., acting executive director. I sent a letter to Miss Burghard. Was there any way ACT could help me? She sent my letter to her friend Mrs. Olive Felt Kennedy, who was founder of Helping Hands, Inc., a halfway house in Minneapolis for expatients.

Helping Hands agreed to send someone down to escort me to Minneapolis. There was enough in my office account to pay for all transportation, plus a couple of months at the house if that were necessary, plus my continuing Social Security checks if I could not find work. Doctor Gumanis approved the arrangements. My mother said okay. Doctor O'Connor met me in Joe Flake's office and personally approved sending $100 from my account, for my daughter's holding for forwarding to Helping Hands. But, the hospital wrote Helping Hands: "Should he be released from this hospital, he will require very strict supervision, which he would not tolerate. Such a release would be to the parents." Even supposing I had needed supervision, my parents said they were not well enough to give it and Helping Hands was equipped for just that, including daily psychological and psychiatric counseling. Who countermanded O'Connor?

How were the doctors reacting, otherwise, to all this activity on my part? Doctor Gumanis made this Progress Note (9/4/63): "Patient was denied a petition of Habeas Corpus and he shows no improvement mentally."

The "Summary and Conclusions" of the psychological examination was written by Julian C. Davis (12/16/63): "This patient refused to come in for interview. According to the Psychiatric Aide who talked to him, the patient stated that the Examiner is a liar. . . ."

Those reports would not have surprised us on Ward 7 nor deterred our activity. Everyone was writing Representative Stallings. I wrote him for the third time while my petition was before the Supreme Court. It was the day I watched the spectacle of President Kennedy's funeral, the only time I broke my vow about TV. I was so caught up in the movement and majesty of the moment, I felt that my childhood visions of the promises of justice for all would certainly meet responsiveness, even in 1963, if I but kept seeking. I wrote Stallings:

> For seven years I have been pushed around by writhing liars. Are the ranks of the law-abiding in Florida so thin that no one dares publicly to reach into the pit that is Chattahoochee to rescue an honest man?

On the last day of the year, Mr. Stallings, under age forty, a tall erudite gentleman of the southern school, visited me. We met in the office next to Doctor Gumanis's and I saw there were open grilles at floor and ceiling between offices. Gumanis was in his.

Mr. Stallings rose from the desk to shake hands, saying, "I want you to know, Mr. Donaldson, there are honest people in this state. And I have taken your case before the others because you have been the most persistent. I want you to go to staff again, as a first step."

"I would rather not," I said.

"You think it's cut and dried?"

"Yes. Besides, they could let me go without staff."

"It's worth a try. Furthermore, I'll write a letter to the superintendent and put a duplicate on file with the Speaker of the House, so the doctors will know we mean business. If they don't pass you, we'll get a doctor and go to court. First, though, I want you to promise me one thing—that you'll come to work in my office. We'll get to the bottom of this and you'll help me get these others out. Will you do that?"

I was not about to turn down a seat in paradise.

IN THE COURTS, 1963

(When the state grand jury ignored me, I wrote to the United States Attorney: ". . . When a man loses his constitutional rights thru the fraud of public officials, is not that a matter for the federal grand jury, especially after state officials refuse to investigate?"

(The reply was a letter from Clinton Ashmore, United States Attorney, to Dr. W. D. Rogers: "We have received a number of letters from this inmate stating that he is falsely imprisoned and other abuses visited on him. No doubt the subject's mental condition is such that he is psychotic in some respects. I would appreciate so much if you would give us a copy of your mental findings on this person. . . .")

(vii)

Gadsden County Court   5/23/63

This is the court of original jurisdiction for noncriminal patients in Chattahoochee. The judge, Hon. H. Y. Reynolds, ignored my petition for writ of habeas corpus.

(viii)

Circuit Court in and for Gadsden County   8/15/63

My petition for writ of habeas corpus was denied without a hearing and without calling for papers from the state. The judge, the Hon. Hugh M. Taylor, said: ". . . The petitioner seeks a writ of habeas corpus on the ground that he was committed to the Florida State Hospital through fraud and yet no facts constituting fraud are alleged. . . ." [!]

(ix)

District Court of Appeal,   9/5/63
First District of Florida

My petition for writ of habeas corpus was denied without a hearing and without calling for papers from the state.

(x)

Supreme Court of the State of Florida   10/31/63

My petition for writ of habeas corpus was denied without a hearing and without calling for papers from the state.

CHAPTER 13

1964 ✶

No Question about Agreeing

WHEN I GOT BACK TO THE WARD FROM THE PSYCHOLOGIST'S, B & E said, "The psychologist can write your ticket with one word."

"But the fact that he certified me for staff must mean I passed," I said.

"That doesn't mean he thinks you're sane. This is Chattahoochee."

That made me think of one of psychologist Cunningham's implications, that I had used code to keep attendants from stealing my ideas. Had he really—

Just then, a shattering "you son of a mammyjamming bitch!" rang out above the squawk of the idiot box. Huey-the-Bluey was improved enough to be advanced from the Back Yard. The path of my thoughts turned to watch his walk to his bed. His hands, flappingly turned out, represented the total degradation of an individuality, a mind shrugging its shoulders after its pithless cry.

A visitor seeing Huey-the-Bluey (had a visitor been allowed on the wards) would have got the impression that the place was an asylum and that we must all be crazy to be locked up with such a patient. But the doctors at staff, wouldn't they be able to see a difference between Huey and me? have proper judgment (which was their own favorite term)?

With these questions in mind, I went to staff. The following entry in my journal gives the doctors' performance:

9 JAN. 1964

I was not in the least nervous. All week the words of Sophocles had been foremost in my mind: "Truth is always the strongest argument." I was prepared to answer the doctors' every question honestly and fully . . . and if it got down to a point-blank question of what I thought of them, I was ready to answer that too. . . . This time I hoped that the influence of Representative Stallings would be enough to see me through successfully.

Doctor Gumanis called me in as the first case. When we were seated, he and I at the end of the long table facing about eighteen men, Gumanis said, "Tell these men your story."

Me: "I'll tell them what I told you last week: I came up here two years ago and told an honest and straightforward story and you refused to believe me. If you wouldn't believe me then I can't see how you would believe me now . . . but I am willing to answer any of your questions to the best of my ability."

Doctor O'Connor and another doctor asked questions about my work, then O'Connor said, "You weren't working up north, so you came down here?"

Me: "No, I was working up north."

At this point I tried to bring up the question that O'Connor had used to poison the minds of the other doctors two years previously: Isn't it true that you were in jail for three years before you were committed? However, O'Connor prevented it.

Other topics that came up included the following, not necessarily in this order:

Gumanis: "What about your mother?"
O'C: "You weren't corresponding with her?"
G: "Would you accept a furlough to her?"
Me: "I would never trust her judgment again. I don't hate her and I'd never hurt her, but I surely could not go with her. I tried to explain the true picture to her but she refuses to believe me. And only two months ago she got word from the hospital that I hadn't

changed a bit since the day I was committed." [I remarked forcefully on the accuracy of that diagnosis.] "Also, she was told that I needed twenty-four-hours-a-day supervision at this time—which is not so."

G: "Didn't you have a halfway house in Philadelphia to go to?"

Me: "Yes—in Minneapolis [but somebody behind the scenes blocked it] . . . but I would rather go out on my own."

G: "What would you do if we released you?"

Me: "I would first of all like to make a phone call to Representative Stallings to see if he wants me to come to Jacksonville at this time to help him." [While this was an honest statement of exactly what I wanted to do and which I could not very well have asked permission for later on if not included now, still in a sudden spirit of orneriness I left it hanging as an implied threat to whatever guilt possessed their souls. However, at no time during the hearing did I feel any levity or try to make a joke of anything. I was completely serious . . .] "Then, if he did not want me now, I would go directly to Syracuse. I would get a part-time job, if one were available, and work on my book."

Cunningham: "Is any of your book written in code?"

Me: "No."

G: "Have you shown it to a publisher yet?"

Me: "No, none of it is ready yet."

Questioner (from far end of table): "What do you think is the underlying reason you have been held so long?"

Me: "It is impossible for anyone to get out of here without outside help. Those with charges or those from Raiford [State Penitentiary] can be released to the authorities—but for people like me—they can't get out until someone comes for them."

G (excitedly): "What do you mean? nobody can get out of here? Why—last year we let 250 go! Would you call that nobody—250?"

Me: "Yes, on furlough."

G (angrily): "Sure—on furlough! That's going, isn't it?"

Me: "That's what I said—those on furlough had someone—"

(Gumanis drowned me out, then piped down.)

Me (to questioner at far end): "Do you understand my answer?"

Questioner: "Yes. What would you say was the cause of this condition?"

Me: "Stupidity and indifference." [There were knowing looks passed at the table and faint smiles between some neighbors. I could have rounded this out with "dishonesty, arrogance, and facetiousness," but the former two are the principal ones.]

Doctor Dunin (seated first on the left): "Were you in a mental hospital before?"

Me: "Yes, in New York State twenty years ago."

D: "Were you committed by a judge?"

Me: "No." [I have since, in 1972, learned that an Onondaga County judge did sign my commitment papers for Marcy.]

D: "Explain what happened."

Me: "I blacked out one night. . . . I was given treatment and released after three months to my wife. . . ."

D: "Would you say you were ever mentally ill?"

Me: "No."

D: "But you were committed to a hospital after examination by doctors, weren't you?"

Me: "Yes, for two minutes by one doctor."

D: "But you were committed by a judge?"

Me: "No."

D: "But you were examined by two doctors?"

Me: "No—one doctor—but the examination was like here—two minutes or less. The hospitals in New York were in poor condition at that time—just like Chattahoochee now. Doctor Gumanis can tell you—he was there then."

There was silence. There was no smile on the face of Mr. Cunningham, who was representing the psychology department in the absence of Mr. Davis [though the latter is listed in the report].

Next, one of the banana-boat quackiatrists asked what I thought of Dr. Char, who incidentally was absent. As I had seen Char twice after that disastrous interview and found him to be sympathetic to my case, I answered honestly that "he seems to be sincere, but he doesn't have a very good understanding of English."

"Would you say," the banana-boater continued, "that you were ever mentally ill?"

Me (after thinking carefully): "At one time, not mentally ill, but mentally injured." [As an afterthought] "All the gossip in the world doesn't make me guilty of any crime, and all the accusations don't give me a mental illness."

A question from the other side of the table, from a young Doctor Erdag. . . .

Erdag: "You say the New York hospital was bad then. How do you mean?"

Me: "Things were a mess in general—just like here before the investigation. A year after I was there, Governor Dewey was elected . . . and one of the first things he did was clean out the state hospitals. . . ."

E: "Did the Communists have anything to do with your case?"

Me: "No. I wouldn't say so. . . ."

Gumanis: "You spoke about medicine being put in your food. Was this done in a public place?"

Me: "Yes."

G: "How was it done? How would they know who to give it to? Do you mean that everyone served in the restaurant was poisoned?"

Me: "No."

G: "How would they have known you were the one? Did you just walk into the restaurant and get poisoned?"

Me: "It did not happen the first time I ate there. Someone could have told the waitress to do it. It could have been the proprietor or someone from the outside who knew I ate there and told the waitress to do it. It was codeine—not a very powerful drug to be sure—but I never took codeine in my life. It's the principle of the thing. I went to a doctor and we agreed that I would take urine samples and he would have them analyzed at a laboratory. That's how we found out what they were using. I have a report from the laboratory in my files—down in Largo."

Dunin: "Both times you say you were railroaded—yet in New York you put yourself in!"

Me: "That is rather involved. I do not believe I needed to be sent to the state hospital for treatment. . . ."

D: "Now here in Florida you say again that you were railroaded—but you say two doctors—you admit two doctors saw you. How can you say you weren't examined when two doctors saw you?"

Me: "That was some weeks after the sanity committee filed their report that they had examined me thoroughly physically and mentally—they never saw me—they committed perjury!"

D: "But two doctors saw you!"

Me: "Yes—some weeks after the report had been filed."

D: "But they saw you—that's all that counts!" (Suddenly Dunin partly raised himself on the arms of the mahogany chair and screamed.) "You're lying!"

Me (in normal voice): "I told you the truth."

D: "No, you didn't! That's not what happened—you're lying!"

Me (calmly): "If you say I'm lying, then you're the one who's lying, not me."

Dunin stood all the way up. But Doctor O'Connor interrupted with a word and a gesture of his hands to Dunin to knock it off. Dunin's act is an example of what I call pure unadulterated chicken plucking psychology. . . .

D: "Tell me about your work with Representative Stallings when you go to Jacksonville to serve as his advisor."

Me (smiling inwardly at their having risen to the bait I had so mischievously dangled before them): "I did not say I was going to serve as an advisor to a legislator. He—"

D: "What is your business with him then?"

Me: "Representative Stallings is going to look into the matter of my commitment. He believes I was railroaded."

D: "How do you know that?"

Me: "Because he told me."

D: "And he is going to look into it?"

Me: "Yes."

D: "That's all then."

O'Connor: "That clarifies that. I'm glad to have that point cleared up."

D: "So am I."

Erdag: "You admit that you like it here. Would you say that you like it more—"

Me: "That's not a sensible way to put it."

E: "Would you rather stay here year after year than take some medication—even if you knew you could get out if you took some?"

Me: "Why should I take medication if I don't need it?"

E: "Did you ever take any here?"

Me: "No."

O'C: "Tell them why you never took any."

Me: "I am a believer in Christian Science."

O'C: "But you were offered medication?"

Me: "Yes."

O'C: "And you refused it?"

Me: "Yes, I refused to take any." (Factually, no medication had been offered me. ... To Erdag:) "Let me explain about Christian Scientists. They are intelligent people—they are not against doctors and medicine just for the sake of being against. If a Christian Scientist found he needed medicine he would ask a doctor for it."

E: "Supposing you were told that you couldn't leave unless you took some medicine?"

Me: "That would be blackmail!"

E: "Yes—but if it meant you must stay here many more years?"

Me: "Bullshit! Pills don't cure anything!" (Smiles and almost a couple of giggles around the table. A rather rash statement I knew as soon as I had made it. ...) "I know [I was quick to add] that when a person is upset emotionally, tranquilizers can calm him. But if a person is not upset he doesn't need any pills!"

O'Connor: "Are there any more questions?" [After scanning both sides of the table, he turned to me.] "Do you have any questions?"

Me: "No."

O'C: "You may leave then."

As I went out the door a small roll of toilet paper, flattened out for use as paper handkerchiefs, dropped out of my pocket with a plunk on the floor. Before I could look back to see what it was, Gumanis reached down and got it for me.

G: "Here—you forgot something." (He grinned.)

The above verbatim account was written down one hour afterward on the ward. Doctor Gumanis's summaries, before I entered the room and after (see end of this chapter) give the other side, which I was ignorant of until getting a copy through the federal court in 1965. I left the staff room, believing they had to pass me. Three of the eight doctors had never seen me before that staff; three had seen me only once before, at staff in 1962. I leave to the reader a judgment as to how they found me to be in a "dangerous to others" condition, which Doctor O'Connor reported as a "consensus."

And as I write this in 1975, I am reliving the first page of this chapter. I had been interviewed by the psychologist on January 2. I had, at first, refused to take more tests. Instead, we visited pleasantly. I had taken him some newspaper clippings, which he asked to keep.

"This one," I said, "tells of a ten-year survey in Manhattan, taking in all levels of society—a case sample called typical of the country as a whole—showing that 85 percent of the people are so-called mentally ill. I agree wholeheartedly, Mr. Cunningham, and I belong out there with the 85 percent, not locked in here with the 15."

That brought his easy smile. We talked over every angle of my case; reluctantly then I took some tests. On the Rorschach, I said: "I have a good imagination and I can easily pick out many things in the blots, though I know they aren't exactly so. Do you want me to tell you everything I can imagine?"

"Let's limit it to three answers for each card then," he said.

Doing that, a free-world psychologist told me, made it impossible for anyone to score the testee accurately.

He had me write out the actual happenings of my case, about two pages.

Cunningham's vote at staff made it unanimous against me. Gumanis called me down at the end of his workday to tell me I had not passed. What astounded me was, a week later, his telling me, "You were nasty at staff."

Of less surprise was the staff's report to Stallings, which he sent me: "... mentally ill ... by his demands and allegations against them, and even may present some degree of danger to others."

One side of the picture I was presenting was not altogether meek. My Progress Note stated: "(1/17/64) Patient is demanding. . . . He became infuriated. . . ." But if I were "infuriated," the Lord only knows why I did not get ECT.

Representative Stallings arranged for a Jacksonville psychologist, F. J. Calhoun, a former college professor, to examine me. Doctor O'Connor called me down to Joe Flake's office to see if I approved sending $90 from my account to Doctor Calhoun, which I did.

"You could save all this expense by letting me go to the halfway house up north," I said next.

"Why didn't you bring that up at staff three weeks ago?" O'Connor said.

"You even approved my sending $100 to my daughter to hold toward the expense of the trip down after me. Why can't you let me do that and save all this other expense—and the expense of putting my case in court?"

O'Connor's little moustache was firm above the lips. "I can't do a thing for you. The matter of your release is solely in the hands of Doctor Gumanis."

"But he says it's up to you."

"There's nothing I can do for you."

You can bet your bottom dollar, that if I had voiced my indignation and asserted my rights that morning, as a human being born under the protection of the United States Constitution, I would not have been allowed to retain the ability to write this book, let alone ever get out.

A few days after Groundhog Day, a young attendant came to the breakfast table. I had just put the first spoonful of cereal in my mouth, after stirring the milky solution to inspect for mice turds.

"Come along," the attendant said.

"I'm going to eat first," I said.

"It's visitors. They said to get you quick."

"I know who it is. He won't begrudge my taking time to eat."

That day they didn't dare bulldoze me; however, I left without touching the bacon and the biscuits. I was taken first to the barbershop and given a shave, then to the ward and given all new clothes. Then I waited in the pill room while attendants awaiting assignments talked.

"Maybe they'll let him go now," Call Jesstar said.

"Gumanis's letting a lot of them go," somebody said.

"Like peas out of a half-bushel," big A.B. said. "How long you been here, Donaldson?"

"Seven years."

"That's a life sentence at Raiford," A.B. said. "Seems they should be satisfied now. What'd you do? Rape?"

"That's all I've heard since I've been here. That and mammyjamming."

"Didn't mean nothing by it, friend. I mean there's nothing wrong with you. Why they holding you?"

"Nobody can figure it out," Call said. "There's the doctor, Kenneth. Ready?"

Doctor Gumanis stood in the doorway next his office with Mr. Stallings.

"Good luck to you, Kenneth," Gumanis said.

Stallings shook hands and introduced Doctor Calhoun, who arose behind the desk. Then Stallings and Gumanis left.

The doctor and I plowed ahead through a series of tests. For an hour I answered by rote and repeated my story. Calhoun was

keen about the "poisoning" in a restaurant. Then he asked his way
through the life histories of everyone in my family.

"Now, let's talk about your book," Calhoun said.

For the life of me I couldn't think of its latest title, so I said, "I
wrote one before I came here. It was titled *Ruptured Heritage*."

"Is that what you think happened? Is it fiction or nonfiction?"

"In fiction form."

"What's the protagonist's name?"

"Manton Sigg."

"Is that you?"

"He is fictional, though his experiences paralleled mine, as far
as Chattahoochee goes."

"Was this Mr. Sigg locked up before?"

"Yes, in New York State once."

"And before that?"

"His troubles all started overseas—North Africa—where a
couple of curious—you might say, trigger-happy—doctors gave him
shock treatments."

"So that's what you think, eh?"

"In his case—yes, it was uncalled for in his case."

"Is that what you've been saying all along?"

"Certainly."

"Is that what the book's about?"

"That and the slander that grew up around it."

"You think everybody's against you?"

"I never said that."

"Yet you think people followed you all over the country, and
yet you say you were not an important person. It should be a very
interesting book." Calhoun looked at his watch. "Hm, ten thirty.
I've got to go over and see your record and then talk to Doctor
O'Connor. If we make the plane out of Tallahassee, I'll have to
hurry. Thank you for talking to me, Mr. Donaldson."

"Are you an M.D., Doctor?"

"No."

Back on the ward, my new buddy, Hezekiah Jones, wanted to
go over every sentence of the interview. "They're all the same,"
Hezekiah said. "You shouldn't have talked about your book."

"I guess you're right," I said. "But his being an outside doctor—"

"You don't know the breed—not in this state." Hezy was disgusted.

But a week later I did know. Stallings wrote me that Calhoun, while not saying I was mentally ill, had the opinion that I needed treatment. (The basis for Calhoun's reasoning and his surprising report, which I was not to know until my later trial, was to fill me with both glee and wonder.) But, Stallings said, "The authorities at the Florida State Hospital indicate to me that they would be happy to have another state relieve them of your presence. If Helping Hands . . ."

To sum it up, then, I had told the staff and an outside psychologist the God's honest truth, for which they labeled me sick. Now the hospital said they would let me go out of state, yet they didn't. What was I to do?

I had come across a battered copy of *How to Win Friends and Influence People*. I would try its principles. I wrote Doctor O'Connor:

> I wonder if you'd help me now. . . . I readily admit that had I stood in your shoes I certainly would have judged myself exactly as you have done, considering all the "charges" on record. I also confess to the mistake of hardheadedness in everything pertaining to my case. Yet, against this, are there not redeeming things? A life of honesty and industry . . . the complete absence of violence and lawbreaking? . . . Just what do you want me to do? . . .

There was no reply from O'Connor.

I even softened my opposition to going with my parents. This is recorded in a Progress Note: "(4/2/64) Patient today for the first time accepted to be furloughed to his parents. Wrote a letter to Dr. O'Connor explaining matters. . . ."

In this period, I began to avoid the early rush up the three levels of stairs, in order to be able to walk more slowly and not attract attention when I stopped on the last landing to let the tightness in my chest go away. I believed at the time that it was due to the constant debilitating medication in the chow. My hair was falling out faster. When I got angry at something said behind my back, or someone elbowed me on the stairs, there would be that tightness.

Another straw was Robert McRobert, doing time for the untried murder of a sister over some trifle. When first on the ward, he was attracted to me by our mutual interest in scientific news.

But he objected to my respect for Christian Science and his words became insulting when I stood my ground. Soon McRobert was going down to Gumanis's twice a week. Then he started following me to the toilet, varied with coughing every time we passed in the aisle. In a short time, every one of the dozens of murderers on the ward was doing the same.

Both John Lembcke and Jack, a former fellow patient, were ready to put up the money for lawyer Orshale. Jack sent the $50 from Miami. I wrote Orshale that I would under no circumstances go before staff again.

I sat in the dressing room late in the afternoon, waiting while Orshale talked with Gumanis. Afterward he said, "You must bear in mind, Kenneth, that when your head is in the lion's mouth you don't have much choice. . . . Doctor Gumanis is willing for your furlough to your mother, and he believes that Doctor O'Connor will consent. Well, I have to go up the street and talk about it with Doctor O'Connor. Then I'll write your friend, Mr. Jack."

On July 30, Orshale wrote Jack: ". . . It is my opinion that he is going to have to change his attitude to justify a release. . . ."

Upon seeing that, B & E said, "You can't fight city hall. You want more proof?"

"It looks like they didn't give me a choice," I said.

That summer, a related item appeared in *Newsweek*, June 22:

> Gideon turned out to be . . . the guardhouse lawyer, the crank who will not rest until an injustice has been righted, the crackpot nuisance who will move heaven and earth for a fair shake. Once in prison, Gideon set about trying to do what is nearly impossible for his sort in a faceless, bureaucratic society: Make himself . . . heard in a world which has ceased to listen to the lone voice. . . .

If Gideon could do it—

I had chosen a private correspondent, having found the grapevine unreliable for briefs, and so I was allowed to send one (although the law did not limit it) sealed letter every Thursday. Joe Flake said, "I don't care how big it is, so long as it's only one." So, under Chattahoochee "law," some of my letters took $4 in stamps. All but two of my private letters, first via Doctor Birnbaum, then my children, then friends, were accounted for.

During this time, John tried twice more to get me released to his custody. On July 7, the clinical director, Doctor Rich, wrote John: "If Mr. Donaldson is released, he will require complete supervision because of his poor judgment."

On the wards, new problems continually grew out of small pleasures. It happened that one day late in the summer, the chunks of roast beef on the dinner trays were browned just right to taste good, such a change from the usual blubber that B & E went around gathering it from toothless old men. There were mashed potatoes too ("Somebody's here from Tallahassee," B & E said) and a new brown pudding, though it tasted like the old yellow kind. We both had more than one helping of everything.

"Whew!" I said when we got to the yard. "I've got to walk this pot off."

It was a blistering day and I took my blue shirt off. We walked for an hour in and out of the sun under the trees, my back and chest covered with sweat.

At 3:00, we were unexpectedly returned to the wards and I took my shoes off and sat back on the bed to enjoy my Philadelphia papers. It was not long before I had to go to the toilet. Before I got there, I felt dizzy and threw my arms over the dividing wall for support. Next thing, I was being helped off the floor by some little patient who kept asking, "Don't you want me to call the attendant? Don't you want something? Don't you want to go down to the dressing room?"

"Don't tell the attendant," I said, knowing that would mean confinement on sick bay, and worse, medication, which in my weakened condition no doubt would have finished me off. "I'm all right. Just blacked out. Gee, it's the first time in my life. Thanks, pal, but don't say anything, will you?"

Two days later, on a Saturday afternoon, I was all alone in the bathroom, hunkering on the seatless toilet, when my head started to roll. It banged the pale-green tile partition on my right, slammed over to smash into the one on the left, then back to the right. Hurt as it did, I was thinking that the blows would certainly straighten me up when I pitched straight forward off my perch. I picked myself up and was sitting on the cold commode when a houseman hurried in. I said I was okay.

That night I read several extra pages in *Science and Health*. I made a conscious prayer, too, to a personal God, "I've got to make it, God." I asked for a little more strength. "I WILL make it, God," was my wording.

As for other things, the more they changed the more they stayed the same. There was Tomas, a little brown amigo, who was installed as the No. 1 boy by the night attendants, because he sold grilled cheese sandwiches, hot off a smuggled-in grill. One of the outside patients stole the cheese from the commissary. There were repeated questionings by the day crew and shakedowns for the grill, but nobody would spoil this joke on the establishment. The second-shift attendants had less respect for Joe Flake & Co. than did the criminals.

Tomas had appeared several times at staff and been given a good going over each time. What had brought about his rest cure, he said, was going out one night and coldly killing five of his girl friend's relatives on a hillside, after some imagined slight of hers to him. Then he had given himself up. After his last appearance at staff, Gumanis advised him to get another lawyer, and so his folks borrowed more money and hired their third lawyer. Under threat of action under Stallings's new laws, Tomas went to staff again.

"Know what they asked me?" Tomas said beaming. "Doctor O'Connor said, 'Do you know the day you arrived at this hospital?' I told him. That was all there was to it. Gumanis let me out the door and whispered that I passed all right."

"How do you like that?" Grandma said.

(I first read this in 1965. K.D.)

Re: Kenneth Donaldson A-25738
GENERAL STAFF CONFERENCE
January 9, 1964

Doctor Gumanis:
SUMMARY:

> This is the case of Kenneth Donaldson, white male, aged 55, who was committed from Pinellas County on January 3, 1957, and was admitted to the Florida State Hospital on January 15, 1957.

The past history indicates that he was born in Erie, Pennsylvania, on May 1, 1906 [*sic*], and had lived in Florida four years prior to his commitment. His occupation is listed as a painter and carpenter. He was hospitalized at the Marcy State Hospital in New York during 1943 for a period of three months and received electroshock treatments. He was diagnosed Dementia Praecox, Paranoid Type.

On the Receiving Service of the Florida State Hospital he was delusional and paranoid, with defective insight and judgment. He believed that the Republicans had stolen many of his good ideas which he had recommended to the Foreign Police Association. [**The one word "Police" is an enigma. It could have been an innocent error—"Police" for "Policy." I had mentioned writing letters on foreign affairs. But it could have been an attempt at discrediting me totally—the old paranoid charge. The reader should understand that I was totally oblivious of any of this till the following year.**] He also felt that they had attempted to poison him by putting chemicals in his food.

On the General Wards this past year he has shown no particular changes. Basically he is still delusional with ideas of reference. He now has Representative Stallings from Duval County representing him.

He is being presented today for evaluation and further disposition of his case. He refuses to be furloughed to his parents, and definitely does not answer any of their letters.

Post Staff Dictation: This patient has been hospitalized here since 1957. His past history reveals that he was hospitalized for a period of three months at the Marcy State Hospital in New York, and received electroconvulsive treatment. After that he was placed on convalescence care in the care of his wife. Since his admission here he has spent most of his time writing letters to various officials explaining to them about his hospitalization. He definitely is still paranoid. He has ideas of reference against his parents, with whom he refuses to correspond or hear from the doctor about their correspondence.

Since his last presentation, I do not see any change in this patient. I believe he should remain here. We have tried in the past to furlough him to his parents, but he definitely refuses this. I know even if he is released to his parents he will require supervision. I don't think he is mentally competent at this time to be released. Diagnosis is the same, Schizophrenic Reaction, Paranoid Type.

Doctor Hanenson: This is a case of paranoia, who has been hospitalized in the past. This afternoon he is very hostile. He shows evasiveness. Every question is answered, "This is a long story." The patient is still very sick mentally, and I do not believe that he is ready to be released, even on a Trial Visit basis because he will never accept any supervision. He is incompetent and I diagnose him as a Paranoia State. I believe he should remain in the Hospital.

Mr. Davis: I think he is a paranoia and has been since he has been in this institution. I think he should remain in the Hospital.

Mr. Cunningham: I agree that he should remain here.

Doctor Chacon: Basically he has shown no insight. He is paranoid and incompetent and should remain in the Hospital.

Doctor Dunin: I agree with the examiner.

Doctor Erdag: I also agree that the patient does not show any change in his mental condition. He still remains paranoid. He uses denial mechanisms as a defense and I also believe he is not ready for a Trial Visit.

Doctor Ravenet: I agree.

Doctor Rich: I agree.

Doctor O'Connor: No question about me agreeing. The consensus of opinion is to hold him in the Hospital; that he is incompetent and considered to be dangerous to others; and that he should be held in the Hospital until further improvement.

CONSENSUS OF OPINION: HOLD—He is incompetent and considered to be dangerous to others and should be held in the hospital until further improvement.

CHAPTER 14

1965

Charlie Fongju Schemes

IT HAPPENED IN THE AFTERNOON. IT WAS ONE OF THE OVERRIPE FRUITS on the Chattahoochee tree. All but three in the whole building were on the hot yard. Two young "crims," Darrold and Rainton, had coaxed attendant Kanrelk to stay up on the ward and wash windows. Kanrelk was in charge of Ward 7 during Yillabar's vacation and was doing the two weeks without a charge attendant's premium pay, thus having no incentive to do more than the minimum. But he was faced with two facts: one, Supervisor Flake's standing orders pertaining to windows being done every month, and the other, Yillabar's foresight in leaving the windows to these last two weeks. So Kanrelk stayed in out of the sun.

Nothing was noticed amiss until shifts changed at three. There was no trace of Kanrelk and the two housemen. All the men on both yards were hurriedly driven indoors for a bed check. Lying on his bed in the pen next mine, young Nassy "by chance" spotted the two small holes in the soundproofing ceiling over Darrold's bed and strolled over to point them out to Grandma. In short order, the evening attendant had a look, then the supervisor. Soon the grapevine was vibrating with all stops pulled, about a phone call from Tallahassee. The state police had found Kanrelk tied to a tree ten miles north of the capital. The two patients, was the report, had put two slugs through the ceiling to convince Kanrelk it was for real. Then the three had left in Kanrelk's car from a front parking lot. After tying the attendant, the patients headed south. The final flash came over the idiot box. An off-duty policeman happened to be listening to a description of the fleeing men when they passed on the road to Tampa. He turned about and caught them single-handed.

The next day, both heroes were back on Ward 7. Darrold boasted how the gun had been smuggled in in his new record player. But privately he stopped swanking in explaining his capture to his pal Nassy.

Nassy had turned down the chance to wash windows and escape, on the advice of his boy friend, deputy Wormen. When Wormen told the doctor about it, the doctor rewarded Nassy with a discharge. This came for Nassy after doing only one year for the suffocation of a little girl in a dry cleaner's garment bag. Unluckily, Nassy had not finished his cure, because he tried to stuff another little girl into a bag and had to be sent back for another few months of pills.

Those were our two choices: shoot a hole in the ceiling or take your pills and tell Gumanis he had cured your headaches.

But neither way was my style in 1965 and I still had faith in the courts. It was all or nothing. I wasn't going to plead that I did not know what I had been talking about. There had to be honesty someplace in the structure of our country. And if eight years wasn't preposterous enough, I showed the courts that the original order that saw me thrown into the hole of the jail was not an arrest warrant.

In April, the United States Court of Appeals, Fifth Circuit, transferred my case to Federal District Court, where Judge Carswell numbered it as Tallahassee Civil Action No. 1067 and ordered the state to respond.

On May 19, I was summoned on the run from the yard to John Gumanis's.

"You have a writ in federal court in Tallahassee?" Gumanis asked.

"Yes," I said.

"Why don't you stop writing them and get yourself ready for

staff? As long as you fight the doctors you'll stay."

"I'm not staying to fight the doctors. I didn't pick this for a career—it was forced on me."

"Why do you keep saying that you were sent here without seeing any doctors?"

"Because that's exactly what happened."

"But your papers say different."

"I know. I have copies of them."

"You have copies?"

"From the state Supreme Court."

"You still say you never lived in Florida?"

"That's right."

Gumanis reached for the three-by-five box, then drew his hand back and said, "I've tried to help you. I've said all along you're only stubborn. That's the only thing that is wrong with you. That will be all."

A few days later, I was sitting on a slatted bench, tipped back in the dusty heat. The limping mailman had just brought the Respondent's brief. A medicated shaker plopped down on the other end of my bench, teetering it a bit. Rhythmically he vibrated his torso and the bench, his legs jiggling to a different tune. It was the perfect background for an amazing document. I reread Gumanis's two-page notarized statement:

> This is to certify that I have this date, again interviewed Kenneth Donaldson . . . he does not realize he is mentally ill. . . . He states that if he is released he will obtain a civilian job and publish a book of his hospitalization for the past 20 years which illustrates he has little insight of his own condition . . . actually he could be considered potentially dangerous.

The Respondent's reply also carried a copy of my January 9, 1964, staff appearance. Two ideas attributed to me—"the Republicans had stolen many of his good ideas which he had recommended to the Foreign Police [*sic*] Association" and "they had attempted to poison him by putting chemicals in his food") almost made me jump up to pull my hair in anger and laughter. Those statements illustrate why Doctor Birnbaum says my experience was something out of *Alice in Wonderland*.

I realized that nothing I wrote would convince Judge Carswell that the doctors were acting out Kafka. There was even the danger that my simple recital of the facts had already given him the impression that I was creating a fantasy. My words begged, implored, demanded that I be given a hearing in person with the right to subpoena witnesses, including attendants who had volunteered. Lawyer Charles M. Butterworth III, in McSorley's office in Philadelphia, notified me that that was my right under the writ of habeas corpus, which had been grudgingly issued on order from Fifth Circuit. Carswell's words in granting the writ were: "In accordance with this directive [from the Fifth Circuit], and in order to clarify the record herein this Court concludes that an order must be entered authorizing the filing of the writ of habeas corpus in forma pauperis."

I sensed that my second writ would go down the drain unless I could get someone, anyone (a shoemaker, a grocer, a doctor, a lawyer) to speak up for me in person before the judge. I wrote to dozens (the bar association in Tallahassee, medical societies in neighboring counties, to doctors, lawyers, the American Civil Liberties Union). Here was an almost unprecedented situation, a mental patient getting a writ of habeas corpus (my third too! including the one for Narrel Damascus) and no one in the free world would step in to see that I got a fair shake. One psychiatrist, to whom both Jack and I appealed, replied to neither of us; instead, my letter came back to the hospital via the county medical society.

Jack wrote the bar association: "They cannot commit a sane man and keep him locked up except through falsification and deception. Examine him and you will find him sane, it follows then that the record is false." But they did not examine me.

Nevertheless, things looked bright for a time. I had got the ear of the newly elected Congressman from Syracuse, the Hon. James M. Hanley, who was "shocked" at what Florida had done to me. He asked the Florida bar to help. They sent me, on the day before the writ was issued, a list of their members in Quincy, the county seat. I wrote them all. A half dozen replied, with legitimate excuses of why they could not help me, thus allowing a little more strength to ebb out of us on the ward.

On June 17, Judge Carswell ordered the case closed.

I stuffed the order inside my shirt and paced the far end of the yard along the fence. Across the valley on the ridge, the trees were still green; on this side, inside the fence, the sun was still bright.

"What is it, Kenny?" said Hezy falling in.

"They threw it out."

"They're all the same. Better start packing—we'll leave some night—about one thirty."

"Rembin Rollen! Rembin Rollen!" came the call down the tunnel.

"What is it?" I said. "That's you," B & E said.

"Visitors," the young attendant said. "You look good enough. Come along."

After I was seated, a handsome young man in an expensive gray suit and blue tie came from the direction of Gumanis's office.

"I'm Jackson Beatty," he said shaking hands. "I'm a lawyer in Quincy. You did not write me but your letter was referred to me."

"Then you'll speak to the court about reopening my case?"

"No. I shall work with you, though, until we get you freed. You look and act well. Doctor Gumanis has no objection to your going free. I am going to get a doctor from outside. Then Chattahoochee should let you go. Have you any funds?"

"A few hundred."

"That will be enough. I'll charge no fee for my services. I'll be back as soon as arrangements are complete."

Going back to the ward, I felt that my long sentence was near an end.

At this same time, a patient, Whiteburn, on Ward 7 had an examination by a Tallahassee psychiatrist for $75. But no requests from Stallings, Jack, Beatty, or myself could get any doctor to examine me. Then Beatty wrote to psychologist Calhoun. Unknown to me, the latter's answer found its way to my chart: "This man has the type of mental illness that is the most difficult for lay persons to detect."

Then Doctor Szasz was willing to come down from Syracuse to testify for me. One of my correspondents, Zena, a member of ACT, offered to pay his expenses and I could have borrowed enough on my life insurance to pay his fee. But he would not come unless a lawyer made the arrangements, and Mr. Beatty would not.

One afternoon that summer, when I was going through a pile of five newspapers, B & E leaned over the wall and said, "There's someone on the other end I think you know." B & E's heavy features were lit by a smile. "You ought to talk to him."

I put the papers under the pillow to prevent their being borrowed and not returned. I found a tall big-boned man in his late thirties, walking back and forth in the corridor across the middle of the ward connecting with the other buildings.

"My friend tells me I might know you," I said.

"Were you at Raiford?"

"No. He says you were in the Pinellas County Jail. I was there December and January, '56 and '57."

"You were two cells down from me."

"Kenneth Donaldson."

"That's right. I'm Albert."

"I'd never have known you. You were skin and bones. We took a shower together. You showed me the plate in your head."

"It's grown over now."

"You must be three times your weight then."

"I played big-league ball. I'm at my playing weight. Do you remember the song sessions? And could Mabel sing! And she sent out for lettuce the last day you were there. Remember? What became of her?"

"She wrote me from the receiving ward. I didn't answer—what was there to say? Been here long?"

"My second time. I got life you know. The doctors say this time I'll stay until I'm pardoned. How come you're still here? I thought you'd be in Philadelphia. There doesn't seem to be anything wrong with you."

"I've given up my plans of going to Philly and being admitted to the bar. I thought I'd go back to northern Jersey."

"You'd like the Oranges. That's my home. But I like it down here—if they'll let me stay after this."

"The weather is all right—but I wouldn't stay one day after I was freed."

"You've had a poor deal."

"Gumanis's told me I don't belong here—that is, to my face."

Another day and Albert wanted to talk about his problems.

"Do you go to Catholic church?" he said.

"I went to mass here twice. Catholics have helped me, but I never intended to join. I'm partly Christian Science."

"Do you think I'll go to heaven? I've talked to the priest about purgatory. He says God will let me know when the time comes. I'd like to make it right with God. I'm taking a Bible course—the Apostles church, by mail. The Bible says we'll be pardoned. Do you believe that Jesus has atoned for our sins? I would like forgiveness. I can't get it off my mind what I did. They gave me shock treatments. Did you ever have them?"

"Once, many years ago. They're rough. I've never told anyone here except the doctors."

"They made me forget for a while," Albert said. "But I can see it all. I came home from work tired. My wife seemed to be scared. She had me taken to the V.A. Hospital. They sent me home the third day. We saw our family doctor. He didn't see I should be locked up. It happened in the middle of the night. There was a storm—lightning, wind off the Gulf. I thought I had to save the family from being taken away from me. I grabbed the butcher knife and slit their throats where they lay in bed. I just had to do it. I had a compulsion that I had to save them that way. They put me in the jail. Did you hear what I told the doctors there?"

"Only one thing. You said it was compulsion."

"Do you think God will have a place for my soul?"

"His ways are beyond our understanding."

"That's what the priest tells me. You have learned a great deal from your religion. Walk with me every day, will you, Kenneth?" He paused. "After I did it I blacked out. Don't you see why I wanted the chair?"

"Yes, your soul would have been easier."

Albert was the exception to one of Goffman's points, that inmates in "total institutions" take on the characteristics of their guards. Albert was quiet, resigned to what life had left him.

In reverse, Albert's example was too isolated to have any influence on the attendants. The attendants had taken on the cloak of anger of the abused and frustrated patients; however, some of these same gung-ho attendants later became reasonable men, helpful to the inmates, when assigned to open wards.

These same influences worked on the doctors, making them hate their patients. The exception was the first few weeks for a new doctor in the department, which meant a fresh breeze of intelligence blowing on the lucky few who happened to get interviews. So when Hezekiah, as A. B.'s right-hand man, got word that a Doctor Chacon was coming to take over part of Doctor Gumanis's 1,300 men, Hezy urged me to get my name in early. I sent it in, though knowing that one drop of chocolate syrup could not flavor a tank of sludge.

I did not connect my request with what later happened. I was called down to the basement of our building, to the half ward next the baggage room. I was seated beside a desk in a small room. The attendant said someone would see me, then went out, leaving the door open. Everything done in Chattahoochee was always so mysterious. This was the way they set up lobotomies and shock.

A middle-aged middle-sized Doctor Chacon came in.

Doctor Chacon: "I am having a group of four, twice a week— to discuss your problems and see what's wrong. You're the first one I've called. We're going to straighten out your thinking and get you out of here."

Me: "There was nothing wrong with my thinking when I was put in here. I don't want any group therapy."

Chacon: "It has helped many patients—not in here—this is the first in Chattahoochee—but—"

Me: "I don't need that kind of help." (And I thought: I'll be damned if after eight years I'll let them take credit for getting me well.)

C: "I've heard some nice things about you. I am your friend, Donaldson. I'll go through your chart and see what I can do. I'll talk to you anytime you want."

A couple of weeks later, I wrote and asked to see him. To counteract my excessive weakness, I had ordered through my private mail some wheat germ and brewer's yeast. Supervisor Flake would not let me have them, saying we'd make beer on the wards.

C: "He means the criminals. But why did you send for them?"

Me: "After eight years of bone stew, I need a supplement."

C: "Did you ask Gumanis for vitamins?"

Me: "I don't want anything from this state. Besides, brewer's yeast is the best source of B vitamins, isn't it?"

C: "I'll give the order to Nurse Park for you to have them. I'm going to get your chart."

In three days, he called me again.

Chacon (leafing through a thick file): "I see you passed all your psychological tests. I've talked to Gumanis and he's agreed to my putting you to staff this week."

Me: "I won't go before that bunch again."

C: "How'll you get out?"

Me: "Through the courts."

C: "As long as you write the courts, these doctors will go to any length to defend themselves."

Me: "I've had a half-dozen ways—somebody always blocks them."

C: "You're not sick. Have one of your children come talk to me."

Me: "Would you write them?"

C: "I couldn't. Have them ask for me, I'll tell them."

Years later, I was shocked to find that the first entry by Doctor Chacon in my chart was: "5/17/65 Mentally unchanged. Dr. Chacon: jp."

During the larger part of the year when nobody went to the yard, the aisle was often crowded by bully-boy criminals refusing to share the path. I walked little those days. Boogerisch had found, before he was transferred, what happens when one crosses them. He had cheated in his clandestine numbers game and one of them got him in the back with the ragged bottom half of a broken coffee jar. The fact that the attacker fell, stretching around the dividing wall and cutting his own hand, saved Boogerisch. But he never made so much as a derogatory remark about a criminal again on the ward.

On a Sunday afternoon when most were asleep, I was too restless to lie on the bed contemplating passages of Mrs. Eddy's. My refreshed spirit raged against the punishment of being in a building that got sunshine inside for only fifteen minutes at 7:00 A.M. and again at 5:00 P.M. I stood up. B & E, off medication, got up too.

"Let's walk," he said. "I'd sure like to be on the Boardwalk at Atlantic City on a day like this."

"Yeh." After a silence I said, "I can't wait to pay these people for what they're doing to us."

"Boogerisch does it wrong. You can't win by shooting your mouth off. I never told you the story about Charlie Fongju, did I? He worked in the galley of our ship—a little Chinaman. Good-natured, always smiling—they loved him and took to teasing him. They short-sheeted him. They sewed his socks across the middle. While he slept they tied his pants around the overhead pipes and put so many knots in his shoelaces the captain himself couldn't have undone them. On the last night out on a long voyage, they raised a pool and allocated ten dollars to Charlie. His eyes almost broke their slits.

" 'You're one helluva guy, Charlie,' they told him. 'We won't bother you no more. No more knots on your shoes.'

"The money was real but Charlie was skeptical. 'No more short-sheet Charlie?'

" 'No.'

" 'No more tie to pipe?'

" 'Naw. You're the best damn cook in the navy.'

" 'Then Charlie no more pee pee in the coffee.' "

That bolstered me for months. I'd keep right on pee peeing in the coffee until they let me go—on my terms, now.

There was always something, like Charlie Fongju, almost miraculously it seemed in those days, to help my spirits. From another new correspondent, Hegel Kirk, from San Francisco, a member of ACT, who had done volunteer work, putting on dances in Bay Area mental hospitals, came this:

> ... you certainly have a wonderful constitution to live in such a
> crowded place and still not become sullen and bitter. . . . Living in a
> slum environment breaks most people down. Their health can't
> stand it.

It was good to know I was making a positive impression on my correspondents. On the other hand, that letter gave me morbid thoughts. I could rest on the landing for ten seconds. But what about Carter? I had not heard from him in months. And Grandma was ailing—and Damascus dead.

All right then, I'd be damned! Those were three going down the drain. I'd resist, survive, reveal the truth. I refused to see Gumanis when Call Jesstar told me the doctor had the hunch he ought to let me go. I put my reasons in a letter through the censors to lawyer Beatty, with references to the May 19th statement. "You can't do business with a liar," I have always said.

Beatty's reply went no further than to say: "I see no harm in your consulting with Dr. Gumanis." The letter had been addressed to "Kenneth Donaldson, White Male Department," though I had headed mine with "Department A," pointing out that the first Negroes had arrived on Ward 7 in the beginning of Chattahoochee's integration.

"I hate to see it happen," I said to B & E when the first six came up on the ward. "These antisociables here are the last ones ready for it."

At supper, the attendants and supervisors thought the same, because the six were seated isolated by a ring of attendants and escorted back to the ward ahead of the rest, to a pen cleared of whites.

The next day, one of the six, Sammy, came over to me. He was disturbed to the degree that he made noises like a fair candidate for Chattahoochee. He resented the housemen's stealing his coffee—a full ten ounces—while the bugs were on the yard. It was evident that Department C (formerly Colored Male) had shipped out their worst pests, which was reciprocated by Department A (formerly White Male) in sending Beelzebub in the first exchange. One of Sammy's buddies screamed and swung his left arm in the manner of a zoo ape. He left for the Back Yard the second night. Sammy was crying when he came over: "They stole two dollars' worth. Coffee, sugar, cream. Will you keep this new jar for me, Mr. Man?"

I hated to give the troublemakers something more to agitate on, and so I told Sammy, "They'd only steal it from me."

"No, suh! I see'd your muscles. They wouldn't steal from this Mr. Man. Do it for me and I'll have mah wife send you a red snapper from Jacksonville. She come up in mah red Cadillac. She bring you a red snapper."

"Okay." I laughed. "See it's cooked good."

"Yazzuh, yazzuh."

When things were quieted, my neighbor came over to talk: "Did you hear that Big Pasquale went home?"

"Yeah, Hezy," I said. "He gets out of his car at a gas station and kills the attendant in cold blood. Then after six months here— no trial—he goes scot-free. Last week he showed his colors. He was lying on Daniel's bed with his dirty shoes on the spread. Daniel told him to get off. He got up and knocked Daniel clear out of the pen with a blow to the teeth."

"I wondered how it happened. What about Daniel?"

"I told him not to report it, otherwise Gumanis would never let him be furloughed to the job he has set up at a gas station."

"You get your things ready," Hezy said without a smile, "what you can carry. Not too much. Send to your kids what you can't manage. The less, the faster we'll go."

A friend got me a small carton from the dope stand. I cut it in two, around the middle, covered both halves with wrappers from my papers, and when it was telescoped together it held an extra pair of shorts, socks, and two shirts, besides Bible, pocket dictionary, and a few recent letters. All the rest I sent out. I sent fifty dollars to my daughter and bought two pairs of pants to bring my balance down in the office.

"Get some money ahead," Hezy kept urging. "How much you got?"

"Ten bucks."

"Draw every week."

"But they'd suspect."

"No matter, we'll need every cent. Starting tonight we'll take turns watching. You start tonight. About 12:50, one attendant goes down to the dining room for coffee. The other stays in the back of the TV room with his feet on a chair. Some nights he dozes. When you see it's clear, you wake me. I've got a key to the back stairs. Don't ask me to show it. I've got it where no one can find it."

It was rough going. After years of going to sleep at dusk, so as to sleep through the almost-unbearable night hours and then up before dawn to have a few peaceful moments for meditation, I had to force myself. Finally the first attendant went to supper. We would have thirty minutes. Boy, was it cold. They would use the dogs too, because Hezy had charges. Wonder if they were all barks and no bites. They growl so viciously and you can hear them for five miles in the swamp. I was fully dressed except for shoes. I reached over to ease the drawer open for the box. I put my shoes on by sticking my feet out from under the blanket. Hezy looked so peaceful. What was that—a door? It was the pill man from the dressing room. Somebody was having a seizure. Then the third-shift supervisor showed up and the lights went on in the TV section. It was no use calling Hezy now.

The next day Jason Bennock and three of his attendants from the Back Yard shook Hezy down. They even cut the mattress in two places. But the key was not found.

"Anyway, you're going back with us," Jason told Hezy.

Thus another road to freedom was blocked; another year behind bars was totted up. At the end of nine years, all my efforts to find ways out were so much banging my head on the walls.

Re: Kenneth Donaldson   May 19, 1965
     Florida State Hospital
     Chattahoochee, Florida

This is to certify that I have this date, again interviewed Kenneth Donaldson, patient at this Hospital who has been here for the past eight years and I find the following to be my evaluation of his current mental status.

This patient has shown no changes in his mental condition, he is still delusional and paranoid and has delusions against certain persons. His insight and judgment are defective and he does not realize he is mentally ill. He spends most of his time writing letters to various officials about his release and believes that he was committed in this Hospital illegally. He further states that he has never been mentally ill and the Electroconvulsive treatments that he received in Marcy State Hospital in New York were a mistake. He has not corresponded with his parents until lately but will receive letters from them and answer a few questions. He states that if he is released he will obtain a civilian job and publish a book of his hospitalization for the past 20 years which illustrates he has little insight of his own condition and what little judgment he displays in thinking he can adjust in the world when his history shows he has been unable to do so for almost the past 25 years.

This patient has appeared before the General Staff of this Hospital on several occasions and it was the unanimous consensus of opinion on each occasion that he could not adjust outside of the institution and that he was suffering from a chronic type of mental disorder, namely Schizophrenic Reaction, Paranoid Type and that actually he could be considered potentially dangerous.

Most of his time in this Hospital is spent in writing to prominent individuals and also various courts and attorneys and most of such endeavors are to convince them that he has never been mentally ill and that he has been persecuted all these years and illegally placed in mental institutions. He has applied for writs to Florida Supreme Courts and other courts and these have been denied, and he has previously written the Federal courts, as correspondence in his file will show. It is my considered opinion that this patient remains chronically mentally ill to the degree that he is mentally incompetent and that he could not adjust outside an institution except under most stringent supervision, and because of the nature of his mental illness, he would not accept such supervision since he does not realize he has ever been mentally ill. His release from the Hospital is not recommended at this time, but if marked improvement should develop in the future, it could of course, then be recommended.

JOHN GUMANIS, M.D.   Attending Psychiatrist

IN THE COURTS, 1965

(xi)

U.S. Court of Appeals, Fifth Circuit	No. 176 3/25/65
U.S. District Court, Tallahassee	No. 1067 4/30/65

My brief to Fifth Circuit said: ". . . (Petitioner) is aware of the shadow line beyond which the judiciary do not grant writs of habeas corpus in noncriminal cases; but, as he points out below, his is a struggle bearing on the very fundamentals of our society: the struggle of a decent, law-abiding, sane man to regain his constitutionally guaranteed freedom from unjust and illegal incarceration. . . .

"Whereas, fraud nullifies every subsequent action based on that fraud; and,

"Whereas, fiction and deliberate lies are no legal basis for holding a man as a prisoner. . . ."

The Fifth Circuit sent it back to the District Court, for the Northern District of Florida. The District Court ruled: ". . . In accordance with this directive, and in order to clarify the record . . . this Court concludes that the State of Florida . . . should make response thereto by brief of authorities. . . ."

Respondent's Return, May 19, said: ". . . petitioner, through the intervention of Representative Stallings, was examined by an independent psychologist, and such psychologist found that petitioner was mentally incompetent. . . ." The return included Doctor Gumanis's notarized statement, supra.

My Rebuttal said: ". . . the State of Florida has never proved that (1) Petitioner ever made his domicile in Florida or (2) that any doctor in the State of Florida, outside of the Hospital, ever examined Petitioner and found him needing to be confined. . . ."

The District Court quashed the writ, June 17.

I petitioned for an extension until I could "procure either . . . proper legal counsel [or] unbiased psychiatric testimony." Further, I said: "Even if things were true of Petitioner as his department doctor . . . claims in his statement of date 19 May 1965, still those things of themselves would not invalidate Petitioner's right to his freedom."

The District Court denied an extension, August 8.

CHAPTER 15

1966

Convulsions

THERE WAS A VERY TALL WELL-BUILT MAN IN A BLUE SUIT SLUMPED IN a chair in front of Gumanis's desk, his legs protruding so far that I had to sit sideways.

"I'm Rich—Clinical Director. Remember me?"

"Yes—from staff," I said.

Gumanis came in.

"Mr. Beatty, your lawyer," Rich said, "has been here about your going to your friend's in Binghamton. What are you going to do? Work? Jobs are not hanging on trees like they used to be."

"I can work as a carpenter—or that job he offered."

"Well, I think we can arrange it, don't you, Doctor Gumanis?"

"Why, certainly," Gumanis said.

"You work it out then," Rich said. "I'll put it through." But there must have been something gnawing at the back of his brain, for he glanced through a four-page letter I had sent him. "You say here that Chattahoochee doctors have repeatedly lied about you. Can you give me a concrete example?"

223

As he put the letter in his briefcase and stretched his legs farther yet, I told about that "certain senator from Arizona."

"That was not a lie. That was an interpretation of what you said. We do that all the time. What other statement do you object to?"

"The report Gumanis made to—"

But Rich had turned to Gumanis and was talking about something else, one of their customary rude tricks to put an inmate in his place. But I had not learned mine yet and kept on until I had finished my sentence and Rich gave me a withering look.

When they were through, he said: "Why couldn't you talk to Gumanis for two years?"

"What did I ever do to you?" Gumanis said.

"You lied."

"Who? Me?"

"Yes, you're a liar."

"Tell me what he said," Rich said.

"He made a statement to—"

"I didn't make it. O'Connor made it out and I signed it."

"What was so out of the way?" Rich said.

"For some years now, Doctor Gumanis has been telling me that there is nothing wrong with me. Then he told the court that I think the international police association is after me. He made that one up out of whole cloth."

"We've got Gumanis's statement right here," Rich said. He read through the two pages. "There's nothing in it like that."

"But I've got a photocopy of it from the state's attorney general."

"You mean they changed the copy they gave me?"

"No."

"Then you find it."

I read through the statement and my face fell. "But I have a copy which contains it."

Rich said, "You're schizophrenic. I'll tell you what, Donaldson. I promise to let you go one year from now if you'll take a course of medication for six months."

"No," I said. That would give them the proof they needed and leave me no recourse. "I don't need any medication."

"What do you say, Gumanis?"

"I agree with you, Doctor Rich. Why don't you try it, Kenny? You've tried everything else."

"But I don't need any pills."

"Then you'll stay here forever!" Rich said. "Either you take pills for six months or I'll never let you go."

"That's coercion," I said.

"We could give you the needle. That would be coercion, wouldn't it?"

Any further remarks by me, I feared, would only cause him to double whatever the pill man was bound to have for me at supper.

"Don't you know we have the right to treat you when they send you here?"

I answered with a craven "Yes."

Back on the ward, I didn't dare let my indignation seethe over the edge. "I hope you don't get pills," Hezy said. "They'd tear you up." I was considerably brighter when I got through supper and breakfast without being in the pill book. I found the foreign-police statement in the 1964 staff report, which was part of the respondent's brief in 1965, along with Gumanis's statement. Triumphantly I told Hezy I was going to send Rich a note.

"A waste of good paper," Hezy said. "You know how much they care about what comes out of their mouths. Ever ride behind a loose mule?"

Still, I knew I was not out of danger. Thus, when a strange attendant leaned over the wall shortly after 3:00 and asked, "You Kenneth? Kenneth Donaldson?" shock waves went through me, as in the jail when they came for me in the middle of the night.

"I'm from the Back Yard," he said.

As transfers were made on the second shift, did this mean I was on the list for special treatment for talking up to Rich?

"Your friend Carter went home this evening and he wanted me to tell you that he would help you just as soon as he got there. You know his address?"

"He gave it to me," I said, and my shoulders relaxed.

"It's very important you send it to the right place. Just put down what you want him to do."

"He knows what to do. But thanks."

Good old Carter. Funny how a guy always runs into a first-rate soul wherever he lands. I had not thought I'd find a way around Rich so soon. Then followed two days of sorting papers and discarding work sheets. I was in good shape to travel, having held to a minimum since the night they shook Hezy down for the key.

"Kenny!" It was Yillabar calling as the ward came back from dinner. "Did you know your friend Carter died two days ago?"

"They told me he went home," I said.

"No, he died. I saw the report in the office."

"Why! the mammyjamming sons of bitches!"

Next there was a letter from John Lembcke. Lawyer Beatty
had suggested John come to the hospital and contact the doctors
directly. Superintendent Rogers had already assured John and
Stallings that if John got my father's permission and gave me
adequate supervision, he could take me back to Binghamton.
Thus, no battle would have to be fought in the courts. I would
settle for that, letting my book finish the job.

I was relaxed enough now to enjoy farmer Anson Netherington, who greeted each morning and each evening with: "Dogs
do it and stick to it, birds do it and fly." He had a murder charge
("a crime of passion"). For cleaning the showers and toilets on the
far end, he was allowed to keep a kit of tools: a set of needles and a
skate key, the latter for the louvered windows.

He asked me one day about Grandma: "Have you noticed
lately she lies down a lot?"

"He looked bad this morning," I said. In fact, Grandma had
lost fifty pounds and had even gone to Christian Science services,
then asked me what I knew about healing.

"But you're an atheist," I had said.

"I've been so weak. I have to lie down some days all day,"
Grandma said, lying on the bed with hands over his eyes.

Nether continued, "She's one charge patient without all her
marbles."

"I've never been sure," I said. "He throws the stuff out by the
forkful, but he could be the ace of con artists."

"No, she believes it. That's why the doctors won't let the
bastard go."

"Doctor Rogers says there is no one here can't be cured."

"You could cut her balls off."

"Would you advocate that?"

"No. She has constitutional rights. That wouldn't change her
ideas anyway."

"But they didn't lock Barnum up."

"You may have a point there."

"And a homo won't add to the population explosion."

"That's for sure."

"Then what right does the state have to keep him locked up?"

Two days afterward, Grandma was stretchered up to the
"hospital." A fortnight later, wavy-gray-haired Mr. Looper, eve-

ning foreman on the Front Yard, told me after supper, "Grandma died."

Then there were indications on all sides that things were working for me. My newspapers came uninterrupted for a whole month and the attendants did not give me a hard time on library run; however, to be on the safe side I kept on with my letter writing.

The next event was comparable to the finding of the Dead Sea scrolls. Doctor Rogers consented to letting a reporter from the St. Petersburg *Times,* Mr. Harold Rummel, interview me. I gave my permission for him to see my chart, for, as I told him, there was nothing to hide. If there were any statements in my chart damning to me, I expected him to discuss them with me, then write an exposé. After that, I felt that the weight of public opinion would free me.

Gumanis made sure that one of the two visiting rooms would have no other visitors. He escorted me and threw an arm about my shoulders as I was shaking hands, holding me so tight that I would have had to duck through Rummel's legs to shake him off.

"I've had Kenneth many years," Gumanis said with his broad official smile, "haven't I, son? I'm going to get him out one of these days too. Don't you believe that, Kenneth?" With a pat on my back, he left.

"I've come from O'Connor's office," Mr. Rummel said. "Went over your chart with the doctor—about two hours. You've had an interesting stay."

"But not pleasant."

"What I am interested in now is what led up to this commitment. I talked with your father and mother in Largo. They say that you never were dangerous."

I was silent a long time.

Then Rummel said, "I've had two long telephone conversations with Stallings. He says some of you were instrumental in preventing a riot. Have any regrets?"

"I've had many a long look at freedom since, but I'm not sorry. The others are all out. It's cost me five years—but it's the best road. The only permanent solution can come through law and order."

"That is one reason why my editor was interested."

"The *Times* won its Pulitzer last year for saving the state millions in graft. There's something here that's more important. The price to the state in Chattahoochee is measured in lives—

hundreds, thousands—needlessly destroyed." I got heated going over the doctors at staff. "There's no excuse for what they do to a person." My voice rose. "I've just started to fight. I've sworn to fight these doctors all the way down to the gates of Hell, if necessary, where I'm sure to find some way to push them in ahead of me. They—"

"I've read your briefs in Tallahassee, Kenneth. I know how you feel. What interests me now is what happened out west—up in Philadelphia—in St. Pete. Do you have any qualms in talking about it?"

"None at all."

"Let's start way back in Syracuse then."

"I was found walking the street by my wife and my father. . . ."

We took one break at noon for a coke, the attendants letting me skip the slop.

At the end of three hours, he put his pen in his pocket and his note pad in a big brown envelope, saying: "Do one more thing for me, Kenneth. Write down all these dates and anything else you have upstairs and send them to me through your friend in Los Angeles."

That was Zena, who was now my private correspondent.

Then I had two weeks to brood. Had I been too dramatic? A letter from Rummel explained: "I've talked it over with Stallings. There's nothing we can do until we get an independent doctor."

That meant that they could not accept the story, the same one as told in chapters 2 to 4 in this book. I would have preferred separating the two parts. But, as with Rummel, the first questions by every audience always are about what led up to Chattahoochee, what led up to Marcy. It is a dilemma without a solution.

I set about getting whatever proof I could for Rummel and Stallings. Both wanted a copy of my examination report from the Philadelphia clinic, which Rummel said was not in my chart. My requests for that report were to extend over the next six years. First, the clinic in Philadelphia wanted $2.00. Then they wanted my mother's maiden name.

But other letters were bringing replies. Doctor Birnbaum wrote that he had "been engaged in constant litigation in New York State in one case for more than six years. . . . The truth is that the courts will not listen to a case such as yours at present, because they do not understand the problems involved. . . . The only [thing] is to convince the authorities that you should be released now. Unfortunately, bureaucrats are bureaucrats, whether they are doctors, lawyers, or laymen."

Still and all, there was some force at work for me, whether perseverance or luck. On one of those quiet afternoons, with half the ward at the movies, A.B. leaned over the wall as though to peer at my paper.

"I've got something of value for you," he said. "Did you know how a patient got out—off this ward too—Albert Plevins? Slept that next pen there. His father got a court order in 1964 on the basis of his being held by an untrained doctor. Did you know that Gumanis is licensed by the state only as a woman's doctor?"

"Obstetrician?" I said.

"That's it. He tried the state exam twice for psychiatrist. Couldn't pass it nary the once. Thought you might be able to use that."

I got the information off to Rummel and others in my private mail. He did not answer. Stallings did not answer either. ACLU, Miami, sent a two-page questionnaire, fashioned for the inmates at Raiford.

Another letter astonished me. I had sent Jack, seeing that he was staying in the fight with Zena and Stallings, a copy of the list I had furnished Rummel, thinking that Jack would like to know the whole story too.

His reply was short: "I am beginning to doubt that anyone can help you. All this stuff about the little green men. It is a pity what one of those institutions can do to a fine mind. But I will, however, still do what I can."

Zena wrote: "I have a copy of Jack's letter. I must agree with him about the little green men, and I am sending you a pack-age."

It contained six papier-mâché green monkeys in sitting positions, which I mounted on a folded carton on my stand. I loved them, but I was heart-weary at Zena's disaffection.

Yet, I was far from ready to give up and lie quiet for the knockout count. And, following Nether's rule: "The best way to get a thing done is to fuel the mule yourself," I had been working on a version of my story in diary form, entitled *3000 Days—For What?* Zena sent it to a New York paperback publisher, in hopes of earning enough to get some outstanding northern lawyer for my case. It was 43,000 words, which I had neatly hand lettered in 18-point. It never came back, though they said they mailed it. Anyway, it brought Zena around.

But the business of the little green men made me mad. If no one was going to believe me anyway, there was no need to crawl to improve my position. So, when a fellow patient told me, "If my sister ever wrote these doctors without my permission, I've told her we'd be through, once and for all. And that's the stand you should take, Kenneth. If I did as many years as you, I'd have it my way at the end."

I agreed. It is "maddening" as you wait month after month on the wards, after telling people outside what goes on in the name of medicine, to have them remain silent, as if they had some superior source of information.

I wrote all three children: "I am not going to be viewed like a monkey in a cage. If you want to see me, you must promise to believe that what I tell you is the truth. You don't have to do one damn thing about getting me out." But don't write the doctors about me, I laid down the law, until you have first cleared it with me.

Taking that action might have been a mistake. I could see how it was letting my anger spill over to affect the lives of my children, though it was not anger directed at them. It seemed better, at the time, though, to sacrifice normal relationships with them, rather than give them the slightest notion that I accepted any of the doctors' judgments. My hopes always were that, when I had won the larger battle, i.e., had won my unconditional release, my children would see that I had been right.

The older son obeyed me. I can appreciate the feelings of the other children, in light of the outsider's vague picture of the operation of an asylum.

Two weeks later, Gumanis called me down. Keeping his hands off the file box and skipping the three questions, he handed me an unfolded letter to read. It began: "It is my understanding that my father is sick. Would you please tell me the true condition of his present state?"

It was from my younger son. I handed it back.

"Go on, read all of it," Gumanis said.

"I told my children explicitly that if they communicated with the hospital without first clearing it with me, they were through," I said.

"You shouldn't be like that. You can't get along with any of your family. How do you expect to get out if you can't get along with your children?"

"How I decide to handle my contacts with my children

doesn't make me dangerous. It is no excuse for these people holding me for nine years. Why, some of the most despicable criminals—armed assault, beating up and raping little children—they do six months or a year—and you want to keep me because I tell my children I am the father, they aren't.''

Gumanis was a bit sheepish.

Things lay quiet for some weeks until I was called for visitors. I refused to go without knowing who it was.

Yillabar got Jesstar on the phone, and he came running. "Goodness gracious, son! It's your own flesh and blood—your daughter." He tried to encircle my shoulders. "They're with Gumanis. They'll be back after dinner to see you."

After dinner I refused to budge. Joe Flake talked to me out on the landing by the elevator, standing with one foot up on the gray radiator cover.

"Haven't I treated you all right?" he said.

I thought: "Except for one time on the Back Yard when I lost a Christmas Shirt." But this wasn't the time to remind him.

"I talked to them," he said. "Your daughter wants to take you out."

"I explained to my children that I'm not going to be subjected to indignities ladled out by a bunch of goddamned mammyjamming honey-dippers. If my children can't decide that I wouldn't lie to them, let them wait until they can."

Ten minutes later, a cold heart looked down from the third-floor window onto a tall straight son-in-law with the baby in his arms and the other two boys skipping ahead. And Beverly—she was a pretty woman.

That seemed to me a wise decision in 1966. If I gave one inch and let my daughter sign me out, I would lose the whole case against institutional psychiatry, for then the doctors could say they had cured me and let me go. My next decision was also weighed on the scales against the nine years already down the drain. The slim man in the brown suit in the visitor's room was smiling. His hair was whitish but otherwise he was the same red-headed John Lembcke I had gone to school with.

"I came to Atlanta for a seminar," John said. "I've got four days before I have to be back. Would you go down to your mother and father's with me, before we drive north?"

"Of course," I said. "Did Gumanis say he'd let me go?"

"I haven't seen him yet."

"I'll go back to the ward now, so's you can see him this

morning. You haven't changed, except for the hair. I'd have known you on Market Street."

"You look good, Kenneth."

But I realized I only looked good to other patients. The big circles under our eyes and the lines in our faces did not match the free world's freshness.

After dinner, John said, "He says you have to go to staff."

"Didn't the lawyer Beatty tell you they'd let me go?" I said.

"Yes."

"Then call him."

In the morning John said Beatty told him to see Doctor Rich.

"He's been rough," I said. "I say to see Doctor O'Connor. After all, he has to pass on whatever Rich does and he's always been nice to my face." And if Beatty wasn't going to come over and help, what good was his advice?

After dinner John said, "Doctor O'Connor was very nice. He said he didn't think you would want to do what I wanted you to. I told him that I could swear you would. I've got a job for you in my office. Would you take it?"

"There's no question about it. I don't think I'd want to make a career of bookkeeping but I believe I could handle it."

"That's what I told O'Connor." John reached over and shook hands warmly. His eyes were moist.

"Then I could leave without going to staff?"

"O'Connor said it was solely up to Gumanis."

"It's a runaround, John. Gumanis says it's solely up to O'Connor. They let lots of guys go out of state without staff. Is Jackson Beatty coming over?"

"No."

After a minute, John said, "Sure you won't try staff once more?"

"No."

"All right."

The day after John drove away from Chattahoochee, I imploded. I was walking the center aisle, deaf to the suggestions of a friendly criminal about walking being a signal of disturbance to the attendants. It was time to lay the cards on the table in such a way that doctors Gumanis and O'Connor would be under no misapprehension about my going to staff. If they had wanted to be fair at all, they could have let me go with John without staff. Their refusal meant one of two things: they intended to make me get on my knees to them or they intended to keep me forever. I would accept neither. I thought for two hours and found the exact words that could not be mistaken, words that I could swear to on the witness stand, words that meant I would find some way out other than with the help of these doctors. Thus, in my tenth year, here was the point of no return with these two doctors. Only one of us would win. I put my words in identical letters to Doctor Szasz and Representative Stallings. I sent them through the censors, knowing that photocopies would be made for the doctors. I followed one note of caution. Taking a new friend's advice, I attacked only O'Connor, thus not burning my last bridge of possible compromise in the event Gumanis was not guilty with O'Connor. The letters said:

16 May 1966

Dear Mr. Stallings:
This is the final straw: Whereas, written permission had been given for Mr. Lembcke to sign me out and, whereas, dozens of other inmates have been so released, Mr. Lembcke is gone and I am not.
Who stopped me?

My answer, of course, described O'Connor in well-seasoned terms.

I was called down to Gumanis's the following afternoon.

Doctor Gumanis (much heated): "What's the idea of sending those letters? Here I had it all set for you to go to staff this week and you do something like this." [Screaming] "I sent them over to the office. They made photostats of them for your record. Then they mailed them—I want you to know they were mailed. The doctors called them paranoid."

Me: "I don't care what they called them."

Gumanis: "How you going to get out? I can still talk the doctors into passing you. . . . Stallings can't help you. I don't care what he does."

Me: "I'll tell him that."

G (rising to another yell): "I don't care what you tell him. He doesn't pay my salary."

Me: "I'll tell him that too."

G (frothing): "Go ahead—tell him anything!"

Me: "I will. But I didn't come down here to argue."

G: "If you don't go to staff, you'll stay here forever." [After I got up] "I've spent more time on your case than on any other patient's. You should see the number of letters I have written."

Me (at the door): "Then I feel sorry for the others."

The next day there was a letter from Mother:

> Just a line to tell you that we are going along with John's plans and are waiting for the Hospital papers to sign, which we will do and send them on. Kenny, we are happy but not building our hopes too high. We love you, dear boy, and long for happy days for you.

I was glad to see, after years of wondering where my parents stood, that they had finally come around to a position which could be helpful.

Others were taking steps in my behalf too. Zena sent me a thousand sheets of legal-size paper and a box of carbon paper.

Although things advanced slowly, it seemed that everything was confirming my new confidence in getting out on my own terms. In my fishing for some way to pressure the institution, I came up with a letter from Zena, quoting Doctor Szasz. He was willing to come and examine me. I dropped that news to Stallings through the censors. It got me called down promptly by young Zaffler, a social worker. He said I was now well enough to be released. He asked to see my Social Security records in the morning. Sitting in with him for the experience was a sociology graduate, young Looper, son of our evening foreman. He spotted the four months where there had been no record when I had been self-employed in Charleston, South Carolina. "That proves," Looper said, "that you might have been a citizen of Florida for four months."

"I've been here long enough," I retorted, "to know that there are some honest people in Florida, but none of them have been involved in my case."

Looper's face was crimson.

The two social workers had, during the talks, asked if I did not think my parents were the only ones to blame for my commitment. Then Gumanis carried on the theme that only my parents were to blame. I rejected that argument, telling them every time that my parents were neither the county judge who could commit me nor the doctors who could hold me.

Yet I was beginning to worry about my parents' health. Mother had had several operations, including one for cataracts. I wrote them: "This is an awful way for us to end our lives. . . . But, if you live a little longer, you will see my faith entirely vindicated." Again, I wrote: "Your last letter sounded, once again, like the parents I thought I had. . . . Just believe me, and this business will turn out all right as far as you and I are concerned."

The last letter from Mother said: "We have not forgotten our dear boy. Your mother has been sick. . . . I can't see where I am writing, but keep going. . . ."

I like to think that only age kept my parents in the group that seemed to be convinced of the effectiveness of psychiatry.

Whether or not psychiatry will ever be a science, the rankest phoniness of institutional psychiatry is shown in the treatment of prisoners. The one mystery was why the men from Raiford, who might be inclined to swat anyone who called them a bug and who said food and other living conditions were better at Raiford, would choose to stay in a bughouse. The explanation came from Albert, one morning as we walked: "In Chattahoochee they can draw their Social Security."

One "criminal" on the wards with me who did not want to stay was Jesse Daniels, a slow, timorous individual. He did fourteen years while the state Supreme Court refused to hear his case. He had been arrested in his teens "for the rape of a Florida woman who said she had been attacked by a black man. Daniels is white," said an Associated Press dispatch, Syracuse *Herald-Journal,* April 17, 1974. Jesse was neither retarded nor crazy but "he remained at the hospital until the Supreme Court ordered his release in 1971." Incidentally, in perhaps the only such action ever in Florida, the legislature voted him $75,000 in 1974 in payment for his illegal confinement.

Some hardened criminals and young punks cured themselves of the illness that kept them in small cells in the Flattop by tearing it up, ripping out plumbing and beds, throwing soggy mattresses at guards, who came on the run to see why water was flowing down the stairs. Doctor Gumanis had to distribute them through the wards. Their second night on Ward 7, three of them held a razor to foreman Looper's throat. He unlocked every door to the street, handed over his keys, and accompanied his captors on the back seat of his car.

It happened at 8:50, so quietly that I missed the main part of the show. The aftermath was noisier. Three more criminals jumped an attendant who had already been slashed on the back in the first attack. He held them off with a chair while other attendants stood some distance away, two even locking themselves in the clothes room. Bloodhounds were put on the trail. City and county police, day-shift supervisors and attendants, and doctors all milled around outside the office in the warm night. The one dog left in its cage on a trailer was center stage, giving a deep growl from time to time.

Looper was returned by state police before morning and the three escapees before noon. They got a needle in the rump at the beginning of each shift.

More criminal was the treatment meted out to Vittorio.

I was standing, one morning, waiting while Airtrane passed out letters before he got to the bottom of his bag for my papers, when Yillabar called me.

"Don't you think Vittorio Dacker looks better?" he said, as Vittorio was being brought across Ward 7 on the way from the Back Yard to the dressing room. Vitt had two black eyes, was tied up in a straitjacket, and drooped like wilted beet greens.

Ten months previously, he had been a robust sixty, all five foot six. An amateur boxer, an opera baritone, he had last been the prosperous proprietor of Vitt's Spaghetti House, in St. Pete. Domestic strife (accusations of someone else's husband and someone else's wife) put him in Chattahoochee. Doctor Gumanis had been coaxing him to go to staff, but he refused, vowing like me, though we were not cognizant of each other's plans at the time, to get a clear-cut discharge through the courts, so as to be free from his wife's vendetta.

Vitt had arrived on old Ward 1 about the time of the investigation. His rollicking *Barber of Seville* flooded the ward every morning for a week. Then he cooled on the Back Yard. There he saw too much senseless sadism for his sensitive soul. He dedicated his remaining years to fighting for humaneness for the so-called mentally ill. For a few years he was on the open ward, until his friend Joe Doppling died. It was not an easy death. Joe went downhill fast, then lingered for four months. Intelligent, he claimed Gumanis was injuring him with new medication and his friends believed him. When Joe died, Vitt fired a letter off to Governor Hayden Burns. It came back through channels, down to Gumanis's desk. Without the doctor's seeing him, which other psychiatrists label as second-hand head-shrinking, Vitt was put on a locked ward, he told me, with an increase in medication.

Joe Doppling died in July 1965. The following summer Vitt was seated at a small table in the patio under the rear building when Ward 7 was let out. He called me over.

"I hear you're fighting this place in the courts," he said. "Any chance you'll be released soon?"

Sitting down, I said, "It can't be much longer. This has been going on six years. I got a writ in 1960 and I thought every month since then that I was just about to be freed."

"Can't do it alone," Vitt said. "But I stopped you to tell you I appreciated your *Christian Science Monitors*. Grandma used to save them. I'll be glad when these warehouses are run on Mrs. Eddy's principles, not Gumanis's. I am writing to people I met when I was in the chorus at the Met and when I was assistant to my senator from New Hampshire. After I get out I'm going to do something for you and then I'm going to see Gumanis pay for Joe Doppling's death."

As he told me, Vitt began to shake. His voice left. Then he whispered, "Do you think I've got the strength to do it?"

"God provides us with the strength we need whenever we need it," I said. "With a body like yours, there's no question about it. It could be the medication making you nervous."

"Yes, that's it. I'm all right now. It's hard to be alone in here. I know you're right. I'll be all right."

It was like that every morning for a couple of weeks. But the goons were working on him. One day he did not show on the yard. One of the brainwashers sitting with the attendants had called Vitt an s.o.b. His temperament carried him over the desk and he knocked the guy to the floor. They had Vitt trapped. They put a big goon on the bed next him to pick a fight, and for fighting, Vitt landed on the worst ward in the Back Yard. Fellows on the far end of Ward 7 could see Vitt throw the drawers out of his stand, across the pen and into the aisle. Each outburst, whether he was goaded into it or not, brought larger and larger doses of tranquilizers, until the pill man used two needles. Vitt was so angry—mad, really, to all appearances—that he figured to straighten out Chattahoochee with his own hands. He was a morsel of delight for the meat grinder. He came through Ward 7 so full of liquid Thorazine, the morning Yillabar called my attention to him, that his eyes were frozen open and he had to be led by hand.

"Tearing up a ward at 3:00 A.M." is often stated by administrators as a reason for maintaining an inmate's involuntary commitment. Which came first, Vitt's egg or the goon's chicken?

Perhaps it would have been more humane to handle Vitt with Chemical Mace as is done to "violent patients" at the New Jersey State Hospital in Trenton, where "its use has improved staff morale," as reported in *Freedom-Scientology,* No. 4, 1970. "The spray, effective at 12 to 15 feet, is directed at the face and eyes of the patient and is usually used by the hospital at a distance of 6 feet.

Often more than the 'recommended' single one-second spray is used by Trenton State staff. Once hit by the spray, the patient abruptly stops, holds his eyes and tries not to breathe. Suffering an uncertainty in physical orientation, the patient usually sinks to the floor to avoid falling and to gain firm support."

But Chattahoochee had its way and Vitt did not choose my way. Instead, like the men and boys being driven into the ovens at Auschwitz, he used his last ounce of strength to "spit on the guards."

Yillabar was surprised when I told him the whole story, having been told that Vittorio was having one of his periodical relapses. Provocation or relapse?

One day, they brought Vitt into the dining room on a trial run to see if he could be rehabilitated. He happened to spot my table. Still in a straitjacket and fed by attendants, he reached over with his teeth and pulled an empty ballpoint from my shirt pocket. His mind wandered, but he released his bite when I explained the pen was only for opening letters.

Later in the summer, when I saw him again, in the Back Yard, he would take off all his clothes, sometimes ripping them to pieces, and standing behind the fence between the yards would holler, "Kenneth Donaldson! Kenneth Donaldson!"

"You know my name?" he would ask.

"Yes," I would say.

"What is it?"

"Vittorio Dacker."

"That name is going to mean something when these places are cleaned up. Do you still read the *Monitor?* Still read *Science and Health?* Good boy. And that representative's name? Stallings. You don't have to tell me."

Then Vitt would twirl in the majesty of his superb nakedness. A gathering audience of the top criminals would catcall. He would cuss them roundly. More catcalls and the throwing of small stones by each side. Then I would ease away while he screamed, "Kenneth Donaldson! Kenneth Donaldson!"

Every afternoon Vitt would stand quiet, intensely interested in the smallest bit of news from Stallings and the possibility that my case might generate another investigation. But the performance, like a four-year-old, for the new fellows on my side of the fence went on for a full hour. Singing, making obscene naked gestures, urinating while he twirled was too much for me. I had to walk away.

CHAPTER 16

1967

Layering-in
the Pork

IT WAS A FLORIDA JANUARY DAY FORETELLING SPRING. THE WARM AIR brushed our faces as I laid my pencil and clipboard on the bed. Netherington and I talked and watched attendants cut across the short parkway bordering the main offices. Bright winter flowers, on tall stems in circular plots, waved to the few visitors.

I said, "You know, when I go see my children in Arizona, I think I'll rent a long red wig—down to my shoulders—and a purple serape—then trudge up the road in sandals."

"You'd never make it," Nether said. "The sheriff'd have you."

"Or the grandchildren would bushwhack me."

Our laughter was interrupted by an attendant coming for me for doctor's call, my first since John Lembcke's visit.

"That means Gumanis will have his feet off the desk this afternoon," Nether said. "He reads girlie mags. I've seen him."

Doctor Gumanis handed me a letter to read: "I am asking you to inform Kenneth Donaldson that his mother has passed away. . . ."

It was not a shock, because of her sickness and age.

I handed it back, saying, "I'm sorry. I'm sorry she died before this could be straightened out." Not having her see my final victory is one of my keenest disappointments.

Gumanis shifted quickly from condolence to the question of staff, getting heated and loud. I noticed his lower teeth had brown stains down the edges from his pipe. I said yes, very much I would like to be released. He brought up the point again, about being anxious to get out the last of the old-timers.

"When you get ready to let me go, then let me know," I said.

"You're not a troublemaker and you should be out," he said.

"Yes, you get all the troublemakers out."

Gumanis snapped: "I don't have anything to do with that!"

It was beginning to look as if he had precious little to do with anything.

Yillabar told Hezy, "He'll be out in sixty days."

But, as weeks went by, I sent off my twelfth petition to the courts, with copies to the several lawyers who had sporadically looked into the case. Doctor Birnbaum, the only one to reply, said he was impressed with my argument and, being in a position finally to devote some time to it, offered to take over conduct of the case and stick with it until my release, on the one condition that I would write no court or no other lawyer without his direction.

To brush up on my homework, I reread his "Comments on the Right to Treatment" from the *Archives of General Psychiatry* (July 1965). His argument was: If an inmate is not being given adequate treatment, he is entitled to his release from a state hospital. And the simplicity of this argument has not been affected in ten years.

I took a week or so to relax and gather my thoughts. With Mother gone, I would make up to Dad what I owed both. He was nearly ninety. But with Doctor Birnbaum's help, maybe I'd make it in time.

About this time, two inmates got away by buying a key from an attendant and stealing a woman attendant's car. Then five murderers, with a .22 pistol, had Ward 3 secured for an hour one evening, beat up an old man and took his thirty dollars, and waited for the night supervisor, Macon, to come along with the cash box with the weekly draws for the inmates. They took the supervisor's car, the cash box, and the supervisor.

On the Back Yard, a white patient was choked to death by black attendants' stuffing rags down his throat. Another Back Yard patient was put in the Flattop and beaten brutally by a goon, for having jumped a "rat." In the department's new high-class infirmary building, an old man kept going into the hall to look at the clock. A nurse told him to stop. He cussed her out. Within a week he was dead from overdoses of cathartics.

With so many things like this being added to my own harassment in Department A, it was not with reluctance that I received a five-minute notice to pack for Department C. Nor was the demotion unexpected, for I had been causing too much trouble for Gumanis with all my talking back and legal maneuvers. I was throwing papers into a carton when Grady Jones came up. This gray-haired foreman of the Front Yard, who always had a kind word for me, said: "You can unpack. I put a stop to it. You belong here on a better ward."

But, as I told Call Jesstar later, I was not averse to going. In fact, in a letter to Doctor O'Connor, I had once volunteered to go to promote integration.

As Department A was neither the hospital nor the prison I thought proper for the State of Florida, I had asked governor-elect Claude R. Kirk to do something about it. After inauguration, as my chart shows, an "administrative aide" sent my letter back to the institution with this note: "This fellow seems rational in his letters. Don't know about his facts. Will you give me a report when you get time?"

When my letter came down to Gumanis's desk, he had me down for a screaming session: "There is no such thing as a brainwashing corps here! . . . I run this department! I don't have to have anybody tell me about the patients! . . . We didn't send for you! . . ."

A 5-foot-wide hall, 18 feet long; eighteen men and three attendants sitting on straight chairs along both sides, feet inter-twined; people coming and going through six doors, including the elevator. I marveled that a laundry cart and a triple-deck food rack could pass, let alone either one even get in the hall. Dimness, low ceilings, antiquity, that was Department C.

I am reminded of what a state hospital superintendent reportedly told Professor David Rothman, Columbia University: "What we need is a better grade of patients. There is nothing wrong with the system."

Later in the morning, while I was being questioned on my medical history by sick bay attendants and given a quick physical by Doctor Sanguinetti, I had left a pair of shower clogs under a guy's mattress, which he said was the only safe place in the whole department. When I went back in thirty minutes, the clogs and the guy were gone. In my pocket now, wrapped in one of my socks, were comb, toothbrush and paste, nail clippers, and pen. Everything else brought over from Department A was in a shoebox on the floor of young Robert Carmichael's office. He had risen from attendant in A to supervisor in C. My papers and books were in A Department's baggage room, which also served the few C men who had anything to store. "Don't have anything you can't carry," Carmichael had warned me. "The attendant will bring you out to your box anytime."

One of the doors in the jammed hall opened into the office of Israel Hanenson, M.D. In the far corner of the 15-foot room, wearing very thick lenses, he peered over 2-foot piles of books along the front of his desk.

He spoke briskly, "What day is this?"

"Nineteenth—let's see—no—eighteenth."

"I didn't ask you that. What day? What day?"

"Wednesday—no, we change linen on Wednesday—Tuesday."

After a few more questions, he said, "I see indications that you are nervous. I am going to put you on a maintenance dose of medication." He disregarded my protests. "In this department we don't believe in Christian Science—you will take medication. Do you prefer liquid or tablet? We give you a choice—or we can even give the needle."

"Tablet."

While he wrote he said, "How often did you see Doctor Gumanis? . . . Well, we don't do as he does. Do you know that I have three hundred more patients than Doctor Gumanis and I manage to see my men every two or three weeks?"

A 50-mg tablet of Thorazine, three times a day, was the dosage. I held the first tablet under my tongue until I could spit it into the toilet. At the second meal, attendants threatened me with the needle if I spit out another. The Thorazine caused a narrow purple ring beneath each eye, by the second day. The third day it covered both eye sockets and a spot on the left nostril. I sent word to the doctor but was not called.

My hopes were at an all-time low. This was how Carter and Vittorio had been taken care of.

Then, again, a miracle. On the fifth morning I went to sick

bay and the pill man took me in to Hanenson. The doctor discontinued the medication. That was Thursday and the spots were gone by Saturday.

On Monday, more depression. The doctor put me on Mellaril. Again the spots. Other reactions from the medicines were a slight fever for several hours, a pounding in the ears for an hour, and a distinct impairment of hearing. There was a numbing around the edge of the cranium, drowsiness all day—a miserable insatiable drowsiness and a tiredness, without being able to actually sleep more than five minutes at a time during the day and fitful sleep during a long night of tossing. I got up and dressed at 3:30 one night, thinking it breakfast time. After three more days, the pill man said the doctor had discontinued all medication except a vitamin capsule.

On second doctor's call, Hanenson had my file open. "It was O'Connor who asked to have you examined by the psychologist last time. Would you refuse again?"

"No," I said, "I made a clean break with the past when I came to this department." Before leaving, I said, "You might chew a patient's head off, but I don't think you'd lie to him."

I was applying Warden Lawes's principle: When dealing with a criminal [in this case a doctor] let him think you believe him.

Hanenson was quick to pick me up. "You mean a doctor here would lie to his patient?"

It was a ticklish moment. But I got away without answering.

Out on the wards, I showed around a letter that happened to come from Senator Robert Kennedy, in answer to a suggestion of mine. It had a great effect on the attendants, who were mostly Negro. Kennedy was of course a hero to the Negro attendants, whereas he was scorned by white attendants. Here was the working Christianity I had witnessed in Georgia and South Carolina. Negro day foreman Ronny Po was typical: laughing, quick to do a favor, with time to sympathize with any patient, black or white. While I marked time, I volunteered for houseman and wrote the doctor about working in the laundry with two hundred sweating Negroes, men and women, who got no pay.

My bed was narrow, with a foot-deep hole in the middle. There was a foot between beds in row after row. Six fifteen-watt bulbs complemented the TV, which blasted until 11:00.

When we stayed in, there were 240 mission rockers for 260 men on opposite sides of the porch, which was L-shaped, 280 feet by 11 feet, with heavy grilles on double-hung sashes. Walking meant bumping into others and hopping over legs. Sleeping meant abandoning one's medically twitching body in the damp space around the spit trough or pressing one's throbbing forehead into the arm of the rocker. Once a day someone would crash in a fit. Thieving cardplayers erupted into fistfights. All day someone or other was moaning or screaming or beseeching God for deliverance.

When we stayed on the yard, a thousand souls abandoned by the twentieth century kicked up dust or took shelter under magnificent live oaks. Some of the young threw a basketball at a hoop and picked the pockets of the helpless, who were scared to tell. When I could overcome, for a while, the weakness remaining from the medication, I would take my shirt off and walk in the sun. One or another of the white men I had known on A, who could not for long sit, stand, sleep, or stay awake from medication, might fall in step with me for a minute. Each one's story was alike, in heartbreak, in senselessness, in finality. Forgotten by flesh and blood, abhorred by society, we were 1,350 souls dependent on one nearsighted doctor.

This is from an entry in my journal, telling about my next break, a transfer to a better ward:

> I have been two nights in Building 41, in Ward 10 (#41 has two wards with a total of one hundred men, all on one floor, formerly TB wards for both men and women). Fritz D. calls it the country club. We have a small private "dog run," a porch to sit on with household screening (I sat out there until 9:00 last night . . .), cookies and punch in midmorning every Friday, use of the kitchen (electric stove) to make coffee or cook up an omelet . . . and graham crackers and peanut butter to nibble on. I could, of course, be having a dream, but it all still seems real.
>
> It all came about on Thursday when I asked the doctor if I might go to Occupational Therapy while I was waiting for release and he suggested I be transferred to 41, where OT is held in the basement and where I would be free from the "roughnecks" (his word), as there are no charge patients in 41. . . .

Before I had left the big building, a Negro attendant, Raymas Little, sat down beside me one day. As we looked through the wire mesh at dripping oak leaves, I told Raymas my story.

"You're not sick," Raymas said. "The doctor listens to me. I'm going to tell him to let you go."

While I waited, I found OT fun. Young, overweight Baldy-locks had about five of us. He was a zealous worker in his church, and did not swear, drink, or smoke. He translated his religion to his work by showing compassion and understanding to all of us. He let me spend afternoons learning the touch system of typing.

"How much of your book is ready?" Baldylocks said.

"About half," I said.

"You are going to be kind to us Chattahoocheeans?"

"Where deserved. I'm going to show Doctor Gumanis for what he is."

"I have to report these things, you know."

"I don't give a damn. I told Gumanis to his face. I've found an honest doctor who's going to put me to staff next week."

Mornings, I worked on number paintings, at first. Then Fritz showed me how to turn wooden bowls on the lathe. After two items made for the state, which were sold at OT headquarters, the patient kept the third. In time, I was able to send bowls to Zena, John, and Morton Birnbaum.

Baldylocks agreed with Fritz that we should have a cooking class upstairs each Friday. The first week Baldylocks stewed a chicken and dumplings. I fixed the tomatoes and lettuce and poured the cocoa. Over the weeks I became chief cook and only potwasher. Yet it was true relaxation to scrape a jar of mustard experimentally into a meat loaf and to layer-in pork chops, potatoes, and onions in a roaster.

Still, pleasures in Chattahoochee always carried a grim side. Walking into the general kitchen with Baldylocks for supplies was a shock, upon realizing it was ten years since I had come fresh off the streets without an all-encompassing hatred for everything Floridian.

A screen door opened on the downhill side of OT, offering long looks at life in the vacation sun. There were blue jays and lawn, oaks and firs against powerhouse smokestack and ware-houses. Outside the door, the neighborhood dogs, cringing curs called fices, lolled in the sun and raised their noses only at the prospect of a bone. They seemed to tell something about sadistic masters.

Baldylocks started taking the OT men and a half dozen from

upstairs for a two-hour walk on the grounds each Wednesday. Under the umbrella of all this warmth, I began watching the news on TV again. This was not breaking my vow, I decided, for I was out of Department A.

Things were improving so rapidly that it seemed the whole world was conspiring to save me. At the direction of Doctor Hanenson, so that there would be something concrete to show Doctor Rich, John Lembcke wrote me: "I will be happy to have you come and stay with me in Binghamton, New York."

In July, Morton Birnbaum felt we could win in the courts. He wrote: "If I did not, however, think that there was some chance of success, I would not bother to involve myself in this matter or cause you the added psychological burden of yet another legal proceeding."

I replied that "After ten years, defeat is no longer a psychological strain. Rather my troubles are physical."

I was doubly glad I had said that, for Samuel Cunningham flunked me on the psychological test again.

When Morton Birnbaum was turned down by the Court of Appeals for the Fifth Circuit, he filed with the Supreme Court of the United States.

Altogether, 1967 had been the most portentous year by far. It was such an improvement in my living conditions that it seemed possible the charge attendant was right when he said, "This place will be a hospital yet."

IN THE COURTS, 1967

(xii)

U.S. District Court, Tampa   No. 67-182 Civ. T.   4/6/67

My brief said: ". . . Everything decided about me in my case has been done when I was not there. . . . My petitions in court have been decided on the words of an absent doctor who has seen neither the court nor me, but who "interprets" to the court what he has heard from some third party about me. . . .

"There is no need for this Honorable Court to make a ruling on my mental health from a medical viewpoint but simply to determine if I and my witnesses are credible."

It was denied April 27.

U.S. Court of Appeals, Fifth Circuit   No. 839   8/7/67

In petition for Certificate of Probable Cause, filed by Morton Birnbaum, he said: ". . . The simple question being raised by petitioner is really nothing more or less than the question of whether the State of Florida can establish a human storage bin for the mentally ill without violating the provisions of the due process of law and equal protection of law requirements of the Fourteenth Amendment."

The court denied the petition on September 19, saying that petitioner has not exhausted the state's available remedies.

(xiv)

The Supreme Court of the United States   390 U.S. 971   12/18/67

In petition for certiorari, Morton Birnbaum said: ". . . Respondents submitted no answering papers to the petition presented by the petitioner to the District Court.

"QUESTIONS PRESENTED:

"A. Is the petitioner sufficiently mentally ill to constitutionally allow involuntary institutionalization in a public mental institution?

"B. Does an involuntary inmate of a public mental institution who has been committed by remedial procedural methods solely because the State claims that he is sufficiently mentally ill to need care and treatment in a public mental institution, and who now receives grossly inadequate care and treatment, have a constitutional right to adequate care and treatment so that he may regain his health, and thereafter his liberty, as soon as possible?

"C. Is it constitutionally required to offer to a petitioner in a habeas corpus proceeding who is alleged to be severely mentally ill, the services of counsel and of an expert witness on his behalf?

"FACTS: . . . At present, respondents contend that Donaldson's involuntary institutionalization may continue until his death. . . . .

". . . we see a continuation of the underlying theme of American forensic psychiatry that it should concern itself primarily with those mentally ill who are accused of committing criminal acts.

"If Donaldson had looted, plundered and maimed, if he were a narcotic addict, or if he were a criminal psychopath, great interest might well have been shown in his case by the courts, by law reviews, by civil liberty groups, etc. to assure that all of his substantive and procedural rights had been protected."

CHAPTER 17

1968

So Many Skeletons

"I JUST CAN'T BELIEVE IT," I SAID, THE MORNING THE REV. TELFORD Sixx died.

"I kept telling you," Fritz Demsy said, "that C Department was no different from A. They're a little more subtle here, that's all."

Sixx was a retired Canadian Episcopal priest. He landed in Chattahoochee after a hassle with his wife over his church pension. All we in Building 41 could see wrong was his stinginess and his habit of pushing another patient's pan to a back burner when he wanted to fix a can of soup. And having once written a series of children's books, he was sarcastic about my aspirations to authorship. Doctor Hanenson would not hear anything against Sixx, however. He would have released him but Sixx had required gallbladder surgery.

The Canadian was weak recovering and, in his misery, sharptongued. Because he was losing two pounds a day and bitching about the lack of food, the "hospital" sent him back to C

Department on a stretcher, early. Sick bay having a waiting list, the ambulance rolled him out at 41. Fritz cooked him a cheese omelet and on Friday I braised him two pork chops. It being a pretty time of year, with the H-shaped one-story building surrounded by purple and pink azaleas, the charge attendant, Nessley Wisston, would tote a heavy rocker for him out onto the lawn.

But Telford Sixx's strength did not return. He slept next to Fritz, who would get up in the middle of the night and make him some bouillon. And Fritz consoled him for two days when his wife died. Then a brother priest invited him to his mission in Mexico, where he could lie in the sun. The doctor okayed that and Sixx got ready by dictating long letters to Fritz, for Mexico, the pension board, and his daughter downstate. That brought a visit by the daughter and husband, a native Floridian.

"But we need the pension for payments on the house we just bought," the son-in-law said in the visiting room. "You just don't appreciate all that us Floridians are doing for you."

"You psalm-singing bastard!" the reverend bellowed, upsetting the quiet dignity that Department C's new visiting room projected to the public.

That called for a new sheet in 41's huge sturdy pill book: 150 mg. Thorazine, four times a day for Telford Sixx.

Fritz got a letter off to Mexico through the grapevine and the missionary flew up the next week. But Doctor Hanenson, in his interpretation of the reports of the situation, refused to let the missionary see Telford. That brought an educated castigation of the good doctor from the bed in 41. And to 41 came another order adding 150 mg Mellaril to the Thorazine. The second day following, the ambulance reswallowed the priest. On the fifth day, word came down that Sixx's daughter refused to claim the body. Baldylocks closed OT for the afternoon and attended the rites in the tiny morgue back of the women's buildings.

Older people were going to die, I knew; however, seeing them pushed over the brink left a continuous tension.

During this period of most intense waiting, Doctor Hanenson and the rest of the department were ignorant of the significance of Birnbaum's work. Affably, they were taking credit for getting me well. Cunningham's only 1968 psychological testing revealed: "... There are no basic alterations in his disorder but he does appear to have become more composed, less sure of his delusions, and generally more cooperative. . . ."

Proving that in every walk of life, people will see what they want to see.

This is what Hanenson saw: "(March 12, 1968) . . . There were times during the interviews the patient exhibited a number of paranoid delusions and ideas of reference mostly centered toward a previous examiner and the Hospital administration. There were other times during the interviews this patient appeared to be under a satisfactory control, elaborating in detail his hospitalization in Chattahoochee. . . ."

Nonetheless, it remained a precarious situation. I was not going to give them one bit of credit for making me well. But I also knew that, lacking Vittorio Dacker's physique, I could go down Telford Sixx's path. The difference—and God bless Morton Birnbaum—was having his hand. He told me in 1968: "You have fought this long for justice, you might as well keep on fighting."

In a note for my book, I wrote: "Sitting on the porch in the warm early-morning sunshine of a spring day takes the mind back to former days, when lazing on a soft summer day had decided charm. The sun is the same today and I know spring still invigorates. But hatred turns the honey into vinegar. In a way, a person should be horrified at what these fiends have done. Horror, though, cannot span weeks, months, years. A deep-seated anger is mortised in and pegged."

Somebody brought a new radio on the porch. Miraculously, it was playing symphonic music. But after years of raucous tunes, I got up and left, afraid that I might slip back into normalcy and stop fighting city hall.

To protect my resolution, I set a limit. If nothing concrete developed in the court by April, then I would run.

I notified Doctor Birnbaum. In March he visited, his first time since we'd met in the antiquated White Male visitor's room. He marveled at the new offices, though I told him that the locked wards of Department C had not changed.

Birnbaum said, "The court denied certiorari."

As my face fell, Doctor Hanenson appeared, saying, "And you are Doctor Birnbaum, I see." They shook hands, then Hanenson went up the street.

Birnbaum then explained: "I came down to discuss the next move. We'll proceed to county court. If we get a hearing, I'll come down. Now, here is what I suggest you put in your brief. Keep it short—judges don't read long petitions. I wouldn't go into your commitment. That isn't important at this time. What we want now is your freedom."

"But the fraudulent commitment is covered specifically under Florida statutes. It should strengthen the case."

"All right. But include it only as one point."

Again we stood as Hanenson dashed in, saying, "I hope I may be pardoned. I am going to put Kenneth to staff this week. What do you say?"

"I'd rather not," I said.

"But it would be better, Mr. Donaldson," Birnbaum said. "It would look better to the court and we can still go back."

To me, that amounted to a sell-out. My dejection was extended the next day, as Hanenson postponed staff until we got a letter prepared, from John Lembcke to Doctor Rich: "I have a place for Kenneth Donaldson to stay; and I will see that he gets adequate supervision; and I will see that he seeks the help of a psychiatrist."

But Rich wanted a more detailed statement regarding a home and supervision. To this John replied: "Kenneth would have a room at the home of a person who has known him a great many years and will be interested in his welfare. He would be readily accessible to medical doctors licensed by the State of New York. He has promised to make use of medical services."

The day of staff, March 21, Hanenson called me to say: "You must not show any hostility. Hostility is the one thing that bothers Rich. Don't argue. If some doctor says something you don't like, don't answer. Do I make myself clear? You don't belong in here, I've got the votes to get you out. Don't argue with the doctors."

I was the first one called. O'Connor was not present. My chart, top one of five, lay open in front of Rich, who leafed a few pages. The two letters from John Lembcke were on the very top.

Rich: "The next time you come to staff, I hope you have a plan to present."

Me: "There—"

Rich: "The only reason the hospital has not released Mr. Donaldson to his friend in New York is because his friend has not shown interest enough to so much as notify the hospital he is willing to take him out."

Hanenson (with his hand on my arm): "I will work something out for Kenneth."

(There were a number of questions by younger doctors on the details of the case.)

Dunin (sitting at far end of table this time, which was half filled, about fifteen present): "You remember me. . . . You say your parents put you in here. Didn't they?"

Me: "They requested I be examined."

Dunin: "That's the same thing."

Me: "But they're not doctors."

Dunin: "But members of families know best. The only thing wrong with you is that you don't know you're sick. Look at me—I have diabetes. So I take medicine for it. You have mental illness and don't know it. You can't see it—that's why you are mentally ill. But instead of being sensible like me and taking some medication for it—no, you'd rather stay here the rest of your life. That's your illness, Donaldson—you are so sick you won't admit it."

An unidentified doctor: "Florida law says you must be examined by two doctors before commitment."

Me: "I know that. That's why I object. It's fraud—absolute fraud in my case."

Doctor: "If the law says you must be examined by two doctors, then you were examined by two doctors."

For the next two hours, back in 41, I thought of many things. I could have told staff that I had (1) found more time to write in Chattahoochee and (2) learned of the inner workings of an asylum, which made clear what had happened to me in Marcy. Still and all, I was satisfied with having told staff that my time in Chattahoochee had been "wasted."

Also, I had in mind clearly Al Siebert's experience in his first week as a psychologist at a large hospital. He wrote: ". . . I was invited by my supervisor to participate in a staff conference on a teen-age girl. I said, 'I'd like to meet her and talk to her.' 'Why?' he asked. I answered, 'If I'm going to participate in any discussion and decisions about a person's life I want to hear their side of the story from them.' He told me in no uncertain terms, 'We don't do that sort of thing here.' "

At five o'clock, I was sitting in Hanenson's office.

Hanenson: "You did very well. But Rich says there has to be a new authorization. You don't mind writing for one, do you?"

Me: "But my father won't sign any more papers—his lawyer won't let him. The one you have is legitimate."

Hanenson: "I'm going to work something out. Rich said you made the best impression of anyone today."

The change in my "disease" shows in Hanenson's post staff remarks, perhaps because there was in Department C no attendant with any reason to funnel upward false reports on me and no doctor afraid of what I would say after I got out:

Doctor Hanenson:

. . . He still does not want to accept the idea that he has been mentally ill and still harbors a great deal of his residuals, in spite of the fact that he does not show any anger or hostility today, I still believe that there is hidden. For the past eleven months he has been at department C, and we took him off his medication in May of 1966 [1967], because I was of the opinion it would not do any good anyway, but he was placed in occupational therapy. He doesn't show any management problem. At the present time I don't believe that he is competent to be released, but I will recommend if there is a possibility that we should receive a statement from Mr. John Lembcke of Binghamton, who claims to be a friend of his, stating explicitly his plans and if he is able to give him supervision while outside of the Hospital atmosphere, then I will recommend him for an out of state discharge. . . .

Doctor Dunin:
I think this patient will never show any further improvement. . . .

Doctor Rich:
I doubt if this patient will ever be released from the Hospital. . . . We have agreed to let this patient go in the past, but so far suitable plans have not ever been arranged.

CONSENSUS OF OPINION:
RECOMMEND RELEASE ON TRIAL VISIT OR OUT OF STATE DISCHARGE.

Bear in mind that I did not read the above until 1974. The fact that the doctors voted for my release and yet did not release me made me wonder once again if they were being honest with me.

The remarks quoted are both amusing and sobering to read. I have no doubt today that they believed what they said, at least some of them. The question I would like answered is: What kind of science is it that can see so many skeletons in the closet of a man who has never *done* anything crazy in sixty-seven years?

I was still waiting in June, when the United States Circuit Court of Appeals for the Tenth Circuit held (in *Herryford v. Parker*) that persons cannot be confined in state mental institutions against their will without having been represented by an attorney at commitment proceedings.

That meant, I thought, that our case was won. Fritz and Nessley celebrated with me over Cokes. But in July's visit, Birnbaum said the local courts were not bound by it.

"And I must ask you to wait sixty days," he said.

"But that'll take us into fall," I said, not foreseeing what he did.

"It's the wisest thing—not to rush now."

His primary aim was to free me. He knew the doctors would put a freeze on my discharge as soon as he went back to court and he foresaw years of delaying tactics in state courts before we could get our case back into federal court.

The closer I got to freedom, the unpleasanter the going. A whole mess of homosexuals was transferred from Department A to Building 41. They quarreled among themselves and raised havoc with the ward's routine.

An evening attendant, at eight o'clock, put a rocker on black Joshua's bed, astraddle the sleeping Joshua, and rocked. The resulting five minutes of screaming should have shattered the windows of Lunacy Hall, 200 feet away. Again, it might be a relief attendant following Dan around the ward and saying, "Dan burned the biscuits," until Dan went into a paroxysm of screaming and stomping. Was it the constant hazing that had driven Joshua to insanity, like Vittorio Dacker? And when during his forty years of working in the hospital bakery had it overtaken Dan? And when would the constant hazing in the toilet, the threats of medication and other bodily harm, the screaming, the crowding in the dining room overtake Kenneth Donaldson?

But I was not ready to give in. A former patient contacted the FBI in Tampa for me and I petitioned the federal and state grand juries. I started a series of letters to all my former correspondents.

"But why," Birnbaum asked on his next visit, "write such long letters?"

"I thought I could make them understand," I said.

"If they don't understand by now, you're wasting your time.

Don't ask anybody. You've asked a thousand people in eleven years. And what have they done? Forget all of them—do the job yourself. We're going to win this—if we live long enough."

But there was still help inside. On my next call to Hanenson's, he sent the assistant out and pulled my chair around by his, behind the desk, and offered his hand to me.

He said he was only one man, that if he were in a position to do so he really would raise a stink about my case.

That emboldened me to say, "May I ask one thing? I can talk to you without your getting angry."

"Of course, go right ahead."

"If Rich or O'Connor wanted someone out, they would go, isn't that so?"

Hanenson did not answer.

"I have just finished writing you a letter." I handed it to him.

"What's this—Superintendent?" His voice was upset, with an edge of controlled choler. "There is only one superintendent here. I am not the superintendent."

"Of Department C," I said. I had used it as a mark of respect. O'Connor had told me that Department A had its own superintendent to handle my case.

Hanenson must have been shouting. He drowned me out. This was during two months when I was almost stone deaf. From sleeping by a damp wall, built into the side of the hill, I had a cold in both ears. Thinking to help me, Hanenson had rinsed them out with a B-17-size syringe. The resulting deafness lasted.

Hanenson read the letter. "You get the wrong interpretation of everything," he yelled in my face.

At our next meeting, Hanenson had to swallow a big white pill he took from his pocket. He said if I didn't stop making him yell at me he'd have a heart attack. I had been arguing that the hospital usually let patients go without a signed authorization from the family. Again he cried that I misinterpreted everything.

In August, before Hanenson went to a Tallahassee hospital for heart treatment, he told me several hundred men had been cleared out of C Department, which I thought might have been accelerated by my pounding away in the courts.

In September, under Birnbaum's direction, I submitted a brief to Gadsden County Court, asking for a hearing on these basics: (1) that I was not now sufficiently mentally ill to be involuntarily incarcerated and was not so in 1957; (2) that I was not receiving

proper care and treatment and had not since 1957; and (3) that at
the time of my commitment and at subsequent hearings in the
courts I was not represented by counsel. Then, beginning with the
Circuit Court, in Gadsden County, we added what I thought was
the incontestable clincher: (4) that I was being held on a
technicality (the unusual request by Rich for a second authorization from my father) and that my sanity was not an issue (because
the doctors had voted to release me).

Two weeks later, back from the hospital, Hanenson saw me.
"I know all the judges in this part of the state. They won't go
against the doctors. As long as you write writs, the doctors will say
you are sick."

"I have no choice," I said.

"I don't blame you."

Then Hanenson began weekly stops in 41, on his way to his
office. One time it would be: "I talked to your friend Mr. Lembcke
on the phone. He's working for you." Another time it would be:
"I'm going up the street and do something for you, Kenneth." And
he was mailing all my letters personally, taking them from my
hand, sealed.

Birnbaum was not letting me down. He telephoned both
courts in the county. As a result, after eleven years, County Judge
H. Y. Reynolds wrote me, including this: "Certainly the State
Hospital authorities have no desire to detain you in the hospital
any longer than your condition requires."

I remarked to my private correspondent Hegel Kirk, in San
Francisco (Zena had gone abroad for several months), "Florida
courts work directly under God, they bypass the laws and the U.S.
Constitution."

IN THE COURTS, 1968

(xiv, cont.)

The Supreme Court of the United States refused certiorari, in March (390 U.S. 971).

(xv)

Gadsden County Court   9/11/68

After Morton Birnbaum telephoned the court, this court finally recognized my case, in a letter to me, October 5, which said they would take no action.

(xvi)

Circuit Court of the Second Judicial Circuit   10/7/68

On December 12, I wrote the clerk of the court, in Quincy: "I would like to know when I may expect an answer to my petition." On December 27, I wrote the clerk: "If I do not hear from you within two weeks, I will consider going to a higher court."

CHAPTER 18

1969

A Butterfly
Chases Us

WHERE-SHALL-I-GO WAS A BEFUDDLED LITTLE OLD WRECK, WHOSE wife had tired of his questions. All day he asked his thing. Should he lie down? stand up? go eat dinner? go to bed? Not satisfied with one answer, he would ask five men in a row, then come back in fifteen minutes and do a repeat.

I could put up with his questions sixty-four times a day and I knew he should have been in a boarding home where the operator was prepared to do likewise. Where-shall-I-go did not need psychiatric therapy. Nor did he need the milieu therapy of Building 41 and the heavy medication, which reduced his questions by three-quarters but did not relieve or release his "psychoses." The milieu also reduced him in size as an individual, with his bed jammed up to the next, his dining table jammed up to others, his moments free from noise nil, his chance to ask his guard a question free from a cursing rejoinder uncertain.

With the first let-up in twelve years from constant agitation, I was able to get an insight into these people who are supposed to illustrate the need for insane asylums. Admittedly, they were loud, but only when teased by an attendant. Building 41 was like the inside of a drum, which was contantly being bonged by some attendant's turning the TV up, then going back to the quiet office between the two wards.

If left undisturbed, black Four o'Clock would rock sixteen hours a day, saying "fo' o'clock, fo' o'clock," like a broken record, interspersed every fifteen seconds with "hehn-hehn-hehn" or "ha-ha-ha." But even he cut it off when seventy-five of us went outside to our $12' \times 30'$ fenced yard.

In the bathroom an old black ran water enough from four spigots to wash an elephant. He would dip his finger and run it along his gums. After twenty years in Building 41, to hell with ecology. Was he too being held for psychiatric treatment?

All of the hundred men in 41 could feed, dress, and bathe themselves, but all except the half-dozen in OT were slated to remain in that resounding drum for life.

Figmont Nobes, who was in OT, talked to the intercom box (dead since the installation of telephones), then asked the black evening attendant Clorange Filers, was it full moon?

"That shows good sense," I told Filers, "recognizing that the force working on him wasn't supernatural."

Figmont came to my bed. Did I think he was being poisoned by the medicine?

"I am not afraid of the medicine," he said, "but I think I may be getting too much. My mind is going faster than the clock."

"You are demonstrating one of the applications of Einstein's theory of relativity. You are getting the same effect as someone going on a long voyage through space for a few years and coming back to a world a thousand years older."

"No, no, it has nothing to do with Einstein. My brain seems to be standing out to one side of my body, as if waiting for me to catch up with it."

"Like LSD," I said hopefully.

"No, not like LSD and not like Einstein. I have nothing to do with space. I think it's silly going out into space while we have problems unsolved here on earth. All I want to know is if you think I might be getting too much medication."

"It is logical to think that."

Afterward, Filers told me, "He's on 400 Thorazine."

"I've seen more than one go berserk on that amount," I said.

Elsewhere in Department C, two men on the open ward saved

and stole $500 and took the Greyhound west. It was the first such
event for C Department in years. As a result, to straighten us all
out, Doctor O'Connor then took all money away from all C men.

Across the ocean where sane people are "kept with the insane"
and where escape is even more difficult, this is reported about one
of the victims in a Russian institution: "The gaunt figure in the
striped uniform of a repeater, sick and ghastly, reminded one of the
frightful photographs of the surviving victims of Auschwitz. The
prison rags hung on him as if on a wire skeleton." (This is about
Valentyn Moroz, on the op-ed page, *New York Times,* Nov. 9, 1974.)

Only the uniform differed in Chattahoochee, as I found in
going through the porch of sick bay for supplies with a young
attendant. I had my hands grabbed by Vittorio Dacker. He was a
little shrunken man in leather cuffs, naked as a jaybird. He didn't
say a thing, just smiled.

The attendant was impatient. "Give the old nuts your knee.
Come on."

But I waited and pulled away easy. "I'll see you," I said.

There was the smile again.

I had to get something done. When the local circuit court
ruled against me, I flared up.

When Hanenson stopped in Building 41, three days afterward, I seethed: "There is no excuse for their taking so long."

"I admire your guts," he said. "And good luck. You'll need
patience and patience and patience."

Doctor Birnbaum had advice too: "I should also like to
emphasize that you should always argue your case. Do not expend
so much time answering the contention of the lower court or of the
state that they set forth six or ten years ago. This is a 1969 case, not
a 1957 or a 1963 case."

There were other matters to consider too. Birnbaum had
predicted it would all be over in three months or so; now, already
the two local judges had taken four months. While I did not want
to nullify a lot of work on Birnbaum's part and while I knew things
were at the showdown stage, I had to be realistic. I could not take
the strain much longer. I wrote him: "I am not going to jump off
the dock, but in three months I will give things a close
reappraisal."

Next, Birnbaum wrote: "The courts are not the only forum
which you can plead your case in." He was preparing an article for
the *Georgetown Law Journal*'s symposium on the Right to Treatment
(57:768). Would I have the time, would I care to submit an article

on what a right to treatment would have meant to me and my fellow inmates during eleven years?

Would I! But they wouldn't print it. They'd be like the lawyers in Quincy, who thought every letter from the bughouse was a Chinese fortune cookie. I must, therefore, be restrained. Also, if I went into details, the Joe Flakes, the Robert Carmichaels, the J. B. O'Connors were sure to see its author on the shock table. In the safe quiet of the night, I awoke at 3:00 A.M. and wrote it out in an hour.

Birnbaum was disappointed: "Your average letter is better."

There was excitement, nevertheless, on the ward as Fritz, Baldylocks, and the attendants read the article in the *Journal.* "Son of a gun!" Jennerull said, but Clorange Filers shunned me for two days.

Fritz called my attention to Birnbaum's words in the law journal: "Although most Americans fail to recognize the fact, much of the disturbing behavior of the severely mentally ill results not from their illness but from the way they are treated in our present-day overcrowded, understaffed institutions."

Doctor Hanenson ordered a copy of the symposium. His other reaction was telling me that his department did give treatment, more than any other in the hospital, giving $4,000 worth of pills a month. Also, he said, "I told 250 state judges and attorneys that too many of them tried to practice psychiatry. There is no such thing as temporary insanity."

Thus, I was seeing a little bit of sense creeping into the worlds on both sides of the green door. Maybe, if I kept on, I could even come up with proof that I was not sick when I came to Florida; however, the clinical director in Philadelphia reported: "Since the date of your treatment was over twelve years ago, we are not in possession of a record at this time." My follow-up to Travelers Aid brought this: "Our records of 1956 are no longer available. They are destroyed at the end of an eight-year period."

Fritz and I were summarily waltzed up to the dressing room for "something to do with education." We waited with forty-five men and thirty chairs from 12:30 to 2:00 for a couple of students from Florida State University to arrive to administer a three-hundred-word personality test. In sixty days we took a second test. Then I told them I was not interested in group therapy. My reasoning was that it was both a six-month deal and a trap to show the courts that I was being cured. And what if Birnbaum agreed to wait the six months to see how things turned out?

"Anyway, you've got a real friend in Doctor Hanenson," the student in charge said. "Too bad he went to the hospital yesterday—his heart."

If we lost Hanenson, I told Birnbaum on his next trip, I would no longer feel safe. Birnbaum said he could get a Florida lawyer for me. "On the other hand, your case will be much stronger and you will be helping others if you force the court to give you an attorney."

"All right," I said. "You said we'd win this, if we lived long enough."

In about a week, Hanenson was back. Holding up a two-page legal paper in a blue folder, he said, "Doctor Rich asked me what I thought of Doctor Birnbaum. 'I can describe him in two words,' I said. 'A prince of a fellow. He likes to help those whom he believes deserve it.' " Before I left the office, Hanenson said, "There'll be justice in your case one of these days."

But I could have lost the whole fight at the next encounter. I was under orders from Doctor Birnbaum to get out any way I could, short of admitting I had been sick. Only the "miasma of stupidity" that is institutional psychiatry saved me.

At 12:30 on April 30, Jennerull and I were summoned, cutting short our dinner, to go to Doctor Hanenson and then to Doctor Rich. Rich kept his door open and Jennerull stayed outside.

Rich: "Come in for three minutes, Donaldson. Be seated. Doctor Hanenson tells me you want to go to Tallahassee."

Me: "State law allows me to represent my own case in the courts. A preliminary hearing is being held next Monday, and as my own attorney I am entitled to be there to speak for myself."

Rich (reads letter and announcement, handed over by me): "The District Court of Appeal. Motion Day Calendar. It would be a lot of trouble for the hospital to get you there. I don't see why you want to go."

Me: "This is the first concrete action any court has ever taken in my case, and being unable to get a Florida lawyer I am entitled to attend."

R: "Why did Stallings quit you?"

Me: "He couldn't proceed without a psychiatrist."

[As the reader knows, I had been unable to get Szasz to come. Stallings had encouraged me to believe that no Florida psychiatrist would speak against another of the "brethren." Birnbaum told me that psychiatrists shunned court cases because the frequent judicial postponements, after they were in the courtroom, often wasted many of their valuable days.]

R: "How can you say the hospital is holding you for an authorization? That is not so. We are willing to let you go without authorization by your father, as we have already let Mr. Lembcke know. But he won't do anything about it. It isn't our fault that nobody will do anything for you. Here is our last letter to Mr. Lembcke, of last September."

Me (after reading letter): "It says in the last paragraph that you 'will not let Mr. Donaldson be released without the prior authorization of his father dated later than 1966.' "

R (reads the last paragraph.): "Oh, yes, that was then. Why didn't you agree to go to the halfway house in Minneapolis? I would have thought you would have jumped at that. I could release you to one of the neighborhood rest homes."

[I did not reply; by now I wanted an unconditional discharge.]

R: "You admit yourself that you are not getting medication because of your own request. As a psychiatrist I say that medication is all the treatment you need. So how can you complain of inadequate treatment?"

Me: "I am complaining about my close confinement all these years. And although I'm getting good treatment from the attendants now and satisfactory food, for years there was brutality on the wards and the food was poor. No attendant ever laid a hand on me, but anyone seeing the brutality twenty-four hours a day suffered."

R: "Your thinking is wrong along several lines. But that could be cured by a short course of one of the new drugs. If you were my patient I would force you to take medication until your thinking was corrected."

[I turned aside from those dark eyes. Speaking out of turn to this man had brought heavy medication to Hezekiah. Talking back to Gumanis had brought no-return treatment for Carter and Vittorio.]

R: "In a rare few cases I have changed my diagnosis."

[I prayed inwardly not to say the wrong word until this demigod had finished reversing his diagnosis. An admission would be victory too and quicker than the courts, which could drag on for years.]

R: "If you will cooperate with the hospital now and if Mr. Lembcke can come up with a plan." [In turning pages of the chart,

he came to a picture of Doctor Birnbaum and article about him.]
"But he has the facts on your case all wrong. He'll have to sit down
and talk with me so I can straighten him out about those things."
[Turns more pages.] "I see nothing in the record that shows you
ever were dangerous. It's just that your thinking is wrong. You
made illusionary statements at my interview in Gumanis's office."

[Foreign Police Association was on the tip of my tongue. But
wasn't I bucking for a discharge?]

R: "I wonder at your refusal to take medication here when
you state you are ready to accept any and all treatment from a
doctor in New York, including medication. You see, your thinking
is not right."

[Doctor Birnbaum had told me that no New York doctor that
he knew would prescribe pills for me.]

R: "It says on your commitment papers: 'The prospective
patient is indigent and is entitled to be kept at the said hospital
without payment of fees or other charges.' "

Me: "I'm glad you read that. The first papers I saw said the
same things. Today, the attorney general's office has furnished
copies which say 'is not indigent' and 'is not entitled.' " [This came
about after I started drawing Social Security.]

R: "You mean they changed it after your commitment? They
couldn't have. They probably just forgot to type in the 'not' in the
spaces."

Me: "That copy is a photostat, isn't it?"

[That indicated that some bureaucrat had typed in the "not"
after I began drawing Social Security benefits, so that "everything
would be in order" on my papers and they could legally collect my
benefits.]

R: "An example of your thinking are these two paranoid
letters—"

Me: "To Stallings and Szasz?"

R: "Yes."

Me (Catching anger in Rich's eyes but venturing a reply):
"Isn't a man entitled to his own opinions?"

R: "Yes."

[I wanted to jump up and shout that, after this performance
of walking across a river of eggs, I had finally scored a point.]

R: "If you had been my patient, I would have forced you to
take medication and I would have got you out long ago—maybe in
1957. . . . But why have you been so against medication?"

Me: "I am a long-time student of Christian Science. Besides, I was not upset."

R: "But as a trained psychiatrist, I know you are sick."

Me: "But how? I am not nervous. I don't bother other people. I don't write poison-pen letters. I don't imagine things."

R: "Along certain lines your thinking is wrong."

Me: "But pills can't change that."

R: "Oh, yes they can. There are some new drugs that can change one's thinking. Do you know what your diagnosis is?"

Me: " 'Schizophrenic paranoia' and 'possibly dangerous to the people of the State of Florida' and 'seeing and hearing things.' "

R (Reading in chart): "Yes."

Me: "My commitment papers are wholly fraudulent. The doctors did not see me."

R: "I have in some cases been known to change a diagnosis. But you are sick. As a psychiatrist I know you are sick. And all these other doctors here can't be wrong."

Back at 41, I told Nessley, "The time for ultimatums is past— at least for me—so I made none today. But the hospital could do whatever was needed whenever they wanted to get me out fast."

Nessley said, "Why is it the goodies seem to catch it but the baddies don't?"

"It's probably because the goodies go around openly while baddies always have an angle."

When I showed Hanenson the permission from the Florida Supreme Court for Doctor Birnbaum to appear in my behalf, Hanenson said, "I'll go into court for you." He then divulged that Rich would be out by mid-July. "And mail no more letters through the censors. No matter what the letter pertains to, bring it up to me."

On August 20, Doctor Hanenson read to me a Progress Note he had earlier inserted in my chart:

April 30, 1969
The above-named patient has been seen on numerous occasions in this examiner's office and also visiting in Building 41 where patient resides. I watched this patient very carefully in every respect and it was noted that this patient has been helping a great deal with the patients who are unable to write to their relatives. He was helping them in that respect. Furthermore this patient was constantly occupying himself with reading material and in Occupational

Therapy painting a great deal. We discussed a great deal his long period of hospitalization here and at the present time it was the opinion of this examiner that this patient is most definitely in remission of his past psychotic symptoms and has been so for some time.

When Birnbaum had me file an original petition in habeas corpus concurrently with the appeal because the courts were using all manner of delaying tactics, I asked Hanenson if he would submit a statement.

Seeing me alone, he said, "I would not want to be put in the middle right now, but I would if I were subpoenaed."

"Is O'Connor the liar, then, in sheep's clothing?" I said.

"You'll have to draw your own conclusions. The little person with the little moustache yelled at me, and moustache's door is not open to me."

Then Hanenson asked me to repeat that I was glad I was under him. I did as he asked, wondering at his insecurity. But I added, "I told Doctor Birnbaum once that you sometimes acted like an army sergeant."

"You did?" Then he laughed.

Then I said I was glad the case was coming out this way—in the courts—and there was that rare spine-tingling rapport between us.

Morton Birnbaum wrote: "I hope that the personnel changes at the hospital do allow you to be discharged without having to wait for the Florida Supreme Court. However, just in case, I shall plan on keeping the court cases going."

In August I wrote Birnbaum: "Now, Doctor Hanenson tells me he is leaving by December for someplace that appreciates him. Thus, if the court doesn't remove me, that leaves only my feet."

When Birnbaum visited on September 4, he said, "You'd always feel guilty if you ran now."

Fritz and I were transferred to the open ward. It meant that we could also go to town whenever we wished; however, I went to town only to shop, not for pleasure. My only real pleasure was getting out in the fields, away from people and buildings.

We took a long walk around the back of the women's buildings.

"The freedom is welcome," I said, "but it doesn't taste as good as it would have had it come years earlier." Passing the strawber-rybed, I said, "It's twelve years since I took off. It hardly seems that long."

"I made a break two years later," Fritz said. "Slid down sheets from old Ward 2. I couldn't run now. I've lost sixty pounds. That stuff in my coffee chews up my stomach."

"It's a frightening thought—standing here and seeing twelve years down the drain."

A monarch butterfly chased us for two blocks.

"A butterfly chasing the last two roses of summer," I said.

"Good to have something but punks after us."

The best part was the sunshine. Then rest from constant hazing. Not least was the breeze taking the stink out of one's clothes. And in four days, free of the barn drafts inside, my ears were twice as good. But a feeling of uneasiness grabbed me every time I saw an attendant walking or driving by.

Doctor Hanenson said he had talked to "somebody" about staff for me, and when "somebody" learned about the grounds' privilege card "somebody" said, "How nice." The date was set for October 9.

Hanenson kept calling me often. My chart was so thick he had to postpone staff three weeks. Then O'Connor told him I had not passed staff. But Hanenson was not much concerned about O'Connor's opinion, for he believed he had the three votes needed for my competency discharge. However, one vote began fluctuat-ing. "Is Gumanis afraid of something if you get out?" Hanenson said.

Then the attendants and housemen started hard-timing me, "I'll put a stop to it," Hanenson said. "And rest assured, I won't put it down to schizophrenia or paranoia on your part. What do you hear from the court? How much longer?"

The next morning there was a letter from Birnbaum. I hurried up to the doctor's car as he parked.

"The court—a month yet," I said.

"Pardon me while I take this," he said, pulling out a "horse pill."

After a minute, I said, "If I'm here much longer, I'll be taking them too."

Then in September, Hanenson called me in to inform me my father had died.

Then in October, I sent the following letter:

11 October 1969

Morton Birnbaum, M.D., LL.B.:
    A catastrophe: Doctor Hanenson died last night.

I got a scare, for Doctor Dunin was sent down to take over. At staff it had been a matter of his insolence, rather than "deceit and trickery," but there was nothing in the actions of any Chattahoochee doctor to earn one's trust. But the next day we got a permanent replacement, a younger doctor, Jesus Rodriguez, Jr., M.D. Fidelio, formerly on old Ward 1, was quickly installed as the doctor's special confidant.

At his urging, I wrote Doctor Rodriguez: "My case is on appeal in the Supreme Court of Florida, and while I am awaiting further word from my lawyer, I thought you might like to be acquainted with the following facts. . . . Doctor Birnbaum has no objection to the hospital's releasing me."

Dr. Jesus Rodriguez, Jr. (wavy black hair, rimless glasses, Spanish accent): "Because you passed staff last year, I am going to let you go. Your case is of much interest to me. You have a lawyer?"

Me: "Morton Birnbaum—both practicing M.D. and lawyer from Brooklyn."

Rodriguez: "In Supreme Court. Is that the highest? Tell me about your case."

Me (after going through details): "Will you notify Mr. Lembcke to come after me?"

R: "Certainly. How is it he didn't take you out last year?"

Me: "Doctor Rich wouldn't let him."

R: "You are sick." [Once again, my stating a simple truth is taken as proof of my illness.] "It says here that you passed staff and would be released on trial visit to Mr. John Lembcke. You should be on medication. I am going to put you on medication."

Me: "Doctor, I am a Christian Scientist. Every doctor here except Hanenson has respected my belief and not forced medication on me."

R: "This is a hospital."

Me: "I appreciate that."

R: "You are sick."

Me: "I am not trying to convert anyone or force my belief on others."

R: "I respect other people's beliefs. But I will have to consider medication in this case."

Me: "Doctor Hanenson put a statement in the chart, not too many months ago, that my illness has long been in remission."

R (leafing back): "Yes, I see it. Well, I am going to have you talk to Mr. Hatcher."

At one o'clock, I was in the next office, talking with Mr. Willard Hatcher, a big, pleasant, brown-haired social worker, who was the first one assigned permanently to C Department.

He shook hands and said: "The doctor asked me to talk to you—thought we could establish better communication. The hospital is going to do what they should have a long time ago—let you go. The doctor is extremely interested in your case. Tell me about it."

We discussed in detail everything written in this book up to here.

"Your long stay," Hatcher said, "is due to lack of communication with the institution."

We talked for hours and I gave him a copy of the law journal. Then we had two long sessions the next day.

"The doctor wants to arrange your release through one of your children. Is that all right?" Hatcher said.

"Sure," I said.

"I found nothing in your talk or manner to indicate any paranoia. We will find out if you are all right or incurable. If your psychological test is against you, I will study it myself to find out why and then go over it with you. Do you have any objection to seeing Davis?"

I told him that, since Doctor Hanenson assured me Davis was okay, I had no objection.

"I do not know why the hospital did not release you eighteen months ago," Mr. Davis said.

We discussed my refusal to see him after the first two examinations and we agreed that "hallucinations" had been injected by Gumanis. We covered the commitment and the cause therefore.

"You know," Davis said, "psychologists are sometimes used as whipping boys by the doctors. There is no such thing as passing or failing the psychological." He spoke quietly, not cutting me off in midsentence. "Sometime we would like to give you an intelligence test. I don't know why they have not in thirteen years."

At the end, catching my eye in what seemed an honest glance, he said, "I hope your book is successful."

Before Hatcher got the psychological report, the state Supreme Court, on November 19, dismissed my case without prejudice. On November 25, Birnbaum wrote: ". . . if your case goes to the U.S. Supreme Court, I intend to make the briefs on it . . . available to the press. . . . In the past I have always shied away from discussing any case . . . in public; however, I believe very little—if anything—has been gained by keeping silent . . . however, the decision is yours. . . ."

I replied, certified and special delivery: "By all means: the U.S. Supreme Court and all the publicity we can get. In the meantime, if these people [in Florida] want to get off their fannies and do something, they can—and they can act fast when they want to, too."

Then, for a short time, while I waited on the new broom to sweep me out, the harassment, as Fritz predicted, stopped. It was a good time to bring my notes up to date. Where-shall-I-go had long been demoted to an upper floor in the nursery, which was the Back Yard of C Department. Here the men lived in strong odors of both body waste and food. Many were naked. They were like pigs in a muddy sty. Massive doses of institutional "psychiatric treatment" had reduced Where-shall-I-go to one of these many.

One with even less apparent benefit from his "psychiatric treatment" was Stan. Of the estimated 10,000 men, with whom I rubbed shoulders in the changing populations of the wards in 15 years, Stan was one of the three actually schizophrenic patients I knew. The other two were a very old man at the receiving ward and Figmont Nobes, though the latter's aberrations might have been induced solely by medication. Stan stood first in line for each of the bulletins I was getting from the American Schizophrenia Association, as a member of ACT. They kept us abreast of the research which was uncovering diet deficiency as the trigger for this frightening condition.

For two years, Stan had slept in uneasy tranquility, currently taking three drugs, afraid to be on the open ward, too frightened of women to go to the dances or movies. For part of his unsettled waking hours, he did not know who he was and it frightened him. He had his mother send for some of the bulletins. Immediately, she made arrangements to take him home as an outpatient of a local clinic. With person-to-person therapy, within a month, Stan wrote back, he was dancing with girls; within two months he had a steady job and was going to night school to earn a promotion.

Smokey, who had been in 41 for a couple of months, was

another not benefiting from "psychiatry." He definitely was in the category of trainable. "Educators feel that 75 percent of the physically disabled and 90 percent of the mentally retarded could work if given the proper education and training" (York *Dispatch*, p. 21, Jan. 28, 1975). The test Smokey failed was keeping his mouth shut. For reporting a night attendant's sleeping, Smokey had his first "relapse," which took him to the nursery.

For the rest in 41, under their regimen of beneficence, they went on September 9 to the yard for the first time since winter. That was encouraging, for the rest of C and all of A had not been out in the sunshine once during the year.

One who did not go to the yard that day was Tommy "Peepee." He had been out on a privilege card most of the time since I worked with him in the kitchen. He had kept happy until desegregation knocked out the dances, where he was a star. With no outlet for his energy, he was on and off the open ward, seemingly acting the cripple when he was locked in. Then, when he got his card back, he would take off on the double and not stop until jailed again for resenting some attendant's mocking his stammering.

The previous night, he had come back from sick bay, where he had been sent for not eating. He came back to 41 with his face wet with blood, without shoes, his socks soaked, for it had been raining. Night attendant Ettleton was incensed when neither sick bay nor night supervisor would take him back to sick bay. Tommy had fallen getting into the ambulance, which accounted for his skinned face. The next day he lay in bed unable to go to meals and urinating on himself, his urine dripping through the mattress to a big puddle on the floor. When I told Gawch about it and how Tommy had been brought back the night before, Gawch went up to the office straightaway and got Tommy moved.

A week later, Tommy died. He had lived a life of complaints in Chattahoochee. He died hard. Afterward they found an infection in his leg. Attendant Ettleton was incensed again and urged me to write Tommy's father. But after all these years when a father had never visited, I said honestly, "I wouldn't know how to put it to him."

"That's what's wrong with Chattahoochee," Ettleton said. "Nobody'll do a damn thing."

How different was the outcome for one for whom something did get done? On December 26, I sent a clipping to Birnbaum on this case. An eighteen-year-old, Joe Harding in Department A, wrote his mother that the attendants were going to kill him. He came back from an afternoon session with them with his shirt torn off. The next day he was dead. At the mother's request, the FBI "investigated." It was death from natural causes, the clipping reported O'Connor's saying.

I carried in my heart for a long time, something from one of Hegel Kirk's letters:

> I am reminded of something said by Eugene Debs, "As long as one human being is in prison, I cannot be free."

IN THE COURTS, 1969
(xvi, cont.)

The Circuit Court of the Second Judicial Circuit denied my petition for writ of habeas corpus, January 8, without a hearing and without calling for papers from the state.

(xvii)
District Court of Appeal, First District   Case No. L-265   1/21/69

My petition for writ of habeas corpus on appeal was returned by the clerk of court, because it had not met certain procedural rules pertaining to criminal procedure, although I was not a criminal. It was refiled, dated February 10. My Notice of Appeal, dated February 3, but in my ignorance sent to the Appeal court instead of the Circuit court, was received, filed, and docketed in the Appeal court on February 24. The state Attorney General's office filed a motion to dismiss on March 3, saying I had filed late. My petition for counsel to be appointed by the court was dismissed on April 8. The court dismissed the petition for habeas corpus on May 5.

And so once again, the spirit of the law was lost in observance of the letter.

(xviii)
Supreme Court of the State of Florida   Case No. 38,610   9/3/69

My Notice of Appeal was filed by the clerk of court on May 12. The court issued an order, June 18, allowing Morton Birnbaum to appear as my counsel. The only paper filed by the state was a motion to dismiss. The petition for habeas corpus on appeal was dismissed on November 19, "without prejudice to whatever rights appellant may have under Chapter 394, Florida Statutes."

The Chief Justice, specially concurring, told us to go back to Pinellas County for a sanity hearing; then, if it were resolved against the petitioner, he would consider the merits of our petition for habeas corpus. But, because Florida statute said a sanity hearing involving a noncriminal had to be in the county where he was being held (in my case, Gadsden) Birnbaum and I decided to go to the United States Supreme Court.

CHAPTER 19

1970

Up the *Apple Tree*

PREACHER AND I WERE SITTING ON THE STEPS OF LUNACY HALL, IN THE shade of ornamental firs. I was brushing a few flecks of white paint from the concrete while Preacher talked:

"When Doctor O'Connor asked me, 'What have you on your mind?' I told him, 'God's law.' He said, 'You've got to have more than that.' I said, 'That's a lie.' I also told him, 'If I'm not fit to leave, then you're not fit to stay.' Praise the Lord! O Glory! That's right! Isn't it the truth?"

The first words of praise were shouted; all were the words of other people passing through his lips, the blessed people he had met on his journeys.

Preacher had traveled the country, working sometimes, then moving on. Back in Michigan he had met a "Mother" of a Pentacostal sect, seen the light himself, and set off to preach the Gospel—to talk, to preach to any who would listen. He took off penniless, leaving his wife with a debt-free house and money in the bank. He saw almost every state, got punched in the nose and pistol-whipped by a deputy in South Carolina, slept out in a sleeping bag in a freezing rain, picked grapes in Oregon.

Something directed him to Ocala, Florida. He found there two rival evangelists who had carved out the territory for themselves. Preacher's sitting in their tents bugged them enough to call the chief of police.

Preacher continued: " 'I'm the law,' the chief said. 'I've got the law too,' I said. 'Let's see your identification then.' 'I've got the Holy Ghost and I can catch a crook quicker than you can.' "

Preacher was jailed and ordered to appear before Judge Carbox, or be represented by someone. But Preacher was allowed neither to appear nor to have a representative. Two doctors signed papers that he was schizophrenic paranoid.

" I'm going back there someday," he told me, "and repeat what I said to them in 1950, that they didn't have God's law."

Talk about meat for the grinder. The attendants had a field day around the clock. Often, as soon as each shift came on the ward, they would tell him a half-dozen times, "You're no preacher." If he ignored them, they would yank his Bible or his newspaper out of his thin hands. Then he would denounce their sins of adultery and smoking. For a reward, cigar smoke was blown in his face. Some of the abused inmates, too, seeing this gentle man as an outlet for their own frustrations, broke his nose, spat on him, overturned his bed, all because of the way he would tell them that they were not going to heaven.

Looking at it another way, just saying, "You're no man of God, you've got the devil in you," a dozen times a day for a dozen years to a baboon would have him swinging across his cage to slap you. Not so Preacher. The second time I talked to him, he was sounding off about the blackness of the Roman Catholic Church and what the nuns had done to his daughter when a judge ordered her tonsils out in a Catholic hospital. A Raiford man at our table in A Department had got up and slapped Preacher off his chair. I jumped between them. But never once would Preacher, by no means a weakling, raise a hand in defense.

Our first meeting had been in 1958, when I used to pass by where Preacher sat at the milk table with a few of the older men. At supper he always saved his milk for me. "Here, you need it more than I do" was what the extended arm meant.

"I'll put it on your account," I said.

"And see," Preacher said in 1970, sitting on the steps of Lunacy Hall with me, "see how my account is paying off. You've brought me sugar cookies again—my favorite. There must be forty in this sack. I put one in my vessel and run hot water on it. They want to give me phony teeth. When I first came here, the barbers left a little Hitler moustache on me. They wanted to make me look like the devil. 'Like you,' I told O'Connor."

"Did you get Thorazine for that?" I asked.

"He never called me again and the barbers cut it off. Sure you won't get in trouble bringing me these cookies?"

"No, they'd only get thrown out. The old men don't want them."

To pay for my privilege card, I did two hours' work in 41, cleaning toilets and showers. That also entitled me to 41's leftovers. In the afternoon, I always took Preacher some baked goods or fruit.

Preacher said, "When Joe Flake isn't there, the boys will give me four or five dips of oatmeal. This morning one handed me a sack of rolls. Last night another brought me a dozen hard-boiled eggs. Joe Flake says I'm going to take a tray like everybody else, or go hungry. I told him I'll go a year without eating before I'll take a tray with meat on it. The fellows used to let me have one—Miss Brack stopped that. I called her a bitch. They put me on the Back Yard for five years."

Other than taunting people until they wanted to hit him, Preacher was like Carter, Narrel, and myself. All of us had a right to our own lives. We were driven to the insane asylum, not driven insane. Preacher does not even come close to being on the thin borderline between sanity and insanity. He never slipped over into the world of make-believe. He hardly ever lost his temper when he was mercilessly teased. He did not need the jokes of the wonderful doctors in the great institution.

Nor did Vittorio. He threw his dresser drawers across the pen. He tore his clothes off. But did he attack people? And never once did he fail to recognize me. Never once did he twist my words or forget them. Also, was his anger excessive for what happened? He had asked for an investigation about the death of a friend. Instead of getting an investigation and without seeing the doctor, he was taken from an open ward to a closed ward. He was baited by a stool pigeon into fighting. As punishment for fighting he was put on a back ward and given the needle for protecting himself.

I told Doctor Birnbaum on his next visit, "Let's get a clear-cut decision from the courts. If these people offer me a competency discharge, then I would reconsider. I hope you believe I know what I'm doing."

"I'm not interfering with your handling of the local front," he said.

"That makes me feel good."

"How many times did Doctor Hanenson put you to staff?"

"Just once."

"Oh. I was led to believe that you were going regularly every so many months."

"Maybe there's one other misconception. After Hanenson talked to John Lembcke on the phone, John never wrote me again. It's a mystery to me."

"It does seem that he turned your friend away. All in all, your case sounds like something out of *Alice in Wonderland,* or Kafka, rather than a case in the American courts. The difference, however, is not that you are in a Florida institution or that you have been in the Florida courts, for almost identical problems arose in the New York case I handled. The difference is that the courts refuse to consider openly the problems of a petitioner who is an inmate of a mental institution. But I am feeling quite optimistic at the present time, and I am sure you feel the same. The only trouble is that I am sure we have felt the same way before this litigation."

"Another thing," I said, "I'm afraid to tell Doctor Rodriguez about the hazing on the wards. He might put me on heavy medication."

"He had better not!"

"That's a relief to hear."

There were other words that were also as unexpected as change in a coke machine. Some were Doctor Gumanis's. I had been avoiding him, turning my head, crossing to the other side of the street; but he caught me one day, where I was reading my paper on a patio, my back to the walk. He came up behind and asked what were my chances of getting out. I told him about the case in Washington.

"What does your doctor say?" Gumanis said.

"He said he was going to let me go," I said. "But that was two months ago. I haven't seen him since. Hanenson told me that O'Connor was holding me."

Gumanis looked both ways to see if anyone was listening. "Yes, I told you that."

The immediate problem was holding off the blandishments of a whole new set of characters, including two more social workers, who were interested only in getting me to staff. I was not going to destroy the credibility of my book by accepting less than a competency discharge. I patiently explained to each social worker what Hanenson had told me, that only three votes were needed for passing staff.

"Oh, Doctor Rodriguez couldn't do that," Mr. Hatcher said.

"He ought to be able to get two of his Spanish friends to side with him," I said. I declined suggestions of talking to him again, however, not wanting to appear stubborn and risk getting medication. But I did tell my friends that I would have to learn to laugh in Spanish, because the Cuban inmates laughed with the doctor and got competency discharges. That story must have got back to him, for he called me in.

Dr. J. Rodriguez: "Do you want to go to staff?"

Me: "Not at this time. My lawyer does not want me to complicate the case in court."

R: "How do you expect to get out then?"

Me: "The court will free me someday."

R: "They'll never do that. Why do you believe that?"

Me: "That's what my lawyer told me."

R: "I'd like to put you to staff. But I couldn't get you a competency discharge. You are schizophrenic. You've been schizophrenic all your life. But you're not dangerous. There are lots of schizophrenic people outside—they don't hurt anyone. But you'd have to have somebody be responsible for you."

Me: "I had someone."

R: "No you didn't. Nobody wants you. Your family doesn't want you. Why is your family against you?"

Me: "That's not so."

R: "But your mother won't take you out. Why not?"

Me: "She's dead. And my father died last year."

R: "It says in here your children don't want you."

Me: "My children tried to get me out."

R: "All these doctors here have said the same thing. Why do you think everybody is against you?"

Me: "I never said that. The whole case consists of presumptions and assumptions. And lies."

R: "And how about all your psychological tests here? Did you know that you didn't pass them?"

Me: "Doctor Chacon told me that I had passed the last four times."

R: "I'll let you go out of state whenever you can get anyone responsible to take you." [Then, after reading in my chart.] "Here—Doctor Hanenson wrote your friend Mr. Lembcke not to ever write you again or ever to take you out, because you would never be well."

Me: "That explains that."

[In 1975, there is no such letter in the chart.]

When I was a hundred feet outside the office building, I always felt like a man who has driven ten miles away from an atomic plant which has cracked lead shields—out of sight but not out of danger. Careful as I was about irritating (to their faces) the O'Connor machine (for I had learned from my Bible what Preacher had missed in his, about a soft answer turning away wrath) some accident could pour death over me, as it had over Carter, Reverend Sixx, and others before my eyes. Nevertheless, my hopes were up that I could hold out against their well-affected friendliness and alternative bluff until Birnbaum could move our case to a court victory. The newspapers had reported his press conference in New York, announcing that four groups had filed amicus curiae briefs with our petition for certiorari (400 U.S. 869).

Doctor Birnbaum's brief stated: "What member of this Court would not consider it a tale of horror if he or a member of his family were to be involuntarily committed to a state mental institution where there were only one doctor to more than 950 inmates? ... Petitioner contends that after more than ten years of appealing to the courts, that after more than 18 different attempts to have his rights vindicated before the courts, that after three appearances here, that *he is entitled to at least one hearing—to repeat, at least one hearing*—in some court somewhere in the United States."

New York and Florida newspapers carried accounts of the case. This was a pretty heady period for me. On April 20, the court asked the state to file a reply to our petitions.

The publicity was beginning to look like a barn fire to some of the bureaucrats up the street, so firemen were dispatched to a large office with two desks by adjoining walls. Psychologist Davis was there to greet me.

Davis: "As I understand it, there are two parts to your case— the Right to Treatment and the fact that you don't need treatment."

Me: "Yes, and there's another part—illegality—fraud."

D: "There's a chance that your case could establish a

precedent—like that case a few years back for prisoners—the Gideon case."

Me: "And to help others. We could help a thousand others right here."

D: "We could say, then, that all these years here—what has happened to you has been unfortunate."

Me: "We can say unfortunate all right."

[Davis got a phone call. Then a Dr. Francis G. Walls came in and shook my hand. Davis said Walls was from the Women's Department.]

Doctor Walls: "Doctor O'Connor asked me to read your file. It's quite thick—three folders. And he asked me to have some talks with you."

D: "I was just telling Mr. Donaldson that he might go down—"

Me: "Down—I'm down as far as I can go." [An honest-to-goodness laugh came out of me, rather hearty, too, considering the gravity of the interviewers. It went over like a lead balloon.]

W: "I've got a few questions I would like to ask you." [He gets out a pencil and a piece of paper the size of a large postage stamp.] "We doctors wonder how come you don't run?"

Me: "On advice of Doctor Birnbaum. Besides, he's spent a lot of time and money on the case and it wouldn't be right to waste all that."

W: "You thought someone put medicine in your food in Los Angeles."

Me: "Not thought—I have a laboratory report proving it."

W: "How come all these people—in all these cities where you lived—these judges, doctors, all these professional people—all found you to be mentally ill?"

Me: "Nobody found me to be mentally ill."

W: "How do you think others get out?"

Me: "With a lot of the others, they were sick when they came here, or said they were sick. They tell the doctor how pleased they are because he has got them well. Then the doctor lets them go."

W: "What have the doctors got against you? What can they gain by keeping you here?"

Me: "It's what they won't give. They won't give an inch—won't admit that somebody made a mistake."

W: "Let me tell you an anecdote." [Tells about a thousand

soldiers marching—one out of step.] "Why aren't you in that same position?"

Me: "Because it isn't a thousand to one."

W: "But your doctor is the only one against all these doctors in this hospital."

Me: "Doctor Birnbaum told me that state doctors just copy over from one year to the next what is on one's commitment papers." [Then I pointed out how Doctor Adair had planned to release me from the receiving ward; how Doctor O'Connor had given permission for anyone up north to sign me out; how Doctor Hanenson had come around to my side. I did not know, of course, in 1970, that my chart, which Walls had read, was largely a collection of reports from these people's imaginations, i.e., psychiatric interpretations.]

W: "Would you say these doctors down through the years, who've found you sick, are fools or knaves?"

Me: "Neither the one nor the other—somewhere in between. I have had time to study my case. Here is a fact: No doctor outside of a state hospital ever found the first thing wrong with me mentally."

W: "What I would like to know is why the staff did not pass you two years ago."

Me: "They did."

D: "That's right, he did pass."

W: "Why are they holding you then?"

Me: "That's the question I'd like to have an answer to."

W: "There's something wrong here."

D: "There is."

Dr. Rich had said he was holding me for a second authorization from my father; however, there is no provision in Florida statute requiring such an authorization.

On June 30, Birnbaum wrote: "The Supreme Court did not decide the petition on June 29, 1970. Accordingly, you must wait until September, 1970, for a decision unless an opinion is handed down in the interim. Let's hope no news is good news. At least, it means the Court is interested in the case."

A letter from Hegel said: "Murphy's law is so true: If anything bad can happen it will."

An enormous scandal gave me a respite, because everybody's

attention was held by front-page headlines of another exposé of Chattahoochee. Reporters Skip Johnson of the Tampa *Tribune* and Norma Jean Hill of *Today* detailed that blood poisoning from unchecked bedsores had killed at least fifteen patients. Old men die like flies in the heat of the "hospital" wards without air conditioning. Coroner's records show that patients starved to death. Doctors, only, use the golf course.

Superintendent O'Connor was indignant. The Florida Medical Association sent an investigating team. During their stay, the bread, which was wheeled down the dusty street amid fluttering pigeons, came wrapped—for two weeks.

The Jacksonville *Times-Union*, May 8, reported the association's summary: "The patients are well fed, clean, and humanely treated with kindness and dedication by the staff at all levels."

I saw the next headline in my case in the Pensacola *Journal*, October 20: "COURT DENIES INMATE CASE."

There was a hurry-up call that morning. Doctor Rodriguez saw me with another doctor and supervisor Carmichael.

Dr. J. Rodriguez (points to story in middle of page): "I don't mind your writing, but why did you write this?" [He spoke with some warmth, so that I had no trouble understanding him.]

Me: "I didn't write anything."

R: "You said you are not getting any treatment. Tell these men here—I want you to tell it before witnesses. I'm a conscientious doctor. My patients take medication. My patients have group therapy. Tell these witnesses you refused it."

Me (getting out of it fast): "You must remember that my case was filed two and a half years ago—it happened long before you came here. I want to say in front of these witnesses that I do not put any blame on you."

R: "How do you feel now about staff?"

Me: "Whatever my lawyer decides."

After supper, at a bench up the street, Sedge Wicks said, "It's hard to say anything good about this place, isn't it?"

"And it's hard to say anything without going into superlatives," I said.

But other people up north were still pushing for some meaningful solutions. On the front page, the *Wall Street Journal*, November 3, headlined: "Lawyers, Doctors Push for Fairer Treatment of Nation's Mentally Ill." The article by Stephen J. Sansweet

began: "You would think Kenneth Donaldson was a criminal. . . .
Florida officials refuse to discuss the case with *The Wall Street
Journal.*"

Doctor's call this time started with Mr. Hatcher.

Hatcher (holds up clipping): "You didn't write this?" [Again,
I was amazed at their stupidity about newspapers.] "And now,
where to?"

Me: "Federal District court—habeas corpus."

In a few moments, the doctor came in.

Doctor Rodriguez: "You could be a lawyer."

[Hatcher then explained the steps through the courts.]

R: "Wasn't there a case where a lawyer in jail fought for years
and wound up in the chair?"

Me: "Yes—Chessman."

R: "Then things could go on for a long time yet?"

H: "It could take years."

R: "What do you expect to get now?"

Me: "Habeas corpus."

R: "Then you'll get a hearing?"

H: "Or his lawyer will appear for him."

Me: "No—this time we're asking for a personal hearing."

R: "You'll never get it."

I knew in my bones, though, that with my "powerful friends"
(as Hegel called them) I would someday, someplace in the United
States get that hearing. But, with the repetitious letdown by the
court in my nineteenth round of appeals, there came an opening of
floodgates of filth again on the wards. The black attendants in 41
tried to stop it, but dozens, literally, who should have appreciated
the battle I was waging for them too, went out of their way to curse
me and to interfere with my rest. They picked on Fritz too, calling
us "Hans and Fritz, the homo twins," until in fear he shunned me,
then asked for medication and turned in his privilege card. On
reflection, in 1975, I see that they had merely taken on the garment
of their guards (see Goffman's *Asylums*). In a world of hopeless
frustration, where everyone suspects others of stealing or hiding his
possessions (attendants, as well as patients) I knew this behavior
was only the crying out from their angry souls, not ingratitude.

Walking out after supper one day, one of his henchmen said to
Fidelio, "There'll be a slip of paper in the morning saying to give
him some medication." Thus, it was always with fear that I went
when called to the office. It was a constant tightening up inside,

then partial relaxation, as on my next call, which turned out to be two social workers. They grilled me for an hour and a half.

Mr. Hatcher: "We want you to consider us your friends. We are not trying to pry into your affairs. As I told you, Miss Freeman here is curious to know the background of your case. You don't mind talking to us, do you?"

Me: "Certainly not."

Miss Freeman: "I would like to know what led up to this."

[A half hour later, here came the pitch.]

Miss F: "Why do you want to stay and fight when you could be free?"

Me: "I didn't ask for this. I didn't choose the nuthouse for a career."

[At the hour mark, they were still prying.]

Miss F: "How is Birnbaum going to argue the case?"

Me: "He says we have nothing to discuss with the hospital."

H: "But we want to help you."

[After an hour and a half, this came out of a clear blue sky:]

Miss F (to me): "You are evasive."

But the equal and opposing force was more in evidence too. In December, Doctor Birnbaum visited again. In the new brief he was asking for $100,000 in damages from the hospital doctors too.

Doctor Birnbaum: "I delayed filing because the American Civil Liberties Union blew hot and cold. They keep asking what your politics are. I'm a member myself and I keep telling them what's the difference, he's incarcerated unconstitutionally. Finally, I told them I would proceed without them. But they definitely are in now. Mr. Ennis works for the New York Civil Liberties Union— he's done pioneering work in reforming mental hospital law in this area—he's loaned to ACLU for this case. He suggests we delay the action for damages, as it would complicate the matter. At the present, Mr. Ennis has agreed to bring a class proceeding in habeas corpus and we are awaiting your opinion." [I agreed.] "Bringing a class suit is the best way to point out to the public the gross mistreatment of the inmates."

Me: "What we can do for the others has always been the prime reason for this battle."

B: "Mr. Ennis has suggested that we drop Point 4—the matter of fraudulent commitment. That was thirteen years ago—Florida law has changed in the interim. A victory on procedural irregularities in 1957 would have no real significance. The District

284 INSANITY INSIDE OUT

Court judge will be primarily interested in what is happening in 1970, not 1957. But I keep telling ACLU members that we should put in everything, including the kitchen sink. But if it is left in, Mr. Ennis might not enter the case. That's why I came down. It's important that we have your thinking on this."

Me: "If the decision is left to me, Point 4 stays in."

[There was the first discouraged look I had ever seen on my friend's face.]

B: "That's what I told him."

Me: "But I'll leave it up to you."

B: "What time is it? I must meet the plane."

Me: "I leave it up to you."

B: "All right. I'm going back and write the brief Monday and I'll put it all in."

Me: "I don't care if Point 4 is argued or not—just so long as it is on the record. That would guarantee not forfeiting my birthright of a square deal in America."

[I accompanied Birnbaum to his car.]

B: "We'll win this if I live long enough."

Me: "As a student of Christian Science, I know I'll be on earth until this thing is over."

B: "That's like the man who was being chased by Death and kept shooing Death away, saying, 'I'm not ready yet.' Then one day the man was up an apple tree when Death came again, and the man said, 'Go away. I'm not ready yet.' But Death did not go away."

(I first read this in 1975. K.D.)

NAME: Kenneth Donaldson, A-25738 TYPE ADMISSION: Regular
AGE: 61   DATE: 2-6-70
EDUC: 2 yrs. college
REFERRED BY: Dr. Rodriguez

REASON FOR ADMISSION: Incompetent because of paranoid schizophrenia.

ATTITUDE AND PSYCHOLOGICAL CHARACTERISTICS AT TIME OF INTERVIEW: This patient has been evaluated on ten occasions by this service and at least on one occasion by a psychologist not associated with this hospital. As this patient was last evaluated three months ago, it is felt that he need not be seen for further psychological evaluation at the present time, for reasons that will become obvious. Instead, a summary will be presented of all the previous psychological evaluations:

9-19-58—Rorschach, MMPI and DAP in accordance in that the patient is a paranoid individual.

7-28-60—No change from earlier findings. Rorschach content indicates bizarre content and deteriorated logic.

6- 1-61—Considered to be emotionally volatile and oversuspicious. Shown some notes about hospital, taken in a "code" that not even the patient could understand.

4- 3-62—Refused testing, but expressed same beliefs as before.

1- 2-64—Patient's test results, behavior, and beliefs continue to reflect a paranoid thinking disorder.

1- 6-64—Report on the patient summarizes above findings.

8- 9-65—Letter from Doctor F. J. Calhoun, psychologist who made an independent evaluation, agrees with the above findings.

3- 4-66—Patient refused testing and left the room.

7-13-67—Test results and behavioral observations indicated the patient to still be incompetent.

3-19-68—Some progress noted. No basic alterations in his disorder were seen, but appeared to be more composed, less sure of his delusions, and generally more cooperative. However, was not considered to be fully competent.

11-12-69—Rorschach record renders a "classic paranoid protocol." Although the patient's thinking was considered to still be distorted, it was suggested that further change is unlikely. Some plan to get him out of the hospital was recommended, as the patient has been in the hospital for a number of years.

SUMMARY: It should be evident that the patient is suffering from a chronic disorder and that further progress is quite unlikely. The recommendation set forth on the report of 11-12-69 should be given consideration.

AVD:fhp

(I first read this in 1975. K.D.)

March 26, 1970

Re: Mr. Kenneth Donaldson   A 25 738

On March 25, 1970, Doctor O'Connor requested the undersigned to familiarize himself with the three copious files of the above patient, and when convenient, to interview the said patient with Mr. Davis, the psychologist. . . .

. . . he was then asked if all the MDs in medical profession were individually agreed over long period of years that he was mentally ill, and required confining to a mental institution, were all such people either knaves or fools. The patient stated that they were somewhere in between and when pressed further to be more specific, evaded further answering and introduced a new topic. . . .

Similar question was asked regarding the various members of the Legislation and legal profession who throughout the years had been involved in his case, whether they too were somewhere between knaves and fools. The patient again evaded the issue by repeating in a somewhat confusing manner, to the undersigned, the difference between writs and other legal documents. . . .

The initial conclusion drawn from this interview confirmed the findings, the conclusion rather one had obtained from the viewing of the records. . . . At this time I could not fault in any way past findings that the patient was not competent. . . .

F. G. Walls, M.D.
FGW/cb

IN THE COURTS, 1970

(xix)

Supreme Court of the United States   Oct. Term, 1969
                                            Case No. 1711, Misc.
                                            2/13/70

This was a petition for writ of certiorari, filed by Doctor Birnbaum. The Supreme Court asked the state to file answering papers, then on October 20, 1970, dismissed the case without prejudice to return to the District Court.

CHAPTER 20

1971

A Duty

ON JANUARY 14, I WROTE DOCTOR BIRNBAUM A LETTER OF REGRET IN having to send the following clipping from the Florida *Times-Union:*

> Dr. James B. O'Connor, superintendent of Florida State Hospital at Chattahoochee, has announced his retirement for February 1.

O'Connor might be gone, but I still had the awesome power of the hospital chart to contend with. It was going to be a fight to the end. Sometimes, there would be a step back, as when the ACLU stalled for four months and Birnbaum decided to proceed without them. There was a step ahead when a reporter for the *National Enquirer* decided to come with Birnbaum and interview me. We both thought that publicity would bring us more helpers.

Thus, I expected an angry scene on my next doctor's call, ten days later. But Rodriguez was mild, saying that everybody told him that I was having such a good time that I did not want to leave. I reminded him that everybody once said that the world was flat, too.

"But why won't you go to staff?" he said.

"You won't give me a competency discharge."

"You're paranoid."

Three days later, at 8:00 A.M. Saturday, I was called by Gawch: "Let's hook up to the ass wagon, old buddy. They want you in the office."

It was Mr. Dykes, waiting: "Let Gawch go with you, Kenneth. Get your things and take them down to 41."

"What for?"

"We have to keep you confined for a few days so you'll be available for visitors."

"That's pure hogwash!"

"You go with him. Gawch!"

This note was inserted in my chart by Doctor Walls, acting superintendent, February 25: "I am personally familiar with this patient, and his constant wandering around the Hospital grounds and the town, which makes any proposed interview with Doctor Morton Birnbaum rather difficult. Because of the above . . . I have suggested . . . that the patient be retained temporarily in a closed building . . . and for the protection of the said Doctor . . . a reliable psychiatric aide should be in attendance for the purpose of protecting the said Doctor should the interview become difficult to handle. . . ."

The above statement is curious. I had been given unlimited grounds and town privileges between morning and evening bed checks. Several times a month, I would walk down the four blocks of stores, enjoying the feeling of freedom, not buying, as we were not supposed to have money in our pockets. My real pleasure was in a long walk on the grounds and in a half-day's work on the book under a tree. The last thing that I would have done was to create a difficulty for Doctor Birnbaum.

I saw Doctor Birnbaum in the afternoon, but not the reporter. Birnbaum protested to Doctor Walls; nonetheless, I went back behind bars and the reporter went without his interview. (Later I was able to sneak out a snapshot, which a friend took on the street. The *Enquirer* ran the story May 16.)

"But there is good news too," Birnbaum had said. "I filed yesterday. It's a three-part suit: a combined Civil Rights Action and Habeas Corpus Proceeding, and we're asking $100,000 in damages."

And before leaving, he said, "If they don't free you from 41 in a few days, I'll get a court order."

On the following Monday morning, Doctor Rodriguez was shouting at me: "Orders have to be obeyed around here."

"I haven't broken any," I said.

"You will be locked in and put on medication unless you agree to go to staff. I might be able to get you a competency discharge. But it is all up to the other doctors. With O'Connor gone, things are different. And you are to see the medicine doctor in the morning."

"It is nothing but coercive punishment."

I wrote Birnbaum about it, through the censors.

There was a sleepless night. Should I refuse to go to staff at any price? If I did and I took medication, I could wind up like Carter or Vittorio, for I was no longer strong. By morning I saw there was more to gain and practically nothing to lose by going to staff now. With three suits, staff would end only habeas corpus; furthermore, Doctor Birnbaum said the judge did not have to hear the habeas corpus plea anyway.

At 7:00 A.M. I had Gawch call the pill man and tell him staff was on if medication was off.

At 9:00 I faced Rodriguez, who said, "And to think, you could have been out this whole year. About the letter to Doctor Birnbaum, Mr. Carmichael will take you in his office and explain how I want you to change it."

Afterward Carmichael said, "Well, you won't have to go to court now."

"The court could still beat these people—the papers were filed Friday," I said.

"Son of a gun!" Carmichael dropped his pencil.

The letter, which was mailed, came out like this:

March 2

Morton Birnbaum, M.D., LL.B.:

I have had two days of discussions with Doctor Rodriguez, and I have for several reasons agreed to obey Doctor Walls's order and go to staff for evaluation. . . .

I am still locked up in Building 41.

Kenneth Donaldson

Even without use of the word "coercion," Birnbaum would know that it had been used to make me agree to staff.

On March 4, in the morning, I was escorted up to the office.

Doctor Walls (with pencil and tiny paper ready): "What do you want from the hospital?"

Me: "An out-of-state discharge with no strings." (We went over the details of my returning to Syracuse.)

Walls: "We are interested in your condition now—not what it was in the past."

Doctor Rodriguez: "Yes, that is so."

Me: "I am glad to hear that. . . . May I have my privilege card back?"

Walls: "Sure."

Me: "May I stay down in Building 41?"

Walls: "Sure. Anything you want."

In the afternoon, Carmichael had an attendant escort me across the square to Doctor Walls's.

"Didn't you get your card?" the attendant said.

"Yes, maybe they're going to take it away from me," I said.

"Or transfer you to the receiving ward. They give shock there."

Again, there was that feeling that I might soon be needing some of Hanenson's horse pills.

Doctor Walls motioned me to a chair by the window in the expensively furnished office and sat opposite. The attendant waited outside.

Me: "There's something I forgot to tell you."

Walls: "Wait till I tell you. I have just had a call from Tallahassee. You told us your lawyer was doing something. He named Doctor O'Connor and me, even though I am only the temporary superintendent."

Me: "I thought you knew about it. They were filed last Friday, and I thought the papers would have been served last Monday."

(Doctor Walls then took notes on my family members.)

Me: "What I forgot to tell you—Doctor Birnbaum filed three suits. Besides habeas corpus, one of them is for damages."

Walls: "What was the third?"

Me: "A class suit—in behalf of all the other patients, except the criminals."

Walls: "You mean all the patients in the country?"

Me: "Just in Florida State Hospital."

On March 5, in a 1½-hour interview with Mr. Davis, I took a

True-or-False 500-question personality test and a 15-minute intelligence test.

(This is from the Summary of the psychological report by Mr. Davis: "The Minnesota Multiphasic Personality Inventory shows essentially the same pattern as that recorded on 9/19/58. The profile is usually found in people who tend to overlook faults in themselves and individuals who are rigid, touchy, stubborn, and readily project. In view of the striking similarity of these test profiles twelve years apart, Mr. Donaldson's statement at the beginning of the interview was most interesting. He said in a rather lighthearted and frivolous manner, 'If I thought I have changed one bit since I have been here I would kill myself.' . . . I do believe he will have a very good chance of maintaining himself outside the institution.")

On March 8, Monday, I was back in the splendid office in the antebellum building.

Doctor Walls: "The world has changed a lot in fourteen years. You have to lock your car now. Someone might throw a rock at you. You never know nowadays."

Me: "The world outside has got worse and the world in here has got better."

Walls: "I will say the world out there is worse."

Walls spent five minutes trying to convince me that waiting on the court was useless. I said, then Birnbaum would appeal, and appeal again.

"When I went to staff before, my lawyer told me to get out any way I could. I would have crawled. But not now," I said. "And I don't like to be threatened as I was last Monday by Doctor Rodriguez."

Walls: "There'll be no more threats while your case is in the courts. Tell me" [pointing to the file lying open on his desk] "why you refused to go with your friend—Mr. Lembcke?—in 1967."

Me: "I didn't refuse to go with him."

On March 29, Doctor Birnbaum wrote me the following:

> . . . Judge Middlebrooks denied the petition . . . habeas corpus without a hearing. In support of his decision, he cited several cases involving dangerous criminally committed prisoners; however, I called the Judge's clerk and pointed out that you have been civilly committed, was not a prisoner, and not dangerous, etc., and he suggested that I apply for a rehearing.

... I intend to submit the new papers to the Judge at the end of the week. . . .

On April 13, Tuesday, I went alone to Walls's, which he asked me to do as soon as I got news.

Doctor Walls: "Is the news good or bad?"

Me: "Rather good for me."

The doctor brought his cup of coffee over to the large bay window where I was already seated. He indulged in a few pleasantries.

Me: "Doctor Birnbaum has asked for a personal appearance in court next week. I don't know whether this would include me. That's April 22."

W (goes over to his desk calendar): "In England that is the feast of St. George."

Me: "Then we'll have something to celebrate here."

W (smiles): "Yes."

Me: "You know, Doctor Walls, I thought as I was sitting out there, what an appropriate scene this is—so appropriate to the bughouse—my consulting with the person I am suing."

W: [As we arose and started out, he put an arm around my shoulders.] "I know this—that you won't get any money from me."

I reassured him that we did not hold him to blame. He was named in the suit only because he was acting superintendent. But our fraternizing when we were legal antagonists bothered me. Thinking it over, I decided to get an okay from Birnbaum.

April 14

Morton Birnbaum, M.D., LL.B.:

... My visiting with Doctor Walls presents itself as not exactly the correct thing to do. On the other hand, I believe it is necessary for me to keep his friendship. Without it, and being without that of my department doctor, I might long ago have been a vegetable on a locked ward under heavy medication, as has happened to friends of mine. . . .

On April 19, Monday, I was called by Rodriguez. After discussing Thursday's court hearing, he said somewhat heatedly, "I'd like to go to court. I'd tell them what's wrong with you!"

On April 24, Saturday, Birnbaum visited. He had not seen the judge on Thursday. He did not tell me why. But he was going to see Mr. Mahorner, the lawyer from the Division of Mental Health and ask why Mahorner wanted to oppose my case. (In the *Wyatt* case, a Right to Treatment case in Alabama, the court clerk had asked the attorney for the state, "Don't you believe the inmate is entitled to adequate treatment?" And the state attorney had not opposed the case.)

On April 26, Monday, there was this ORDER from Judge Middlebrooks:

> Turning now to petitioner's motion for rehearing and reconsideration, this Court is of the view that the motion is well taken. Previously, this Court had determined that petitioner had not exhausted available state remedies.

I was sitting on the highest tee of the golf course, reading a letter from Hegel: "A weaker person would just run away. But you are standing your ground, determined that wrong shall be exposed."

I thought, what a price to pay! The sun warmed. The blue jay entertained. And I had wondrous recreation: "walking alone and communing with the squirrels and the ants," as I had written to my children. But the meaning, which bright skies and quiet pines offered, only half cheered. There was a sack filled with a stone of fifteen years tied to my neck in a sea of futility.

Back on the wards, I was facing yet another variation of torture. One who did not scream was put in the third bed from me. At 1:00 A.M. he stood up on his bed and, with the form of a diver from a hundred-foot ladder, took off for the thick smooth gray concrete floor. That brought the attendant and the lights. The attendant, after loudly cursing the diver back to bed, pulled the covers off Joshua, setting off ghastly screams. Then lights off. Two A.M., another dive.

The next night, the diver bloodied his forehead. The third night, with one side of his face already black and blue, a gash over the eye called for an ambulance ride to sick bay. At 4:00 A.M. he was back on 41. He got no extra medication, only was tied down with sheets, which he wriggled out of as soon as the attendant was out of sight. Then he took another dive.

"Why do you do it?" I asked him.

"They won't let me out of here, so I want to die."

"That shows good sense. But it's rough on the rest of us."

"I suppose it is."

During several months of vacation and sick leave on the second shift, little Immensley was charge attendant in Building 41.

He was a kindly, cheerful, decent sort, another white transferee from Department A, who would call out, "Here! Who ain't had no supper? Who ain't done et?" So I could not refuse when halfway through the aftersupper dispensing of medicine he called me the first night. Forty men were backed up in the halls while he tried to sort through the B.I.D.s and T.I.D.s in the ledger and find the right "color" in the several dozen cups of the pill tray. So I took over the ledger, a huge thing fit for recording the meals of elephants.

"100 Thorazine T.I.D.," I would sing out. Then together we'd search for the label in the tray. With a dropper he dispensed liquids into Kool-Aid or water, which he poured into Dixie cups. To soothe my Christian Science valuations, as we did not check off the men, I never said anything if some soul did not get off his bed and come to be "destroyed," unless he was a loud-mouthed homo. Then I would say, "I didn't see Rackass, did you?" Then Smiley would be dispatched to wake up the laggard. After a week, though, even this small abuse of power bothered me and I played favorites with none, sparing everyone what I could.

For the readers who recall the surreptitious medication I complained about in 1962 in A Department, consider that in helping Immy I could have taken handfuls of any kind, with or without his knowledge, just as could have many of the other two thousand employees.

On June 28, Monday, in a copy of Attorney Ennis's letter to Attorney Mahorner, which I received that morning, I learned that the hearing on my case, TCA No. 1693, was set for August 12. I went at once to Doctor Walls. I was just in time to have a cup of coffee. He talked a long time.

What he said at the end pleased me much: "Haven't you noticed a different spirit around the place?"

"Yes, I have," I said.

"It's quite a change when employees don't get sarcastic answers when they come to the superintendent."

Then he told me we would have a new superintendent, in July, Doctor Hirshberg, and a new clinical director, Doctor Pinell.

I said, "I am going to miss seeing you. This will probably be my last time here."

"Why? You just come on over anytime."

He then gave a summation of his philosophy of these places, which I enjoyed hearing, because it made so much sense. I asked if institutional psychiatry was not analogous to education, which had grown beyond its fundamental purpose of educating in the basics. He seemed to like that.

"These hospitals," he said, "should not be trying to be everything. I have watched it over the last ten years. First it was OT, then industrial training and education. If a man can't read and write, it should be the job of his home county and not Gadsden County's job. Similarly, if he wants to be an auto mechanic, some other unit of state government should teach him. It should not be the job for a hospital. We need to get down to fundamental questions. What is the purpose of this hospital? It should not be a dumping ground for every county in the state for their geriatrics and morons. They don't belong in a psychiatric facility. And we shouldn't have to have guards to keep criminals from escaping. This can't be a cure-all. It's gotten to be a third-grade college. It should be limited to psychiatric cases, if it is to be a hospital. Say, keep 25 percent of the ones here. Then we could have something we could manage and do something for."

"Busy?" It was a handsome young attendant. "You Donaldson? I hope you win your suit. Something has got to be done. I used to be in A Department. Name's James Reynoldson. Working on a writ?"

"Some notes for my book," I said. "No rush."

"If you could arrange it, I'd like to see a reporter next time. I wouldn't talk to a lawyer—word would get back and I'd lose my job. On March 6, 1970, it appeared to me that an old man was dying. The charge let me take him down to the dressing room. The pill man said Gumanis had too many to see, but if I'd wait until noon it might be all right. I took the man back to the ward, then down again at noon. 'What the goddam hell's the fuss?' Gumanis yelled. 'I think the man is dying,' I said. 'Take him the hell out of here, I'm busy.' The man died on the ward. My supervisor told me that people die all the time. He tried to get two of my friends to sign statements so they could fire me. Then they transferred me. If you can let me know, I'd talk to a reporter."

The next amazing piece of business was the following:

July 23

Kenneth Donaldson:

... I just spoke by telephone with Mr. Mahorner and he informs me that the hospital has (miraculously) decided that you no longer need to be hospitalized . . . it is to be an absolute rather than a conditional discharge . . . and . . . dropping the action is not a prerequisite to absolute discharge. . . .

Bruce Ennis

26 July (Monday):
1:00 P.M.

(New superintendent Dr. Milton Hirshberg and I meet alone in Carmichael's office.)

Doctor Hirshberg: "I believe in voluntary patients. It should be like a university—the students can see what they are accomplishing. . . . When the patient finds out that he can gain no more, he should be free to leave."

Me: "That's splendid."

H: "Tell me something about conditions here." [I do.] "I am astounded at what you have told me. I had no idea the place was so bad. That is not the picture they gave me. But I can tell you that I do not intend to stay here if the legislature does not give me the money to do the job. Now, about staff. We could have staff tomorrow. In some states—and I believe that is the way it is in Florida—the court cannot free a patient. It has to be done by the staff. But I'll check with Mr. Mahorner. In the meantime, would you make a call to Doctor Birnbaum and find out their final decision about staff?"

Me (in the front office, with Doctor Hirshberg at my side): "I want to make a phone call to New York. I have Doctor Hirshberg's permission."

Mr. Dykes: "But I can't let you make a phone call."

Me: "But Doctor Hirshberg okayed it."

Dykes: "I can't give you permission to make a phone call!"

H: "But I can. And I am the only one who can."

In five seconds after I got an outside line, I was talking to Doctor Birnbaum, but he was unable to get Mr. Ennis and so he arranged a conference call for the three of us in the morning.

4:00 P.M.

I was back in Carmichael's office alone to take a call from Doctor Hirshberg. Being unable to get Mr. Mahorner in Tallahassee and after reading the state laws on the matter, he concluded that I could be freed only by the staff.

27 July (Tuesday):

11:00 A.M.

At the conference phone call, taken in Carmichael's office, I was warned by Birnbaum, "You are gambling with your life, remember, Mr. Donaldson."

"I've been doing that for fifteen years," I said.

So, Birnbaum, Ennis, and I agreed: no staff unless the court ordered it.

11:45 A.M.

Me (on phone): "On the advice of two of my counsel, I shall not go before staff before my appearance in court."

Doctor Hirshberg (after five minutes of our arguing over the phone): "Here I am brand new on the job—with a record of always helping the little man—and you want to spoil my record the first month." [Gets heated, talks faster] "I don't see why you can't do it for all the other men."

Me: "I am sorry that it has to spoil your record. I have suffered fifteen years of abuse—real abuse—and that comes first. After that is straightened out—"

H (cooler): "So, all you want really is a place for board and room until August 12. What if I tell you we are going to charge you a hundred dollars a month if you stay?"

Me: "You're already getting more than that. The hospital takes most of my Social Security and has for years—and many Floridians don't pay a cent. If anybody owes money, it's the hospital."

H: "Well, Mr. Donaldson, take care. I'll be calling you."

3:30 P.M.

Doctor Pinell, Clinical Director: "Tell me about your case."

Me (giving résumé): "So, you can understand my position after fifteen years?"

P: "Yes, I can. The law is not as Doctor Hirshberg has been told by the lawyer in Tallahassee, for I have read it. It says the patient must be released by the staff."

Me: "Which does not mean before any certain number of them—nor in any certain place."

P: "Right."

(Doctor Rodriguez comes in.)

P: "I think this man should be released."

Rodriguez: "I've felt that way all along."

30 July (Friday):

12:55

(This meeting in Carmichael's office)

Doctor Hirshberg: "I am letting you go. When do you want to leave?"

Me: "First thing in the morning would be all right."

H: "I am considering that we three doctors were the staff. Would it be all right if we gave your name to a social worker, so one could call on you?"

Me: "I don't want a thing to do with any of them."

H: "Mr. Dykes will call the office and see that you get everything."

(We shake hands.)

Over the phone the treasurer, after Hirshberg had left, offered forty dollars cash and the rest to be mailed in two weeks. Was it needed for room rent, et cetera?

"It doesn't make any difference what it's for," I said. "I'll stay right here and let the court give it to me."

Dykes grabbed the phone away and said something to the treasurer. So Jennerull took me up to the treasurer's.

Treasurer: "We can't give you over one hundred dollars and I'll mail you the rest."

Me: "I'll wait right here until the court gives it to me."

Treasurer: "Take a state check for two hundred."

Me: "No. I'll stay until I get cash. I don't want anything Florida."

Treasurer: "But I haven't got that much."

Me: "I'll take it to the bank and get traveler's checks then."

With a check for $216 and a hundred dollars in my pocket, Jennerull drove me to the bank five minutes before closing.

Saturday, the discharge papers weren't ready in time for the first bus, but I got to Tallahassee by noon, where the hearing was still scheduled for August 12.

I walked several blocks and got a room in a tourist home for nine dollars a week, in the off-season.

"I was just discharged from Chattahoochee," I said.

"You don't cause trouble, do you?" asked the landlady.

"No."

"It's perfectly all right then."

That afternoon I bought an umbrella and on Monday, shoes,

sneakers, and hot-weather clothes. Restaurant food was out of this world. I walked from early until late, contented to be alone, just looking, soaking up life. The hospital forwarded bundles of newspapers. I wrote all my regular correspondents and soon had mail every day.

Hegel wrote: "If I had a hat, I would throw it up in the air . . . [but] I note Shirley's warnings about the prejudice against exes in Syracuse."

In a phone conversation on Monday, Birnbaum said: "Let me ask you one thing. If you want to drop the whole thing, it will be all right with me. There will be a lot of unpleasantness before this is over. If you would like a little peace—and you certainly deserve it after fifteen years of incarceration—I want you to know it will be all right with me. And I speak for Mr. Ennis too. And if at any time in the future you decide the pressures are too much, I will understand."

"This is all I have left in life," I said. "Whatever they can do to me now can't match the last fifteen years. If you stick with me, we'll win this together. If I have to do it alone, with the book, I'll do that too."

But I walked away from the phone with a feeling of having nailed down my anchor rope to the deck. However, my feeling of *hopelessly* drifting was gone.

On August 12, Thursday, I entered the following in my journal:

Who needs Perry Mason?

Mr. Ennis and Doctor Birnbaum were terrific. This is only preliminary skirmishing to limit the issues for a trial if the judge grants it.

Tomorrow I'll give my deposition in the morning, mostly being cross-examination by the state's lawyers.

In the afternoon Doctor Walls gives his. O'Connor very conveniently has heart weakness and has been excused for the time being from a personal appearance.

I got a few points in before the judge—points of fact which no one else had any response to.

At the close of the hearing, Judge Middlebrooks rode Birnbaum hard. "Somebody goofed, not getting Mr. Donaldson out years ago on a writ of habeas corpus," said Middlebrooks.

Ennis interceded: "Mr. Donaldson got lost in a shuffle of

papers. That's why we say judicial review should be automatic."

Said Birnbaum: "Your Honor, the people who goofed have been the honorable judges of the courts."

My journal continued:

> ... In the afternoon Ennis and Birnbaum and I went to Chattahoochee and they pawed over my record. It seems to have been thinned out. . . .
>
> I left [my] place before 7:30 A.M. and got home after 7:30 P.M., then did an hour's research for Mr. Ennis.

Visiting with the Wallses in the corridor, before the depositions the next day, I was flabbergasted when Mrs. Walls said, "How do you feel, Kenneth? This is a terrible thing to do to you."

[What she thought was mental torture was for me the most exquisite ecstasy, an almost unbelievable event.]

This is from the deposition of Doctor Walls, August 13:

> Q. (by Ennis): "Are you able, Doctor, to give an opinion as to whether or not you observed any difference in Mr. Donaldson's mental condition today from his mental condition when you observed him in March of 1970?"
>
> A. (by Walls): "I thought he was worse today than 1970."
>
> Q. "Well, you're speaking in terms of 'maybe,' 'possibly.' What I'm talking about is you've been involuntarily depriving a man of his liberty for fifteen years on the basis of possibilities. Is that correct?"
>
> A. "No, no, no, no, no, on the basis of professional diagnostic conditions of a serious mental illness, which has shown no improvement and has shown deterioration."
>
> Q. "In other words, if you had had the final say, am I correct, you would not have discharged Mr. Donaldson on July 31 of this year?"
>
> A. "If I had been on that staff, presuming a staff was held, my vote would have been 'no.' "
>
> Q. (by Mr. Mahorner): "Is it your opinion that Mr. Donaldson is unable to handle a job right now?"
>
> A. (by Walls): "I don't think he could. . . ."

Two days later, the train slid to a quick stop at 2:00 A.M. in pastureland at East Syracuse. With fifty other silent people, I descended to the platform, with "two suitcases crammed with law books and briefs" (as a friend said later) and a double-thick attaché case with the manuscript. Three days later, I was handling a job.

On December 21, my Christmas card to Vittorio Dacker arrived back in Syracuse, marked "deceased."

DEPARTMENT OF HEALTH AND REHABILITATIVE SERVICES
Division of Administrative Services

July 23, 1971

Dr. Milton J. Hirshberg
Superintendent
Florida State Hospital
Chattahoochee, Florida 32324

Re: Dr. F. G. Walls's letter of June 2, 1971 to me
concerning Mr. Kenneth Donaldson, A 25 738

Dear Dr. Hirshberg:
A copy of the above letter is enclosed for your information.
In reference to the Kenneth Donaldson case, my research has indicated there are two (2) reasons for retaining mentally ill patients against their wishes. One is to protect the public, and the other reason is to protect the individual. An involuntarily committed patient must be released (1) if he is no longer mentally ill, or (2) although he remains mentally ill, he is no longer likely to injure himself or other persons. Every case which has inquired into the question has concluded that it is impermissible to detain mentally ill individuals against their wishes if they are no longer likely to injure themselves or other persons. In Dr. Walls's letter to me of June 2, 1971, he stated that Mr. Donaldson has both ground and town privileges and that neither he nor anyone else on the staff considers him to be a danger to either himself or to others. I recommend that we release Mr. Donaldson if that is the case. Mr. Donaldson's attorney has stated that that is all they actually seek. To continue with this case would only result in adverse publicity being generated against the Division of Mental Health.
Perhaps you contend that a periodic examination which would result in the release of Mr. Donaldson is a privilege for which he must apply. The courts have stated that such periodic examination is not a right of the patient but a statutory duty of the hospital staff. In other words, it is the duty of the hospital staff to make periodic examinations of those who are involuntarily detained in the institution to determine whether they

are likely to injure themselves or other persons or not. If they are not prone to injure themselves or other persons, they must be released.

I am not certain whether you are familiar with the recent law applying to the mental health field which was passed by this session of our Legislature. I enclose a copy of it for your information.

Sincerely,

B. R. PATTERSON
Assistant General Counsel

Staff Meeting
Re: Mr. Kenneth Donaldson, A-25738
July 30, 1971
Doctor Hirshberg: Mr. Kenneth Donaldson is a sixty-five years old divorced man who was admitted to Florida State Hospital on January 15, 1957, on a commitment dated January 3, 1957. He was admitted under Section 394.22, Florida Statutes, following adjudication of mental incompetency.

He has a history of hospitalization in the Marcy State Hospital in New York in 1943 when he was approximately thirty-seven years of age. He had electroshock treatment at that time. Subsequently he became divorced, had lived in Arizona for a while, and then came to Florida to be with his parents. He tended to think that people were slandering him, stealing his ideas, or threatening to put poison in his food, and as his judgment at home evidently deteriorated his father applied for hospitalization.

When I met with him on July 26, 1971, we were in the supervisor's office of Department C. He appeared to have the physical vigor and health appropriate to his age. He was pleasant and he spoke with me in a direct, logical, and coherent fashion. We discussed his hospitalization, and he talked about this in a reasonable way with many suitable and appropriate comments which indicated an intellectual competency with somewhat complex facts. He said that if he were to leave the hospital, he would be able to take a bus to Tallahassee and register at a hotel and await the appearance in

Court which is to be scheduled sometime in August. On the basis of his demonstrated assurance that he could look after himself if he were to leave the hospital, that his thinking was clear and logical, that he had a realistic appreciation that the transition from the hospital to community life would be challenging, that there was no defect of his intellect, that he had a successful adjustment in managing ground privileges, was not in need of medication, it was my impression that as long as he did not wish further treatment, that he should be discharged. When I told him this, he asked to reach his attorney, and he placed a long-distance call to New York City to his attorney to inform him of my wish to bring him to Staff because of my opinion that he could be discharged. The next day, we learned that his attorney had instructed him not to go to staff.

It was my belief that the patient should not remain in the hospital in any prolonged way, if the need for hospitalization had terminated, merely because his attorney told him to. On the other hand, in view of this man's long-standing hospitalization and the challenge he would face in adjusting if he were to leave the hospital against his will, I was willing to give him time to think over the prospects of leaving at this time. I then asked Doctor Jesus S. Rodriguez and Doctor Octavio Pinell, the Florida State Hospital Clinical Director, to independently evaluate Mr. Donaldson on the question of his readiness to leave the hospital. I have now received the extensive findings of these two psychiatrists, and they concur with my own. Accordingly, it is our decision that Mr. Donaldson be given a competency discharge from Florida State Hospital. I talked with Mr. Donaldson in the Supervisor's office of Department C at 1:00 P.M. today and he said he wanted to leave the hospital and would depart tomorrow for Tallahassee. He did not want after-care contact with any mental health agency whatever.

Doctor Pinell: Concurred with Doctor Hirshberg.
Doctor Rodriguez: Concurred with Doctor Hirshberg also.
RECOMMENDATION: Discharge with competency.

MJH/mg/vgg

IN THE COURTS, 1971

(xx)

United States District Court   Tal. Civil Action No. 1693
Northern District of Florida,
    Tallahassee Division   brief dated 3/24/71

This was a three-part petition filed by Doctor Birnbaum, seeking plaintiff Donaldson's release through habeas corpus. It asked $100,000 damages for plaintiff. It was a class action in favor of all other involuntary patients in Chattahoochee, asking for a declaration that Florida commitment statutes were unconstitutional and asking for an injunction barring the hospital staff from holding patients without adequate treatment.

On March 10, this court denied habeas corpus, without prejudice to return to the state courts, and without action on the other two parts of the suit. On March 27, Birnbaum filed notice of appeal to the U.S. Court of Appeals, Fifth Circuit. On April 20, again back in Tallahassee, the District Court denied the plaintiff's petition to proceed in forma pauperis. On April 20, Birnbaum filed a motion for a rehearing, which this court granted on April 26, but transferring the case to the Tampa Division. Birnbaum and Ennis flew down to Tampa for a hearing, only to have the judge transfer the case back to Tallahassee. This court set August 6 as the date for plaintiff's oral deposition. Somewhere along the line, this court let plaintiff proceed as a pauper.

On July 27, Bruce Ennis filed a motion asking that the state be made to file answering papers. On July 29, Ennis filed notice to take oral depositions of the defending doctors on August 13.

On August 12, Judge Middlebrooks held the first hearing for opposing counsel. On August 13, the plaintiff and Doctor Walls made oral depositions in the Leon County Courthouse.

The rest of 1971 and all of 1972 were a series of legal skirmishes on both sides; proddings by Bruce Ennis to get things under way; and numerous interrogatories by opposing counsel, attempting to sort out the facts for the trial.

CHAPTER 21

Essence
of Sanity

THE CROWDED SECOND-FLOOR CORRIDOR OF THE UNITED STATES POST
Office and Courthouse, Tallahassee, with its marble floor and its
two sets of oak double doors to the high-ceilinged courtroom, held
the cast of the final act in an obscure American drama. For the first
time, the small group of people who for fifteen years had wielded
unlimited power against me would meet me today on an equal
footing.

For all the long years of incarceration I had asked for nothing
more than a fair and open hearing. For all those years, my
petitions to the courts reached no higher than the level of the
wastebasket. My claims had simply been denied by the doctors and
those denials had been accepted as conclusive. Now, before a jury,
our versions would be tested. The doctors, up to this point, had
been my only judges; today the people would judge them; and I
would judge the reality of the American dream of justice.

I had often said on the wards, "The Florida state courts work
directly under God. They bypass the laws and the U.S. Constitution." But inside, would there be a difference? Hadn't half of my

nineteen previous pleas been to federal courts? The difference this time was the jury—ironically because the state's lawyers had demanded a jury, in the belief the judge was biased for not having thrown the case out. Understandably now, we were worried, for here we were, a swarm of Yankees, trying to win over some small-town southerners against one of their own, Doctor O'Connor. In the end, though, my reasoning told me this was the best way. At least one of the jurors was bound to be like Nessley or A. B. or Yillabar. Could a jury stomach what I had been through? Let lawyer talk to lawyer and doctor to doctor, but here today, let the little man talk to the hearts of Americans.

Their decision, that of a jury of my peers, was all the answer I wanted. The amount of money which might be awarded me was not of importance in comparison.

By 9:00 A.M. the veniremen took most of the benches and all of two small rooms, leaving the contestants to cluster twenty feet apart. Doctor Walls crossed over to shake my hand warmly. He was introduced around our circle before going back. Doctor Gumanis understood the blank abhorrence on my face and remained chatting with Mr. Mahorner and Mr. Robert E. Carmichael, though the latter was appearing as plaintiff's witness.

At 10:00, lawyer Birnbaum, in his well-filled dark suit, came up the circling stone stairs. He was attending as a spectator. "Too many cooks spoil it," he said. "Mr. Ennis and Mr. DuBose are doing a top-notch job. But what's the tie-up? I thought Mr. Donaldson would have his money by now."

"The jury hasn't come in in an accident case," Dean said. He was an experienced trial lawyer, a Florida member of ACLU, who was offering a steadying hand to the two young lawyers in their first case before a jury. "Here they are now," he said. "But this changes our plans. We wanted Kenneth first, as his testimony is the strongest. Now it means we're going to have to put John and Walter on first, so they can get back home."

Neither young counsel had eaten a full meal for two days. It was eagerness, I could see, and my confidence rose each day as I worked with Ennis and saw the strategy develop. "You'd have to be a lawyer to appreciate the tremendous job they are doing," Birnbaum said. "You'd think it was the Pentagon Papers case."

Then Judge Middlebrooks had another matter to take up with a large group of lawyers, and Civil Action No. 1693 was postponed until Tuesday.

Overnight, I pondered Birnbaum's words: Why was the state opposing us at all? "Are you against adequate treatment for the patients?" he had asked the state's lawyer. Perhaps it was rather, as William F. Buckley wrote about the case of Edgar Smith in New Jersey, who did fourteen years on death row: "But pride is an addiction, and the State is not disposed to take the position that it made a mistake."

Why was society trying to disprove my sanity? I had spent many years thinking about it. Freud had said that the abilities to work and to love are the best indicators of health. To the best of my ability, I had been a loving son, husband, and father. Times had been hard but I had cared deeply about my people. As to work, I had enjoyed pursuing several trades, developing a considerable skill in each. THESE THINGS WERE AT THE HEART OF THE MATTER FOR ME.

For my lawyers, there were a number of issues. For Birnbaum, who had fought shoulder to shoulder with me for years to obtain my freedom, this trial was part of a broad offensive to improve the state hospital system. He saw my case as an important opportunity to argue the Right to Treatment.

For Ennis there were four main issues. First, the federal courts had traditionally examined only commitment procedures, and this case examined postcommitment rights. It afforded a chance to contest the hands-off attitude of the courts. Here, perhaps, the Constitution could be brought *into* the asylum. Second, since I was absolutely nondangerous, the state plainly had no business interfering in my life for fifteen years. Only procedural limitations had been imposed before; now a hard look could be given to substantive limitations. Third, the sham and pretense of patient treatment ought to be revealed. That patients stay the same or get worse is the fact. And fourth, since most Right to Treatment cases were *affirmative* and resulted in orders to improve treatment, the worst that could happen to a doctor would be an order to release the patient. Here was a case which, because of the assessability of money damages, could put teeth into the sanctions against doctors.

Legal details were that I was not a bona fide resident of Florida before my commitment, and that the requirement of parental consent to an out-of-state discharge was unlawful and unconstitutional.

For my opponents, the issue was: Is the court to make medical decisions?

For the public in general, the issue was: Can a person be locked up against his will on the sole basis of someone's saying he has delusions?

Trial, Tuesday, November 21, 1972:

The opening moments of the trial were solemn for us. Underneath, there was exhilaration that things were under way. But there was also knowledge that no state hospital doctor had ever lost a cent in a damage suit to one of his patients.

The jury was chosen with two scratches by the defense. Those thrown out were a bright-painted lady and a dull-black woman. Plaintiff's lawyers challenged no one, so as not to give the impression of finding fault with the local populace. The jury was three men and three women, all middle-aged and white. Alternates were a youngish black woman and a white man.

Defense lawyer Mahorner objected because there were no doctors of medicine on the panel. Judge Middlebrooks, astounded, pointed out that "the court has no control over that."

Our lawyers called Doctor Fox first. The Tallahassee *Democrat* reported the next day:

> A consultant with the National Institute of Mental Health said in U.S. District Court yesterday that former mental patient Kenneth Donaldson should have been hospitalized for only two to three months at the most, not fifteen years.
>
> Dr. Walter Fox, who is also the director of Arizona's mental health services, said the state hospital at Chattahoochee appeared for the first few years to be indifferent to discharging Donaldson, "Almost like this wasn't one of their goals."
>
> Thereafter, he said, there even seemed to be some resistance to discharging him. . . .
>
> Fox said there was nothing in Donaldson's past history to indicate that he was not a responsible person who should have been given as much freedom as possible at the hospital. . . .
>
> "Donaldson has a great deal more strength than most persons," said Fox, "the experience did not rob him of his independence. . . ."

After lunch, John Lembcke was called. He was as indignant as I at what the state had done. His was the first voice my tired ears could catch distinctly. He spoke in a rhythm of carefully selected phrases. The recording stenographer looked around at him. "Nervous," Dean said, and Ennis and DuBose nodded. But I watched the jury. For the first time, they seemed alive. Good old

John, he would be the last to flub when he got the ball. Not even Mahorner questioned that he meant what he said. Asked why I had been divorced, John replied that others had told him that my wife was not as mature as I. "No, I did not hear it from Kenneth," he said to Mahorner. In answer to why the hospital might have refused to let him take me out, he said, "The hospital thought Kenneth was dangerous because he would write and say things about them after his discharge."

I testified from 3:00 to 6:00. My voice almost broke at the beginning. Such a feeling of relief came over me—of pride that this room was not an *Alice in Wonderland* setting, that one who had been humbled was being listened to. I felt no pity for myself. I was not begging. I did not run out of breath, nor did I hurry, nor stumble. I was speaking for Carter and Narrel. I told of the fears, the humiliations, the indignities that reduce a strong man. I was thinking of Vittorio.

When I told why I had refused to see my daughter ("I love my daughter. I wasn't going to let her see her father cowering in a cage"), the juror who wore the Stetson Western and a string bow tie, and who was chief of an Indian tribe, took a tear away with his finger.

Bruce Ennis was building, in direct examination, the story presented by this book. I had been a competent worker. I had had no delusions. I had made no threats. There had been no examination before commitment. We brought out all the opportunities for my release, which had been blocked. Supporting my mental competence, we noted that I had not read my hospital chart, making my testimony entirely from memory.

What Ennis said next warmed me. From the hospital chart, he showed that Mrs. Marjorie Katherine Donaldson had not requested that her son be given electroshock. This differed with Adair's version, which had been that my mother had requested ECT.

To display my ability to the jury, during the time the hospital said I was incompetent, Ennis sought to enter copies of my article in the *Georgetown Law Journal* as evidence. The defense objected and the judge ruled that only my original manuscript could be submitted. The original was with my papers in my apartment in Syracuse. We were on the verge of telephoning a cousin in Syracuse to get a key from my landlady and look for the original, before deciding it was not needed because we had already made our point for the benefit of the jury.

Entered, though, were copies of my letters to the White House and prominent people, *giving* them my ideas, plus the laboratory report showing codeine.

Trial, Wednesday, November 22:

In cross-examining me, Mr. Mahorner was trying to build a case of persecution complex. He tried to show I had been sick all my life and dwelled on my Marcy experience.

At one point, Judge Middlebrooks turned to me and asked, "What do you think is the reason that no court would hear your case?"

"Because when they received a petition from the hospital they figured it was from somebody who belonged in the nuthouse," I said.

"You mean this court?"

And though this court had once sent my case to Tampa, instead of tackling it itself, I answered, "Of course not, or I wouldn't be here today."

The whole courtroom laughed.

I had not noticed the tension. I was exhausted when I stepped down.

Our next two witnesses were psychologists. Julian Davis, chief psychologist at the hospital, swore that he had advocated for years that I be furloughed. Then Dr. Raymond D. Fowler, University of Alabama, took the stand. He explained in great detail the definitions in current usage for so-called mental illness.

The following is from Respondent's brief, in the Supreme Court of the United States, October Term 1974, Case No. 74–8, on page 20:

Dr. Raymond D. Fowler, Chairman of the Department of Psychology at the University of Alabama, reviewed respondent's record, including all of respondent's psychological tests and the underlying raw data. He found no evidence that respondent had been schizophrenic, and testified further that "at least 10 percent and probably more" of all "college students would have profiles as deviant or more deviant than" respondent's in the Minnesota Multiphasic Personality Index ("MMPI"); that the raw data from these examinations showed that respondent's behavior was "quite well organized"; and that he doubted that he would ever have recommended hospitalization for respondent.

The following, also from our Supreme Court brief, well describes the deposition of the Syracuse hotel owner, Mr. Emil Colozzi:

> After his discharge respondent took a bus to Syracuse, New York, where, within a week, he found a steady and responsible hotel job which he had held over a year by the time of trial. His employer, John Colozzi, testified that respondent "caught on very fast and very well," "conducted himself as a normal individual," showed up on time and never missed a day of work, ran the entire hotel from midnight until 8:00 A.M., balanced the accounts, received all monies, and "handled the job very well."

Eugene DuBose had done the legwork for us in Chattahoochee. It was his inspiration to include Gumanis, after talking to him. He was to handle Gumanis on the stand. He started slowly, then drilled into him and Gumanis backtracked all the way round Robin Hood's barn. At times, DuBose asked the same question three or four times without getting a clear-cut answer from Gumanis. The early questions set the background for the jury.

Q "Are you licensed to practice medicine in the State of Florida?"
A "No."
Q "Are you licensed in any state of the Union?"
A "No, I am not. I am licensed to practice in Athens, Greece."
[DuBose questioned Gumanis about the bylaws of the hospital and asked him to read certain of them.]
A " 'It is required that each physician read this manual in its entirety and sign a statement that he has done so. He should often refer to it to refresh his memory of its contents.' "
Q "So you were required to read all of these rules, weren't you?"
A "Yes, sir."
Q "And you have only read some of them, is that correct?"
A "Yes."

DuBose brought out a 4 × 6-foot chart with each of my 5,300 (approximately) days of incarceration ruled. While he questioned Gumanis, he started to black out each day I had been seen by a doctor. The black spots were lost on the huge whiteness.
Q "Now, why did you have this staff conference on Mr. Donaldson?"
A "Well, we were trying to release the man."

Q   "You were trying to release him?"
A   "We were trying to release him, and, as I said, if the other
doctors thought that he was ready to go, and if a psychological
examination was satisfactory, at times I did not receive the
psychological examination until that date, but my opinion at that
time was that the patient was still psychotic."
Q   "Well, if you were trying to release him, why did you advise the
staff in the post-staff dictation—"
A   "I have that here."

THE COURT: "Doctor, wait until you are sure you hear the
question."
THE WITNESS: "Excuse me, sir."

Q (by DuBose)   "If you were trying to release him, why did you
say that he should still remain in the hospital? He should 'remain'
in the hospital, I think that is the word."
A   "Our objective was always trying to release the patient, but on
this particular staff I made the recommendation that the patient
remain at the hospital. We thought he was still psychotic."
Q   "So that staff was not for the purpose of releasing the plaintiff,
was it?"
A   "If the patient received the correct number of votes he would
have been released."
Q   "But you—"
A   "No matter what we said."
Q   "You were not going to vote for his release, were you?"
A   "No, sir."

Judge Middlebrooks put the trial over to Monday, because of
the Thanksgiving weekend.

In a holiday mood, on Friday, I took the bus to Chat-
tahoochee for a visit with Sedge Wicks and several attendants. It
was fun, though a little scary, going into the locked wards again.
A.B., who had retired, hearing I was in town, drove over to tell
me to see the piece in the evening *Democrat,* a second installment of
my testimony.
"We're mighty proud to see you get justice," A.B. said.
At a hamburger joint, I ran into psychologist Cunningham.
Holding up the V sign, I said, "Mr. Davis testified for us."
"Oh, I didn't know that," Cunningham said. "I'm so weak. I
told them I couldn't take the stand. Mr. Mahorner said they'd
have to subpoena me. Oh, I can't go. I've been off work for weeks."

Another with the O'Connor syndrome!

The bus-station lady discussed the case with me: "It's like the rain after the drought. It was inevitable. Somebody had to start it. We're all so glad. Your case is responsible for a big improvement at the hospital."

And all the workers at the hotel in Tallahassee were pulling for us.

By Sunday, two more expert witnesses had flown in, one from New York, one from Oregon. But, led by Dean, our counsel began speculating on not calling any more witnesses.

"We have a wonderful momentum built up," Dean said. "Let's cut it off here."

"When it goes to appeal," Ennis said, "it's the quality of the evidence that counts, not the quantity."

However, while we would call no more expert witnesses, there remained considerably more questioning of the defendants.

Trial, Monday, November 27:

Mr. DuBose continued questioning Doctor Gumanis:

Q "... Now, you say that Doctor O'Connor knew of Mr. Donaldson's case?"

A "He knew of Mr. Donaldson's case because he was the attending Psychiatrist from December 1957 until October of 1959. He was not Assistant Clinical Director or Clinical Director or Superintendent. His position at the hospital was Staff Psychiatrist of Department A."

Q "So he was Staff Psychiatrist up until 1959 and where was he located in the department?"

A "Department A."

Q "That was the department that you are now on?"

A "Yes."

Q "And you were on then?"

A "I was there with him, his associate, yes, sir."

Q "And Doctor O'Connor was in charge of the department?"

A "Yes."

Q "And he was also plaintiff's attending Psychiatrist?"

A "That is right."

[This corroboration of the plaintiff's story contradicts O'Connor's deposition read into the record later in the day.]

Q "Now, what were Mr. Donaldson's strengths? What were his good points?"

A   "Pardon me?"
Q   "What were Mr. Donaldson's strengths?"
A   "Mr. Donaldson's what?"
Q   "Strengths?"
A   "I didn't understand you."
Q   "Strengths, good points."
A   "I–"
Q   "Why was he strong in what things he could do?"
A   "In which way? What are you referring to?"
Q   "When you treat a patient isn't it important to know what he can do rather than what he cannot do?"
A   "All right, yes."
Q   "So what were Mr. Donaldson's strong points? What could he do?"
A   "What could he do if he helped himself, is that what you mean?"
Q   "In what areas was his functioning unimpaired?"
A   "Oh."

(This was the testimony of the man charged with understanding me—and a thousand other men.)

The following is from the *Democrat's* reporting of Gumanis's testimony:

> Former mental patient Kenneth Donaldson's commitment to Florida State Hospital helped protect him from delusions which could have been worse without treatment, a psychiatrist testified in U.S. District Court today.
> Dr. John Gumanis said Donaldson was "unable to realize he was mentally ill."
> The therapy he did receive involved going to dances, movies, and church. This, Gumanis said, was referred to as musical therapy, recreational therapy, and religious therapy. . . .

Doctor Walls was called. In cross-examination Ennis asked some of the same questions he had at Walls's deposition on August 13, 1972. Walls repeated that he would have voted against my discharge on July 31, 1972, if he had been at the staff that day.

> Q (by Ennis)   "Did you think at the time of the deposition two weeks after Mr. Donaldson was discharged that he was capable at that time of holding down a job?"
> A   "No."

Q "In fact, didn't you say that in your opinion that he would not be capable of holding down a job?"

A "Yes, sir."

Q "Now, you have heard his testimony that nine days after that deposition he went to Syracuse and got a job?"

A "Yes."

Q "Which he has held down steadily ever since?"

A "Yes."

Q "Would you be willing to admit that experience has proved you wrong in that instance?"

A "Yes, sir."

Q "Do you think that you might have been wrong about other matters concerning Mr. Donaldson?"

A "What matters, Mr. Ennis?"

Q "Well, for example, his ability to adjust to live in the community after a prolonged period of hospitalization? Don't you concede now that you might have been wrong in thinking he could not adjust to community life?"

A "Yes."

Q "And might it not have been a sensible thing to do to at least give him a trial visit or a chance to prove that he could?"

A "No, sir."

A deposition by Dr. Frank Calhoun had been put into the record as evidence. Calhoun was the psychologist whom Representative Stallings had taken to Chattahoochee from Jacksonville. Upon first examining me, he had recommended that I be released. After studying the tests he had given me, he had decided I was sick; and one of the things that he pointed to when asked on deposition to identify those characteristics of the profile of the tests that made him conclude that I was paranoid-schizophrenic was the fact that I had not put pupils in the eyes of the stickmen I had drawn. It was brought out in the questioning that Little Orphan Annie also has no pupils in her eyes. This information was given to the courtroom by one of our expert witnesses, Doctor Fowler.

The defense paraded the brass of the health department, from all over the state, and there was a deposition from Doctor Rich, who now worked in Georgia. Doctor Adair's well-tanned head seemed larger, now that it was so gray. Each doctor, in terms most appropriate, was finding, symbolically, no pupils in the eyes.

The trial transcript continued:

These are answers from three sets of interrogatories served on the defendant O'Connor:

Set 2, number three, What was your relationship to plaintiff when you first met him? I had general supervision over the area where the plaintiff was housed and I had general supervision over the plaintiff's doctor.

Set 2, number four, Were you ever the psychiatrist in charge of plaintiff? I was never the plaintiff's only psychiatrist, but I had an interest in the plaintiff as well as in all of the other patients in my capacity as assistant clinical director and the superintendent.

Set 3, number 15, Who was plaintiff's attending psychiatrist? Doctor John Gumanis.

Set 2, 24, State in detail what transpired during your interview with John Lembcke when he visited Florida State Hospital in Chattahoochee in May of 1966. To the best of my knowledge, Mr. Lembcke did not have an interview with me.

(Doctor Gumanis had already deposed that he had "escorted (Lembcke) over to Dr. O'Connor's office.")

Trial, Tuesday, November 28:
Another deposition of Doctor O'Connor, on written interrogatories, was read to the jury, it being introduced into evidence because he was otherwise unable to appear. Concerning my treatment, O'Connor said:

This patient on numerous occasions was offered treatment and would categorically refuse to accept treatment, that on the basis of his opinion there had never been anything wrong with his mind, including the particular times when such treatment would be offered him.

The reader knows very well the treatment offered to me on numerous occasions—drugs. When asked, however, what the appropriate treatment for my alleged condition was, here is O'Connor's answer:

I would think that the most acceptable form of treatment, though this may not be universal, would be to attempt to explain to the patient what actually was the case, hoping he might at some future time accept the explanation.

In other words, the wrong treatment, which was drugs, had always been offered me, and I had always refused. But serious discussion, which I had always requested and which was never allowed, is now what Doctor O'Connor says is the right treatment. Because I was sane and demanded the right treatment, O'Connor called me insane and kept me in Chattahoochee.

Part of Doctor O'Connor's defense was that Florida law gave him the right to hold me since I had been committed as "possibly dangerous" (a label put on me without a scrap of reason by the doctors in Pinellas County who had not seen me). This defense, though, had already been struck down by the state's attorney general, who pointed out that under Florida law I could not be held when not dangerous, which all the other doctors had acknowledged.

The other part of O'Connor's defense was that he should not be held liable for denying me a right (the Right to Treatment) before it was ruled as being a Constitutional Right.

At the end, there was a 45-minute summary by Mr. Ennis. He said that Florida State Hospital was no different from a prison, that there was nothing that I got in the hospital that I could not have got at Raiford State Penitentiary.

Then Mr. Mahorner spoke for the defense. He said that since I was such a good witness the hospital must have helped me.

The final word was by Mr. Dean. Speaking in a low voice, right in front of the jury, he said, "Let's see what the hospital did to help Donaldson." He looked at the first entry in the progress notes in my hospital file, which said to "continue custodial care." Then he pointed to the second entry, four months later. Then five months later there was another. "Then after another nine months of nothing, there was another," he said. And the fifth entry said, "Continue custodial care." This, of course, had been the refrain about my treatment.

The Tallahassee *Democrat* summed up the case thus:

> At issue is whether or not the state had a right to commit and involuntarily hold Donaldson, or any person, in a state mental institution because he is "potentially" dangerous due to illusions.
>
> "Doctors at the hospital admitted that Donaldson posed no physical threat to himself or others and that he had no past record of arrest or trouble with police prior to his commitment.

The judge's charge to the jury was the first in a Right to Treatment case. He said the jury should rule for the former mental patient, Kenneth Donaldson, if it found he was not given such individual "treatment as will give him a realistic opportunity to be cured or to improve his mental condition."

Not one bit of evidence was introduced at the trial, of anything I did in forty-eight years before Chattahoochee or in fifteen years at Chattahoochee, that showed I should be locked up for as much as one day.

But when the jury went out at 3:30, I agonized.

At 5:30, the jury came in.

When the words "punitive damages" were read, I was gratified. Two doctors had acted "maliciously or wantonly or oppressively."

I couldn't hear too well, but when Doctor Walls came over to shake hands, I knew he had been let off, which was as I wanted. I thought in 1972 that Walls was honest, based on his actions and his testimony. In 1975, after reading his entries in my chart, I still do. His finding "skeletons in my closet" represents the classic sensitivity of a state-institutional psychiatrist to any inmate who disagrees with him or objects to being held.

The jury award was $5,000 each in punitive damages against Gumanis and O'Connor, and compensatory damages of $11,500 against Gumanis and of $17,000 against O'Connor.

I believe these are the first judgments ever against a state asylum doctor in this country.

We celebrated the victory. But the many in unhappier circumstances tempered our cheer.

IN THE COURTS, 1972, 1974

(xx, cont.)

United States District Court
Northern District of Florida,
Tallahassee Division

Tal. Civil Action No. 1693
Trial 11/21,22,27,28/72

This was a trial for damages against several hospital doctors, before a jury, conducted by lawyers for the plaintiff, Bruce J. Ennis, Eugene Z. DuBose, and George Dean. The jury awarded $38,500 in compensatory and punitive damages against J. B. O'Connor, M.D. and John Gumanis, M.D.

(xxi)

United States Court of Appeals
Fifth Circuit

Case No. 73-1843
Oral Argument 12/5/73
Lower Court's Decision Affirmed 4/26/74

This was the appeal of doctors O'Connor and Gumanis. Donaldson's lawyers were Bruce J. Ennis and Paul R. Friedman, both of the Mental Health Law Project, Washington. Oral argument was heard in New Orleans.

"The Court of Appeals, Wisdom, Circuit Judge, held that patient had constitutional right to such treatment as would help him to be cured or to improve his mental condition; that evidence supported finding that attending physicians had acted in bad faith with respect to their treatment of patient and were personally liable for his injuries or deprivations of his constitutional rights. . . . Affirmed."

(xxii)

Supreme Court of the United States

Oct. Term 1974
Case No. 74-8

This was an appeal in certiorari by J. B. O'Connor, M.D. Donaldson's lawyers were Bruce J. Ennis, Eugene Z. Dubose, Jr., Paul R. Friedman, and Benjamin W. Heineman, Jr. It is the first Right to Treatment case ever taken by this court and also the first case involving a non-criminal mental patient in modern times.

CHAPTER 22

Essence
of Sanism

SIXTEEN YEARS AFTER THE FACT, FINDING THE 1956 CHRISTMAS CARD,
which my parents had put in with the gifts I had refused at the
Pinellas County jail, was jarring. Their added note said: "Please
have faith in thought that we are doing all we can to make things
better for you. Our hearts are heavy. Lots of love, Mother and
Dad."

They had done everything but send a lawyer. They just didn't
understand.

Tears also wash the slate clean. For the second time in my
adult life, they ran down my cheeks. It came over me suddenly,
with the card in hand, while I was working on the book, sitting in
an easy chair in the warm bedroom by the double windows, the
manuscript on the coffee table in front of me and papers spread all
over the bed beside me. Suddenly, the inutility of the fifteen years,
the simple fact that my whole family life, both with parents and
with children, had irrevocably gone down the drain, overwhelmed
me.

What had my parents done and why had they done it? They

had loved me and had taken the signs of turbulence in my life to heart. I was a grown man and yet I seemed to them rootless and problematical. Twenty years before, they had accepted a psychiatric diagnosis which forever rent the fabric of my life. Thereafter, not only society at large but members of my family would see not Ken the son and father and friend, but Ken the mental patient. From this would flow unimagined misery, a fog which would envelop all our lives. And our situation would be, of course, representative of millions. The fog would seep into my employment, my relations with doctors, my access to lawyers and the courts. Every enterprise in which I would engage would be poisoned by the label. It haunted me and frightened others.

As is clear now to the reader, my earlier episode at Marcy, meant to be therapeutic, had not only mistakenly injured me, it had become in the eyes of the world an indisputable illness which might recur at any time. I had to be watched for signs of relapse. Having people breathing down one's neck creates an oppressive atmosphere. These suspicions of the world go a long way, of course, toward inducing prickly responses.

So what have we? An explosive atmosphere which makes the victim continuously vulnerable. Neighbors, colleagues, employers, police, all are drawn as if by magnet to the simplistic formula: mental illness. For every problem the same solution—institutionalization. In light of this, my parents' behavior becomes comprehensible; the doctors' signing the papers without seeing me becomes acceptable medical practice; the judge's commitment order merely endorses the medical method.

As a naïve participant in this long-rehearsed play, it was still my belief two decades ago that there was a Birnbaum and an Ennis in every city and village. It was my belief that the provisions of Florida statutes had to be obeyed. I thought that if fraud were committed, someone among the press, the bar, the medical societies, and the judiciary would undertake to get things put right.

In a post-Watergate year, few people should say that I was more naïve than my fellow citizens in trusting my case to lawyers. Nor were my parents more astute. They did not get me a lawyer because they thought my "trouble" was medical. They had faith in the integrity of the doctors in jail and then in Chattahoochee.

My hope is that this book will help families see through the fog of sanism, to be more skeptical of the premixed formulas of state psychiatry. Families should think a million times before allowing one of their own to be committed. If they have a loved one in an institution, they should question the value of keeping him there.

In some places, there is more careful screening of the people committed than there was two decades ago. But patients in many parts of the country report no change. Also, the same abuses and the same back wards continue, much as I saw them in Chattahoochee. While the average stay is shorter now, patients still face indefinite incarceration of years and years.

The only way to eliminate the abuses is to outlaw involuntary commitments. Alternatives to commitment are working in many cities. There are local clinics, with both day and overnight patients, which sharply reduce the treatment periods, sometimes to a few days. There are crises intervention centers to handle overwrought families or individuals. There are trained volunteers to talk to upset people, on the telephone or in person. Often that is all that is required to calm a person. Compare these things with what being dumped into Chattahoochee means.

There have been advances made by some states in cutting down the population of the big custodial institutions. There are fewer troubles getting out younger patients, who usually have families and who can more easily find employment. With older patients, locked up as much as twenty, thirty, forty years, many have been so beaten down (institutionalized) that their will to survive independently has been destroyed. In some states, these old-timers have been dumped into communities without proper planning. Doctor Birnbaum tells of old people lodged in firetraps in neighborhoods where you don't dare walk on the street. One illustration he gives is an old woman returned to a street where even prowl cars will go only two at a time. In some cities, as in my hometown, York, Pennsylvania, the York County Mental Health Association under Mrs. Mildred Johnson, director, polices the houses boarding ex-patients and provides recreation and transportation for them.

The situation is plainly one in flux. The catalyzing views and experience of R. D. Laing have played quite an important role. Halfway houses and other experimental programs are being funded and realized in many areas. A sympathetic and informed public must advance these programs for both altruistic and selfish reasons. The present trend continuing, one out of seven Americans will be labeled mentally ill.

Necessary and desirable as halfway houses are, many communities will not readily accept them. In ignorance too many of us fear the unknown and magnify the threat of strangers in a crime-ridden age. Recognizing this, when the patient comes out from the institution, usually he or she keeps that fact as guarded as possible. Nonetheless, in many cities they are kept under surveillance by the police and overly zealous telephone and postal workers.

The cost of this expression of sanism is exacted not only from the ex-patient but from society at large in the loss of energy and skill. I asked one "ex" who did not lie about her past to prepare a statement for this book. She is Shirley Burghard, R.N., the editor of *Constructive Action,* a person with more devoted followers than any other I have known.

> My first great shock relating to the stigma and shame of mental illness came about in this way. The Supervisor in Chief, Miss P., of Crouse Irving Hospital came to see me. (I was in Syracuse Psychiatric Hospital.) She promised that when I recovered I could have my old job back on the medical-surgical floor or anyplace else I wished to work. A little over eighteen months later, I went to get my job back and was told by Miss P. that "I wouldn't hire you if you were the last nurse on the face of the earth. I don't want former mental patients, right out of institutions, working here!!!!"
>
> So I worked for several years in a number of incredibly bad nursing homes where they checked nothing, not even my nursing license. They would have hired anybody off the street because they were that desperate for help. But to work in one of these homes meant virtual "slave labor," far overworked and extremely underpaid....
>
> In due time, I took a chance and went and applied at St. Joseph's Hospital where Sister M. B. told me, "You will have to prove yourself." What she meant was—I was hired as a Registered Nurse and paid as one, but did the work of a nurse's aide, that is, I washed dishes in the floor kitchen, I ran for the mop when anything got spilled, I folded linen and put it away, I changed the clothes on the statue of the Infant of Prague. In due time, I worked in the newborn nursery, but even there I was not allowed to even give the newborn his shot of vitamin K. A Licensed Practical Nurse came in and did it for me. After 1½ years of this, I felt I had something better coming so I tried to talk to Sister M. B., who would not even discuss the matter with me ...
>
> When the Plaza Rehabilitation Home opened I applied for a job and was told I was too rigid to work with their team system of

nursing; and at Hutchings Psychiatric Hospital (state) I was told I was too lenient to work with their team system of nursing. . . .

I forgot one important incident. I left Syracuse and moved to Cortland and got a job at Memorial Hospital. I was doing well. The Chief Supervisor of Nurses told me so. Four days later, she called me into her office and asked, "Have you ever been a patient in a mental hospital?" When I answered truthfully, "Yes," I was fired right on the spot. . . . I never realized that a supposedly sane person could have such a hatred for somebody whom society had once labeled insane. We must get rid of these labels, if it is the last thing we ever do.

When I arrived in Syracuse from Florida, Shirley was being subjected to any-hour noises, like horn-blowing in the daytime and drum-beating under her second-floor apartment at 2:00 A.M. I had to side with two of my friends who said that Shirley must have said something unpleasant to a neighbor's cat, or done some other equally vicious and dangerous "paranoid" thing. But, then, I soon had my own twelve months of hammering on the ceiling and wall, blowing of a horn every time I turned on my bathroom light at night, and so I knew that Shirley was not the one who was sick.

Once this harassing starts on an ex-patient, there is nothing he can do to stop it. A Syracuse doctor warned me not to appeal to the police for help for, with my record, they would lock me up immediately and I'd have a tough time ever getting out. If the patient told his family, they could feel sorry for him or have him recommitted.

When I came back triumphant from the trial in Tallahassee, WSYR-TV gave me a big slot on the evening news, at 7:00 and 11:00. The next day, a neighbor, Mr. Oronzo Lotito, real estate broker, stopped around and introduced himself. Then he said, "I wish I had known. I would have stopped you. Going on TV is the worst thing you could do in this town." And from what Oronzo told me, I was beginning to wonder if the chief of police really was paranoid.

With the man in the street, the fellow worker on the job, the nervous storekeeper, the hazing sometimes took on a nasty edge. It is part of the "pathology of oppression," Birnbaum's friend Florynce Kennedy, a black feminist lawyer, told him. "Our society oppresses state mental-hospital patients by niggerizing them."

I have told you about two of the three things, sanism and harassment, that are the ex-patient's lot on his return to the free world. They were both expected. The third was not'. It is psychic shock, similar to that experienced by an air crash survivor.

In March, at a bus stop on Market Street, I saw a thin fellow with big sunglasses, bundled against the weather, standing with shoulders and neck sagging forward. I recognized it at once—the nuthouse stance. It signaled that he had been washed out emotionally and mentally.

It has taken massive doses of vitamins and sardines, under the encouragement of New York City nutritionist Benjamin Frank, M.D., and much meat to straighten my backbone. It has taken thousands of encouragements from interested audiences and much loving by family and friends to bend back the kinks in the spirit. Time has done the rest.

I tell now what I told nobody during my first two years out of Chattahoochee: I did not expect to live over two years, I did not want to live over two years. I came out of the institution with what I call pre-angina. Besides that, I felt age one hundred and twenty inside. It is a curious thing, looking back at those two years, for it never once occurred to me that Death would find me before the book was done. It was just that beyond the two years there was no desire, one way or the other.

Nonetheless, I popped vitamins. I ate lean meat, vegetables, yogurt, wheat germ, blackstrap molasses, and ice cream and cookies, the latter two a sop to my weaknesses.

Psychic shock eased simultaneously as physical health improved, so that I could not see any separation of the two. My brain was stunned, simply bruised so much that it halted normal activities where possible until the fouled-up blood from fifteen years of beatings drained away. I could read newspapers twice as fast the second year, four times as fast this year.

Some of the results of psychic shock were not unlike those of ECT, although not as pronounced. During the hotel stint in Syracuse, when I was pushing so hard, I would waken from a sound sleep with a flash in my head like ECT. I assumed it was Nature's way of housecleaning and simplifying things by using a path already burned in. But I also wondered if it were a warning that the brain was being pushed too hard; however, Christian Science fought that one off. Besides, I have been pushing even harder this last year, on lectures and the book, for months now getting the least sleep in my life, but there have been no more flashes during the stretch run.

My greatest pleasure in Syracuse was to sit and rock in the dark—no radio, no phone, no TV. I had an insatiable need for quiet. This was misunderstood by people, who thought I needed to be prodded to become more gregarious.

For a year, I felt uneasy about not being home for seven o'clock bed check. At the hotel, it was on the tip of my tongue to ask guests, when they came up to the desk, "What ward are you on?"

I have told of the death of emotions, which I noticed during my last years in Chattahoochee. A full complement of feelings has returned gradually over the years of freedom. During the long fight for vindication, anger has waned and friendships have grown.

"Go placidly amid the noise and haste, & remember what peace there may be in silence. As far as possible without surrender be on good terms with all persons," says the *Desiderata,* found in Old Saint Paul's Church, Baltimore, dated 1692, a copy of which was sent me by my perspicacious friends Margery and Roy Sonnleitner, Central City, Colorado. I hung it on my wall that first month in Syracuse. It still hangs beside my bookshelves.

CHAPTER 23

A Constitutional
Right Interpreted

IT WAS AN EXCITING MOMENT FOR MY LAWYERS AND ME. WE HAD just won a major victory in the Supreme Court of the United States. We were ringed by reporters and cameramen outside the brownstone headquarters of the Mental Health Law Project, at 1751 N Street, N.W., Washington.

By a vote of 9 to 0, in the case of *O'Connor* v. *Donaldson,* No. 74-8, the court had that morning, June 26, 1975, ruled on "every man's constitutional right to liberty":

"In short, a State cannot constitutionally confine without more a nondangerous individual who is capable of surviving safely in freedom by himself or with the help of willing and responsible family members or friends. Since the jury found, upon ample evidence, that O'Connor, as an agent of the State, knowingly did so confine Donaldson, it properly concluded that O'Connor violated Donaldson's constitutional right to freedom."

After thirty-two years of fighting for my right to be a free man, I had won vindication. Gratifying, yet somber too in the thought of the fellow sufferers who had already perished. The cameramen had to ask me to smile.

When the microphone was thrust at me, I said: "It is a victory for common sense." Speaking from the heart, I then said that I was proud of my country. Proud that we had a system that could work to right a wrong.

Caught in the first flush of victory, I answered one question, saying, "It's hard to say what fifteen years is worth." But after getting the enthusiastic response of hundreds of people and seeing concrete hope for the release of thousands of mental patients, my ready answer today is, "Yes, it was worth fifteen years."

Thus, on a sunny morning, the so-called mentally ill, for the first time in the two hundred years of our nation, had been given some standing in the law. No longer would it be sufficient to point your finger at someone and say he's crazy, then have him legally locked away, as has been done under the emergency provisions in the statutes of many states. From now on, a nondangerous person could use the leverage of the decision in his refusal to go to a psychiatric facility.

The numerous press conferences that day pointed up the role of the press in keeping my case before the public. Initially, through a series of articles, the Tampa *Tribune* had been instrumental in getting my case into court for the first time—Federal Court, Tallahassee. Now the press was alerting patients on every ward to their new rights. As long as there is a free press, there will be the promise of justice.

The court's opinion, written by Justice Potter Stewart, made several points, including the following:

> The jury found that Donaldson was neither dangerous to himself nor dangerous to others, and also found that, if mentally ill, Donaldson had not received treatment. That verdict, based on abundant evidence, makes the issue before the Court a narrow one. We need not decide whether, when, or by what procedures, a mentally ill person may be confined by the State on any of the grounds which, under contemporary statutes, are generally advanced to justify involuntary confinement of such a person—to prevent injury to the public, to ensure his survival or safety, or to alleviate or cure his illness. See *Jackson* v. *Indiana*, 406 U.S. 715, 736–737; *Humphrey* v. *Cady*, 405 U.S. 504, 509. For the jury found that none of the above grounds for continued confinement was present in Donaldson's case.

Given the jury's findings, what was left as justification for keeping Donaldson in continued confinement? The fact that state law may have authorized confinement of the harmless mentally ill does not itself establish a constitutionally adequate purpose for the confinement. See *Jackson* v. *Indiana, supra*, 720–723; *McNeil* v. *Director, Patuxent Institution*, 407 U.S. 245, 248–250. Nor was it enough that Donaldson's original confinement was founded upon a constitutionally adequate basis, if in fact it was, because even if his involuntary confinement was initially permissible, it could not constitutionally continue after that basis no longer existed. *Jackson* v. *Indiana, supra*, at 738; *McNeil* v. *Director, Patuxent Institution, supra*.

A finding of "mental illness" alone cannot justify a State's locking a person up against his will and keeping him indefinitely in simple custodial confinement. Assuming that that term can be given a reasonably precise content and the "mentally ill" can be identified with reasonable accuracy, there is still no constitutional basis for confining such persons involuntarily if they are dangerous to no one and can live safely in freedom.

May the State confine the mentally ill merely to ensure them a living standard superior to that they enjoy in the private community? That the State has a proper interest in providing care and assistance to the unfortunate goes without saying. But the mere presence of mental illness does not disqualify a person from preferring his home to the comforts of an institution. Moreover, while the State may arguably confine a person to save him from harm, incarceration is rarely if ever a necessary condition for raising the living standards of those capable of surviving safely in freedom, on their own or with the help of family or friends. See *Shelton* v. *Tucker*, 364 U.S. 479, 488–490.

May the State fence in the harmless mentally ill solely to save its citizens from exposure to those whose ways are different? One might as well ask if the State, to avoid public unease, could incarcerate all who are physically unattractive or socially eccentric. Mere public intolerance or animosity cannot constitutionally justify the deprivation of a person's physical liberty. See, e.g., *Cohen* v. *California*, 403 U.S. 15, 24–26; *Coates* v. *City of Cincinnati*, 402 U.S. 611, 615; *Street* v. *New York*, 394 U.S. 576, 592; cf. *United States Dept. of Agric.* v. *Moreno*, 413 U.S. 528, 534.

On the whole, the decision marks the judicial recognition that the populace is turning away from the easy incarceration in asylums of anybody and everybody.

Still, strong as the decision is, there are many people not entirely satisfied with it. Those following the progress of Right to

Treatment cases through the courts were disappointed that the Supreme Court did not rule on that issue.

"The first time they had the issue squarely before them, they sidestepped it," Morton Birnbaum said. "The Constitution already guaranteed us our freedom. But what about the sick patients who are rotting in crowded warehouses without proper food and with no psychiatric care? Can't those jokers see that this inhumane issue must be tackled?"

The court put its reasoning thus:

> We have concluded that the difficult issues of constitutional law dealt with by the Court of Appeals are not presented by this case in its present posture. Specifically, there is no reason now to decide whether mentally ill persons dangerous to themselves or to others have a right to treatment upon compulsory confinement by the State, or whether the State may compulsorily confine a nondangerous mentally ill individual for the purpose of treatment. As we view it, this case raises a single, relatively simple, but nonetheless important question concerning every man's constitutional right to liberty.

Ennis and I were content with the decision. My view is that the world's troubles are solved step by step. Given the facts of my case, no court could possibly fail to find that I had been held unnecessarily. Thus, we were almost sure of winning on that score. Then, too, the concurring opinion of Chief Justice Warren E. Burger bore out Ennis's belief that a vote on the right to treatment could possibly be close and possibly unfavorable. It was better, we felt, to win one step than to lose all in trying for a second step.

Nonetheless, the strong wording and the scope of the opinion gave us as important a victory as we had hoped for. In fact, *The New York Times* in an editorial said the ruling "on the [Constitutional] rights of confined mental patients ... could be more significant than the comparatively limited extension of their legal rights [e.g., the right to treatment]."

Furthermore, looking at it from my own viewpoint as a patient, I always felt that the right to proper treatment amounted to the same thing as the right to freedom. In other words, as Ennis put it, we were asking for "a right to treatment or release." Birnbaum had accepted that view for this case. He turned the case over willingly to Ennis and let it go in a slightly different direction to arrive at the present court decision.

My original involvement with the right-to-treatment argument was not as paradoxical as it might seem. Although both Birnbaum and I knew that I needed no treatment, we had learned through hard experience that the courts just would not hear the claims of a man being held in an asylum. But Birnbaum did know that the courts were becoming interested in the fact that thousands of people were locked up for treatment but given no treatment. By establishing a precedent, we hoped to benefit my fellow patients languishing in wards all over the country, which was always our primary object.

That is why the present Supreme Court decision brought diverse reactions. Birnbaum is thinking in terms of the right to treatment for sick people. Ennis and I are both thinking in terms of "patients" who have been ostracized for social reasons.

Interestingly, Burger goes to the heart of the matter as it pertains to people not already committed. To some of them the concept of a right to treatment has been frightening. It meant to them that if a state offered you treatment, then the state had the right to lock you up. Burger wrote:

> . . . [I]t has been argued that a Fourteenth Amendment right to treatment for involuntarily confined mental patients derives from the fact that many of the safeguards of the criminal process are not present in civil commitment. The Court of Appeals described this theory as follows:
>
> "[A] due process right to treatment is based on the principle that when the three central limitations on the government's power to detain—that detention be in retribution for a specific offense; that it be limited to a fixed term; and that it be permitted after a proceeding where the fundamental procedural safeguards are observed—are absent, there must be a *quid pro quo* extended by the government to justify confinement. And the *quid pro quo* most commonly recognized is the provision of rehabilitative treatment." 493 F. 2d, at 522.
>
> To the extent that this theory may be read to permit a State to confine an individual simply because it is willing to provide treatment, regardless of the subject's ability to function in society, it raises the gravest of constitutional problems. . . .
> . . . Given the present state of medical knowledge regarding abnormal human behavior and its treatment, few things would be more fraught with peril than to irrevocably condition a State's

power to protect the mentally ill upon providing of "such treatment as will give [them] a realistic opportunity to be cured." . . . Our concepts of due process would not tolerate such a "trade-off."

But, as I said, the right to uproot people and incarcerate them for mandatory treatment is not the right to treatment I was fighting for. In our briefs for fifteen years, Birnbaum and I were fighting for rights for people already in asylums—for the Carters, the Narrels, the Vittorios. Either give them proper/adequate treatment or give them a writ of habeas corpus for a hearing on their release.

While this book is primarily concerned with the overwhelming majority of state-hospital inmates who are not sick, the question always arises at my interviews and lectures about what to do for the disturbed person, the so-called mentally ill. There is widespread belief that this kind of person makes up a large percentage of our population, who will then suffer if they are not forced behind bars to be "treated" as were my fellow patients in Chattahoochee. In the first place, there is no large percentage of our population which is suffering from mental illness. Judging from the ten thousand souls who filtered through the system and rubbed shoulders with me in fifteen years, there is no epidemiology of mental illness. With rare exceptions, the problems of these ten thousand could have been solved by talking them out with almost any sympathetic person—the corner grocer, the neighborhood minister, a Dutch uncle.

Still, some newsmen and social workers, who have toured the wards of other state hospitals, tell me that they encountered types of patients different from those I pictured in Chattahoochee. They were patients who apparently needed to be confined. My argument is that those patients would in the main behave normally in a normal setting. An extreme example from Building 41, Chattahoochee, is Rackass. He refused to get up on time or to come to meals; he was rude to nearly all patients and attendants; he made the most horrible threats against people both inside and outside the hospital; he viciously beat up an old man who subsequently died. Rackass was one person who I was sure was rightfully confined against his will. Yet he was given a competency discharge and now lives on his own in a Florida city.

The experience of other hospitals, which suddenly opened

their closed wards and gave town privileges to all patients, is that even unkempt and ill-natured patients usually "straightened out and flew right" when they were freed from the abuses and pressures of closed wards. Much as Rackass did, they could take the next step and live as free men in the community.

But what about the person who goes about muttering to himself and saying he is Napoleon? If he is living safely and bothering no one, leave him alone.

As for treatment for the really sick, the Chattahoochees should be the last place assigned them. Rather, the place for them must be like one outlined in the letter, following, from Walter Fox, M.D.

Doctor Fox is past president of the Association of Medical Superintendents of State Mental Hospitals. For some years, he has acted as consultant, evaluating the treatment programs of many state hospitals and setting up realistic goals for their improvement. He is now, as his letter points out, at a regional institute concerned with the planning of mental health services for the future.

> Georgia Mental Health Institute
> Atlanta, Georgia 30306
> March 20, 1975

Mr. Kenneth Donaldson
York, Pennsylvania 17405:

... The questions you asked in your letter would really take a book to reply to and some of the questions I really, of course, don't have answers for. President Kennedy inspired Community Mental Health legislation in 1963, and 1965 foresaw the demise of large state hospitals. Probably for the 1980s this legislation also foresaw a complete network of community mental health centers—some 2,000 in all, and I believe the deadline for getting them operational was 1980. However, since that time we have had the terrible intensification of war in South Vietnam and the Far East. We've experienced in President Nixon, a man who has not only a pretty indifferent attitude to human services generally, but who had an active dislike for mental health services generally, and now, of course, we are in a recession with inflation, so I don't know how long it will take to get adequate mental health in every little county. I guess as long as it takes for people to care badly enough. One thing that would help in this is if we can demonstrate that the services we give really make a difference.

As mentioned earlier, I see mental-health services as being part of general-health services. I would see smaller communities having general practitioners who might diagnose a physical problem or let's say a mental one and then plug in by telephone or TV to a larger center where further consultation would be given and perhaps even some treatment started if that were indicated. I see all of this being paid for by some form of National Health Insurance, and I see the providers more and more coming under the scrutiny of the consumer, and having to demonstrate their ability to provide proficiently. I don't necessarily see the Federal Government getting into the act as far as providing services is concerned. I do see them, however, as a people who will monitor the services. Ideally, it would seem to me that an individual should be able to choose between competing health maintenance organizations. If groups of health-service people had to compete for patients with the goal to keep them well, I think that we would get the best level of service—at the lowest cost. The difficulties facing state health officials today are, of course, numerous; one problem is the bureaucracy itself. Often a state official has inherited a huge and cumbersome bureaucracy with unions and merit systems which make it very difficult to affect change. Then there are all the difficulties of measuring the effectiveness of the services given, and without condensing evidence it is difficult for the lawmakers to commit a sizable proportion of tax money to mental-health services. One of the biggest difficulties of the public right now is being able to evaluate quality of care. The public really needs brokers to guide them to quality care and I think that this is coming. Also, health services people have to learn from the department stores that services need to be more readily available when the most people can conveniently take advantage of them.

As far as state asylums ever being phased out, I am optimistic about this. I think the vast majority of the people who in the past and even to a lesser extent who now live on large wards and are labeled "chronic patients" will be able to be maintained in the community. The community will have to develop new and more support systems than it has now, but this should be able to be done without any real new knowledge and probably more cheaply than maintaining the asylums. It may be that there will be a few very sick people who can never remain for long in the community. If this turns out to be so, they will be able to be housed in relatively small and I would hope very expensive facilities where a complete spectrum of treatment, particularly new treatment, would be available. I like to think that this "most restrictive alternative" would also be the most expensive alternative. This would be one way of guaranteeing that it would not be overused. . . .

Walter Fox, M.D.
Deputy Superintendent, Medical

To return to the import of the ruling on a right to liberty, I note that four states, according to newspaper reports, already grant the right to liberty. I am not familiar with their statutes. But I do know about states which allow their patients to sign themselves in as voluntary patients with the right to sign themselves out whenever they choose. Thus, they presumably implement rights guaranteed by the Constitution. In these states (among them, Florida, New York, and California) patients are often coerced, however, into signing in as voluntary under threat of being designated involuntary under an emergency provision, which permits their being locked up without examination by a doctor or appearance before a judge. Under that latter deprivation their commitment papers are made out and signed by a county judge the next day. In these states the legislatures are going to have to enact this right to liberty into law so that "prospective" patients, such as I was, can refuse to go to a mental facility and so that those patients already in the facility, such as I was, can sign themselves out.

While as many as two hundred thousand patients may now be entitled to immediate release, liberty will not be automatic for every mental "victim." For one thing, little men in administrative jobs in state hospitals are going to disregard the edict unless pushed by outsiders in individual cases. For another, some judges in all parts of the country are going to throw petitions from patients for habeas corpus into the trash can unless a lawyer intervenes.

In still other instances, as telephone calls since the ruling from ex-patients in Florida and New Jersey have informed me, local authorities are being pressured by relatives and other people to railroad these ex-patients. The New Jersey call came from a man who has fled his home in another state because someone told the police that the ex-patient had a houseful of guns and was going to kill his business competitors. In a case like this, when a substantial citizen makes such a charge against an ex-patient, the police or the judge are liable to take the easy way and commit the man under

emergency provisions. In the state the ex-patient fled, police have a
statutory right to do this without even getting a court order. Such
usurpation of Constitutional rights has been outlawed by the
ruling in *O'Connor* v. *Donaldson,* but that does not guarantee ready
compliance in every local jurisdiction.

These victims whose rights will not be accorded them are
going to need a lawyer. Those without a lawyer should contact one
of the following for advice:

> Mental Health Law Project, Washington, D.C.
> New York Civil Liberties Union, or local ACLU chapter.
> American Bar Association Commission on the Mentally Dis-
>   abled, Washington, D.C.
> Citizens Commission on Human Rights, The Church of Sci-
>   entology.

At the present time, life for many former mental patients is
extremely lonely. For them, there is encouragement to be found in
sharing experiences with other ex-patients through the pages of
Constructive Action magazine, which has been published for fifteen
years by ex-nurse/ex-victim Shirley Burghard. The address is:
B-1104 Ross Towers, 710 Lodi Street, Syracuse, New York 13203.

I have said nothing up to now about the second part of the
decision in my case, that concerning the award of $38,500 in
damages from two doctors. Because of a technicality, the matter of
the award has been remanded to the lower courts. Admittedly, the
sum is small compensation for fifteen years of unjustified incarceration; but it would be a satisfaction, coming as it should, from the
doctors' own pockets. Neither they nor the state had insurance for
this.

Finally, the man who did more than anybody else to free me,
Morton Birnbaum, puts the blame for my long incarceration
squarely on the judges, all the way from the lowest court to the
highest. "They are the ones who had the power to free you," he
says. "Not once in fifteen years, not once in nineteen tries would
they grant you a full hearing. Now they say the doctors are to
blame. Why—you can't blame the doctors when the state does not
provide enough money to staff the hospitals adequately. I have
rapport with doctors who have a thousand patients. How can
anyone blame them if they do a poor job? Justice Stewart—or
Justice Douglas—four times could have given you habeas corpus.

No, they couldn't be bothered. Now they put all the blame on the doctors. Why—the judges are the ones who should pay a fine!"

That would be poetic justice.

The court itself in its decision noted some of the problems remaining in this field for the judiciary. I, for one, welcome their resolution in the courts. But slow as the wheels of justice grind, a decision such as that in *O'Connor* v. *Donaldson* uses the Constitution to tear open the straitjacket of state-institutional insanity.

IN THE COURTS, 1975

(xxii, cont.)

Supreme Court of the United States

Oct. Term, 1974
Case No. 74-8
Argued 1/15/75
Decided 6/26/75

(1) Held that Kenneth Donaldson's Constitutional right to liberty had been violated by Doctor O'Connor; and

(2) Remanded the matter of monetary damages to the Fifth Circuit Court of Appeals for a rehearing, in light of *Wood* v. *Strickland*, 420 U.S. 308.

On October 9, 1975, the Fifth Circuit Court of Appeals refused plaintiff a rehearing and sent the action for damages back to the District Court in Tallahassee for reconsideration.

Postscript

I STOOD ALONE OVER MY PARENTS' GRAVES IN A QUIET RURAL CEMETERY, where the land creeps up from the Hudson River to form the Catskills.

On the nearby hills, there was new growth springing up from the roots after a forest fire. Taking inspiration from Nature, I renewed vows made in Chattahoochee. I would do everything in my power to prevent what had been done to me from overtaking my grandchildren, or Carter's or Vittorio's . . . or yours.

INSANITY INSIDE OUT

is the story of Kenneth Donaldson, a man whose faith in himself has built a road to freedom for many whom we label mentally ill.

His is a tragic story of fifteen wasted years, stolen from him as a result of involuntary commitment to a Florida state mental hospital. For fifteen years he sought to procure his release, to assert his sanity, to demand his constitutional rights. And for fifteen years the more he struggled, the more he stood erect, rejecting the label of incompetence, the more he refused the drugs which he saw destroying his comrades, the more deeply was he plunged into the nightmare of incarceration. To claim sanity was to prove insanity; to claim health and refuse drugs was to demonstrate illness; to say he could care for himself was to reveal incompetence; to scorn such doctoring was to be paranoid; to keep records and say that "one day a book will tell all" was delusional.

A tragic story of wasted years . . . yet also a brave and useful one. For Ken Donaldson is an American hero, the principal in a landmark Supreme Court case which ascertains the right to freedom for tens of thousands of involuntary mental patients. Perhaps the most important ruling on mental patients' rights in the history of the nation, the Donaldson Case promises to restructure our incarcerative mental health system. The Supreme Court ruling is only the undersea quake which may produce a tidal wave: freedom for involuntary patients, financial threat to irresponsible psychiatrists, tightened responsibility for the courts, a virtual revolution in the administration and budgeting of our gargantuan mental health apparatus.